THE LETTERS OF MARGARET FULLER

Margaret Fuller Ossoli. Courtesy of Constance Fuller Threinen.

THE LETTERS OF
Margaret Fuller

Edited by

ROBERT N. HUDSPETH

VOLUME VI · 1850 AND UNDATED

Cornell University Press

ITHACA AND LONDON

PUBLICATION OF THIS BOOK WAS ASSISTED BY A GRANT
FROM THE PUBLICATIONS PROGRAM OF THE NATIONAL ENDOWMENT
FOR THE HUMANITIES, AN INDEPENDENT FEDERAL AGENCY.

Copyright © 1994 by Cornell University

First published 1994 by Cornell University Press.

Library of Congress Cataloging-in-Publication Data

Fuller, Margaret, 1810–1850.
  The letters of Margaret Fuller.
  Includes bibliographies and indexes.
Contents: v. 1. 1817–38 — v. 2. 1839–41 — [etc.] — v. 6. 1850 and undated.
    1. Fuller, Margaret, 1810–1850—Correspondence. 2. Authors, American—19th
century—Correspondence. I. Hudspeth, Robert N. II. Title.
PS2506.A4 1983   818′ .309 [B]   82.22098
ISBN 0-8014-3069-0

Printed in the United States of America

PREFACE

In this final volume of *The Letters of Margaret Fuller* the reader will find three groups of letters: those that were written in the last six months of Fuller's life, those that are undated, and those that have come to light since the first volume of the edition was published. Most notable of the latter are eighty-four letters written to James Freeman Clarke. Inevitably this grouping makes Volume 6 a miscellany, but the letters in it provide a cross section of Fuller's epistolary self-history, for the final section of letters begins when Fuller was a young woman and ends in the midst of the Roman revolution. The volume is at once a conclusion and a recapitulation.

The correspondents of the surviving letters of 1850 are predominantly the people who shared her European life: the Springs and the Storys, Costanza Arconati-Visconti and Lewis Cass, Jr. There are few surviving family letters in 1850, only fragment copies to William Henry Channing, and none to Emerson, Carrie Tappan, or James Clarke. Of course, Fuller may have sent letters to American friends and more to her family, but probably what we have faithfully mirrors what she wrote. The intensity of her Italian life, with its secrets and emotional stress, with its involvement with Roman politics, and with the failed opportunity for historic change, had made her a stranger to the United States and to many people who had earlier meant so much to her.

As 1850 began, Fuller was relieved to have a quiet time after the Roman revolution of 1849. The horror of the French attack, the collapse of Mazzini's republic, and the sure return of the hated Piux IX had forced her and Ossoli to leave Rome for Florence, which she thought the inferior city. There she not only had the leisure to read (though not to write because of an unusually bitter Tuscan winter), but she and Ossoli took part in the expatriate social life in Florence. They became familiar with the sculptor Horatio Greenough and his wife; they met the inevitable array of traveling Americans, some of whom had known Fuller in her youth. In fact, she seems to have had her past life suddenly paraded before her: the brother of one of her Providence students came to Florence, as did friends of her father. Even the Greenoughs were old acquaintances who had known Timothy and Margarett Fuller in Cambridgeport. Life outside the family was further enriched by evenings with Robert and Elizabeth Browning, to whom Fuller became much attached.

The quiet of the winter, however, could not put off the certain knowledge that the Ossolis must return to the United States. The Tuscan political situation was bearable and certainly better than the sure repression descending on Rome, but Fuller knew that she must resume her writing. To do so she needed to publish her history of the Italian revolutions. She had written to Thomas Carlyle in the summer of 1849 to seek his help in finding a British publisher. He wrote on 9 August to John Chapman of Chapman and Hall. He described her to Hall and concluded that "she is . . . *considerably* a higher-minded and cleverer woman than any of the Lady Lions yet on your Books."[1] But by 17 August Chapman had declined to make an agreement for a book as yet unwritten. This failure to secure an English house convinced Fuller that she had to be in the United States to publish her work.[2]

Then, too, she had been away almost four years. The flow of marriages, births, and deaths had reshaped not only her life but the lives of her family and friends: Carrie Sturgis was married and a mother; the Wards and Springs had new children; her brothers Arthur and Richard had married; Pickie Greeley, her uncle Abraham Fuller, and Ellen Sturgis Hooper had died. Certainly it was time for Fuller to renew her place in the lives of those who had meant so much to her, and she had every reason to introduce her Italian family to her American circle.

Her decision to return emerges quickly in the 1850 letters, fraught as they are with hope, fear, longing, and perplexity. As always, her

1. *The Correspondence of Emerson and Carlyle*, ed. Joseph Slater (New York: Columbia University Press, 1964), p. 456.
2. ? to Margaret Fuller, 17 August 1849 (AL MH: fMS AM 1086). Fuller's correspondent is not Chapman but an intermediary.

poverty harried her. She preferred passage on one of the safer steamers, but they were more expensive, so Fuller, who had to borrow money from Marcus Spring as it was, had no choice but to take passage on a sailing ship. As the letters in 1850 show, she immediately had forebodings about the crossing. She read the many news stories about wrecks; she speaks openly to her correspondents about how much she dreads the trip. Since we know she did indeed die in a shipwreck, we are struck by Fuller's prescience, but we ought not to make too much of what was common sense: travel by sail was hazardous; many ships went down.

After spending her last night in Florence with the Brownings, Fuller, Ossoli, and their son set out for Leghorn and thence to the new world. She narrates the first half of the unfolding drama in a letter to the in-laws of the ill-fated captain, Seth Hasty. A week into their voyage, Hasty became ill and showed all the signs of smallpox. He grew worse through the remainder of the trip to Gibraltar and died the day after they arrived. The local authorities quarantined the ship, so Hasty's body was buried at sea, and the first mate, Henry P. Bangs, assumed command of the *Elizabeth* for the trip across the Atlantic.

All went well until their arrival off the coast of New York. Bangs miscalculated their position and thought they were off the New Jersey coast. The *Elizabeth* was in fact near Long Island, where the ship hit a sandbar shortly after four A.M. on 19 July. The heavy sea immediately broke into the forecastle. Beginning about nine in the morning, some of the survivors managed to swim the 300 yards to land. The sea was running too high for people on shore to help those remaining on board, though the wreck was clearly in sight of land. By midafternoon several more had swum ashore, but about three-thirty the *Elizabeth* broke apart. Apparently by this time Ossoli and Nino had drowned. Margaret was sitting at the foot of a mast when she was swept away. The child's body was washed to shore; those of Margaret and Giovanni were never recovered. Of the twenty-two on board, seven died.[3]

The news spread rapidly. Henry James (then a child) later remembered that Washington Irving told his father of Fuller's death as they steamed from New York to Fort Hamilton, within a few miles of the wreck.[4] When word of the disaster arrived in New England, Emerson

3. For details of the wreck I have drawn on the collections of the Marine Museum of Suffolk County in West Sayville, New York, especially the folder "Elizabeth" in their manuscript collection "Shipwrecks."

4. Henry James, *Autobiography*, ed. Frederick W. Dupee (London: W. H. Allen, 1956), p. 37.

asked Henry Thoreau to go to New York to see what might be done and to learn what he could of the wreck. Thoreau left on 23 July and arrived the next day. William H. Channing joined him there; Marcus Spring and Charles Sumner, whose brother Horace died in the wreck, had already visited the site.[5] On the twenty-fifth, Thoreau gave a sketchy account of the situation in a letter to Emerson and reported the recovery of Nino's body and of some quantity of books, papers, and personal effects.[6] The papers included some letters, but the manuscript of the Italian revolutions was lost. According to Channing, there was an immediate mystery about its whereabouts. Conflicting accounts about which trunk or desk contained it came from members of the crew who were with Fuller at the end.[7] Undoubtedly the confusion of the time and the trauma of the aftermath blurred memories so that it was impossible to remember exactly what happened when.

The repercussions of the disaster were felt for months. About the first of August eight people were arrested and charged with plundering the wreck; an unidentifiable body, perhaps one of the *Elizabeth*'s victims, floated to shore. On the last day of October, Hiram Powers' portrait bust of Senator John Calhoun, which had gone down with the ship, was recovered, slightly damaged but in good condition.[8] It found its way to South Carolina, where it survived until the national wreck of the Civil War.

Fuller's family and friends slowly adjusted their lives to her death. For Mrs. Fuller it was a shattering loss of an adult child (the first of several losses she was fated to endure). Ellen was left to deal with an increasingly difficult husband without the counsel of her elder sister; the brothers, all but Lloyd now married, were left without the person who had been the family's center since the day their father died.

The responses among Fuller's friends varied. We know they felt an undercurrent of apprehension and mistrust when she announced her decision to return to the United States. Surviving letters from Marcus and Rebecca Spring, for instance, disingenuously but clearly press her to stay abroad. Rebecca wrote: "Much as we should love to see you and strange as it may seem, we, as well as all your friends who have spoken to us about it, believe it will be undesirable for you to return at

5. Ralph Waldo Emerson, *The Letters of Ralph Waldo Emerson*, ed. Ralph L. Rusk (New York: Columbia University Press, 1939), 4:219–20; Henry David Thoreau, *The Correspondence of Henry David Thoreau*, ed. Walter Harding and Carl Bode (New York: New York University Press, 1958), p. 262.

6. *Correspondence of Thoreau*, pp. 262–63.

7. William Henry Channing to Ralph Waldo Emerson, n.d., manuscript copy in Channing's hand, Boston Public Library.

8. Suffolk County Marine Museum records.

present."[9] Marcus wrote that he and W. H. Channing agreed that she had better prospects of publishing if she remained in Italy. Her letter to Channing shows that he had written directly to her of his concerns about her return.[10] These views came from New York, but the attitudes in New England appear to have been little different. Immediately after her death, Emerson wrote in his journal, "The timorous said, What shall we do? how shall she be received, now that she brings a husband & child home?" Even such a good friend as Almira Penniman Barlow was one of the "timorous": "The death seems to [Mrs. Barlow] a fit & good conclusion to the life. Her life was romantic & exceptional: So let her death be; it sets the seal on her marriage, avoids all questions of Society, all of employment, poverty, & old age."[11]

Apparently the sexual implications surrounding the secrecy of her marriage and Nino's birth and the overall "strangeness" of Fuller's life in Italy were more than American society wanted to confront. Her long-time friend Sarah Clarke straightforwardly addressed the gossip in a letter to Fuller in March 1850: "You say your friends appear to lay extraordinary stress upon your marriage— It is not exactly that but we were placed in a most unpleasant position because the world said injurious things of you which we were not authorized to deny— not one of us could say that we knew of your marriage beforehand, nor could we tell when it occurred or answer any question about— If people chose to make unpleasant inferences from this secrecy we had nothing to say beyond expressing our respect for you— This was annoying." Clarke closed with a typically sharp and perhaps accurate surmise: "To me it seemed that you were more afraid of being thought to have submitted to the ceremony of marriage than to have omitted it."[12]

A conversation between two of her friends in April 1858 symbolizes the disrepute that shadowed Fuller's last days. Unhappily, the conversation makes a double betrayal by two men whom Fuller valued highly, Nathaniel Hawthorne and Joseph Mozier. In his journal, after a sharp and unflattering portrait of Mozier, Hawthorne recorded in great detail the sculptor's comments on Fuller and Ossoli. The substance of Mozier's gossip is this: Far from being a nobleman, Ossoli was an illiterate servant who hardly knew his own language; Fuller's

9. Rebecca Spring to Margaret Fuller, 14 April 1850 (Houghton Library, Harvard University, hereafter cited as MH).

10. Marcus Spring to Margaret Fuller, 17 April 1850 (MH).

11. Ralph Waldo Emerson, *The Journals and Miscellaneous Notebooks of Ralph Waldo Emerson*, ed. William Gilman et al., 16 vols. (Cambridge: Belknap Press of Harvard University Press, 1960–82), 11:256, 259 (hereafter cited as *JMN*).

12. Sarah Ann Clarke to Margaret Fuller, 5 March 1850 (MH).

interest in Ossoli was "purely sensual"; and finally, Fuller had never written a history of the Italian revolutions.

From this "news" Hawthorne drew an extended analysis of Fuller's character, calling it "strong, heavy, unpliable, and, in many respects, defective and evil." She was, Hawthorne wrote to himself, "a great humbug," though "of course with much talent, and much moral reality, or else she could not have been so great a humbug."[13] For their individual reasons, Mozier and Hawthorne had to make Margaret Fuller into a fallen woman whose sexuality triumphed over her intellectual pretensions. Nothing external accounts for the hostility Hawthorne records: in 1847, Mozier had taken an ill Fuller into his home; she remained on the most cordial of terms with him. Fuller admired Hawthorne and had shared good talk with him. He was probably jealous of the emotional warmth his beloved Sophia had once felt for Fuller; he consistently distrusted women writers, but we know of no overt insult that Fuller had ever offered such as would lead to his self-satisfied journal portrait. The episode stands starkly as a sign of how deeply Fuller could disturb people who knew her; it reveals how threatening was her combination of sex and intellect, and it sadly reveals Hawthorne's lack of faith.

Emerson, too, felt the powerfully mixed emotions Fuller could arouse. His first comment on her death acknowledges this "inhospitable" attitude but he goes on to remember her as a "brave, eloquent, subtle, accomplished, devoted, constant soul."[14] From then to the publication of the *Memoirs* in 1852, Fuller was seldom far from Emerson's mind. His journals record the interweaving of his thoughts about her with his meditations on fate, power, chance, and circumstance (all themes that inform *The Conduct of Life*). He had hardly gotten the full details of the wreck and deaths when he received a letter from Horace Greeley written on 27 July, saying that the Fuller family had asked him to see to the publication of a "proper edition of Margaret's works, with extracts from her unprinted writings." Greeley declined to take on the task, but he urged Emerson to do it. Close on this letter came a conversation with William Henry Channing proposing "Margaret & Her Friends." On 1 September Emerson wrote Richard Fuller saying that he, Channing, and Sam Ward would write and edit the volumes.[15]

The result was *Memoirs of Margaret Fuller Ossoli* (1852), with James

13. Nathaniel Hawthorne, *The French and Italian Notebooks*, ed. Thomas Woodson (Columbus: Ohio State University Press, 1980), pp. 154–57.
14. Emerson, *JMN*, 11:256.
15. Rusk, *Letters of RWE*, 4:225–27.

Clarke replacing Ward as the third editor. Ever the keen business-man, Greeley had originally urged Emerson to have the book in readers' hands "by the middle of September or at farthest the first of October."[16] It took almost two years, in part because the necessary Fuller manuscripts had to be recovered from scattered portfolios, in part because W. H. Channing was as inattentive as Greeley was impatient, and in part because it was a difficult book to write. Emerson all but lost confidence in the project and fumed to himself, "Margaret's writing does not justify any such research. All that can be said, is, that she represents an interesting hour & group in American cultivation." At other times, however, he recognized the power that underlay his friend's life: "Margaret, wherever she came, fused people into society, & a glowing company was the result. When I think how few persons can do that feat for the intellectual class, I feel our squalid poverty."[17] Emerson, though, never had felt the power of Fuller's writing. She was to him a "presence," a personal force acting on personal lives. Once absent, she became less than real to him, for her writing did not live in his memory.

Emerson erred in his estimate of her published work, but he was keenly perceptive when he thought of her letters, for they were more nearly the representation of the *person*: "She poured a stream of amber over the endless store of private anecdotes, of bosom histories which her wonderful persuasion drew out of all to her." Like Channing and Clarke, Emerson played a part in those "bosom histories," so it was no wonder that he could say that "when I heard that a trunk of her correspondence had been found & opened, I felt what a panic would strike all her friends, for it was as if a clever reporter had got underneath a confessional & agreed to report all that transpired there in Wall street."[18] The *Memoirs* editors conspired to mute the public report and allay the fear, but over the years we have a complete enough record to see how accurate Emerson was in seizing upon her correspondence as an essential history of their times.

The United States toward which Fuller sailed in 1850 was not the same society she had left four years before. The Mexican War, just begun when she left, had come to its conclusion with its physical expansion of American territory. The "forty-niner" gold rush had descended upon the country and lured countless emigrants into the California and Nevada territories. We do not know if Fuller knew of the

16. Ibid., p. 225.
17. Emerson, *JMN*, 11:431, 449.
18. Ibid., p. 258.

Seneca Falls Convention, which began the ongoing struggle for women's rights.

The major political event in the four years of Fuller's absence, the one that had the longest and most somber repercussions, was the Compromise of 1850, and especially the speech Daniel Webster gave on 7 March in support of the measure (which included the Fugitive Slave Law, passed less than two months after her death). At a time when Fuller was fleeing the return of reaction to the Italian states, her native land was increasingly unable to deal with its own betrayal of freedom. Having witnessed one war, Fuller was returning to a United States that was lurching toward a larger one. Ironically, President Zachary Taylor, elected as a hero who had subdued the Mexicans on their own land, died ten days before Fuller, leaving a feeble Millard Fillmore to serve until he was replaced by the even worse Franklin Pierce. Margaret Fuller would have found little in this political landscape to welcome her. The larger struggle between honor and servitude would have been all too familiar.

II

Of the undated letters little needs to be said: some of them can be dated within a decade or half decade, others remain simply divorced from any context. Some of the letters are notes; some are more substantial. Several of the letters in this section are published fragments from the *Memoirs*. I have tried to rely on the wording to determine if a fragment is indeed a letter, though sometimes I have followed her tone. Some of the *Memoirs* material survives in manuscript and is clearly from her journals. The order of the undated letters is explained in the section "Editorial Method."

If the undated letters are less than wholly satisfying, those in the Appendix command and reward our attention. Dominated by the new ones to James Clarke, the letters in this section have important new details about Fuller's friendship with George Davis and Caroline Sturgis; they bring to light a new correspondent, William Channing Russel; and they clarify her relationship with the Springs.

The four new letters to George Davis are especially welcome, for three of them were written in a one-month span in the winter of 1829–30, a time when we know little of Fuller's life. Clearly, at nineteen, Fuller was alive to the books she was reading, especially Byron, whose *Don Juan* was much on her mind. At the other extreme, she makes an effort to analyze *Clarissa* for Davis. As was her habit in her letters, she moves easily from gossip about the young people of their circle to literary analysis, concluding with a pointed suggestion that there were "analogies though not likenesses" between Richardson's Lovelace and Davis—a less than flattering comment to the man she loved.[19] Fuller was pointedly establishing her independence and trying out her considerable wit.

The letters to Sturgis stand out less, given the number between the two we already have, but they, too, bring details that further our understanding of Fuller and her milieu. Her letter of 30 August 1842, for instance, describes her life as a Concord visitor as she draws a careful portrait of Ellery Channing, a man hard to pin down. Fuller is quite aware of how different they are, and she is alive to his limitations, but she also sees the wit, intelligence, and love for his friends that characterized her brother-in-law. If he later failed them all—as inevitably he did—he was in 1842 a fascinating man whom Fuller delighted to know and to record for Sturgis, who earlier had had a romantic interest in him.

It is the letters to James Clarke, however, that form the center of this volume: eighty-four new letters to the same correspondent make an immediate difference in our understanding of Fuller. Twenty-six of the letters have been published in part in the *Memoirs* (and of those fragments twenty have been included in earlier volumes of this edition), but fifty-eight have never before been published. Almost all of the new letters survive in their entirety, so we now have access to complete letters, rather than the altered fragments that Clarke published in the *Memoirs* and that are republished in the early volumes of this edition. These new letters repair some of the damage done by the *Memoirs*. We now depend less on those corrupted texts; we have complete letters where we had fragments; we understand the contexts of the language Fuller uses, and we see more completely the range of her ideas. Fortunately, many of the letters were written in the 1830s, a time when Fuller was maturing intellectually, and when the record is too often scanty.

The number and substance of these letters give them an importance to rival that of Fuller's correspondence with Emerson. Clarke's move to Louisville was fortunate for us, for it gave Fuller occasion to send him news of New England and of her reading. Had he remained in Boston, she would have had less need to write so fully and revealingly, or to write at all. The correspondence all but ended when he returned to Boston in 1841 (save for the months when she was traveling in the West).

19. Fuller to George T. Davis, 29 December 1829.

We immediately recognize how very close Fuller and Clarke were from 1830 until at least 1836. After her disillusionment with George Davis in 1830, Clarke became the most important male in her life for at least five years. The record of these letters and of Clarke's answers to them shows two young people who read the same books and knew that they were in the forefront of literary discussion. Very self-consciously they talked back and forth about the importance of German letters and about how much their taste differed from that of their elders. Both became so proficient at reading German that they could try their hands at translating; they could challenge themselves with an array of German poetry and prose. Clarke himself understood Fuller's importance to him when he wrote that "you gave me to myself."[20]

These letters clearly show Fuller thinking of a writing vocation at an early age. In November 1832 she responds to Clarke's praise with ambivalence and yet with delight. She separates herself from "women authors' mental history," but she cannot yet see a direction for herself that is more satisfactory. Five months later, she confesses her alienation from "a New-England publick with which I have nothing in common." This sense of isolation is common among young intellectuals, but in Fuller's case it reflected reality: she and the *North American Review*, for example, had little use for each other.

Fuller seems to have felt her own lack of vocation as Clarke took up his: "My heart has no proper home only can prefer some of its visiting-places to others and with deep regret I realize that I have at length entered upon the concentrating stage of life."[21] She lacked, in her own words, "the centre of my orbit." Not surprisingly, she fantasized about moving to the West herself and about translating French fiction for western readers.

These letters provide details that make her life even more specific: she originally contracted with George Ripley for her Goethe biography; she carefully kept her publications in the *American Monthly* from Clarke while he was pressing her to write more for his *Western Messenger*. She felt perfectly free to criticize his Schiller translations bluntly, even harshly. Even in the midst of her most intense writing about literature, Fuller was capable of a playful self-mockery that subverts the image of the haughty, self-absorbed Margaret Fuller that some of her acquaintances carried with them and left for posterity.

Still, there remain lacunae, most noticeably from 1 April 1836 to March 1837, a time when she was writing seriously and beginning to

20. James Freeman Clarke, *The Letters of James Freeman Clarke to Margaret Fuller*, ed. John Wesley Thomas (Hamburg: Cram, de Gruyter, 1957), p. 129.
21. Fuller to James Freeman Clarke, 7 October 1833.

publish her work in the *American Monthly*. At the same time, Fuller had finally met Emerson, who at one level displaced Clarke in her emotional life. The months of separation took their toll on Fuller and Clarke; his increasing involvement with his parish and with the *Messenger* kept him focused on Kentucky.

Despite their occasional misunderstandings, their increasingly diverging paths, and their inevitable changes of interest, Fuller and Clarke never broke the bond they forged so early in life. He was given to little kindnesses: he sent her an unsolicited $50 when she was in the West so that she might not have to scrape to enjoy herself. James and his wife opened their home to Fuller for her "conversations"; to the end of her life she wore the ring he gave her, with its motto, "Feed my lambs." Early in 1849, when her Roman prospects were most uncertain, she could say to him: "Spirits that have once been sincerely united and tended together a sacred flame, never become entirely stranger to one another's life."[22] The letters in this Appendix show with great clarity and detail what that "sacred flame" was.

In retrospect, Margaret Fuller's life looks compressed and fragmented. Her public career lasted a bare fifteen years; she died at a moment when her new perspectives could have matched new American needs. In a way homeless and placeless, she died as the de facto citizen of a cosmopolitan world. Multilingual, married to an Italian, a master of several national literatures, Margaret Fuller had many advantages but no genuine home. One may well see her as a quintessentially American writer—venturesome, searching for an adequate voice and literary form but never quite finding them, leaving an incomplete record. As Emerson acknowledged, her letters "are full of probity, talent, wit, friendship, charity, and high aspiration."[23] Her death at forty inevitably leads us to focus too much on what might have been. We need instead to accept the boundaries that exist: the record created by six volumes of her letters needs no defense. What we can now look forward to is a more comprehensive analysis of Margaret Fuller's life and writing.

ROBERT N. HUDSPETH

Redlands, California

22. Margaret Fuller, *The Letters of Margaret Fuller*, ed. Robert N. Hudspeth, 6 vols. (Ithaca: Cornell University Press, 1983–94), 5:173.

23. *Memoirs of Margaret Fuller Ossoli*, ed. R. W. Emerson, W. H. Channing, and J. F. Clarke (Boston: Phillips, Sampson, 1852), 1:279.

CONTENTS

Undated

Contents

Appendix: Newly Discovered Letters

1829

1830

Contents

1834

1835

1836

1837

Contents

1838

1839

1840

1841

1842

1843

1844

1845

1846

Contents

ILLUSTRATIONS

Acknowledgments

I am grateful to Elizabeth Channing Fuller, John C. Fuller, Richard E. Fuller, Willard P. Fuller, and Willard P. Fuller, Jr., for permission to publish Margaret Fuller's letters. I also thank the following institutions and individuals for permission to publish the Fuller letters in their possession that appear in this volume: the Bodleian Library, Oxford University; the Trustees of the Boston Public Library; the Brown University Library; Gene De Gruson; the Fruitlands Museums, Harvard, Massachusetts; the Trustees of the Ralph Waldo Emerson Memorial Association; the Buckminster Fuller Archives; the Harvard College Library and the Houghton Library, Harvard University; the University of Iowa Library; the Maine Historical Society, Local Miscellany collection; the Massachusetts Historical Society; Joel Myerson; the Bryant-Godwin Papers, Rare Books and Manuscripts Division of the New York Public Library, Astor, Lenox, and Tilden Foundations; the Historical Society of Pennsylvania; the Allison-Shelley Collection, Pennsylvania State University Libraries; Manuscripts Division, Department of Rare Books and Special Collections, the Princeton University Libraries; the Caroline Wells Healey Dall Papers, the Margaret Fuller Papers, and the Julia Ward Howe Family Papers in the Arthur and Elizabeth Schlesinger Library, Radcliffe College; the Rebecca Spring Papers (M541), Department of Special Collections, Stanford University Libraries; the Humanities Research Center, the University of Texas; the Watkinson Library, Trinity College, Hartford, Connecticut; the Sarah Margaret Fuller Collection, the Barrett Library, University of Virginia Library; and the Knollenberg Collection, Yale University Library.

Letters to Fuller and her manuscript journal fragments are quoted by the courtesy of the Trustees of the Boston Public Library; the Andover-Harvard Theological Library of Harvard Divinity School; and Harvard College Library and the Houghton Library, Harvard University.

The following librarians have generously aided me in the preparation of this volume: John Alden of the Boston Public Library; Robert Balay of the Yale University Library; Edmund Berkeley, Jr., and Barbara Bettcher of the University of Virginia Library; Patricia L. Bodak, Yale University Library; William H. Bond of the Houghton Library, Harvard University; Herbert Cahoon of the Pierpont Morgan Library; John D. Cushing of the Massachusetts Historical Society; Rodney G. Dennis of the Houghton Library, Harvard University; Peter Drummey of the Massachusetts Historical Society; Ellen S. Dunlap of the Humanities Research Center, the University of Texas; Pamela Dunn of the Stanford University Library; Wayne Furman, the New York Public Library, Manuscripts and Archives Division; Thomas L. Gaffney of the Maine Historical Society; Bonnie Goldstein of the Buckminster Fuller Institute; William Henry Harrison of the Fruitlands Museums; Christine D. Hathaway of the Brown University Library; Jeffrey H. Kaimowitz of the Watkinson Library, Trinity College, Hartford; John D. Kilbourne of the Historical Society of Pennsylvania; Patricia King of the Schlesinger Library, Radcliffe College; Carl Lane of the New Jersey Historical Society; James Lawton of the Boston Public Library; Robert A. McCown of the University of Iowa Library; Sylvia McDowell of the Schlesinger Library, Radcliffe College; Charles W. Mann of the Pennsylvania State University Library; Jeffrey D. Marshall of the Massachusetts Historical Society; Marian Marx of the Schlesinger Library, Radcliffe College; June Moll of the Humanities Research Center, the University of Texas; James E. Mooney of the Historical Society of Pennsylvania; Laura V. Monti of the Boston Public Library; E. J. S. Parsons of the Bodleian Library, Oxford University; Jennie Rathbun of the Houghton Library, Harvard University; Richard S. Reed of the Fruitlands Museums; Stephen T. Riley of the Massachusetts Historical Society; Elizabeth Ryall of the University of Virginia Library; Yvonne Schofer of the University of Wisconsin Library; Alan Seaburg of the Andover-Harvard Theological Library, Harvard Divinity School; Elizabeth Shenton of the Schlesinger Library, Radcliffe College; Margaret M. Sherry of the Princeton University Library; Glenn B. Skillin of the Maine Historical Society; Cornelia Starks of the Bodleian Library, Oxford University; Sandra Stelts of the Pennsylvania State University Library; Linda Thatcher of the Utah State Historical Society Library; Louis L.

Tucker of the Massachusetts Historical Society; Kenneth C. Turino of the Lynn Historical Society; and Melanie Wisner, the Houghton Library. The staff of the library of the New England Historic Genealogical Society was unfailingly helpful. One should take special note of the inexhaustible richness of this collection for the study of New England culture. Sandra Richey of the Armacost Library of the University of Redlands helped me obtain copies of obscure works.

I am grateful to the following individuals for help in securing illustrations for this volume: Teresa Buswell, Houghton Mifflin Company; Pamela Dunn, Stanford University Libraries; Elizabeth Gombosi, Harvard University Art Museums; Charles E. Greene, Princeton University Libraries; H. Thomas Hickerson, Cornell University Library; Kathleen Jacklin, Cornell University Library; Linda J. Long, Stanford University Libraries; Robin McElheny, Harvard University Archives; Constance Fuller Threinen; Rev. Herbert F. Vetter; Patricia White, Stanford University Libraries.

Several people called to my attention the existence of Fuller letters that appear in the Appendix: Konstanze Bäumer, Judith Mattson Bean, Charles Capper, John D. Cushing, Ezra Greenspan, Mary Lillian Haight, Charles Mann, Jeffery D. Marshall, Joel Myerson, and Elizabeth Hall Witherell.

Among the scholars who have answered my many queries are Patricia Barber, Charles Blackburn, Paula Blanchard, Arthur W. Brown, Lynn Cadwallader, Charles T. Cullen, Joseph Jay Deiss, Russell E. Durning, Robert L. Edwards, Alfred R. Ferguson, Robert J. Fitzwilliam, Anna Lisa Goldschen-Ohm, Benjamin Lease, Elizabeth Maxfield-Miller, Howard N. Meyer, Margaret Nussendorfer, Alice De V. Perry, Larry Reynolds, Bruce A. Ronda, Carl F. Strauch, and Richard P. Wunder. I am particularly grateful for the advice of Madeleine B. Stern and Eleanor M. Tilton, who provided me a list of corrections for the first two volumes. Kathy Fuller of the Division of Research Programs at the National Endowment for the Humanities was generous with her help. Mary Lillian Haight extended many kindnesses in making available to me the Fuller letters then in her possession. My colleagues Robert E. Burkholder, Wilma R. Ebbitt, and James Rambeau have given freely of their advice and expertise. Charles Mann, the Rare Books and Manuscripts Librarian of the Pennsylvania State University, helped me gather manuscripts for this edition. Charles Capper has generously shared his work on Fuller's biography with me. It is a pleasure again to acknowledge and impossible to overstate the importance of the assistance I have received from Joel Myerson of the University of South Carolina. For over two decades he has generously shared his information and expertise with me. This edition is much the better for his help.

I am again pleased to be able to acknowledge the expert help given me by several skilled research assistants (each of whom has gone on to a well-established scholarly career), those who worked the longest on the edition—Charles Hackenberry, Larry Carlson, and Robert D. Habich—and the two who focused on this volume: H. Lewis Ulman and Chiara Briganti. Shannon Nichols helped with the comprehensive index. Special thanks go to Barbara H. Salazar of Cornell University Press, who has been the editor for all six volumes of this edition. Her editorial suggestions consistently made the volumes better. As she has done for many years, Kay Hudspeth patiently and cheerfully helped with proofreading but more importantly with love and support.

This volume of Fuller letters has received financial assistance from the University of Washington Graduate School Research Fund, from the Pennsylvania State University College of Liberal Arts Research Fund, the Pennsylvania State University Institute for the Arts and Humanistic Studies, and the University of Redlands Faculty Research Fund. I am grateful for this support. The preparation of this volume was made possible in part by grants from the Program for Editions of the National Endowment for the Humanities, an independent federal agency.

R. N. H.

Editorial Method

This edition brings together for the first time all of the known extant letters written by Margaret Fuller. The texts are presented in their entirety in chronological order. Only conservative emendations, as outlined below under "Text," have been incorporated in the text; all others are recorded in textual notes. The text has been prepared from holographs whenever possible. When a holograph is lacking, the text is based on a manuscript copy of the lost holograph. When two manuscript copies of the same letter survive in the absence of a holograph, the more nearly complete version has been chosen. If both are of the same length, I have chosen the copy prepared by the Fuller family, because a spot comparison of other family copies with their surviving holographs shows them to be more nearly accurate than copies by other hands, if not exact. Only those letters with no manuscript authority have been taken from printed sources. Those letters dated by year only appear at the head of the year; those dated only by month, at the head of the month; undated letters are arranged as follows: arranged alphabetically by recipient when the recipient is known; then alphabetically by manuscript location; then alphabetically by printed source; then by page in the same source. This volume contains an appendix of letters discovered since publication of the edition began and letters whose dates can now be conjectured.

To establish the text, I first gathered microfilm or photocopies of all the manuscript letters and then made typed copies of these photo reproductions. I also typed all of the letters that now exist only in printed versions. I then corrected the typescript twice: first an assistant read aloud to me all of the photo reproductions and the printed versions of the letters; later, other assistants (working with me at different times) accompanied me to the libraries that hold the original manuscripts and read those manuscripts aloud to me as I again corrected the typescript. (Two letters were not read during this second check, for I was unable to visit the Iowa or Weimar libraries.)

The final text was derived from the corrected typescript, and proof was read aloud.

Format

The letters are numbered chronologically and the recipients identified in uniform headings. All dates, locations, salutations, and signatures are regularized in the following manner: dates and locations are set flush against the right margin, salutations flush against the left margin; signatures are set in large and small capitals and indented from the right margin at the bottom of the letter; when two or more initials are used in a signature, they are regularized with a space between each pair.

Text

The text is presented as faithfully as possible with conservative emendations. Fuller's spelling, capitalization, and punctuation are retained, as are her occasional slips of the pen (e.g., *and and*). Punctuation of canceled words and interlined insertions follows Fuller's final intention with the original versions reported in the textual notes. Her end punctuation is often ambiguous, for her period resembles a comma. In all instances this mark is preserved as a period. Punctuation is supplied in brackets only when its absence leads to confusion. A paragraph is often indicated in the holographs only by a space at the end of the preceding line. In all such instances the following paragraph is silently indented. Fuller used the dash as an all-purpose mark of punctuation; her dashes are consistently retained. Abbreviations are not expanded save in those instances where ambiguities might otherwise result. When expanded, the additions are enclosed in square brackets. Cancellations are omitted from the text, and interlined additions are lowered; all such emendations are reported in the textual notes. Cross-hatching (Fuller occasionally turned the sheet and wrote at a right angle across her letter) and all symbols, notes, and marks added by later hands are emended and unreported. The German ß is set as *ss*; & becomes *and*.

Annotation and Index

The text of each letter is followed by a provenance note that indicates the source of the text, any surviving manuscript copies, and any previous publishing history, the name and address of the recipient as written by Fuller, the postmark, and the recipient's endorsement, if any. A brief biography of the recipient follows the provenance note to the first surviving letter to him or her, unless the recipient has already been identified. Then come textual notes listing editorial emendations, Fuller's cancellations, and her interlined insertions. Fuller's words here are set in roman type; editorial interpolations are set in italics. The numbered annotations that follow the textual notes identify all people mentioned in the letter except those well known to readers (e.g., Dante, Shakespeare, Milton) and those previously identified, and all books, literary and historical allusions, and quotations that can be established. Brief biographies of well-known individuals who are not identified in the notes can be found in *Webster's Biographical Dictionary*.

Citations to the Massachusetts vital records office take two forms. Citations to nineteenth-century records refer only to volume and page numbers. Thus "MVR 119:345" cites page 345 of volume 119 of the death record. Beginning in this century, the reference has a preceding date. Thus "MVR 1924 11:167" cites the death record for 1924, volume 11, page 167. Unless otherwise noted, all citations are to death records.

Publication data come from the *National Union Catalog* of the Library of Congress or, when necessary, from the *British Museum General Catalogue of Printed Books*. Occasional notes explain ambiguities in the text, summarize events in Fuller's life, or refer the reader to other letters. The surviving letters written to Fuller have provided explanatory material for many of the annotations. Unidentified items are silently passed over. This volume contains a chronological list of the letters that Fuller is known to have written but that have not survived. The "Errata" section lists corrections and additions to the notes of the previous volumes. Each previous volume of the letters has a separate index. The index for this volume is included in the comprehensive index.

EDITORIAL APPARATUS

Textual Devices

The following devices are used in the text:

[Square brackets] enclose editorial additions.
[*Italics*] indicate editorial comments.
[I] [II] [III] indicate sections of a letter recovered from various sources.
[   ] marks matter missing from the text.
Superscript^n refers the reader to a textual note.
Superscript^1 refers the reader to an explanatory note.

The following devices are used in the textual notes:

⟨Angle brackets⟩ identify recovered cancellations.
⟨?⟩ identifies unrecovered cancellations.
↑ Opposed arrows ↓ indicate interlined insertions.
Italics indicate editorial comments.

Descriptive Symbols

AL	Autograph letter, unsigned
ALfr	Autograph letter fragment, unsigned
ALfrS	Autograph letter fragment, signed with name or initial(s)
ALS	Autograph letter, signed with name or initial(s)
EL	Edited letter, as previously published; holograph now lost
ELfr	Edited letter fragment, as previously published; holograph now lost
MsC	Manuscript copy of a Fuller letter in a hand other than Fuller's; unless otherwise indicated, the holograph has not been recovered

37

MsCfr   Manuscript copy of a fragment of a Fuller letter in a hand
         other than Fuller's; unless otherwise indicated, the holo-
         graph has not been recovered

Location Symbols

CSmH   The Huntington Library
CSt   Stanford University Library
CtHT-W   Watkinson Library, Trinity College, Hartford, Connecticut
CtY   Yale University Library
IaU   University of Iowa Library
MB   Boston Public Library, Department of Rare Books and Manu-
           scripts
MCR-S   Radcliffe College, Schlesinger Library
MeHi   Maine Historical Society Library
MH   Harvard University, Houghton Library
MH-AH   Harvard Divinity School, Andover-Harvard Theological Li-
           brary
MHarF   Fruitlands Museums, Harvard, Massachusetts
MHi   Massachusetts Historical Society
NjHi   New Jersey Historical Society
NjP   Princeton University Library
NN-M   New York Public Library, Manuscripts and Archives Division
NNPM   Pierpont Morgan Library, New York
PHi   Pennsylvania Historical Society Library
PSt   The Pennsylvania State University Library
RPB   Brown University Library
TxU   University of Texas, Humanities Research Center
ViU   University of Virginia Library

Short Titles and Abbreviations

Aspinwall, *Aspinwall Genealogy:* Algernon Akin Aspinwall, *The Aspinwall
    Genealogy* (Rutland, Vt.: Tuttle, [1901]).

At Home and Abroad: Margaret Fuller Ossoli, *At Home and Abroad*, ed. Ar-
    thur B. Fuller (Boston: Crosby, Nichols, 1856).

Berg-Perry, "'Impulses of Human Nature'": Martha L. Berg and Alice
    De V. Perry, "'The Impulses of Human Nature': Margaret Fuller's
    Journal from June through October 1844," *Proceedings of the Massa-
    chusetts Historical Society* 102 (1990): 38–126.

Bolster, *James Freeman Clarke:* Arthur S. Bolster, Jr., *James Freeman Clarke:
    Disciple to Advancing Truth* (Boston: Beacon, 1959).

Briggs, *Cabot Family:* L. Vernon Briggs, *History and Genealogy of the Cabot
    Family*, 2 vols. (Boston: C. E. Goodspeed, 1927).

Capper, *Margaret Fuller:* Charles Capper, *Margaret Fuller: An American Ro-
    mantic Life* (New York: Oxford University Press, 1992).

CC: Columbian Centinel (Boston).

Chevigny: Bell Gale Chevigny, *The Woman and the Myth: Margaret Fuller's Life and Writings* (Old Westbury, N.Y.: Feminist Press, 1976).

Clarke, "Letters of a Sister": Sarah Ann Clarke, "Letters of a Sister," MH: bMS Am 1569.3 (12).

Columbia Catalogue: Officers and Graduates of Columbia University (New York, 1900).

Complete Poetical Works of Shelley: The Complete Poetical Works of Shelley, ed. Thomas Hutchinson (Oxford: Clarendon, 1904).

Crane, *White Silence:* Sylvia E. Crane, *White Silence: Greenough, Powers, and Crawford* (Coral Gables, Fla.: University of Miami Press, 1972).

CVR: *Vital Records of Cambridge, Massachusetts, to the Year 1850*, 2 vols. (Boston: Wright & Potter, 1914–15).

DAB: Dictionary of American Biography, ed. Allen Johnson and Dumas Malone, 20 vols. (New York: Scribner's, 1928–36).

Dalbiac, *Dictionary of Quotations:* Lilian Dalbiac, *Dictionary of Quotations (German)* (New York: Frederick Ungar, n.d.).

Davis, *Suffolk County:* William T. Davis, *Professional and Industrial History of Suffolk County*, 3 vols. (Boston: Boston History Co., 1894).

Detti: Emma Detti, *Margaret Fuller Ossoli e i suoi corrispondenti* (Florence: Felice Le Monnier, 1942).

DivCat: General Catalogue of the Divinity School of Harvard University, 1901 (Cambridge, Mass., 1901).

DNB: Dictionary of National Biography, ed. Leslie Stephen and Sidney Lee, 22 vols. (London: Oxford University Press, 1937–38).

Emerson-Carlyle Correspondence: The Correspondence of Emerson and Carlyle, ed. Joseph Slater (New York: Columbia University Press, 1964).

Frothingham, *Memoir of William Henry Channing:* Octavius Brooks Frothingham, *Memoir of William Henry Channing* (Boston: Houghton Mifflin, 1886).

Goethe, *Sämtliche Werke:* Johann Wolfgang Goethe, *Sämtliche Werke*, 18 vols. (Zurich: Artemis, 1979).

Habich, "Annotated List": Robert D. Habich, "An Annotated List of Contributors to the *Western Messenger*," in *Studies in the American Renaissance, 1984*, ed. Joel Myerson (Charlottesville: University Press of Virginia, 1984), pp. 93–179.

Habich, "JFC's 1833 Letter-journal": Robert D. Habich, "James Freeman Clarke's 1833 Letter-journal for Margaret Fuller," *ESQ* 27 (1981): 47–56.

Habich, *Transcendentalism and the "Western Messenger":* Robert D. Habich, *Transcendentalism and the "Western Messenger": A History of the Magazine and Its Contributors, 1835–1841* (Rutherford, N.J.: Fairleigh Dickinson University Press, 1985).

Heralds: Samuel A. Eliot, *Heralds of a Liberal Faith*, 3 vols. (Boston: American Unitarian Association, 1910).

Higginson, *MFO:* Thomas Wentworth Higginson, *Margaret Fuller Ossoli* (Boston: Houghton Mifflin, 1884).

Howe, *Howe Genealogies:* Daniel Wait Howe, *Howe Genealogies*, 2 vols. (Boston: New England Historic Genealogical Society, 1929).

Hudson, *Browning: Browning to His American Friends*, ed. Gertrude Reese Hudson (New York: Barnes & Noble, 1965).

Hudspeth, "Margaret Fuller's 1839 Journal": Robert N. Hudspeth, "Margaret Fuller's 1839 Journal: Trip to Bristol," *Harvard Library Bulletin* 27 (October 1979): 445–70.

JMN: The Journals and Miscellaneous Notebooks of Ralph Waldo Emerson, ed. William H. Gilman et al., 16 vols. (Cambridge: Belknap Press of Harvard University Press, 1960–82).

Lathrop, *Memories of Hawthorne:* Rose Hawthorne Lathrop, *Memories of Hawthorne* (Boston: Houghton Mifflin, 1898).

Letters of JFC: The Letters of James Freeman Clarke to Margaret Fuller, ed. John Wesley Thomas (Hamburg: Cram, de Gruyter, 1957).

Letters of MF: The Letters of Margaret Fuller, ed. Robert N. Hudspeth, 6 vols. (Ithaca: Cornell University Press, 1983–94).

Memoirs: Memoirs of Margaret Fuller Ossoli, ed. R. W. Emerson, W. H. Channing, and J. F. Clarke, 2 vols. (Boston: Phillips, Sampson, 1852).

Miller: *Margaret Fuller: American Romantic*, ed. Perry Miller (Garden City, N.Y.: Doubleday, 1963).

Milton, *Complete Poetical Works: The Complete Poetical Works of John Milton*, ed. Douglas Bush (Boston: Houghton Mifflin, 1965).

Mt. Auburn: Burial records, Mount Auburn Cemetery, Cambridge, Mass.

MVR: Massachusetts vital records, Boston.

Myerson, "Margaret Fuller's 1842 Journal": Joel Myerson, "Margaret Fuller's 1842 Journal: At Concord with the Emersons," *Harvard Library Bulletin* 21 (July 1973): 320–40.

Myerson, *New England Transcendentalists:* Joel Myerson, *The New England Transcendentalists and the "Dial"* (Rutherford, N.J.: Fairleigh Dickinson University Press, 1980).

National Cyclopaedia: The National Cyclopaedia of American Biography, 62 vols. to date (New York: James T. White, 1898–).

NEHGR: New England Historical and Genealogical Register.

NEHGS: New England Historic Genealogical Society, Boston.

Nichols, "Thomas Fuller": Arthur B. Nichols, "Thomas Fuller and His Descendants," *Publications of the Cambridge Historical Society* 28 (1943): 11–28.

OCGL: Henry and Mary Garland, *The Oxford Companion to German Literature* (Oxford: Clarendon, 1976).

Rusk, *Letters of RWE: The Letters of Ralph Waldo Emerson*, ed. Ralph L. Rusk, 6 vols. (New York: Columbia University Press, 1939).

Sanborn, *Recollections:* Franklin B. Sanborn, *Recollections of Seventy Years*, 2 vols. (Boston: R. G. Badger, 1909).

Sanborn and Harris, *Alcott:* Franklin B. Sanborn and William T. Harris, *A. Bronson Alcott: His Life and Philosophy*, 2 vols. (Boston: Roberts, 1893).

Schillers Werke: Schillers Werke: In zwei Bänden, 2 vols. (Munich: Droemersche, 1957).

Selected Poems of Thomas Hood: Selected Poems of Thomas Hood, ed. John Clubbe (Cambridge: Harvard University Press, 1970).

Tilton, "True Romance": Eleanor M. Tilton, "The True Romance of Anna Hazard Barker and Samuel Gray Ward," in *Studies in the American Renaissance, 1987*, ed. Joel Myerson (Charlottesville: University Press of Virginia, 1987), pp. 53–72.

Van Doren: *The Lost Art: Letters of Seven Famous Women*, ed. Dorothy Van Doren (New York: Coward-McCann, 1929).

VR: vital records.

Wade: *The Writings of Margaret Fuller*, ed. Mason Wade (New York: Viking, 1941).

Wellisz: Leopold Wellisz, *The Friendship of Margaret Fuller D'Ossoli and Adam Mickiewicz* (New York: Polish Book Importing Co., 1947).

Weygant, *Hull Family in America: The Hull Family in America*, comp. Charles H. Weygant (Pittsfield, Mass.: Sun Printing Co., 1913).

WNC: Margaret Fuller Ossoli, *Woman in the Nineteenth Century, and Kindred Papers*, ed. Arthur B. Fuller (Boston: John P. Jewett, 1855).

Works: Manuscript copybooks, Fuller family papers, 3 vols., in Houghton Library, Harvard University.

Works of George Herbert: The Works of George Herbert, ed. F. E. Hutchinson (Oxford: Clarendon, 1941).

THE LETTERS OF MARGARET FULLER

875. To Richard F. Fuller

My dear Richard,

I was just making up a pacquet to send home by a friendly hand, when this morng yours of 4th Decr reached me. I was very glad, having become saddened and indeed surprized not to hear from you. The way you speak now of my marriage is such as I expected from you.[1] Now that we have once exchanged some words on these important changes in our lives, it matters little to write[n] letters. Too much has happened; the changes have been too great to be made clear in writing. I doubt not when we have met face to face; we shall be friends the same as ever, or better than before.

It would not be worthwhile to keep the house thinking of me.[2] I cannot fix precisely the period of my return, though at present, it seems to me probable we may make the voyage in May or[n] June. At first we should go and make a little visit to Mother.[3] I should take counsel with various friends before fixing myself in any place, see what openings there are for me &c. I cannot judge at all before I am personally in U. S. and wish to engage myself noway. Should I finally decide on the neighborhood of N. Y. I could see you all often   I wish, however, to live with Mother, if possible. We will discuss it on all sides when I come. Climate is one thing I must think of; the change from the Roman winter to that of N. England might be very trying for Ossoli. In N. Y. he would see Italns often hear his native tongue and feel less exiled. If we had our affairs in N. Y. and lived in the country we could find places as quiet as Canton, more beautiful and from which access to a city would be as easy by means of steam. On the other hand my family and most cherished friends are in N. England. I shall weigh all advantages at the time and choose as may then seem best.

I feel also the great responsibility about a child, and the mixture of solemn feeling with the joy its sweet ways and caresses give.[4] Yet this is only different in degree, not in kind from what we should feel in other relations; the destiny of all we come in contact with we may more or less impede or brighten. Much as the child lies in our power; still God and nature are there, furnishing a thousand masters to correct our erroneous,[n] fill up our imperfect teachings. I feel impelled to try for go [   ] for the sake of my child, most powerfully, but if I fail, I trust help will be tendered him from some other quarter. I do not wish to trouble myself more than is inevitable or lose the simple innocent pleasure of watching his growth from day to day by thinking of his future. At present my care of him is to keep him clean body and mind, to give for body and mind simple nutriment when he demands it and play with him. Now he lear[ns] playing as we all shall whe[n] we enter a higher state. With him my intercourse thus far has bee[n] satisfactory and if I do not well for *him* he at least has taught *me* a great deal.

My love to your wife.[5] I hear she is very sweet and rejoice she makes you so happy. Ossoli sends his love to you. I may say of him, as you say of your wife, it would be difficult to other than like him, so sweet is his disposition, so [wi]thout an effort disinterested, so simply [w]ise his daily conduct, so harmonious his whole nature. Add that he is a perfectly unconscious character, and never dreams that he does well. He is studying English but makes little progress, for a good while you may not be able to talk with him, but you will like showing him some of your favorite haunts; he is so happy in nature, in sweet tranquil places. Farewell, dear R. every yr affece friend and sister

M.

Direct to me simply *Florence*, Italy. We take our letters now direct fr[om] [   ] just, [   ]

ALS (MH: fMS Am 1086 [9:162]); MsC (MH: fMS Am 1086 [Works, 2:605–11]). Published in part in *WNC*, pp. 378–80; Wade, pp. 591–92; and Miller, pp. 310–12. *Addressed:* Richard F. Fuller / 10 State St. Boston / Massachusetts U.S.A.

Her brother Richard Frederick Fuller was a Boston lawyer.
little to write] little to ⟨exchange⟩ ↑ write ↓
May or] May ⟨and⟩ or
our erroneous,] our ⟨imperfect⟩ ↑ erroneous ↓ ,

1. In his letter, Richard said: "It was *your act*, done at a great distance, and in circumstances not all under my ken; so I confide that it was all for the best. For my part, my own experience of marriage, and my knowledge of your character, make me believe that it was needed by you, and must have developed new veins of experience in relief of your intellectual temperament" (MH).

2. Richard had suggested that the Ossolis rent his father-in-law's Canton home.

3. Margarett Crane Fuller was living with her son Arthur in New Hampshire.

4. Angelo was sixteen months old. Of children, Richard said: "I must gaze on the young spirit with a great intermingling of grief. What a responsibility the birth of a child throws upon the parent to well take care that it attains the second birth of the spirit."

5. Richard married Sarah Batchelder in 1849.

876. To Samuel G. and Anna B. Ward

Florence
8th Jany 1850.

Dear Sam and Anna,

It has seemed getting quite near you to see Mr Haggerty on New Years day, and I accepted it as omen of meeting with yourselves in course of this year, though how I am to get across the great water I do not yet know.[1] But "Providence who is better to us all than any of our Aunts" (certainly much better to me than most of mine) is bound, I think, to get me home somehow, if it is necessary.

I am sorry to have seen Mr H. so little during his brief stay, but Ossoli and I have both been unwell, and could not share the pleasant glow his presence has diffused[n] in the little American circle He seems to have enjoyed himself. To me it seems worse than nothing to come to Italy for so short a time and at this season but he is a better Alchymist.

I would like to have shown him my little boy, but he was asleep the eveg Mr H. called on me. And he could only have told you of a very fat baby, who looks like anything but an Italian. Perhaps he will seem more interesting for others several months hence. To me who have had him so very sick the mere fact of his health seems so very interesting.[n] Till very lately I have feared he might never get over all he had to suffer during the siege of Rome.

I rejoice to hear that your little boy begins to speak; probably then he will quite outgrow the traces of his malady.[2] As far as there is any positive good, I think it is one to be in fair average possession of all natural faculties. No man is fully developed, but to be entirely shut in on any one side, though there may be precious compensations is still a

47

calamity and to the noblest strongest minds brings some portion of morbid suffering. I, perhaps, who have not had so full use of my sight as men in general, value free speech and hearing more, especially the former; many a stone have I rolled off my heart, many a strange mental dilemma lifted by a fluent word, a little rill from the glacier's edge; it carried away but a small portion of the snow-weight but an opening once made, the sun quickly did the rest.

I think of you now in Boston and it pleases me that Sam is using his powers again in the more active scene.[3] There seems to me so much to do that no man of the finer powers can be spared long at a time. Then, being in for Ballagarry fair myself for the rest of my life; my friends seem too far off on the sunny slopes of Mount Pleasant. I should like to know where you are living. Do you not miss Ellen Hooper's lovely eyes and untiring wit.[4] I shall when I come. My friends look very lovely to me in the distance, those who are round you now. I do not find women in Europe to compare with those of[n] America. I have recruited[n] a large band of male friends on this side but among European women have had real intimacy only with three. One of these is indeed a figure of rare dignity and grace, and in mind or honor, perfect in her way.[5] We are every way most unlike, but more friends for that.

My head is aching, I have written too many letters today. My health is vile. I seem so nice and bright when I do nothing; and the moment I exert myself a little suffer. It is the more degrading as fate has annexed[n] me so emphatically to the workies. I have great service offered and cant do enough to merit my salt, to say nothing of bread. Good bye! Prepare me an old, worn, easy chair beside your nursery fire. I am chiefly good now at crooning children to sleep with ballad stories. When childlike minded I will make you doze too meanwhile am only your well-disposed and affece friend

MARGARET.

ALS (MH: bMS Am 1465 [933]). *Addressed:* S. G. Ward Esq. / Boston / Mass / U. S. A. / Kindness of Mr Haggerty. *Endorsed:* Margaret Fuller / 8 Jan.

Samuel Gray and Anna Barker Ward were friends from Fuller's youth. She had once been in love with Ward when she thought he might become an artist (Tilton, "True Romance," pp. 53–72).

has diffused] has ⟨seemed to⟩ diffused
very interesting.] very ⟨u⟩ interesting.
with those of] with ↑ those of ↓
have recruited] have ⟨formed⟩ ↑ recruited ↓
has annexed] has ⟨un⟩ annexed

1. Ogden Haggerty (1810?–75) was a New York auction and commission broker (*New York Times*, 1 September 1875).

2. Thomas Wren Ward (1844–1940), son of Sam and Anna Ward, followed his father and grandfather into the Baring bank. He was a classmate of William James and Justice Holmes, but he never finished his Harvard degree. In 1872 he married Sophia Read Howard (Harvard archives).

3. The Wards had been living in Lenox, Massachusetts, where they were neighbors of Caroline and William Tappan. Hawthorne lived there later in 1850.

4. Ellen Sturgis Hooper, a Boston poet and Fuller's close friend, died in 1848.

5. Fuller refers to Costanza Arconati Visconti of Milan.

877. To Lewis Cass, Jr.

Florence
20th Jany 1850

My dear Mr Cass,

More than three months have passed since I heard from you; two of my letters left unanswered and letters in which I expressed great solicitude to hear, as you were ill at the date of your last. It seems to me there must be some reason for this, beyond the pressure of other affairs on your time, and I beg you to answer me frankly whether it is so or not. You must feel it would be painful for me just at the moment I was most penetrated with the kindness of[n] your acts to be[n] met suddenly by this silence. Add that, beside the cordial way in which you interposed for me as a countrywoman, I had reason, had I not?— to think you felt for me affection and friendship? Our acquaintance had not been long, but amid trying circumstances calculated to promote intimacy more than common days. We had spoken very freely, you had sympathized with my trials, and I had known some of your more hidden feelings. I had supposed a mutual friendliness and good understanding had been founded that could not be disturbed that perhaps we might meet now and then in life, but if we did not, we should still retain a cordial interest in and regard for one another. Was I wrong?

I claim an answer this time; Believe, that I have no desire to occupy your time, if imperatively filled up in other ways, but I do wish to know whether such is the *sole* reason for your silence. Meanwhile, I remain, as before, with sincerest good wishes yours

M. OSSOLI.

ALS (MH: fMS Am 1086 [9:167]); MsC (MH: fMS Am 1086 [Works, 1:351–53]).

Lewis Cass, Jr., the American chargé d'affaires in Rome, helped Fuller and Ossoli escape in 1849.

the kindness of] the ↑ kindness of ↓
to be] to ⟨th⟩ be

Hiram Powers' bust of Anna Barker Ward. In the collection of The Corcoran Gallery of Art, gift of Benjamin Warder Thoron, Louise Thoron MacVeagh, Ellen Warder Thoron MacVeagh, Faith Thoron Knapp, Gray Thoron.

878. To ?

[ca. February? 1850?]

I do not think I shall publish until I can be there in person. I had first meant to in England, but you know this new regulation that a foreigner cannot hold copyright there.[1] I think if I publish in the U. S. I should be there to correct the proofs, see about the form of the work and alterations in M. S. also I hope on the spot I may make better terms than are offered by letter. It will all

MsCfr (MB: Ms. Am. 1450 [112]). Published in Higginson, *MFO*, p. 273.

1. Fuller refers to her manuscript history of the Italian revolution. Although it was possible for an American to secure an English copyright, recent court decisions had not been consistent. The Court of the Exchequer had ruled against foreigners in three major decisions between 1845 and 1849, but the two common law courts had both decided for foreign copyrights in 1848 and 1849 (James J. Barnes, *Authors, Publishers, and Politicians* [Columbus, Ohio, 1974], pp. 153, 167).

879. To ?

[ca. 1? February 1850]

You ask, how I employ myself here. I was much engaged writing; but this last two months our apartment has been very cold, and the only room where I could write in tranquillity quite uninhabitable. I am beginning to use it again; meanwhile I have been more occupied by reading— Louis Blanc's "Ten Years", LaMartine, and other books, which throw light on recent transactions.[1]

There are several delightful persons whom I see in an intimate way. One house where I hear very fine music. Mr. Browning, who enriches every hour I pass with him, is a most cordial, true, and noble man.[2] One of my most prized friends, Marchioness Arconati Visconti, of Milan, is passing the winter here, and I see her almost every day.

MsCfr (MB: Ms. Am. 1450 [173]). Published in *Memoirs*, 2:310–11.

1. Blanc's *Révolution française; Histoire de dix ans, 1830–1840* was first published in 1841–42. An English version, *The History of Ten Years, 1830–1840* was published in London in 1844–45 and in Philadelphia in 1848. Alphonse Marie-Louis de Lamartine's *Histoire de la révolution de 1848* had been published in Brussels and Paris in 1849.

2. Fuller was an early American reviewer of the works of both Robert and Elizabeth Barrett Browning.

880.   To Lewis Cass, Jr.

Florence 5 Feb 1850

To Mr Cass.

I thought before that you had seen too much of the world not to prize a loyal heart and mind open to truth and generous, at least in its desires. In early youth it seems the world must be full of such; but after some experience of the vanities, falsehoods and mean competitions, which throng its walks, somewhat true and warm seems of worth not lightly to be relinquished.

What you say of Rome corresponds with all else I hear. It is the same in Tuscany, that is, in its degree. Tuscany must always be under a regime more mild and liberal than any other of the old forms in Italy.[1] The mind of Leopold left an impression that can never be quite effaced, and the Austrian must act with discretion here. Still the reactionaries, here as elsewhere, are doing their best to prepare for another revolution. I think we would not wish to go to Rome under these circumstances; indeed, all tends to make us bend our eyes towards *America* for the present—

MsCfr (MB: Ms. Am. 1450 [33]).

1. Rome, occupied by the French since July 1849, when the Roman Republic fell, began to endure the power of reaction. Although Pius did not return until 12 April 1850, he had already demonstrated his intention to crush any liberal tendencies in the Papal States. The French, as a foreign occupying force, found their soldiers stabbed in the street. As Fuller says, the situation was less harsh in Florence, where the Austrians depended on Leopold II, grand duke of Tuscany, whose quarter-century reign had been more or less moderate. What Fuller could not know was that Leopold secretly agreed to allow Austria to invade Tuscany. The Austrians crossed the border on 5 April and occupied Florence on 25 May (Bolton King, *A History of Italian Unity* [London, 1899], 1:361–63, 370–72).

881.   To Marcus and Rebecca Spring

Florence 5th February 1850

My dear Marcus and Rebecca

You have no doubt ere this received a letter from me written I think in December, but I must suddenly write again to thank you for the New Years letter. It was a sweet impulse that led you all to write together and had its full reward in the pleasure you gave. I am glad it entered into the heart of Emmeline Story to write that letter:[1] it was in the spirit of that tender and generous friendship both she and her husband always showed me. I trust the tie formed between us will last as long as our lives. It is also pleasant that it should be the Lowells that took pains to show the letter.[2] As to its subject matter I have written as little as possible about Ossoli and our relation, wishing my old friends to form their own impressions naturally when they saw us together. I have all who ever really knew me would feel that I am become somewhat milder, kinder and more worthy to serve all who need for my new relations. I have expected that those who cared for me chiefly for my activity of intellect would not care for him, but that those in whom the moral nature nature predominates would gradually learn to love and admire him and see what a treasure his affection must be to me. But that would be only gradually, for it is by acts, not words, that one so simple, true, delicate and retiring can be known. For me while some of my friends have thought me exacting I may say Ossoli has always outgone my expectations in the disinterestedness, the uncompromising bounty of his every little act. He was the same to his father as to me; his affections are few but profound and thoroughly acted out. His permanent affections are few, but his heart is always open to the humble, suffering, heavy-laden. His mind has little habitual action except in a simple natural poetry that one not very intimate with him would never know any thing about But once opened to a great impulse as it was to the hope of freeing his country it rose to the height of the occasion and staid there. His enthusiasm was quiet but unsleeping. He is very unlike most Italians, but very unlike most Americans too. I do not expect all who cared for me to care for him, nor is it of importance to him; he is wholly without vanity. He is too truly the gentleman not to be respected by all persons of refinement; for the rest if my life is free and not too much troubled, if he can enjoy his domestic affections and fulfil his duties in his own way he will content. Can we find this much for ourselves in bustling America for the next three or four years? I know not but think we shall come and try. I wish much to see you all and exchange the kiss of peace. There will, I trust, be peace within if not without. I thank you most warmly for your gift; be assured it will turn to great profit. I have learned to be a great adept in economy by looking at my little boy. I cannot bear to spend a cent for fear he may come to want it. I understand how the family men get so mean. I shall have to begin soon to pray against that danger. Dear Eddie (much was I pleased with his little but prettily written letter) wishes he could introduce the babies to one another. I hope that will be yet and that I shall find dear little Marcus well.[3] My little Nino as we call him for house and pet name is now in

53

perfect health. I wash and dress and sew for him and think I see a great deal more of his little cunning ways and shall know him better for doing all for him, though 'tis inconvenient and fatiguing at times. His head is singularly formed. I fear the faculties are not in very good balance. He is very gay and laughing, sometimes violent, for he has come to the age when he wants every thing in his own hands, but on the whole sweet as yet and very fond of me. He often calls me to kiss him, he says *kiss* in preference to the Italian word bacio. I do not cherish sanguine visions about him. I shall try to do my best by him and enjoy the present moment.

It was a nice account you gave of your visit to the N.A. with Miss Bremer. She found some neighbours as good as her own.[4] You say she was much pleased by Elizabeth Hoar.[5] Could she know E. she might enrich the world with a portrait as full of little delicate traits as any in her gallery, and of a higher class than any in which she has been successful. I would give much to be a George Sand to paint E. It is wicked she should die and leave the world no copy. Now I must begin "to draw to a close. I am writing by a box of Mr Mosier's and there is very little time more.[6] The Mosiers now live in a very handsome house and receive every Saturday night. I go sometimes but not so often as if the rooms were not heated with stoves which bring on my bad headaches. There may usually be seen all the Americans in Florence but we have not been fortunate in interesting new arrivals. Mr. W. H. Aspinwall is the pleasantest among them I have seen[7] Mr Sullivan who came out with us in the steamer interested me by telling me a good deal about you Marcus. He had with him Miss Prall[?] a lady who had put aside *seven thousand* dollars to buy "Objects of Art and Virtu" but he had managed to get his list made up for two thousand! I don't know how well. I see a good deal of Mr. and Mrs. Browning— that is a great pleasure. Madame Arconati is passing the winter here and to me the same precious friend as ever. I know some most agreeable English ladies who are fine pianists and have the best music. I like the Greenoughs much and they are very friendly[8] All true people seem to like Ossoli and he is particularly pleased with the Arconatis and Mr and Mrs Horatio Greenough. All too speak Italian more or less; thus our position in point of society is very pleasant knowing few people and those every where such as we like. On this account and the cheapness of living here I should have liked to stay a year longer in Florence, but on the whole I believe the nays carry it. I feel extremely grieved at what you write about Mr Delf, to me personally he has been a great disappointment, having depended on his friendship to make some arrangements in England which would have been a great advantage to me, and he never even wrote an answer while I let the opportunity go by as to others, feeling no doubt he would take care for me. Yet I could not have believed he would fail in honor as to money sore beset as I know he has been.[9] Pray write to me precisely if you hear any more about it. Will you ask the Mannings with my love to enclose a list of engravings if Hicks brought them from Paris[10] He has never written me about it but I suppose he did buy for the M s as he promised me some engravings in Paris in addition to what I sent from Rome and want to know the subjects as I shall bring yet a few more when I come and might chance to duplicate About my book, I feel disinclined to publish till I can be on the spot. The terms Mr Putnam offers (thro' a letter from Dr Mayo) do not seem advantageous— then how ill that affair with Wiley turned out—[11] Whenever I have published before I have got at least a hundred or two soon, but if their business is conducted so that the expense of agencies swallows up profits for so long a time that is worse for poor authors than a more limited sale I feel as if I had better come and have the aid of some friend skilful in these affairs and—who cares a little for my interests; if I cannot make any thing out of my present materials my future is dark indeed. I do not wish to throw away the studies and materials of 4 years, paid for by so many hours of bitter care as they have been already Yet to get home seems a great undertaking too. I had hoped so much once Mr Delf would be my friend about these very things——Alas!—Farewell and peace be with you both——The joys of mutual love, duties cheerfully fulfilled and an ever deepening trust in God for the rest.—

MsC (MH: fMS Am 1086 [9:220]); MsC (MH: fMS Am 1086 [Works, 1:277–87]); MsCfr (NjHi); MsCfr (CSmH [46944]). Published in part in *WNC*, pp. 381–84; *Critic* 48 (March 1906): 252–53; Sanborn, *Recollections*, 2:411–12; and Miller, pp. 312–14.

Marcus and Rebecca Spring of New York had been Fuller's traveling companions in Europe.

1. Emelyn Story, wife of William Wetmore Story, had become Fuller's close friend during their months in Rome.

2. The Storys were friends of James Russell and Maria White Lowell. Fuller had published Lowell in the *Dial* and reviewed his work in the *New-York Daily Tribune*. He had created an acid satire on her in his 1848 *Fable for Critics*.

3. Edward Adolphus Spring was born in 1837; Herbert Marcus, third and last of the Spring children, was born a few days after Fuller's child in September 1848.

4. The Springs had taken Fredrika Bremer to the North American Phalanx in New Jersey. Fuller plays on the title of Bremer's novel *Die Nachbarn*.

5. Elizabeth Sherman Hoar of Concord was a close friend.

Marcus Spring. Rebecca Spring Papers, Department of Special Collections, Stanford University Libraries.

6. Joseph Mozier was a businessman turned sculptor with whom Fuller formed a friendship that was later betrayed.

7. William Henry Aspinwall (1807–75) was a wealthy New York businessman. He married Anna L. Breck (1812–94) (*DAB;* Aspinwall, *Aspinwall Genealogy*, p. 110).

8. Both the Henry and Horatio Greenough families were in Florence at this time.

9. Thomas Delf had been employed by the D. Appleton publishing firm in London. Fuller probably refers to letter 635 in vol. 4 of these letters. Her reference here may be to the disclosure that Delf, acting on his own for his own profit, had sold American copies of Irving's works in England and thus had violated John Murray's copyright protecting English sales and had seriously embarrassed Wiley and Putnam, Irving's American publisher (George Haven Putnam, *George Palmer Putnam: A Memoir* [New York, 1912], pp. 198–99).

10. Richard Henry and Mary Weeks Manning were friends of Fuller during her months in New York City. Thomas Hicks, the American painter, had known Fuller in Rome.

11. Having met Fuller in London, George Palmer Putnam accompanied her to Genoa in 1847. William Starbuck Mayo (1811–95) was a New York physician (*DAB*). In 1849, Putnam published Mayo's *Kaloolah,* which became a very popular romance. Fuller had published her *Papers on Literature and Art* with Wiley and Putnam of New York.

882. To William H. Channing

[I] Florence 6th February 1850.
I know there must be a cloud of false rumors and impressions at first, but you will see when we meet that there was a sufficient reason for all I have done, and that if my life be not wholly right, (as it is so difficult to keep a life true in a world full of falsities,) it is not wholly wrong nor fruitless. You would have had true impressions at first if you had received the daguerreotype likeness of O—I had depended on that. It gave a view of his face different from the habitual one, but which represents him as he most is in our relation.

[II] But I have too much to tell you of all that, in which others are also interwoven. My life proceeds so regularly, far more so than the fates of a Greek tragedy, that I can but accept all the pages as they turn.

I: MsCfr (MB: Ms. Am. 1450 [110]); II: MsCfr (MB: Ms. Am. 1450 [115, p. 4]).

William Henry Channing was a reform-minded Unitarian minister with whom Fuller had a close friendship.

883.   To Margarett C. Fuller

Florence
6th Feby 1850.

Dearest Mother

After receiving your letter of Octr I answered immediately, but, as Richard mentions in one dated 4th Decr that you have not heard, I am afraid by some post-office mistake it went into the mail-bag of some sail-ship instead of steamer and so you were very long without hearing. I regret it the more as I wanted so much to respond fully to your letter, so lovely, so generous, and which of all your acts of love was perhaps the one most needed by me and which has[n] touched me the most deeply.

I gave you in that a flattering picture of our life and those pleasant days lasted till the middle of Decr but then came on a cold unknown before[n] to Italy and has lasted ever since. As the apartments are not prepared against such; we suffered a good deal, beside both O. and myself were taken ill at[n] New Year's time and were not quite well again all Jany. Now we are quite well; the weather begins to soften, though still cloudy damp and chilly so that poor baby can go out very little. On that account he does not grow so fast and gets troublesome by evening, as he tires of being shut up so much in two or three little rooms where he has examined every least object hundreds of times. He is always pointing to the door. He suffers much with chilblains as have other children here; however he is with that exception in the best health and[n] great part of the time very gay, laughing, dancing in nursemaid's arms and trying to sing and drum in imitation of the bands which play a great deal in the piazza.

Nothing special has happened to me. The uninhabitableness of the room in which I had expected to write and the need of using our little dining room the only one where is a stove[n] for dressing baby taking care of him, eating and receiving visits and messages has prevented my writing for six and seven weeks past. In the eveg when baby went to bed about 8 I began to have time, but was generally too tired to do other than read. The four hours, however from 9 till 1 beside the bright little fire have been very pleasant. I have thought a great deal of you remembering how you suffer by cold in the winter and hope you are in a warm comfortable house, have pleasant books to read and some pleasant friends to see One does not want many only a few bright faces to look in now and then and help thaw the ice with little rills of genial converse. I have fewer of these than in Rome, but still several. It is odd how many old associations have turned up here, mostly connected with Father[1] There are the Greenoughs you knew their mother, and Father used to keep locks of their sisters' hair in his desk.[2] Mr Horatio Greenough is married to Miss Gore, whom I first saw at Dr Freeman's[3] Mr Henry Greenough to Miss Boott who was a friend of Amelia Greenwood's.[4] They are all very friendly in their conduct towards me. Then Horace Sumner youngest son of Father's Mr Charles Sumner lives near us and comes every evening to read a little while with Ossoli.[5] They exchange some instruction in Engh and Italn. He has been much ill and is too slow and old in his ways for one of his age, so that those who know him slightly do not like him, but he has solid good in his heart and mind; we have a true regard for him and he has shown true and steadfast sympathy for us. When I am ill, or in a hurry he helps me like a brother. He often speaks of Lloyd whom he knew at Brook farm, and appreciated the grain of gold that is mixed up with so much sand to incumber it.[6] Then who should come along but Anna Breck (Mrs Aspinwall) rich in California gold, with a daughter that seemed much older than herself and a son of 15 named Lloyd.[7] Her husband I found pleasant, herself not more congenial than of old, though still pretty, simple and smiling in the way father used to like so much. She enraged one or two persons here that are quite fond of me, by not echoing at all when they praise me. She was very civil, but I suppose thought I was just as odd and disagreeable as ever. Indeed, not one of Father's friends ever became mine, in fact I was an odd and unpleasing girl to people generally. However, it matters not. One thing seems *odd to me*, dear Mother, as I see so much money flow by, that none of us ever gets any. It is quite a destiny. Here has been a fat round-eyed old lady who had taken seven thousand dollars, just for pocket money to buy pictures and engravings. I thought, now if you could just spare me fifty dollars of that to buy little common engravings to illustrate lessons on Italy, if I want to give some when I go home. But the round-eyed can get such a mass of things she cant use, while I have never had a dollar I could spare for what I could make so interesting to others as well as myself.

I wanted too so much to buy several little objects connected with the early days of the baby that in case I do not return with him, now[n] as I hope, would be so precious for him in after life. However! we must not think too much of these clippings and repressions on every side, but just be thankful if we can get our dinner of herbs and love therewith

I am very anxious to hear from you, to know how you are, and Arthur, if any thing new has occurred, and especially if Eugene is fixed to come to the North this summer.[n8] I hope and expect to come, but baby has not yet his teeth, cannot walk and help himself much and we have not yet the money. Mr Mozier wants me not to return yet, but so far all looks to me as if it were important and desirable to delay no longer. I shall see you and all my friends; you especially I feel the need of seeing now. I want to talk with you and know for myself how you are and have you see the baby. Then I would not on any account miss seeing Eugene, if he comes, who knows when another chance might occur. If I am to publish, I had best be there, and I hope to make some arrangement by which we may pass together at least three or four years of our lives. Ossoli looks forward with great desire to seeing you he lost his own mother when very little and now exercises himself much in saying *Mother.* I cannot boast he says it very well. If you have not written, pray do, suddenly on getting this. With love to Arthur, Aunt Abba, Cousin Ellen ever yr affecte[9]

MARGARET.

ALS (MH: fMS Am 1086 [9:176]); MsC (MH: fMS Am 1086 [Works, 1:287–95]). Published in part in *At Home and Abroad,* pp. 438–39. *Addressed:* Mrs Margaret Fuller / ⟨Care Richard F. Fuller / 10 State St / Boston / Massachusetts / U.S.A.⟩ Rev. Arthur B. Fuller / Manchester / N.H.

which has] which ↑ has ↓
unknown before] unknown ↑ before ↓
ill at] ill ⟨?⟩ at
is with that exception in the best health and] is ↑ with that exception in the best health and ↓
room the only one where is a stove] room ↑ the only one where is a stove ↓
him, now] him, ↑ now ↓
this summer.] this ⟨winter⟩ ↑ summer ↓ .

1. Timothy Fuller, who died in 1835, had been a lawyer and congressman.
2. David Greenough (1774–1836) married Elizabeth Bender in 1799. They had four sons, all artists or sculptors: John (1801–52), who married Maria Underwood in 1832; Horatio, Henry, and Richard Saltonstall (1819–1904), who married Sarah Dana Loring (1827–85) in 1846. The Greenough sisters were Louisa (1809–92); Laura (1811–78), who married Thomas Buckminster Curtis in 1838; Ellen (1814–93), who married Charles Phelps Huntington in 1847; and Charlotte (1815–59), who married Charles H. Parker in 1852 (Hamilton Perkins Greenough, *Some Descendants of Captain William Greenough of Boston, Massachusetts* [Santa Barbara, Calif., 1969], pp. 41–42).
3. Louisa Ingersoll Gore married Horatio Greenough in 1837. James Freeman (1759–1835) graduated from Harvard in 1777. The first avowed Unitarian minister in the United States, Freeman was the minister of King's Chapel in Boston from 1787 to 1826. In 1788 he married James Freeman Clarke's grandmother, Martha Curtis Clarke, (1755?–1841), widow of Samuel Clarke (*Heralds,* 2:1–11; William W. Johnson, *Clarke-Clark Genealogy: Records of the Descendants of Thomas Clarke, Plymouth, 1623–1697* [North Greenfield, Wis., 1884], p. 28).
4. Frances Boott married Henry Greenough in 1837. Amelia Greenwood Bartlett, daughter of William Pitt Greenwood, was Fuller's childhood friend.
5. Horace Sumner was the son of Charles Pinckney (1776–1839) and Relief Jacob Sumner (1785–1866). Horace, who lived for a time at Brook Farm, died with the Ossolis in the wreck of the *Elizabeth* (*NEHGR,* 8 [1854], 128k). The elder Sumner, whose more famous son served in the U.S. Senate, graduated from Harvard in 1796, became

a lawyer in Boston, and then was the sheriff of Suffolk County. He and Timothy Fuller were in the commonwealth government together in 1825 (Elias Nason, *The Life and Times of Charles Sumner* [Boston, 1874], pp. 14–17).

6. Lloyd Fuller was Margaret's youngest brother.

7. Anna Breck Aspinwall was the daughter of George (1785–1869) and Catherine Israel Breck. Her daughter was Anna Lloyd Aspinwall (1831–80); the son was Lloyd Aspinwall (1830–86). In later life, Anna married James Renwick of New York; Lloyd fought in the Civil War and became a general in the Union army (Aspinwall, *Aspinwall Genealogy*, pp. 110, 166–68; Samuel Breck, *Genealogy of the Breck Family* [Omaha, 1889], p. 57).

8. Arthur Buckminster Fuller was the Unitarian minister in Manchester, New Hampshire; her oldest brother, Eugene, was a newspaperman in New Orleans.

9. Her maiden aunt was Abigail Crane; Ellen Crane Hill was the daughter of another aunt, Elizabeth Crane.

884. To Emelyn Story

[I] Florence 15th. Feb 1850.

My dear Emelyn,

I have been hoping many weeks past to get some line from you, but to me none comes, and I learn that Mrs. Greenough is not more fortunate. I hope this silence means that your time is so filled up with new enjoyments, acquisitions both of knowledge and friends that you have not time to write but then again I am a[n]xious lest it should be that you and Wm or the children are ill, or that you never received my answer to yours of Venice. If you receive this do write at once, even if you have time only for a few lines. I cannot be content to remain so long ignorant about your life after taking so strong an interest in all its details as well as aims, and motives. The only way I have heard of you was through Mr. Haggerty, who saw you in Berlin, and he could tell nothing but that you were there and at that time well.

We have had a most dismal winter, in point of damp, snow and extreme cold. It has been quite as cold as Boston and one suffers more in apartments not provided against it. Ossoli and I were both ill a little while, but are now quite well; the baby has not suffered except from chilblains, as all the children seem to here; indeed I myself have had them for the first time in my life. For the rest we have enjoyed much repose this winter and it has been balm to me after all the agitations and struggles I had undergone. I consider it but as an oasis, but have prized every moment and feel really refreshed and more courageous to set forth again on the difficult way. I have felt like reading more than for some years past, have read Macaulay's History of the James 2nd Period, Louis Blanc's Ten Years, and many books of that

61

class, where were some facts I wanted.[1] These few evenings past I have lightly skimmed over Lynch's Excursion to the Dead Sea, a book interesting for its subject and as showing the resources for action and the barrenness of thought of the American (so called practical) man in our days.[2] I go out a little every day and see about as many people as I like.

The Americans meet twice a week at the houses of Messrs. Mozier and Chapman.[3] I often go, on account of friendly interest in those residents here, for of the birds of passage, if my ear deceive me not, not one had song. The Messrs Greenough had a box at the Persola and I went with them twice, the music quite bad, but one pretty good ballet. I have been much amused by the Stenterello; he shows the modern Florentine in all his degradation, but with a kind of poetry too.[4]

I see the Brownings often [   ] I feel that for me, just when our little one is unfolding, just when he daily [II] discovers some new trait, to have our acquaintance stopped to give him principally into the care of hirelings and turn my care to a new subject would be so painful. But Mrs. B. seems very glad. Their society affords me great entertainment and pleasure, but I fancy I make little return. I do not feel drawn out, but like to hear them, especially Browning; when he comes here for an hour I feel exhilarated by his full tide of talk, fine talk it is: he tells so many things I want to know, and his generous loyal nature warms one so truly the while.

He is like one of our best American men, I find nothing of the modern Englishman about him. Genuine Saxon! Yes! I go often to the house of some very agreeable English ladies, where I hear some excellent (and German) music. I want to hear from William about the music he gets now. I trust he is not disappointed in that: If he hears of fine things arranged for the piano not likely to be known to me, I wish he would mention them in your letter, and now adieu dear E. My expectation is to go to America in May or June. Shall we meet there or do you stay abroad yet more years.

Mrs. Henry Greenough leaves here on 1st April. She expects to pass a month or two in Paris and then sail for U. S.

All my letters are full of Miss Bremer; people seem to like her very much. How frightful the Phobia will be when Jenny Lind is there.[5] I shrink as I think of the mass movements in our country. I am afraid I shall be trampled under foot, if I can't keep out of the way. My love to William, the children and Uncle Tom if with you, and write quick to your friend Margaret.[6]

Have you seen Carlyle's remarks about the eighteen million Bores his American Cousins?[7]

Have you seen another novel by author of Jane Eyre, and is it good?[8] Is Countess Hahn Hahn in Germany now? Did you know that Browning is acquainted with her?[9]

I: MsCfr (MB: Ms. Am. 1450 [149]); II: MsCfr (MH: fMS Am 1086 [9:235]); MsCfr (MH: fMS Am 1086 [Works, 1:329–35]). Published in part in *Memoirs*, 2:311.

1. Thomas Babington Macaulay, *The History of England from the Accession of James II* (London, 1849), which Fuller described in letter 868.

2. William Francis Lynch, *Narrative of the United States' Expedition to the River Jordan and the Dead Sea* (Philadelphia, 1849). Lynch married Virginia Shaw, Fuller's school friend in Groton.

3. John Gadsby Chapman (1808–89) was a Virginia painter and engraver who published *The American Drawing Book* in 1847 (*DAB*). Fuller had undoubtedly known him in Rome, where he often lived.

4. The Stenterello, a masked figure created by Luigi Del Buono in the second half of the eighteenth century, became a popular feature of the Florentine theater. It stood for a variety of ills: gluttony, idleness, poverty, cowardice, and foolishness (*Grande Dizionario Enciclopedico UTET* [Turin, 1972]).

5. Johanna Maria Lind (1820–87) toured the United States in 1850–52, thanks to Barnum's efforts.

6. Thomas Wetmore, William Story's uncle, was traveling with the Storys in Europe.

7. Carlyle published his acerbic opinion of Americans in the first of his "Latter-Day Pamphlets": "'What have they done?' growls Smelfungus, tired of the subject: 'They have doubled their population every twenty years. They have begotten, with a rapidity beyond recorded example, Eighteen Millions of the greatest *bores* ever seen in this world before,—that hitherto is their feat in History!'" (*Latter-Day Pamphlets* [London, 1907], p. 21).

8. Still using the pseudonym Currer Bell, Charlotte Brontë published *Shirley* on 26 October 1849 (*Shirley*, ed. Herbert Rosengarten and Margaret Smith [Oxford, 1979], p. xxiv).

9. Ida, Gräfin von Hahn-Hahn (1805–80), published poetry and several social novels that portrayed emotionally powerful women. In 1844, four of the novels were made into one series, *Aus der Gesellschaft* (*OCGL*). Browning had met her in London in 1846 (*The Letters of Robert Browning and Elizabeth Barrett Barrett, 1845–1846*, ed. Elvan Kintner [Cambridge, 1969], 2:761).

885. To Arthur Hugh Clough

Florence
16th Feby 1849. [1850]

Dear Mr Clough,

I am going to write, principally with the view of getting a letter back, so you must not disappoint me.

You wrote that you might see me here, might come every now and then to Italy. But you must come to America rather. I think I shall go there this summer. Dearly as I love Italy and incomplete as is my acquaintance with her yet, I do not like to be here at this time of incubus. Often I forget it, but on reawaking" to a sense of the realities round me it is crushing to think, to feel all that is smothered down in mens minds. I care least for these cowed and coward Florentines; they are getting only what the[y] deserve, but do not like to be among them.

The judicious conduct of the Austrians here is quite admirable. One would not think that men installed where they are not wanted and ought not to be could seem so gentlemanly The troops" are kept in great order, still from the very nature of the case the Tuscans gather with each day fresh cause for gloomy brooding. The Austrians at this moment seem in great dread of an outbreak, but I suppose it could only be some trifling street fuss as yet

Yes I shall like to go back and see our "eighteen millions of bores," with their rail-roads, electric telegraphs, mass movements and ridiculous dilettant phobias, but with ever successful rush and bang. I feel as if I should be the greatest bore of all when I get home, so few will care for the thoughts of my head or the feelings of my heart, but there will be some pairs of eyes to see, and a sense of fresh life unknown here.

I have recd an offer from an Amern publisher for my book, but it is not satisfactory and I think to wait till I go myself," perhaps to burn meanwhile. I am not at all sorry it was not to be published in England, (indeed now I see the question whether foreigners can hold copy right is quite decided against us) and I shall not care if prevented from publishing at all. I dare say the experiences if left for seed corn will grow to something better.

As to money I have not got any yet, but probably should not by the book; if it succeeded tolerably, I should get cheated somehow out of the penny fee.

Casting aside the past and the future, and despite the extreme cold which has tormented me much in an Italn apartment, fit only for May and June, I have enjoyed many bright and peaceful hours this winter. My little baby flourishes in my care; his laughing eyes, his stammered words and capricious caresses afford me the first unalloyed quiet joy I have ever known. Tis true! he must grow up to sorrow and to strive and have less and less the sweet music that seems to flow around him now, if like his mother he will be full of faults and much unreasonable, but I hope there will be in him a conquering, purifying energy too. What we call God seems so very near in the presence of a child; we bless the love that gave this soul to put an end to loneliness, we believe in the justice that is bound to provide it at last with all it needs. I like also much living with my husband. You said in your letter you

64

thought I should at any rate be happier now because the position of an unmarried woman in our time is not desirable; to me on the contrary it had seemed that in a state of society where marriage brings so much of trifling business arrangements and various soporifics the liberty of single life[n] was most precious. I liked to see those I loved only in the best way. With Ossoli I liked when no one knew of our relation, and we passed our days together in the mountains, or walked beautiful nights amid the ruins of Rome. But for the child I should have wished to remain as we were, and feared we should lose much by entering on the jog-trot of domestic life. However, I do not find it so; we are of mutual solace and aid about the dish and spoon part, yet enjoy our free rambles as much as ever. Now I have written a good deal of me, will you write some sincere words of you, at least as much so as you have put in your print. Which makes me always so sorry I threw away the chance of knowing you in Rome. Had I known you before we could have talked then, but I was so pressed with excitements, I had not the soul to make a new acquaintance

Is Mazzini in London; have you seen him?[1] if so, do write me how he is and whatever you may know of him. I think of him with unspeakable affection, but do not wish to write.

Adieu, dear Mr Clough, your friend

MARGARET

ALS (Bodleian Library). Published in *Correspondence of Arthur Hugh Clough*, ed. Frederick L. Mulhauser (Oxford, 1957), pp. 280–82. *Addressed:* Mr A H. Clough / University Hall Gordon Square / London / England. *Postmarks:* Firenzi 16 Feb; E Q 25 Fe 1850.

The English poet Arthur Hugh Clough knew Fuller during his stay in Rome during the time of the Republic.

on rewaking] on re⟨viv⟩ ↑ aw ↓ aking
The troops] The ⟨men⟩ ↑ troops ↓
I go myself,] I ⟨am come⟩ ↑ go myself, ↓
soporifics the liberty of single life] soporifics ⟨that⟩ ↑ the ↓ liberty ↑ of single life ↓

1. Mazzini did not arrive in London until the latter part of May, 1850 (Giuseppe Mazzini, *Scritti editi ed inediti* [Imola, 1925], 42:294).

886.   To Richard F. Fuller

Florence
24th Feby 1850.

My dear Richard,

I take the oppory of sending under cover to S Ward, to write you a little note just that the family may hear from you, how I am. Now that

I pay 25 cents here on every single sheet instead of a dollar as I used to through the banker[n] I find my letters do *not* go so swiftly and surely and even of this postage I must be chary

I hoped by this time to say decisively when I come home, but do not yet know, we not being sure yet we can get the money. The voyage, made in the cheapest way we can, must cost us about[n] 150 dollars as, even if we brave the length and discomforts of voyage by a merchant-man, and go without any help for care of the baby in case of being sick, we must still buy stores and have a cow or goat to insure him proper food. We *may* have in this way two months on the ocean. I have always suffered much in my head at sea. However to go by France would be more than double the expense. Happy the fowl of the air who dont have to think so much about these things. I hope by hook (we shant try by crook) to get the means and come somehow.

Days have come here already such as was the May day on which you wrote to me last year, glorious days that expand the heart, uplift the whole nature. Walks here are very charming, because in whatever direction you move on leaving the gates, you immediately find yourself climbing a height, while below lies gently nestled the brown first home of many an eagle,[n] many a song bird, too. You are very sublime and stern, my dear Richard, in your disownings of the lures and ambitions of this life, as well as amazed at the *worldliness* of your sister, who on her side, was not a little surprised, to say nothing of other feelings, at such accusations, more than once repeated, too. At the risk of confirming this dark view of her character, she must observe, she has at times hoped much you would sometime have dollars enough to traverse land and waves and see some beauteous sights that will be to her memory a joy forever. But the little bit of paper ends so only more love to all from

MARGARET.

Admire this war steed I intend to have a donkey engraved with some motto and in this same style beauty. Motto Fier mais soumis

ALS (MH: fMS Am 1086 [9:135]); MsC (MH: fMS Am 1086 [Works, 1:123–27]); MsC (MB: Ms. Am. 1450 [81a]). Published in part in *Memoirs*, 2:365, and Higginson, *MFO*, p. 273. *Addressed:* Richard F. Fuller / 10 State St. / Boston. *Endorsed:* Margaret / 24 Feb 50.

to through the banker] to ↑ through the banker ↓
us about] us ↑ about ↓
an eagle,] an ⟨?⟩ eagle,

887. To Samuel G. Ward

Florence
24th Feby 1850

I ought, dear Sam, to have acknowledged by last steamer the receipt of the money but an accident made me miss the day for writing from here. I lost eighteen dollars here by the exchange; if Caroline (Tappan) comes to you to send me a little sum to buy her engravings, tell her there is now this loss, and the banker says likely to be[n] worse[1] Perhaps her father could send in some way by which I would have all the money to spend for her, a note direct on Leghorn, or the like, or it might be arranged for me to take it direct from Mr Mozier and something bought or done for him in U. S. If she sends fifty dollars, I would not like to have only forty five, for example, to buy her things.

We have had a winter incredibly cold for Italy, and it is very bad here where houses are not prepared. I had attached no importance to having fire-places in the sleeping rooms and we have really suffered, in consequence, our *sala*, where I had expected to write could not be warmed, we have had nothing but a little dining room,[n] to dress, eat, take care of the baby &c; that generally smoky the coldest days; we have scarce had more comfort, and retirement than one might in a Western log cabin. But now begins glorious Spring weather, like the (few)[n] good days of May in N. England. Not withstanding the bad weather, my health has been constantly improving. Since my father's death (which you may remember took place just after we were acquainted,) I have never been so well as at present. I have always looked back to the[n] few weeks we passed on that journey as the last period of tranquillity in my life. During those weeks the persons with whom we were were kindly towards me, and even their defects not uncongenial. Mrs Farrar protected me with a great deal of thoughtful affection, for which I have never ceased to be grateful; in my growing acquaintance with you I found a kind of home, my enjoyment of nature and my own mind was profound.[2] Afterwards I had always griefs or cares to beset me, and allow me free life only for hours or[n] days at a time. In Europe I have had countless plagues all along; many rich joys and grand opportunities, but generally snatched away half known[n] or shut up half tried[n] by failure of health or want of money to do as I wished. This winter there were cares enough, but I have put them aside; we began with the resolve that, having planned our life for these few months as prudently as we could;[n] we would enjoy it as much as we could and leave the rest to Him that careth for the least birds, though He does let so many of them get shot.[3] We are not shot yet, nor frozen, nor starved My little boy on the contrary is very[n] fat though I am afraid he will not do so well after he is weaned from his great stout Roman mother in the flesh. He grows every way; except hair, and people rather jeer at me, for[n] having only a *bald* child. I piously wish them the fate of the scoffers[n] who did not prize that peculiarity in a Prophet, and beside flatter myself that being in temperament so unlike Absalom he will show the opposite conduct towards[n] a fond parent.[4] Now in these fine days I have begun to go sometimes to the galleries; in winter the Uffizi are too cold. I feel works of art more than I have ever yet. I feel the development of my own nature as I look on them; so many hid meanings come out upon me. Two new (old) Raphaels have of late been discovered under the paint. One seems to me only a copy; the other is a lovely Madonna in the earlier manner. Jesi is making an engraving of the Raphael (Last Supper) discovered in the coach-house.[5] It would be good for you to have as companion to Leonardo's. The contrast of mind in the two ways of treating the subject as you see them together speaks[n] like a dialogue. With love to Anna ever yours

M.

ALS (MH: bMS Am 1465 [934]). *Endorsed:* 1850 / S. M. Fuller / Feb. 24.

to be] to ↑ be ↓
dining room,] dining ↑ room, ↓
the (few)] the ↑ (few) ↓
to the] to ↑ the ↓
hours or] hours ⟨and⟩ ↑ or ↓
away half known] away ↑ half known ↓
up half tried] up ↑ half tried ↓
months as prudently as we could;] months ↑ as prudently as we could ↓ ;
the contrary is very] the ⟨g⟩ contrary is ↑ very ↓
me, for] me, ⟨?⟩ for
the scoffers] the ⟨children⟩ ↑ scoffers ↓
conduct towards] conduct ⟨c⟩ towards
together speaks] together ↑ speaks ↓

1. Caroline Sturgis Tappan, daughter of William Sturgis, a Boston merchant, was Fuller's closest woman friend.

2. Eliza Rotch Farrar, a Cambridge author of a guide for young ladies, had befriended Fuller in her youth. Fuller describes in letter 110 the trip that she took to Trenton Falls, New York, in July and August 1835.

3. Fuller plays on the familiar scriptural injunction: "Take no thought for your life, what ye shall eat, or what ye shall drink; nor yet for your body, what ye shall put on. Is not the life more than meat, and the body than raiment? Behold the fowls of the air: for they sow not, neither do they reap, nor gather into barns; yet your heavenly Father feedeth them. Are ye not much better than they?" (Matt. 6:25–26).

4. As the prophet Elisha was going up to Beth-el, he was mocked by a group of children, who said, "Go up, thou bald head; go up, thou bald head." The enraged prophet "cursed them in the name of the Lord. And there came forth two she bears out of the wood, and tare forty and two children of them" (2 Kings 2:23–25). King David's

son Absalom, known for his beauty and luxuriant hair, raised a rebellion against his father but was killed when his hair caught on the branch of an oak tree and he was pulled from his mount (2 Sam. 14–18).

5. Samuel Jesi (1789–1853) was an Italian line engraver (*Bryan's Dictionary of Painters and Engravers*, ed. George C. Williamson [London, 1927]). Fuller often called Ward "Raphael" because he had once thought to pursue painting as a career.

888.   To Lewis Cass, Jr.

[I] Florence.
5th March 1850.

Dear Mr Cass—

This has been a divine day— The most glorious sunshine, and gently flowing airs, crows cawing and searching in gay bands; the birds twittering their first notes of love; the fields enameled with anemones, cowslips and crocuses— the Italian Spring is as good as Paradise. How dreadful it will be hereafter to shiver and pine up to the middle of May; yet I *must* go brave that and many an ugly thing beside.

What do you in Rome these lovely, lovely days? Mount your horse and gallop over the Campagna? that is worth doing, and *there* are beds of narcissus, while here are only crocuses— As indeed Rome every day is worth ten million Florences. And yet I would not stay there steadily, as you do; the atmosphere of Rome is so peculiarly dejecting and enervating; you will find your vital spirits always on the ebb. That is partly the cause you feel so sad, and yet not all, for this world is really a sad place, despite all the sunshine and birds and crocuses. I never felt so near happy as now, when I find always the glad [II] eyes of my little boy to welcome me home. I feel the tie between him and me so real, so deep-rooted, even death shall not part us. I shall not be alone in other worlds, whenever Eternity may call me. So sweet this unimpassioned love; it knows not dark reactions, it does not idealize and cannot be daunted by the faults of its object. I wish you had a child, and the right mother for your child; nothing else can take the worst bitterness out of life: nothing else can break the spell of loneliness. Yet these treasures shall somewhere somehow be given to each heart pure enough to prize them.

No important change has taken place here. The Austrians fortify themselves day by day; but the Tuscans reluct more and more at finding themselves Austrian subjects. The *contegno* of the Austrian troops, both officers and soldiers, is wonderfully discreet. Still both feel the

69

knife not unfrequently, and they would gladly at this moment put even cowardly Florence in state of siege.

At the Opera, in the "Puritani" the singers use the word "beatta" in place of the original "*liberata*," and the People hiss in Grand Duke's presence.[1] Indeed, they now hate and despise in proportion to their original kind feeling toward him. Tis but little I see of all this, living as quiet as possible, and associating only with a few friends. [   ]

I: MsCfr (MB: Ms. Am. 1450 [81b]); II: MsCfr (MB: Ms. Am. 1450 [172]). Published in part in *Memoirs*, 2:333–34.

1. The copyist appears to have misread Fuller's hand, for she probably refers to the last act of Vincenzo Bellini's *I Puritani*, when Riccardo and Giorgio exult in the news of Cromwell's victory: "Ah! L'Anglaterra ha libertà!" (Ah! England has freedom!). It is not clear what insult the singers intended. The opera was first performed on 24 January 1835 in Paris, only months before Bellini died.

889.   To William H. Channing

[I] [Spring 1850]

[   ] God will transplant the root, if he needs to rear it into fruit; one would think that so much fuss could not end in nothing, so Patience Cousin and shuffle the cards, till Fate is ready to deal them out anew.

I hear my little baby crying; he does not seem well and that troubles me always. He had risen into rosy health; the air of Florence agreed with him and that made me love Florence. For his sake indeed, I am become a miserable coward. I fear heat and cold and moschetoes. I fear terribly the voyage home, fear biting poverty. I hope Fate will not force me into being as brave for him as I was for myself and that if I succeed to rear him carefully he will not be a weak or bad man. But I love him too much and feel too freshly the meaning of the words,

"For that lost heart was tender."[1]

[II] I cannot be quite independent of what is called society, as I need to earn our bread, at least for the present. But I trust there will be a sufficient number of persons needing something from me to enable me to earn frugal bread, that is all I want of what is called the world. [   ]

I: MsCfr (MB: Ms. Am. 1450 [115, pp. 2–3]); II: MsCfr (MB: Ms. Am. 1450 [110]). Published in part in *Memoirs*, 2:337.

1. From Shelley's sonnet:

> Lift not the painted veil which those who live
> Call Life: though unreal shapes be pictured there,
> And it but mimic all we would believe
> With colours idly spread,—behind, lurk Fear
> And Hope, twin Destinies; who ever weave
> Their shadows, o'er the chasm, sightless and drear.
> I knew one who had lifted it—he sought,
> For his lost heart was tender, things to love,
> But found them not, alas! nor was there aught
> The world contains, the which he could approve.
> Through the unheeding many he did move,
> A splendour among shadows, a bright blot
> Upon this gloomy scene, a Spirit that strove
> For truth, and like the Preacher found it not.

(*Complete Poetical Works of Shelley*, p. 630)

890. To Emelyn Story

Florence, 15th March 1850

My sweet Emelyn,

I meant to have written at length for tomorrow's mail, but have been interrupted till very late, and all tomorrow morng is engaged, so I will write a few lines, lest Monday's mail should not find you in Dresden. I had your letter by Mr. Gale, then after nothing till yours and M's by Mr. Hurlbert a fortnight since, now I have yours from Berlin, by post, and Browning had one from M. a few days earlier.[1] But the other letter you mention (to care of Maquay) never reached me: it is too bad, I shall make inquiry but I fear uselessly; strange things occur at these Florentine p. o.'s— two letters from Mr. Cass they have kept for themselves; if they read yours I am sure they had, at least, *a chance* to be made better by it. I shall write to both you and M, (love and thanks for the Poems.)[2] at Paris, and inclose a letter of introduction, if I find the person I have in my eye is likely to be there. When you receive this do not fail to write what your address will be in Paris. Mine here is (you ask it *in full*) Siga Marchesa Ossoli, Casa Libri, *Piazza Maria Novella.*

Mrs Henry Greenough called this morning, and wanted me to tell you circumstances had occurred that made it impossible for them to be in Paris earlier than *20th May*, and hopes you may visit England first and so meet her there, but I hope for your own good, you will not, the 12th April, when you plan to be there is an excellent time, you will still have some evenings of music and the theatres, while the beautiful weather will favor your going about by day; a month in Paris will enable you to plan for the next winter, and then you will go to England and find *the* season, and do your delightful English travel in later summer.

I should rejoice, indeed, to see you in Paris, to pass some months with you there, but Fate is not likely to favor anything so pleasant. At present all looks as if we must go to the U. S. and sail direct from Leghorn, which I dread. How I thank you for your letter, it gave so lively a picture of your life. I will pay any attention in my power to your friend when she comes. She will enjoy herself; the Spring here is most glorious. Already it is so warm that we enjoy in the highest going to the Cacine in the mornings; there is hardly any one there and we sit and read, while the birds sing and flowers bloom around, and the sun and breeze are like June in our country. I have there read again Browning's Poems, having borrowed from him the new edition.[3] Lady Alice a very odd for an American book, most amusingly crude yet with a glow of youthful talent.[4] I have seen young persons of talent who would view everything in Italy just so. Taking Puseyism for the centre of Creation, too, a peculiar light is thrown on the various provinces over which that magnificient sceptre is expected to hold sway:[5] next read I the novel by the Author of Jane Eyre, now known as Miss Brontë. Only light books can be read in open air so, with people passing every now and then, (Browning to be sure has weight, but so much fascination too.) but it is high enjoyment to play so. I have not attempted to answer, dear Emelyn, any point that interested me most in your letter last night when I began. I was so tired, this morning it is three minutes before sending to post

I shall answer to some purpose when I write to Paris. Congratulate N. that he has alone something good for his winter. I see he does not forget his milestones. Men will know where he has passed, and of the sadder news you told me. What I thought another time, but ever most Affectionately Yours

M.

Kisses to the dear children.

MsC (MH: fMS Am 1086 [9:228]); MsC (MH: fMS Am 1086 [Works, 1:297–301]).

1. Frederick William Gale (1816–54), from Northborough, Massachusetts, graduated from Harvard in 1836. He became a lawyer in Saint Louis and then in Worcester, Massachusetts. Gale's sister had been Fuller's student in Providence. This meeting in

Florence evoked Gale's contempt: "What a strange story, is it not?" he wrote in his journal. "Now that the scornful, manhating Margaret of 40 has got a husband, really no old maid need despair, while there is life in her body!" After a second meeting five days later, he softened his tone, saying that he "heard nothing like that tone of scorn & contempt which I expected in her conversation." Ironically, Gale's death mirrored Fuller's: he and his wife and child died in the wreck of the steamship *Arctic* off Nova Scotia (Harvard archives; *New England Quarterly* 29 [March 1956]: 98). William Henry Hurlbert (1827–95) graduated from Harvard in 1847 and from its divinity school in 1849. He later left the ministry to become a writer, journalist, and critic. T. W. Higginson, two years ahead of Hurlbert at the divinity school, said that in Italy "he not only was blessed by the Pope, but by the society of the Countess Ossoli whom he admires very much" (*Letters and Journals of Thomas Wentworth Higginson, 1846–1906,* ed. Mary Thacher Higginson [Boston, 1921], p. 29). The copyist apparently misread Fuller's "W" (for William) as "M."

2. Story apparently sent a copy of his *Poems* (Boston, 1847).

3. Browning's *Poems* (London, 1849), his first collected edition, contained *Paracelsus* and the eight *Bells and Pomegranates*.

4. Jedediah Vincent Huntington, *Lady Alice; or, The New Una* (London, 1849).

5. Edward Bouverie Pusey (1800–1882), Regius Professor of Hebrew at Oxford, gave his name to the Anglo-Catholic revival of the 1830s (known also as the Oxford movement). Its adherents, who included John Henry Newman and John Keble, advocated a return to the teaching of the church fathers (*DNB*).

891. To Lewis Cass, Jr.

Wednesday eveg 20th March. [1850]

My dear Mr Cass,

I was very sorry to be out, when you came; your visit here is passing without my seeing you at all; cannot you cut your Zerlinos or Zerlinas, if such there be, and pass an hour with me this moonlight evening? If not, I shall be at home tomorrow any time after 2 p m. but other people are always coming in by day and I wanted *really* to see and talk with you.

I send some other Amern papers, but, if convenient, will you let me have them tomorrow eveg as they are not mine.

Ever your friend

M. O.

If you could only come when you get this we might have a Casa Diez talk! and I, for one, remember those with pleasure.

ALS (MH: fMS Am 1086 [9:168]); MsC (MH: fMS Am 1086 [Works, 1:341–43]). *Addressed:* Mr Cass / Gran Bretagna.

other Amern] other ↑ Amern ↓

892. To Mrs. Greenough

5th April [1850]

Dear Mrs Greenough,

Perhaps you would like these two autographs of women, very unlike to one another, but both of marked character, and who have shown great energy and talent.

I have in a box, left at Paris many that might be valuable to you, but regret to find few among my papers here.

Ever yours

M. OSSOLI

ALS (ViU). *Addressed:* Mrs [   ] / Bel [   ].

893. To Costanza Arconati Visconti

[I] Florence, 6 April
1850.

[   ] Yesterday I had been bled after more than ten days constant headach, and dangerous pressure on the brain. I was lying feeling relieved yet much exhausted too, when your letter came. You cannot know how much good it did me. Its effect was quite talismanic, as the sight of you has often been, seeming to heal, console and strengthen.

With Guisti was extinguished a spark of the true fire of genius.[1] Now Italy seems to me wholly bereft— Mazzini, Berchet, silent, Giusti dead—[2] "The great depart, "And none rise up to fill their vacant seat"—. [II] [   ] I would not for the world have your last thoughts of me mingled with the least unpleasantness, when mine of you must always be all sweet.[3] I say, *last thoughts*. I am absurdly fearful about this voyage. Various little omens have combined to give me a dark feeling. Among others just now, we hear of the wreck of the ship Westmoreland, bearing Powers's Eve.[4] Perhaps we shall live to laugh at these, but in case of mishap, I should perish with my husband and child perhaps to be transferred to some happier state; and my dear mother, whom I so long to see, would soon follow, and embrace me more peaceably elsewhere. You, loved friend, God keep and cherish here and hereafter! is the prayer of your loving and grateful

MARGARET

I: MsCfr (MB: Ms. Am. 1450 [154]); II: MsCfr (MH: bMS Am 1280 [111, pp. 8–9]). Published in part in *Memoirs*, 2:337; Higginson, *MFO*, p. 274; and *JMN*, 11:458–59.

1. Giuseppe Giusti (1808–50) was a satirical poet who had studied law in Pisa. He was a political moderate (thus appealing to Arconati Visconti) who had nevertheless been active in the revolutionary government of Tuscany in 1848 (*Dictionary of Italian Literature*, ed. Peter Bondanella and Julia Conaway Bondanella [Westport, Conn., 1979]).

2. Giovanni Berchet was a Milanese poet who had lived in Florence.

3. In a letter written from Pisa the previous day (MH), Arconati Visconti, who came to Florence immediately upon Giusti's death, expressed regret at not having seen Fuller.

4. The Swedish ship *Westmorland* sank during the night of 5 March about 45 miles east of the Spanish port of Cartagena. On board was Hiram Powers' second *Eve*. The statue suffered little damage, however, and was recovered within three weeks (Donald Martin Reynolds, *Hiram Powers and His Ideal Sculpture* [New York, 1977], pp. 158–60).

894. To Costanza Arconati Visconti

Florence 12 April 1850.

I am suffering as never before from the horrors of indecision. The Barque "Elisabeth" now at Leghorn, will take us; she is said to be an uncommonly good vessel for the merchant service, nearly new, and well kept. And now that I was on the point of deciding to go by her, people come daily to dissuade me, saying I cannot have an idea what a voyage of 60 or 70 days will be for me in point of fatigue and suffering, having the care of the baby without any female service or aid, or chance of medical advice if he should be ill; that the insecurity compared with packet ships or steamers is so great; that the cabin being on deck will be terribly exposed in case of a gale; that I cannot be secure of having good water to drink, far less to wash clothing, and therefore must buy an immense stock of baby-linen; that I cannot go without providing for us poultry, a goat for milk, oranges and lemons, soda hardbread, and a medicine chest, all things which in the passenger line are so much a matter of course if you want them, as in a Hotel of a city; that these things will cost as much as the difference of going round by France, while I shall suffer much more, and be exposed to greater risk.— I am well aware of the proneness of volunteer counsellors to frighten and excite one all they can, and have generally disregarded them. But this time I feel a trembling solicitude on account of the child, and feel harassed, doubtful, and almost sick— The Captain of the *E.* will come here in two or three days, and I hope to feel clearer after talking with him—[1] [   ]

MsCfr (MB: Ms. Am. 1450 [155]). Published in part in *Memoirs*, 2:335–36.

1. Seth Libby Hasty (1812–50), grandson of Justice William Hasty, was born in Scarborough, Maine, the son of John and Libby Hasty (Hasty Genealogy, NEHGS).

895. To Emelyn Story

[I] Florence, 16th April 1850.

Dearest Emelyn,

Your Dresden letter reached me safe. I have vainly inquired for that lost during the winter, I deeply regret that I cannot have it: the loss of letters often makes irreparable gaps in the history of feeling. And tell me did it contain a note from Jane forwarded by your mother to your care for me?[1] Jane is anxious to know the fate of that note.

I should have written at once to you at Paris, but have been doubting from day to day, whether I should not have to go there on my way to U. S. But that way is too expensive for us and as there is a bark at Leghorn highly spoken of, which sails at the end of this month, we shall, very likely take that. You ask me to pass the next year with you in Paris, how much I should have liked it, but I find it imperatively necessary to go to the U. S. if I want to have my arrangements made that may free me from care. Will I be more fortunate in person? I do not know, I am ill adapted to push my claims and my pretensions, but at least it will not be such slow work passing from disappointment to disappointment as here where I wait upon the Post Office, and wait two or three months to know the result of any proposition. Enough! I trust it is not in the power of fate to make me feel bitterly towards any person, though there exist those who by a very little stretch of good will and effort could have made me happy and ransomed for me so many precious hours for the worthier purposes of life. I go home prepared to expect everything that is painful and difficult. It will be a consolation to see my mother, and my dear brother Eugene, whom I have not seen for ten years, hopes to come to N. England this summer; on that account I do wish to go *this* year. I had already heard from many quarters, dear E., of your letter to the Lowells;[2] it had a very happy effect, and I was pleased that they particularly should take pains to show it as they did. I am glad to have people favorably impressed, because I feel lazy and weak, unlike the trouble of friction or the pain of conquest, still I feel a good deal of contempt for those so easily disconcerted or reassured. I was not a child; I had lived in the

76

midst of that blessed society in a way that entitled me to esteem and a favorable interpretation, where there was doubt about my motives or actions. Nor had I had foolish illusions or made mistakes in the objects of love. I pity those who are inclined to think ill, when they might as well have inclined the other way, however let them go; there are many in the world who stand the test, enough to keep us from shivering to death. I am on the whole fortunate in friends that I can truly esteem, where I know the kernel and substance of their being too well to be [II] misled by seemings, and on this occasion as I have never answered what you said of the loss of Maria L's child;[3] these things make me tremble with selfish sympathy, I could not, I think, survive the loss of *my* child. I wonder daily how it can be done.

[III] I am anxious about the baby too as he has not cut his eye teeth. I fear he will do so just when I am not fit to take care of him, and cannot have medical aid if I want it. I am weaning him now: he takes it very kindly and after the first rage, has thought it great fun to sleep with me. He is an intelligent little one, but chiefly remarkable for his archness and gayety. Ossoli is devoted to him and the child, looks on him with the greatest love. I trust if he lives they will have endless gentle joy in one another.

As he unfolds if you do not come home, I shall often write you about him, and I want you to keep me informed as to your children in all the little daily things. I trust we shall be much to them mutually in after days. One cannot resign hope in this life. Mine is not to have learned and suffered quite in vain for the next generation.

17th I resume at least for a few minutes; these days swarm with interruptions as the work people are going on with our preparations and all the time running in, beside, my acquaintance supposing these the last days, come in very often. On Saturday I passed an entire day, very delightfully, with the Brownings. I love and admire them both more, as I know them better; we meet more truly of late. You may have seen B.'s new poem by this time. I suppose he had written to W. he took his address long ago for that purpose.

The Blacks return is expected this very day.[4] In the last letter did you tell where you left Mr. B.'s "Vanity Fair"; he is a man never to forget, I may add *forgive* its loss.[5] More Greenoughs have arrived. John and Richard with his wife. Mrs Henry Greenough really loves you. I like her much on knowing her well, but not the Boston part of her. But of all our mutual acquaintance, whether of persons or things, we shall fully talk when we meet, if so we do meet again. I grieve that I do not know persons at present in Paris who might be most congenial and useful to you. The only one I know of there at present is

77

Madame Mohl to whom I inclose a letter.[6] She was Miss Clark of England. She has lived twenty years in Paris, has know[n] all the best people, is exquisitely witty, original, and no less generous and kind. Some slight defects and oddities at once will be obvious, and will, I suppose, by you as by me never be thought of after.

Her husband is one of the most distinguished scholars of France. If she takes a fancy to you, as I doubt not she will, she can do more than any person I have known in Paris to direct your steps to advantage and give you light on various subjects. You had best consult her as to choice of an apartment for the [IV] coming winter. She is an intimate friend of M.e. Arconati, and I observe from letters I have seen from her this winter that she cannot endure the present regime in France.[7] You will find her little in sympathy with you on more important matters, but thoroughly liberal and lively. I have huddled together these items amid so many calls on my attention; they probably come in droll succession. Let me add two more in the same Winifred Jenkins method.[8] She was the most intimate friend of the celebrated Fauriel.[9] The house used to be 112 Rue du Bac; M.e. Arconati tells me the numbers are changed so that the same house now counts 120. So if you do not find her at one, try at the other. I hope you will have my master, M. Louis Nicauel if you still take French lessons and he still gives them. I think you would prize him as I did. If you have lost his address or it is changed (I think it was 33 rue de Rivoli.) the Walshs will know of him.[10] He knows all about Paris and for me got the entrée to almost any place I thought of. He is a perfect gentleman and most excellent man.

In going to England I hope W will call on the misunderstood Clough University Hall. Through him you may know the Youngest Young England.

I am going E to ask of you an amount of trouble I am truly ashamed of amid the crowded interests of Parisian Days, and yet I do want some one to take it for me, and who so likely as yourself I left in Paris a box at Draper and Co.'s.[11] You will find place on the box may be under my name or that of Marcus Spring Feb 5th 1847 It is not full and being opened and the straw taken out, I think will contain some articles left in care of a certain Miss. Fitton Madame Mohl will tell you where she is. Miss. Fitton persuaded me to leave them with her and the consequence is I have written and sent again and again without being able to get things which I wanted much, especially my muff. She has not answered my letters and therefore I presume she has changed her habitation and never received them. She has my velvet bonnet, which would have to be ripped, a brown merino dress, my muff, a little oval pastille of *Faust and Margaret*, which I want, a drawing give me by the [   ]

At her house or in the box is a blue shawl embroidered with white, it was once considered beautiful: if not now become [   ] and you like it, I wish you would take it for yours and wear it. Storeage you will have to pay at Draper and Co.'s and I will repay. Let the box be sent to the same address as yours are in the U. S. or if that is not convenient to care Marcus Spring and Co. New York, only [   ] [V] me by letter. Dear E pardon me this trouble. I hope to live to take as much for you yet— I know or fear, you will have to do it all yourself, unless Miss Fitton will help you, but it ought to be a friend who opens the box, as I think I left letters and papers as well as well as some books, clothes, and engravings. Use your discretion about these things and if any are not worth it, dont send them, but do what you like with them.

I have a thousand things to say to you, but little head or time now. I shall write from U. S.

When you receive this, if you write me directly a line, I shall probably receive it here but write nothing you are unwilling to have go astray in case we have departed. You might enclose to Mrs. Greenough. In U. S. write to me through Barrings, to care of S. G. Ward, Boston Adieu dearest E. How full of memories those days when last year W was modelling Frank, and you were enjoying his friendship, and I was half hoping for Rome or myself.[12] It was much in those days we went to see the Barricade at Porta Angelica

Here in Florence full incessant heavy rains [   ] as in Rome last season, we have hardly had a fair day since the 1st April. Yet when there is sun for a few hours how exquisite the Cascine. I had no idea it could be so beautiful there: the little flowers in such profusion as I never saw elsewhere and never heard such choruses of birds as in the wilder parts. Adieu for tonight. Many interruptions have prevented my closing the letter for today's mail, perhaps there will be somewhat I want to add tomorrow morning.

18th

After I had finished I took up Galignani and read the following; was it not a strange coincidence? "Died—on Thursday, the 4th inst., at her residence, No. 10, Rue de la Ville 'l Eveĝue, Miss. E. Fitton, third daughter of the late N. Fitton, Esq., of Dublin."

Thus you have the number of the house where my things are. They were in care of the younger sister S. M. Fitton, who had sacrificed her life, in the eyes of men, with over-strained devotion to this now deceased sister. She is now left free, but probably too late to form those ties she earlier resigned. If you see her, give my kindest regards and beg her to write to me. A fixed address for me in America would always be care S. G. Ward, Boston. Adieu dear friend, do write to me here, our going may be delayed. My love to Uncle Tom, I rejoice he is better. My own faith in homeopathy has been great from the first I have seen of its operation Ossoli prays his love to you and W and I am ever Yours,

M.

I: MsCfr (MH: fMS Am 1086 [9:233]); II: MsCfr (MB: Ms. Am. 1450 [118]); III: MsCfr (MB: Ms. Am. 1450 [150]); IV: MsCfr (MH: fMS Am 1086 [9:223]); V: MsCfr (MH: fMS Am 1086 [9:222]); MsCfr (MH: fMS Am 1086 [Works, 1:301–5, 321–25]). Published in part in *Memoirs*, 2:318–19, 334; *WNC*, pp. 385–86; Higginson, *MFO*, p. 272; Miller, pp. 314–15; and Chevigny, p. 495.

1. Jane Tuckerman King was once Fuller's pupil in Boston. Emelyn Story's mother was Hannah Smalley Eldredge (1793–1867) (Hudson, *Browning*, p. 363).

2. In his letter of 21 March 1849 to Lowell, Story tempered his praise of *A Fable for Critics* by observing: "There is but one thing I regretted, and that was, that you drove your arrow so sharply through Miranda. The joke of 'Tiring-woman to the Muses' is too happy—but because fate has really been unkind to her, & because she depends on her pen for her bread & water (& that is nearly all she has to eat) & because she is her own worst enemy, and because through her disappointment & disease, which embitter every one, she has struggled most womanfully & stoutly, I could have wished you had let her pass scot-free." An unforgiving Lowell replied, "Set down the parts about Miss F as errors of the press. You speak of her as poor. I did not know that she was so, but that the departure of her uncle Abraham to his namesake's bosom had made her independent. I only knew that she was malicious, & it was not what she had written of me, but what I had heard of her saying which seemed to demand the intervention of the satiric Nemesis. You may be sure I have felt more sorry about it than any one, only I always reflect *after* the thing is done. Nevertheless I imagine the general verdict was 'served her right', though it was regretted that castigation was inflicted by my particular hand" (Hudson, *Browning*, pp. 241, 247).

3. The Lowells' first child, Blanch, died 19 March 1847, when Maria was pregnant with their second, Mabel. Then on 2 February the third, Rose, died, having been born on 16 July 1849 (Delmar R. Lowell, *The Historic Genealogy of the Lowells of America from 1639 to 1899* [Rutland, Vt., 1899], pp. 226–27). Of the four Lowell children, only Mabel survived to adulthood.

4. Charles Christopher and Catherine F. M. Black, whom Fuller had known in Rome.

5. Thackeray's novel was published in 1848.

6. Mary Clarke (1793–1883), daughter of Charles and Elizabeth Hay Clarke, lived for many years in Paris, where she was a daily visitor to Madame Récamier. She was for forty years the hostess of a brilliant salon. In 1847 she married Julius Mohl (1800–1876), a prominent Orientalist (*DNB*).

7. Foreigners with republican sympathies were distinctly uncomfortable in France in the spring of 1850, for Louis Napoleon was moving steadily toward a dictatorship. Although he had not sided with the Catholic reactionaries who held power in the Assembly, he moved to thwart a suddenly rejuvenated liberal coalition that had won seats

in the election of 10 March 1850. By the end of the first week in June, Louis Napoleon launched a reign of terror against his opponents (A. W. Ward, ed., *The Cambridge Modern History* [New York, 1909], 11:128–32).

8. Winifred Jenkins, a maid to Miss Tabitha Bramble in Tobias Smollett's *Expedition of Humphry Clinker*, is prominent for her misnomers and bad spellings.

9. Claude Charles Fauriel (1772–1844) was a historian and scholar, the author of *Histoire de la Gaule méridionale sous la domination des conquérants germains* (Paris, 1836). For several years he was intimate with Mary Clarke. Julius Mohl published Fauriel's *Histoire de la poésie provençale* (Paris, 1846) after the historian's death.

10. Robert Walsh, an editor and writer, was the American consul general to France. In 1847 Fuller had visited him and his wife, Elizabeth, in Paris.

11. Emerson wrote Sam Ward on 3 December 1850 that "a trunk of papers which she left at Paris under the care of Mr Draper, & which has been supposed to be lost, is on its way home to us" (Rusk, *Letters of RWE*, 4:237).

12. Probably John Francis Heath, a Bostonian whom Fuller had long known and who was in Rome in 1849.

896. To Costanza Arconati Visconti

[Florence 21 April 1850]

[   ] I have written to introduce my friends, the Storys to Madame Mohl; I hope she will like them.

It was an odd combination— I had intended if I went by way of France to take the packet ship "Argo" from Havre; I had just written to Mrs Story that I should *not* do so; and at the same time requested her to find *Miss Fitton*, who had my muff etc.: having closed the letter I took up Galignani, and my eye fell on these words— Died 4th April at No 10 Rue ville l'eveque Miss E. Fitton— turning the leaf I read of the wreck of the "*Argo*" returning from America to France! There were also notices of the wreck of the "Royal Adelaide", a fine English steamer, and of the "John Skiddy" one of the fine American Packets.[1] Thus it seems safety is not [to] be found in the wisest calculation. I shall embark more composedly in my merchant ship; praying, indeed, fervently, that it may not be my lot to lose my babe at sea, either by unsolaced sickness, or amid the howling waves. Or that if I should, it may be brief anguish, and Ossoli he and I go together. Pray with me dear friend as yours ever forever—

MARGARET.

MsCfr (MB: Ms. Am. 1450 [156]); MsCfr (MH: bMS Am 1280 [111, pp. 6–8]). Published in part in *Memoirs*, 2:336, and *JMN*, 11:458; published entire in Higginson, *MFO*, pp. 274–75.

1. The *Argo*, sailing from Le Havre to New York City, went ashore on Mystic Point, 20 miles east of Fire Island, on 17 March. The passengers and cargo were unhurt (*New-York Daily Tribune*, 18 March 1850). Late in the evening of 30 March the *Royal Adelaide*, its entire cargo, and 250 passengers were lost off Margate as it sailed for London (*Times* [London], 2 April 1850, p. 5). The *John A. Skiddy* went aground on the Irish shore late in the evening of 1 April. The crew then ran amok and plundered the passengers, though no lives were lost (*Times* [London], 16 April 1850).

897. To Costanza Arconati Visconti

Florence 25 Apr 50.

[   ] Mr and Mrs Black returned from Egypt taking Greece in their way; and Mr B called on the princess Belgioso. He said she was comfortably situated and kept open table for the Italians. She invited Monzoni, Mr B's courier, to dine. She talked of making the Egyptian journey. Monzoni told me the Italians acted comedies in which the Princess took part, and that she had given a concert. "She must get up something of this kind", observed the red pampered courier, as there are absolutely no amusements at Athens." I am sure the whole affair is a comedy, or rather broad farce![1]

I had a visit from Mr Castiglia; it gave me true pleasure to see him again before going away.[2] Seeing him brought strongly to mind Guerrieri, as they two were the last persons I saw in Milan.[3] Pray tell me if you hear any thing of G. I have lately read over my letters and in so doing the affectionate feelings he had inspired, revive. Be sure his heart is excellent! [   ]

MsCfr (MB: Ms. Am. 1450 [157]).

1. Cristina Belgioioso was an Italian patriot noblewoman whom Fuller had known in Rome during the siege. Arconati Visconti had written Fuller of Belgioioso in her letter of 16 April (MH).

2. Castiglia is unidentified. The copyist probably misread the name, for it is likely that Fuller named Gaetano De Castillia (1794–1870), a Milanese patriot whom she met in 1847 and who was close to Arconati Visconti. He had been arrested and jailed in the infamous Spielberg prison. Castillia was later exiled to the United States, where he became friends with the Sedgwicks in Stockbridge, Massachusetts. After a two-year stay, he traveled to France and England, where he met Mazzini. After his return to Italy in 1840, Castillia resumed his public life (*Dizionario biografico degli Italiani* [Rome, 1987]; Detti, p. 285).

3. Anselmo Guerrieri Gonzaga was a Milanese republican.

898. To Lewis Cass, Jr.

Florence
2d May, 1850.

Dear Mr Cass,

I shall, most probably, leave Florence and Italy the 8th or 10th of this month and am not willing to depart without saying adieu to yourself. I wanted to write the 30th April, but a succession of petty interruptions prevented. That was the day I saw you first and the day the French first assailed Rome. What a crowded day that was! I had been in the morning to visit Ossoli in the garden of the Vatican, just after my return you entered. I then went to the hospital and there passed the night amid the groans of many suffering, some dying men. What a strange first of May it was as I walked the streets of Rome by the first sunlight of next day! Those were to me grand and impassioned hours. Deep sorrow followed, many embarrassments many pains! Let me once more at parting thank you for the sympathy you showed me amid many of these. A thousand years might pass and you would find it unforgotten by me. I shall be glad however if you have destroyed, or will destroy, letters I wrote you during that period. I was heartsick, weary; the future seemed too difficult, and I too weak to face it. What I felt, what I wrote then is below the usual temper of my mind, and I would be glad to cancel all trace of those weaker moods—

I leave Italy with profound regret and with only a vague hope of returning. I could have lived here always, full of bright visions, and expanding in my faculties, had destiny permitted. May you be happy who remain here! it would be well worth while to be happy in Italy.

I had hoped to enjoy some of the last days, but the weather has been steadily bad since you were in Florence.[n] Since the 4th April, we have not had a fine day and all our little plans for visits to favorite spots, and beautiful objects from which we must long be separated, have been marred!

Adieu! I do not feel like writing much. You will, probably, not have time to answer now, but if you feel inclined sometimes to address me in our country, a permanent address would be to care of S. G. Ward, Boston

I sail in the bark Elizabeth f[or] New York. She is laden with mar[ble] and rags, a very appropriate companionship for wares of Italy. She carries Powers's statue of Calhoon.[1] Adieu, remember that we look to you to keep up the dignity of our country; many important occasions are now likely to offer, for the American, (I[n] wish I could write the *Columbian*) man[n] to advocate, more, to *represent* the cause of Truth and Freedom, in face of their foes, and remember me as their lover and your friend

M. O.

ALS (MH: fMS Am 1086 [9:169]); MsC (MH: fMS Am 1086 [Works, 1:355–57]). Published in part in *WNC*, pp. 384–85. *Addressed:* Mr Cass / Chargé d' Affaires des / Etats-Unis d' Amerique / Rome. *Postmark:* Firenzi 3 M 1850.

were in Florence.] were ⟨here⟩ ↑ in Florence ↓.
American (I] American, ⟨wi⟩ (I
man] m⟨en,⟩an

1. In 1845 Powers had been commissioned by the city of Charleston to make a statue that duplicated the face of his 1837 bust of John Calhoun. The statue was salvaged from the wreck of the *Elizabeth* and sent to Charleston, where it remained until it was destroyed when the city was burned in the Civil War (Crane, *White Silence*, pp. 209, 239).

899. To George Henry Calvert

Florence, 10th May, 1850.

Dear Mr. Calvert,

Hearing that you are still in Paris and supposing my friend Mr. Story to be there, too, I feel anxious that, in case you have not met otherwise, this little note may make you acquainted. I will not say why, for if I am not mistaken, a personal interview will show you both good reason for talking again together. Mrs. Story is with her husband and is a no less prized friend of mine. They will be my proxies and tell me something of you in America, for I hear you will now live abroad while I am on the point of going home. Do not quite forget me, if many years pass before we meet again. Please give my cordial regards to Mrs. Calvert, and say the note she gave me to Mrs. Horatio Greenough opened the door to a very agreeable acquaintance.[1] I have seen Mr. and Mrs. G. often during the last six months, and owe to them many memories of refined and exhilarating intercourse. Adieu dear Mr. Calvert and I hope au revoir, though the when, unhappily seems very doubtful.

MARGARET OSSOLI
born Fuller

MsC (MH: fMS Am 1086 [9:231]); MsC (MH: fMS Am 1086 [Works, 1:311–13]).

George Henry Calvert, whom Fuller met in 1838 in Providence, was a writer who often traveled in Europe.

1. Calvert married Elizabeth Steuart in 1829.

900. To William Wetmore Story

Florence, 10th May, 1850.

My dear William,

I wrote you a letter and then burnt it because many disturbances prevented my saying what I would, yet fear this will be no better. We are upon the move and my head full of boxes, bundles, pots of jelly, and phials of medicine. I never thought much about a journey for myself, except to try and return all the things, books, especially, I had been borrowing, but about my child I feel anxious lest I should not take what is necessary for his health and comfort on this long voyage, where omissions are irreparable. The unpropitious weather, (for after our Siberian winter we have rain all the Spring rain from 4th April up to this 10th May,) delays as now from day to day, as our ship the "Elizabeth", look out for news of shipwreck; cannot finish taking in her cargo till come one or two good days. Meanwhile I have been hoping to get a few lines from Emelyn just to tell me where and how you are, and answering briefly to a letter I sent you—Care Green and Co. Paris—more than a fortnight back, but I daresay she was hindered till it seemed too late to write.

I leave Italy with most sad and unsatisfied heart, hoping indeed, to return, but fearing that may not in my "cross-biased" be permitted till strength of feeling and keeness of perception be less than during these bygone rich, if troubled years.[1]

I have read your poems with love several times, once during the only good day I have had amid the trees and flowers. There is not one that bears not its own mark, they are full of tender feeling and fine suggestion, in them aspiration makes melody, and the sorrow is very pure. They do not however seem to me so good as those you read to me written at Sorrento; it seems to me they are not written with as much glow and effusion; am I wrong? There is room for detailed criticism, but I feel no inclination for it as to me they were a part of your life, and I did not feel like using critical spectacles, beside you yourself will see where they are unfinished, after they have lain by a few months. I hope you will send me others to America, if we do not meet again soon.

85

I have acted with great carelessness, but do, if you can, excuse. Browning knowing I was writing to you, gave me a note to put in. There were many persons calling at the time. I laid it on the table for the moment, and before I was aware it was put with other papers in a trunk and sent to Leghorn, and aboard the ship. I am very sorry, but fear that now all I can do will be to send it you from the U. S. I fancy it is matter that will keep, but am very sorry.

I reread the letter with shame, but really I cannot write to those I prize most. I am so sad and weary leaving Italy that I seem paralyzed.

Dear William, dear Emelyn, farewell. I want energy and words now to say what I feel, but it is much affection and much sadness that we are not to meet again in Europe. To you may every Fate be propitious as you merit, and may we meet some day in more peace and amid as generous influences as those of Rome. Ossoli desires his affectionate respects to you both. Kiss your dear children for me. Mine seems to grow and promise well, shows nothing remarkable yet, but enough budding human nature to be a precious study to us. I count on you as friends for his growing years.

I hear my friend Mr. Calvert is in Paris; you have very likely seen him, but if not should like to be the means of an acquaintance that I think will be agreeable to both, and enclose a note, if you incline to use it. Write I pray to me in U. S. care S. G. Ward Boston and ever ever your affectionate

MARGARET.

MsC (MH: fMS Am 1086 [9:229]); MsC (MH: fMS Am 1086 [Works, 1:305–11]); MsC (NNPM). Published in part in Chevigny, pp. 495–96, and in Herbert Cahoon, Thomas V. Lange, and Charles Ryskamp, *American Literary Autographs from Washington Irving to Henry James* (New York, 1977), pp. 42–43, where it is incorrectly described as an autograph letter.

1. Fuller quotes from a favorite poem, George Herbert's "The Church": "Thus doth thy power crosse-bias me, not making / Thine own gift good, yet me from my wayes taking" (*Works of George Herbert*, p. 48).

901. To Margarett C. Fuller

Florence 14 May 1850.

My dearest Mother,

I will believe I shall be welcome with my treasures, my husband and child. For me, I long so very much to see you, should any thing hinder it on earth again (and I say it merely because there seems somewhat more of danger on sea than on land) think of your daughter as one who always wished at least to do her duty, and who always cherished you according as her mind opened to discover excellence.

Give dear love, too, to my brothers, first my eldest, and faithful friend, Eugene, God bless him. Love to my kind and good Aunts, my dear cousin Ellen, a sister's love to Ellen Channing,—[1]

We sail in the "Elizabeth," Capt. Hasty, from Leghorn for New York; and I hope we may arrive by the end of June.

I hope we shall be able to pass some time together yet in this world; but if God decrees otherwise,— here and hereafter, My dearest Mother, Your loving child,

MARGARET.

MsC (MB: Ms. Am. 1450 [80]). Published in part in *At Home and Abroad*, p. 440, and Van Doren, pp. 314–15; published entire in *Memoirs*, 2:337–38.

1. Her sister, Ellen Kilshaw Fuller, married the poet William Ellery Channing.

902.   To Marcus and Rebecca Spring

Florence May [14,] 1850

My dear Marcus and Rebecca,

Your packet did not reach me till I had taken passage for America It contained the first word of encouragement, the first glimpse of aid in case I wished to remain I ever received— I viewed the matter as you do for all the reasons you state.[1] I was most advantageously and happily placed here, if I could only have been sure of a narrow maintenance Should I ever return the little band of fond and noble friends who sweetened my life here will probably be dispersed. But most of all I wished to stay on account of my child. I have suffered terribly from anxiety that I must take him the long voyage just as his most dangerous teeth are coming. The necessity however seemed at the time imperative and your letter came too late. Let us hope Providence has ruled it for the best. Having decided I feel tranquil, though I suffer much on leaving Italy.— Yet I long too to embrace my loved friends at home. Since my face was turned towards them I long much.

Say to my dearest William that in the hurry and fatigue of these days I have not time to write to him as I would but not to feel anxious about people's talk concerning me.[2] It is not directed against the real

Margaret, but a phantom. I have acted not inconsistently with myself. If I have practiced some reserve it was because I thought it wise and best. People when they see me will not generally be inclined to injure me, for they will see the expression of a heart bettered by experience— more humble and tender, more anxious to serve its kind than ever before. I think my path will somehow be made plain before me, though I cannot yet see distinctly how. For the rest the delight of meeting him again would a thousand times overpay annoyances if such should arise. For the rest Americans here in Italy act towards me the same as foreigners— always with respect often with most loving kindness— I dare say it will be the same at home I think it will—My dear Marcus—as the opportunity of going in a ship from Leghorn came unexpectedly favorable and had to take up money at Fenzi's the Arconatis being security and I ventured as Fenzi and Hall would only give me exchange on N. York to draw on you. It was a bill for a hundred days and for three hundred thirty six dollars, beginning 4th May. Should I arrive as I expect I shall meet it. Should I perish at sea I know you will not see it dishonored. Combine with my friends. Since taking it up, Mrs. Farrar writes that she has a hundred dollars for me— A letter from Mother that she has placed a hundred at Barings for me for the rest the means I proposed to raise it by would go to the bottom with me, but mother or my brothers would in such a case raise it I am sure if you show this letter. Please send the inclosed to Mother; it is to advise her of my coming. I sail in the Elizabeth— Captain Hasty for New York. If you know when she arrives, I think you will try to come on board— if not, I shall if possible, come to your store. We expect to sail tomorrow. Dear M. R. and Eddie farewell. God bless you from

MARGARET

MsC (MH: fMS Am 1086 [9:221]); MsC (MH: fMS Am 1086 [Works, 1:313–17]); MsC (NjHi); MsC (CSmH [46944]).

1. Both Marcus and Rebecca Spring urged Fuller to stay abroad. Wrote Rebecca on 14 April: "I must now say my most important thing and stop. And that much as we should love to see you and strange as it may seem, we, as well as all your friends who have spoken to us about it, believe it will be undesirable for you to return at present. . . . It is because we love you we say stay!" (MH). Three days later, Marcus cited professional advantages that Fuller would gain: "Knowing too, how hard it will be for you to make anything like a living here, & how much less it costs to live in Florence than here." Among his points was a strained appeal to Fuller's knowledge of Italy: "considering, too, how much your residence in Italy must be worth to that noble & aspiring people, with all your enlightened & matured views of true republican freedom & how much good you will do your own country writing about it, & to it, somewhat as an 'outside

barbarian' or from the standpoint of a foreigner, with all the advantage of intimate knowledge of our needs, which a foreigner cannot have" (MH).

2. Marcus had said: "Mr. Channing, also, with whom we had a good long talk about your affair, the other evening, agrees with the rest of us in thinking that so far as your publishing matters are concerned, the balance of advantages will turn in favor of you remaining abroad. He intended to write to you also, by this parcel, but has not yet sent anything to put in" (MH).

903. To Marcus Spring

Ship Elizabeth off Gibraltar
June 3rd 1850

My dear Marcus,

You will I trust long ere receiving this have read my letter from Florence of 14th May, enclosing one to my mother informing you under what circumstances I had drawn on you through Fenzi and Hall and mentioning how I wished the bill to be met in case of any accident to me on my homeward course. That course as respects weather has been thus far not unpleasant, but the disaster that has befallen is such as I never dreamed of. I had taken passage with Capt Hasty, one who seemed to me among the best and most highminded of our American men, he showed the kindest interest in me, his wife an excellent woman was with him—[1] I thought during the voyage, if safe, and my child well, to have as much respite from care and pain as sea sickness might permit.

But scarce was that enemy in some measure quelled when the Captain fell sick. At first his disease presented the symptoms of nervous fever. I was with him a great deal— indeed whenever I could relieve his wife from a ministry softened by great love and the heroism of womanly courage, The last days were truly terrible with disgusts and fatigues, for he died we suppose (no physician has been allowed to come on board to see the body) of confluent small pox. I have seen since we parted great suffering but nothing physical to be compared to this, where the once fair and expressive mould of man is thus lost in corruption before life has fled.

He died yesterday morning and was buried in deep water, the American Consul's barge towing out one from this ship which bore the body about six o'clock. It was Sunday a divinely calm soft glowing afternoon had succeeded a morning of bleak cold wind You cannot think how beautiful the whole thing was— the decent array and sad reverence of the sailors—the many ships with their banners flying, the stern pillar of Hercules all veiled in roseate vapor, the little angel white sails diving into the blue depths with that solemn spoil of the poor good man— so still who had been so agonized and gasping as the last sun stooped.—Yes! it was beautiful but how dear a price we pay for the poems of this world. We shall be now in Quarantine a week, no person permitted to come on board till it is seen whether disease may break out in other cases. I have no good reason to think it will *not*, yet do not feel afraid. Ossoli has had it, so is safe; the baby is of course subject to injury In the earlier days before I suspected small pox I carried him twice into the sick room at request of the Captain, who was becoming fond of him. He laughed and pointed. He did not discern danger but only thought it odd to see the old friend there in bed. It is vain by prudence to seek to evade the stern assaults of Destiny. I submit Should all end well you see we shall be in N. York later than we expected— but keep a look out. Should we arrive safe I should like to see a friendly face. Commend me to dear William and other of my dear friends, especially Jane.[2] And Marcus, Rebecca, Eddie, with most affectionate wishes that joy and peace may continue to dwell in your house Adieu and love—as you can your friend

MARGARET

MsC (MH: fMS Am 1086 [9:221]); MsC (MH: fMS Am 1086 [Works, 1:317–21]); MsC (NjHi); MsC (CSmH [49944]). Published in part in Chevigny, 496–97; published in *WNC*, pp. 387–88; *Critic* 48 (March 1906): 253–54; and Sanborn, *Recollections*, 2:413–14.

1. On 28 April 1848, Hasty married Catherine Thompson (1818–52), daughter of Samuel and Hannah Fogg Thompson (Hasty Genealogy, NEHGS).

2. William Henry Channing and Jane Tuckerman King, mutual friends of Fuller and the Springs.

904.   To Samuel and Hannah Fogg Thompson

Bay Gibraltar, [3?] June 50

Mrs Hasty wishes that an outline of the late sad events should be made out for the dear friends. I will begin from our leaving Leghorn. The weather had been unfavorable during the stay of the Elizabeth in that port. Captn Hasty had more than usual fatigue and annoyance in getting the cargo, beside the constant rain and dampness were very bad for his cough. We have no means of knowing how he came in contact with contagion, but it could only have been slight exposure. No doubt he was easily affected because fatigued and unwell. However after getting on board he seemed cheerful, and for about a week had no trouble, except from remains of fatigue and the cough.

One evening he complained of violent pain in the head and back. Next day fever began, and increased to the following Saturday, when a red eruption showed itself on the forehead, then the hands, and gradually the whole body. At first fever having diminished, we flattered ourselves it was being thrown off in that way. Still, Mrs Hasty's anxiety began to be great. It is indeed among the most fiery proofs that life offers, to see a loved being suffer, as she did, without the possibility of calling a physician to advise as to the mode of treatment, or even give a name to the disease. Since however we do know what it was, she has the comfort of knowing the treatment was generally judicious, and that probably all was done that could be to alleviate his sufferings. These now became great, his weakness was extreme, a convulsive and constant cough deprived him of all repose. Then his throat became swolen and irritated that it was impossible for him to swallow. The eruption was turning black, and becoming in parts very painful. He sustained himself with great resolution, and up to the last sustained his the heart of his wife, whenever he had strength to utter a few words. "He hoped to find medical aid at Gibraltar, to recover and live with her, and see again their dear parents and friends" *still* he said, though I wish to live, if God wills it otherwise, I am resigned. He begged her when to distressed to read a chapter in the bible. Once he asked her to play and sing one of their favorite hymns, but she was too much moved to comply. The last day of his life was one of great suffering. The morning of that day, I felt distinctly, from the expression of his face, that the aid we expected at Gibraltar, would come too late. He however still hoped and was very pleasantly excited by weighing anchor in the middle of the night of June 1st up to the land port. His mates came to him to take orders and consel. When hardly able to articulate a syllable his mind was still clear on all that regarded his duties. On the following morning Sunday 2d of June, he began to sink about 7 o'clock, and passed gently away as I have seen a little infant. All around felt this a great mercy. He had suffered so much, and still seemed to have so much power of resistence in his constitution, that we apprehended great agony in the separation of soul and body, but all was sweet, and his face assumed immediately that hallowed calmness, peculiar to the death of those whose spirits have been good and not evil. His death was probably hastened a little by the excitement of arrival in this much desired haven, but we have reason

91

to rejoice that it was so, and he was spared the conflict of feeling and disappointment that must have filled the day, for after much going and coming of boats, the authorities proved inexorable as to the quarrentine regulations. Living, he could not have had a physician, nor would they permit the body to be interred on shore. He was so that afternoon from the ship by the care of his own affectionate men. The hour was beautiful, the influence seemed elevating. We felt that the brave and highminded departed was at peace in his Father's love. The men were solemnly and tenderly impressed, as indeed their conduct all through had been more like the refined sympathy of brothers of the same household, than rough sailors. I do not think 'twas possible to render more, and more useful service than the Steward did. The second mate was anxious to watch with him, the first mate to satisfy him in every way.[1] All feel the same towards your daughter. Every effort will be made by all on board to sooth and aid her so far as is possible. I want words t[o] tell you how beautiful her conduct has been so wise, so tender. Such a heroic spirit of christian love and faith supported her doubts and anguish and enabled her to make exertions that seemed almost miraculous. For ten days and eleven nights she nursed him without an hour that could be called one of refreshment, performing for him the most difficult and repulsive offices with equal judgment, resolution and delicate tenderness. In her desolation she she seeks in the same spirit to sustain herself by the christian's hope. Much as you have prized your child, I am sure she would be even dearer, could you have seen her on that day. Though much worn and very weak, she does not seem ill, and we hope to bring her safe to those who will console her as much as much as mortals can. And that God may bless you also and sustain you under this unsuspected deprivation of a precious child is the warm wish of your

M. Ossoli

MsC (MeHi). Published in part in *Portland* [Maine] *Evening Express and Advertiser*, 2 June 1910. Published entire in *American Literature* 5 (March 1933): 66–69.

Fuller took from Catharine Hasty a dictated letter to her parents and then completed it with one of her own. Catharine Hasty said: Think not my beloved parents, I am ill, because I ask my kind friend Mrs Ossoli to write to you for me. I am in much better health than anyone would have supposed after passing thru' such fiery trials as my Heavenly Father has seen fit to place in my path. The trip was bitter, my dear dear parents, but God gave me strength, and I trust the affliction will be sanctified and I not entirely unfitted for future usefulness. My heart yearns for my home, that I may lay my aching head upon those faithful bosoms who have loved me from my childhood. Life seems very dark to me now, the only bright spot is the hope of meeting friends at home. But I shall ever feel grateful to my Heavenly Father that I was permitted to be with my dear husband in his last sickness and had strength to watch by him night and day until the very last moment. There are many things I wish you to know that I feel I cannot write myself, but when I get home I hope to be able to talk to you of every thing, and shall have much to say which will be a comfort. Be assured I have received every consolation which kind attention and sympathy could give from passengers and will tell you much when we meet, and ship's officers and indeed every one on board. Do not be distressed for me "He who tempers the wind to the shorn lamb" will take care of your child This letter is intended for *all my parents,* my own father will please send it to Kilmonnock with the love of their affectionate child

CATHARINE F. HASTY

1. Henry P. Bangs of Philadelphia, the first mate, assumed command of the *Elizabeth* upon Hasty's death.

905.   To M. W. A., S. F. H., E. M., M. M., M. D. M.,

and M. D. A.

Wednesday

My dear Girls,— I suppose you are more than half in jest, but I will answer you in earnest.

I often regret that you have not a teacher who has more heart, more health, more energy to spend upon you than I have; for truly I esteem you worthy of much more. If I were as fit to meet and use life as I was only three or four years since, I should cultivate the acquaintance of many of my scholars. I should wish to know you in your domestic relations and to help you much more and in more ways than I can now. But my duties in life are at present so many, and my health so precarious, that I dare not be *generous* lest I should thus be unable to be *just,* dare not indulge my feelings lest I should fail to discharge my duties. Since I thus act by you in so miserly a spirit, giving to each and all only what the letter of my obligation requires, let me take this opportunity to say that it is not because I do not value you and even (I use not the word lightly) love you. If I did not wish to *give* my love, some of my scholars would *gain* it by their uniformly honorable conduct and engaging manners. And you will do me justice in believing that I generally feel much more regard than I express. And, though I cannot do for you all that another might in my place, let me assure you that, if, while under my care, or after you leave me, you should feel that I can, by any counsel or words of instruction or act of kindness, benefit you where others could not, my ear and heart will always be ready to attend to your wishes.

Give my love to J.[1] I hope I was not too rough with her this morning. Could I but teach her more confidence and self-possession, I should be satisfied with her as much as I am now interested in her.

Affectionately yours,

S. M. FULLER.

93

ELfr, from *Christian Register*, 21 April 1910, p. 428. Published in *Critical Essays on Margaret Fuller*, ed. Joel Myerson (Boston, 1980), pp. 136–37.

The letter was written to Fuller's students at the Greene-Street School in Providence. M. W. A. is Mary Ware Allen; S. F. H. may be Susan Humphrey; E. M., M. M., and M. D. M. are Evelina, Matilda, and Mary D. Metcalf; M. D. A. is probably Mary D. Angel[?] (Frank Shuffelton, "Margaret Fuller at the Greene Street School: The Journal of Evelina Metcalf," in *Studies in the American Renaissance, 1985*, ed. Joel Myerson [Charlottesville, 1985], p. 45; "Students of Margaret Fuller," n.p., n.d. [MH]). Mary Ware Allen (1819–97), daughter of Rev. Joseph and Lucy Ware Allen of Northborough, attended the school until her aunt Harriet Ware Hall died in June 1838. In September 1840 Mary married Dr. Joshua Jewell Johnson (1809–84) (Elizabeth Waterhouse Allen, *Memorial of Joseph and Lucy Clark Allen* [Boston, 1891], pp. 63, 99; Northborough VR).

1. J. is probably Juliet Graves (Laraine R. Fergenson, "Margaret Fuller as a Teacher in Providence," in *Studies in the American Renaissance, 1991*, ed. Joel Myerson [Charlottesville, 1991], p. 117).

906. To Caroline Clements Brown

Tuesday—

Dear Madam

A friend, who has a child very ill, expects me to stay with her this night.[n] It is also difficult for me to make visits in the eveg as I am alone and have no manservant. I shall see you again some day, when I can return at sunset

With respect

MARGARET FULLER

ALS (RPB). *Addressed*: Mrs Brown.

Caroline Matilda Clements married Nicholas Brown in 1831. Fuller knew them when he was the American consul in Rome.

this night.] this ⟨evening.⟩ ↑ night. ↓

907. To Georgiana Bruce

[   ] I shall probably be at Brook Farm in the course of a month. Yours with affece good will

S. M. F.

ALfrS (TxU). *Addressed:* Miss Georgiana Bruce / Brook Farm.

Georgiana Bruce was a young Englishwoman who lived for a time at Brook Farm and who later became active in the antislavery movement.

908.   To William H. Channing

[n.d.]

[   ] This week has been one of real study and I have gone almost through the works on Greek Art that I have been obliged to keep untouched so many months. I have been most happy, transported to the olive grove and blue Ionian skies. I took all the pretty stories out of the great folio pages, and will copy some of[n] them in briefer form for you and affix to this sheet. [   ]

Thursday I passed with your Uncle William.[1] It was rainy; we had a tete à tete, and a most agreeable one, though the subject was great part of the time *insanity*, which he looked on with his usual calmness of faith and love. [   ]

ALfr (MB: Ms. Am. 1450 [44]).

copy some of] copy ↑some of↓

1. William Ellery Channing, minister of the Federal Street Church in Boston, was the most prominent Unitarian minister of the decades between 1820 and 1840.

909.   To William H. Channing

[n.d.]

How I wish that you would dismiss the past except as the birthplace of the future! In you is an energy which is your divine, lawful heritage; which, if you trust it, will make you wholly strong and always radiant, and a benefactor to all about you if you will let it. How shall I convince you that I do not see falsely? It is because of this sure faith that I abide by you. Strange that I have not the power to make you trust yourself. To-night I lay on the sofa and saw how the flame shot up from beneath through the mass of coal which had been piled upon it. While beautiful jets sprang up, then quickly sank again, and all was black and unsightly, till at length the whole mass was kindled. And thus, thought I, is it with human life at present; and yet, if the fire beneath will but persist and conquer, all the blackness shall become radiant and life-like, fit to light a domestic hearth, or for the altar. Yes, so shall it be if we trust our God with a confidence that never flags. May God show you the true course, and so harmonize your life and thought, giving you so profound an insight that no other lives can bring a jar to you.

Your influence on me, in whatever shape it comes, has always been purifying, ennobling, and of late it has been so suggestive of thoughts on the greatest themes of the time that its influence, though pensive, has been most fruitful. I have seemed to be wandering in an unexplored forest, out of which I have not yet found the way. It is a solemn shade, damp and chill, yet full of forms of quiet life, and gentle flowers around the path, while now and then a star shines through the shadows.

Forget, if you can, all petulant or overstrained tendencies which may have displeased your pure conscience, and commend me in your prayers to my best self; and when in the solitudes of the spirit comes upon you some lofty aspiration of earnest faith and high hope, then believe that the power which has guided me so faithfully emboldens my thoughts to frame a prayer for you. And so, farewell.

ELfr, from Frothingham, *Memoir of William Henry Channing*, pp. 441–42.

910.   To William H. Channing?

[n.d.]

I would have my friends tender of me, not because I am frail, but because I am capable of strength;— patient, because they see in me a principle that must, at last, harmonize all the exuberance of my character. I did not well understand what you felt, but I am willing to admit that what you said of my "over-great impetuosity" is just. You will, perhaps, feel is more and more. It may at times hide my better self. When it does, speak, I entreat, as harshly as you feel. Let me be always sure I know the worst. I believe you will be thus just, thus true, for we are both servants of Truth.

ELfr, from *Memoirs*, 2:65–66.

911.   To William H. Channing?

[n.d.]

When others say to me, and not without apparent ground, that "the Outward Church is a folly which keeps men from enjoying the communion of the Church Invisible, and that in the desire to be helped by, and to help others, men lose sight of the only sufficient help, which they might find by faithful solitary intentness of spirit," I answer it is true, and the present deadness and emptiness summon us to turn our thoughts in that direction. Being now without any positive form of religion, any unattractive symbols, or mysterious rites, we are in the less danger of stopping at surfaces, of accepting a mediator instead of the Father, a sacrament instead of the Holy Ghost. And when I see how little there is to impede and bewilder us, I cannot but accept,— should it be for many years,— the forlornness, the want of fit expression, the darkness as to what is to be expressed, even that characterize our time.

But I do not, therefore, as some of our friends do, believe that it will always be so, and that the church is tottering to its grave, never to rise again. The church was the growth of human nature, and it is so still. It is but one result of the impulse which makes two friends clasp one another's hands, look into one another's eyes at sight of beauty, or the utterance of a feeling of piety. So soon as the Spirit has mourned and sought, and waited long enough to open new depths, and has found something to express, there will again be a Cultus, a Church. The very people who say that none is needed, make one at once. They talk with, they write to one another. They listen to music, they sustain themselves with the poets; they like that one voice should tell the thoughts of several minds, one gesture proclaim that the same life is at the same moment in many breasts.

I am myself most happy in my lonely Sundays, and do not feel the need of any social worship, as I have not for several years, which I have passed in the same way. Sunday is to me priceless as a day of peace and solitary reflection. To all who will, it may be true, that, as Herbert says:—

> Sundays the pillars are
> On which Heaven's palace arched lies;
> The other days fill up the space
> And hollow room with vanities;[1]

and yet in no wise "vanities," when filtered by the Sunday crucible. After much troubling of the waters of my life, a radiant thought of the meaning and beauty of earthly existence will descend like a healing angel. The stillness permits me to hear a pure tone from the One in All. But often I am not alone. The many now, whose hearts, panting for truth and love, have been made known to me, whose lives flow in the same direction as mine, and are enlightened by the same star, are with me. I am in church, the church invisible, undefiled by inadequate expression. Our communion is perfect; it is that of a common aspiration; and where two or three are gathered together in one region, whether in the flesh or the spirit, He will grant their request. Other communion would be a happiness,— to break together the bread of mutual thought, to drink the wine of loving life,— but it is not necessary.

Yet I cannot but feel that the crowd of men whose pursuits are not intellectual, who are not brought by their daily walk into converse with sages and poets, who win their bread from an earth whose mysteries are not open to them, whose worldly intercourse is more likely to stifle than to encourage the sparks of love and faith in their breasts, need on that day quickening more than repose. The church is now rather a lecture-room than a place of worship; it should be a school for mutual instruction. I must rejoice when any one, who lays spiritual things to heart, feels the call rather to mingle with men, than to retire and seek by himself.

You speak of men going up to worship by "households," &c. Were the actual family the intellectual family, this might be; but as social life now is, how can it? Do we not constantly see the child, born in the flesh to one father, choose in the spirit another? No doubt this is wrong, since the sign does not stand for the things signified, but it is one feature of the time. How will it end? Can families worship together till it does end?

ELfr, from *Memoirs*, 2:81–84.
1. From the "Sunday" section of "The Church":

> Sundaies the pillars are,
> On which heav'ns palace arched lies:
> The other dayes fill up the spare
> And hollow room with vanities.
> They are the fruitfull beds and borders
> In Gods rich garden: that is bare,
>   Which parts their ranks and orders.

(*Works of George Herbert*, p. 75)

912. To William H. Channing

[n.d.]

I protest against your applying to me, even in your most transient thought, such an epithet as "determined exaggeration." Exaggeration, if you will; but not determined. No; I would have all open to the light, and would let my boughs be pruned, when they grow rank and unfruitful, even if I felt the knife to the quick of my being. Very fain would I have a rational modesty, without self-distrust; and may the knowledge of my failures leaven my soul, and check its intemperance. If you saw me wholly, you would not, I think, feel as you do; for you would recognize the force, that regulates my life and tempers the ardor with an eventual calmness. You would see, too, that the more I take my flight in poetical enthusiasm, the stronger materials I bring back for my nest. Certainly I am nowise yet an angel; but neither am I an utterly weak woman, and far less a cold intellect. God is rarely afar off. Exquisite nature is all around. Life affords vicissitudes enough to try the energies of the human will. I can pray, I can act, I can learn, I can constantly immerse myself in the Divine Beauty. But I also need to love my fellow-men, and to meet the responsive glance of my spiritual kindred.

ELfr, from *Memoirs*, 2:110–11.

913. To William H. Channing?

[n.d.]

I like to hear you express your sense of my defects. The word "arrogance" does not, indeed, appear to me to be just; probably because I do not understand what you mean. But in due time I doubtless shall; for so repeatedly have you used it, that it must stand for something real in my large and rich, yet irregular and unclarified nature. But though I like to hear you, as I say, and think somehow your reproof does me good, by myself, I return to my native bias, and feel as if there was plenty of room in the universe for my faults, and as if I could not spend time in thinking of them, when so many things interest me more. I have no defiance or coldness, however, as to these spiritual facts which I do not know; but I must follow my own law, and bide my time, even if, like Oedipus, I should return a criminal, blind and outcast, to ask aid from the gods. Such possibilities, I confess, give me great awe; for I have more sense than most, of the tragic depths that may open suddenly in the life. Yet, believing in God, anguish cannot be despair, nor guilt perdition. I feel sure that I have never wilfully chosen, and that my life has been docile to such truth as

99

was shown it. In an environment like mine, what may have seemed too lofty or ambitious in my character was absolutely needed to keep the heart from breaking and enthusiasm from extinction.

ELfr, from *Memoirs*, 2:111–12.

914. To Anna Huidekoper Clarke

[n.d.]

Dear Anna,

The only reason I had not sent the letters was that I had not had time to look them over. I could do so now only slightly; if there is any thing left that does not relate to James, you will keep it for me. As you have all[n] James's present mind these relics of the past would all be intelligible to you, if they could have been put in order. I am very much ashamed to send them as they are, but they have been turned over many[n] times to look for this and that. In greatest haste, dear Anna, your friend

S. M. F.

ALS (MHi). *Addressed:* Mrs James Clarke / Somerset Court / Boston / care / Mr Shippen.

Anna Huidekoper married James Clarke in 1839.

have all] have ↑ all ↓

over many] over man⟨?⟩y

915. To James F. Clarke

Saty Morng

Dear James,

Will you come hither and help admire this eveg? Come at ½ past seven; and be very agreeable

M.

Anna H. Clarke. From Nina Moore Tiffany and Francis Tiffany, *Harm Jan Huidekoper* (Boston: Riverside, 1904).

ALS (MH: bMS Am 1569.7 [469]). *Addressed:* Mr James F. Clarke.
James Freeman Clarke, a distant cousin and one of Fuller's closest friends, shared her enthusiasm for German literature in the 1830s. After a period in Kentucky, Clarke founded the Church of the Disciples in Boston and became a prominent clergyman and writer in later life.

916.   To James F. Clarke

Thursday eveg.

Dear James,

Do not[n] send this parcel unless the oppory be of distinguished discretion. I would not have R. W. E's words[n] lent for much, S. M. F's for—

I had no chance to tell you Sunday eveg how my thoughts had been with you all the day; but you knew it I suppose.

In much fatigue and haste your affectionate

MARGARET

ALS (MHi). *Addressed:* Rev Mr Clark / Central Court.
Do not] ⟨I⟩ Do not
R. W. E's words] R. W. E's wor⟨l⟩ds

917.   To George T. Davis

[n.d.]

When we first seemed to be intimates you [*illegible*] with an insincerity and heartlessness unworthy me and I am also willing to believe of you. I found that during yrs of youth when I had treated you with the most unshrinking sincerity—when you had known *all* that lay in my mind with regard to you, you on yr side had cherished sweet thoughts of me wh you had never announced. I thought at the time that was what I never shld forgive

MsCfr (MB: Ms. Am. 1450 [18]).
George T. Davis was a classmate and friend of James Clarke. Fuller had loved Davis and was deeply wounded to find him indifferent to her. A man noted for both wit and

charm, Davis was a lawyer, a newspaperman in Greenfield, Massachusetts, and then a member of the U.S. House of Representatives.

918. To Ralph Waldo Emerson

[n.d.]

When you send this way, will you let me have the vol of Montaigne in which he speaks of his friend[1] E's Montaigne is not at home.

AL (MH: bMS Am 1280 [2384]). *Addressed:* Mr Emerson.

Ralph Waldo Emerson was a friend, fellow editor on the *Dial*, and intellectual companion to Fuller from 1836 to 1844, after which he faded from her life.

1. Montaigne was perhaps the most important literary influence on Emerson, who owned both a set of the *Essais* and Charles Cotton's 1693 translation (Walter Harding, *Emerson's Library* [Charlottesville, 1967]).

919. To Ralph Waldo Emerson?

[n.d.]

Only through emotion do we know thee, Nature! We lean upon thy breast, and feel its pulses vibrate to our own. That is knowledge, for that is love. Thought will never reach it.

ELfr, from *Memoirs*, 1:265.

920. To Ralph Waldo Emerson?

[n.d.]

Is [   ] there? Does water meet water?— no need of wine, sugar, spice, or even a *soupçon* of lemon to remind of a tropical climate? I fear me not. Yet, dear positives, believe me superlatively yours,

MARGARET.

ELfr, from *Memoirs*, 1:289.

921. To Margarett C. Fuller

Wednesday eveg.

I was and am quite grieved, dearest Mother, to give you pain to-night. I am too well aware that a momentary ebullition of impatience may give more pain than many days of tenderness can atone for. Perhaps, beside being sorry to have me so vehement, you felt as if the girls might suppose I did not value your energy as I ought. But all I feel is that you do not sympathize entirely with my great desire to have a clear space round me for a time. It is very natural you should not; the purposes for which I would free my thoughts are not the same as those that act on your beneficent life. Believe I will not again for a long time be thus ungentle, and show this note to E and B. that they may know how I feel.[1] And the Angel who seconds so many good acts of yours for one good plan of mine shall turn over a new page.

I shall not see you in the course of today, unless you are here between one and two, but will call for you by half past six to go to the lecture. Will you be ready; we shall not wish to come in. I have a ticket you can use, and Lizzie too, if she goes. Always most affectionately your daughter

MARGARET

ALS (MH: fMS Am 1086 [9:53]); MsC (MH: fMS Am 1086 [Works, 1:55, 177–79]). *Addressed:* Mrs Fuller / 20 Winter St.

1. Elizabeth and Belinda Randall were daughters of John Randall of Boston, at whose home on Winter Street Mrs. Fuller was visiting. Fuller and Elizabeth Randall had been close friends in their late teens.

922. To Richard F. Fuller

[n.d.]

Dear Richard,

We have tickets to this eveg's concert for you and Arthur and depend on seeing you. Be here punctually a little after 6 affecy yr sister

M.

ALS (MH: fMS Am 1086 [9:125]); MsC (MH: fMS Am 1086 [Works, 2:789]). *Addressed:* R. F. Fuller / Prospect St / Cambridge Port / G Howe's Express.

923. To Richard F. Fuller

[n.d.]

[   ] you say of Lloyd. I have thought sometimes that we would ere long make you and Arthur his guardians. Your father alone was so to four brothers.[1]

"Why should the death of our friend make us sad?" In the same way as separation does. The soul is present to us but the want of positiveness to [   ] yearned to embrace her also, and ached when the shade refused to fill his longing arms.

I am well now, but begin to need change of air and scene.

very affectionately your sister

MARGARE[T]

ALfrS (ViU).

1. Her four lawyer uncles were Abraham Williams, Henry Holton, William Williams, and Elisha Fuller.

924. To Richard F. Fuller?

[n.d.]

Great and even *fatal* errors (so far as this life is concerned) could not destroy my friendship for one in whom I am sure of the kernel of nobleness.

ELfr, from *Memoirs*, 1:77.

The Memoirs *editors identify the recipient as a brother. The letter was probably written to Richard, her frequent correspondent.*

925. To Richard F. Fuller?

[n.d.]

As a family, we are henceforth to be parted. But though for months I had been preparing for this separation, the last moments were very sad. Such tears are childish tears, I know, and belie a deeper wisdom. It is foolish in me to be so anxious about my family. As I went along, it seemed as if all I did was for God's sake; but if it had been, could I now thus fear? My relations to them are altogether fair, so far as they go. As to their being no more to me than others of my kind, there is surely a mystic thrill betwixt children of one mother, which can never cease to be felt till the soul is quite born anew. The earthly family is the scaffold whereby we build the spiritual one. The glimpses we here obtain of what such relations should be are to me an earnest that the family is of Divine Order, and not a mere school of preparation. And in the state of perfect being which we call Heaven, I am assured that family ties will attain to that glorified beauty of harmonious adaptation, which stellar groups in the pure blue typify.

ELfr, from *Memoirs*, 2:120–21.

The Memoirs *editors identify the recipient as a brother. The letter was probably written to Richard, her frequent correspondent.*

926. To Richard F. Fuller?

[n.d.]

We cannot be sufficiently grateful for our mother,— so fair a blossom of the white amaranth; truly to us a mother in this, that we can venerate her piety. Our relations to her have known no jar. Nothing vulgar has sullied them; and in this respect life has been truly domesticated. Indeed, when I compare my lot with others, it seems to have had a more than usual likeness to home; for relations have been as noble as sincerity could make them, and there has been a frequent breath of refined affection, with its sweet courtesies. Mother thanks God in her prayers for "all the acts of mutual love which have been permitted"; and looking back, I see that these have really been many. I do not recognize this, as the days pass, for to my desires life would be such a flower-chain of symbols, that what is done seems very scanty, and the thread shows too much.

She has just brought me a little bouquet. Her flowers have suffered greatly by my neglect, when I would be engrossed by other things in her absences. But, not to be disgusted or deterred, whenever she can glean one pretty enough, she brings it to me. Here is the bouquet,— a very delicate rose, with its half-blown bud, heliotrope, geranium, lady-pea, heart's-ease; all sweet-scented flowers! Moved by their beauty, I wrote a short note, to which this is the reply. Just like herself

It has been, and still is, hard for me to give up the thought of serenity, and freedom from toil and care, for mother, in the evening of a day which has been all one work of disinterested love. But I am now confident that she will learn from every trial its lesson; and if I cannot be her protector, I can be at least her counsellor and soother.

Elfr, from *Memoirs*, 2:121–24. Published in part in Higginson, *MFO*, p. 19.

The Memoirs *editors identify the recipient as a brother. The letter was probably written to Richard, her frequent correspondent.*

927. To Richard F. Fuller?

[n.d.]

It is a great pleasure to me to give you this book both that I have a brother whom I think worthy to value it, and that I can give him something worthy to be valued more and more through all his life. Whatever height we may attain in knowledge, whatever facility in the expression of thoughts, will only enable us to do more justice to what is drawn from so deep a source of faith and intellect, and arrayed, oftentimes, in the fairest hues of nature. Yet it may not be well for a young mind to dwell too near one tuned to so high a pitch as this writer, lest, by trying to come into concord with him, the natural tones be overstrained, and the strings weakened by untimely pressure. Do not attempt, therefore, to read this book through, but keep it with you, and when the spirit is fresh and earnest turn to it. It is full of the tide-marks of great thoughts, but these can be understood by one only who has gained, by experience, some knowledge of these tides. The ancient sages knew how to greet a brother who had consecrated his life to thought, and was never disturbed from his purpose by a lower aim. But it is only to those perfected in purity that Pythagoras can show a golden thigh.[1]

One word as to your late readings. They came in a timely way to admonish you, amidst mere disciplines, as to the future uses of such disciplines. But systems of philosophy are mere pictures to him, who has not yet learned how to systematize. From an inward opening of your nature these knowledges must begin to be evolved, ere you can apprehend aught beyond their beauty, as revealed in the mind of another. Study in a reverent and patient spirit, blessing the day that leads you the least step onward. Do not ride hobbies. Do not hasten to conclusions. Be not coldly sceptical towards any thinker, neither credulous of his views. A man, whose mind is full of error, may give us the genial sense of truth, as a tropical sun, while it rears crocodiles, yet ripens the wine of the palm-tree.

To turn again to my Ancients: while they believed in self-reliance with a force little known in our day, they dreaded no pains of initiation, but fitted themselves for intelligent recognition of the truths on which our being is based, by slow gradations of travel, study, speech, silence, bravery, and patience. That so it may be with you, dear [   ], hopes your sister and friend.

ELfr, from *Memoirs*, 2:125–27.

The Memoirs *editors identify the recipient as a brother. The letter was probably written to Richard, her frequent correspondent.*

1. Fuller's source is unclear, for several authorities—among them Aristotle, Diogenes Laertius, and Iamblichus—recount the story that at the Olympian games Pythagoras showed that one of his thighs was golden. The story is one of several that suggest Pythagoras was more than mortal (*The Works of Aristotle*, ed. Sir David Ross [Oxford, 1952], 12:134–35).

928.   To Horace Greeley

Monday morng

Dear Mr Greeley,

The rain kept me in town last night now I am going home to scribble I believe there is hardly any paper there will you bring me a parcel tonight.

S. M. F.

ALS (IaU).

Horace Greeley founded and edited the *New-York Daily Tribune*, for which Fuller wrote from 1844 to 1850.

929.   To Amelia Greenwood

One oclock A M.

Dear Amelia,

I presume you will find on your bureau a quantity of lovely chestnut ringlets carefully tied up in whitey brown paper. I say *presume*, for if they be not there I know not to what graceful head the sylphs of the air may have wafted them as an appropriate lodgement. I thought I had them in my bag but can find no trace of them, so conclude they lie perdue among those tomes of rare and far sought lore which decorate aforesaid bureau as I remember airing the miscellaneous contents of said bag on its ample and polished surface, unless indeed Annie has slyly purloined them for her locket.[1] In the meantime there is a great want of symmetry in my appearance; one temple lies open to those rough visitants the winds in forlorn and ghastly relief to the sister temple whose hyacinthine locks "such soft expression give." I prythee send them with the long note which I expect today from your prolific pen. I grow abominably careless and troublesome, I know; if I do not make the publick a particular confidant yet I make it my wardrobe-keeper which is, I fear, much worse. Look to it, Margaret, this year must be amended. That respectable article the bryghte moone must be delighted. I hear her at this moment serenaded by three dogs barking in parts, a jews-harp, and a tree toad Adieu! I proffer the hundred-th part of a salute to the north east corner of your left cheek.

M.

ALS (CtY). *Addressed:* Miss Amelia Greenwood. / Portland St. *Endorsed:* Margaret Fuller.

1. Amelia's sister Angelina.

930. To Amelia Greenwood

[n.d.]

Dear Amelia,

Will you have the bonté to cover with paper and send me a pair of dusty stockings which I carelessly left in your apartment?—

I had a most *irritated* walk home yesterday— The wind blew needles and scorpions!— I found a charming partie carrie assembled in our sitting room composed of Mrs Peck! Mrs Hedge! Mamma and Mr Hillard; All raving about the weather— To-day is equally monstrous I have been dead and alive lisstening to Revd Newell and Doane on *Knowledge* and *Love* (which abstracts they might have personified) But dined with Mrs Farrar between!—[1]

Why do I give you this little account?— I dont know— it answers no purpose, but seems natural now we have passed three days together— I know *you* are again immersed in your usual stream— As indeed my society now only stops your current but turns naught aside.

All this apropos to the couvertures du ley as Mr C. would probably say

M. F.

ALS (CtY). *Addressed:* Miss Amelia Greenwood.

1. Harriet Hilliard (1788–1863), daughter of Rev. Timothy Hilliard, married in 1810 William Dandridge Peck (1763–1822), the first professor of natural history at Harvard (CVR; Lucius R. Paige, *History of Cambridge, Massachusetts, 1630–1877* [Boston, 1877]; MVR 167:240). Mrs. Hedge is Mary Kneeland Hedge, wife of Levi Hedge, a member of the Harvard faculty; Mr. Hillard is probably George Stillman Hillard (1808–79), who graduated from Harvard in 1828. After teaching with George Bancroft in Northampton, he studied law at Harvard and was admitted to practice in 1833. He later became a partner of Charles Sumner. Hillard had a career as a writer and was a close friend of Hawthorne (*DAB*). Rev. William Newell became the minister of the new Unitarian parish in Cambridge in 1830. George Washington Doane (1799–1859) was a graduate of Union College and attended the General Theological Seminary. He was ordained as an Episcopal priest in 1823. From 1828 to 1830 he was the assistant at Trinity church, Boston. In later life he was a bishop and the president of Burlington College (Alfred Alder Doane, *The Doane Family* [Boston, 1902], p. 394).

931.   To Amelia Greenwood

Friday morng.

Très chère Amelia,

I ought not to write to you, for I have not half finished my exercises but I could not resist my desire to be present in your thoughts a few moments this day. I have copied for you the passage I mentioned in Shelley, as applicable to your opinions with regard to those faint and shadowed reminiscences of a former state of being which haunt the troubled soul in this. The lines are from Prince Athanase—[1] His friends are speaking of the mysterious sadness which in earliest youth clouded his pure and noble mind. I was obliged to mangle the passage, but have endeavored to arrange the lines I send in *understandable* order. Presentez mes amities a Mlles vos soeurs, et a vôtre amie, la belle Marian—[2]

Shall I not see you before many days?

S. M F.

ALS (MH: bMS Am 2016 [4]). *Addressed:* Miss Amelia Greenwood. / Portland St. *Endorsed:* from / Margaret Fuller.

1. According to his wife, Shelley wrote "Prince Athanase" in December 1817. She published it for the first time in 1824. The passage Fuller mentions occurs in ll. 86–98:

For all who knew and loved him then perceived
That there was drawn an adamantine veil

Between his heart and mind,—both unrelieved
Wrought in his brain and bosom separate strife.
Some said that he was mad, others believed

That memories of an antenatal life
Made this, where now he dwelt, a penal hell;
And others said that such mysterious grief

From God's displeasure, like a darkness, fell
On souls like his, which owned no higher law
Than love; love calm, steadfast, invincible

By mortal fear or supernatural awe.

(*Complete Poetical Works of Shelley*, pp. 167–68)
  2. Marian Marshall was a childhood Boston friend.

932. To Elizabeth Hoar

Saturday

My dear Elizabeth,

  I do not really, really like to send these precious things away from
me, but seeing its you, I wont refuse. I have had a good letter since I
saw[n] you and a better visit. Mr E. looked like May and September and
talked violets and crocuses. Write a little note by Hannah, reinclose
this letter to me, and let me know whether you will stay till Wednesday, because, if so, I will see you and also get ready a parcel for Concord.[1]

  in truth and love yours

M. F.

ALS (MHarF). *Addressed:* Miss Elizabeth Hoar.
  I saw] I ⟨l⟩ saw
On the outside Fuller wrote: Dear Belinda, if E. H. is gone send this back or give it me
on Wednesday. M. F.
  1. Mr. E is Emerson; Hannah is Hannah Adams Randall, Belinda Randall's sister.

933. To Charles K. Newcomb

[n.d.]

Dearest Charles

  I dont know what feeling impels me to address you thus; it seems a
mournful affection Is the mind's heaven clear with you? You should

let me know and not be so indolent; writing only pencil notes and not exerting yourself to make out the sentence in that. I know what you mean but *still* I hope you are going to Newport. The beach and caves will be good for you. Write me when you shall return. I would not, if I could help it, visit Brook Farm and you away.—

MARGARET.

Your mother desired me to send these to yr care as you would soon visit P she said[1]

ALS (MH: fMS Am 1086 [10:125]). *Addressed:* Charles.

Charles King Newcomb was a Rhode Island man who wrote for the *Dial* and who had lived at Brook Farm. Both Fuller and Emerson thought him a gifted writer, but he never fulfilled their expectations.

1. Newcomb's mother was Rhoda Mardenbrough Newcomb, a strong-willed and prominent member of the Providence intellectual circle among whom Fuller moved during her years at the Greene-Street school. Mrs. Newcomb's letters often mention conversations with Fuller.

934. To Charles K. Newcomb

[n.d.]

Sweet child, for though I feel it is true Charles, what you said, that you are "man within," yet it is by such an address that my thoughts turn to you with gentlest love. Those were happy hours we have now passed together. Whether in the variegated wood, whose golden boughs the autumn sunset seemed to envy, or amid the motley crowd of men amid whose friendly hues *we* stood golden, in this season, with scarce more noise to our lives than is made by the gentle dropping of a leaf, or in[n] the clear moonlight, beside the silent pool, or in your little room ministered to by the symbols of your native ritual. As amid those lonely glades the autumn sunlight lingers, so upon my now silent, fruitless yet many tinted mind rest glimpses of the worlds your keys unlock for me. They were all before us, the old worlds the Greek, the Catholic,— the Romantic, the Indian shown as in the boy, and our own world nearer, fairer, holier, still folded in the seed, resting in the grove.

I could not clasp home to my breast any of this,[n] nothing was mine own, but all the forms of the universe circling gently round. Neither did I wish to clasp *one*. Even in the days when my spirit sparkled like

112

the fire, rushed like the tide, I looked on the sculptures of the sitting Ceres and Proserpine the "great goddesses," and knew that time would come with me, when I would not wish to rise from my seat or detain any thing. So now I needed not to see much of Autumn woods or moon or sun; easily bent over me the bow of the new covenant. I wished not to arrest its glories. Even that last night we were in the pine wood, so dark, so religious I knew I should never have just such a moment again, yet I did not wish to detain it, did not wish to stay but passed over as easily as the wind through the tree tops, but in as deep a music.

We meet as the fire met the incense and though the hour is perfume, it is still as a cloud. I never before so realized that we were by destiny any thing to one another. You called me the priestess who had opened to you a gate, and I thought our relation was thus temporary, but it is natural and permanent, though it may not again thus clearly display itself.

Mr Emerson is desirous you should pass a couple of days with him.

You did not give me back with Iphigenia leaves in the handwriting of E. Hoar, exact translations of my extracts made by her from the Greek for me. I would not lose them for much, if you can find enclose them to me. And salute for me *in the spirit* your young brother, not in vain was the title Conqueror added to the name of William;[1] they come together in the fitness of things

AL (MH: fMS Am 1086 [10:134]). *Addressed:* Charles King Newcomb / Brook Farm / West Roxbury.

or in] or ⟨amid⟩ ↑ in ↓
of this] of th⟨ese⟩is
the title] the ↑ title ↓

1. Fuller's reference is unclear; Newcomb did not have a brother named William.

935. To Charles K. Newcomb

[n.d.]

Dear Charles,

The hour comes not in which I can say to a distant friend, more words than these "I love you— Let me know that you are well"

I reflect with pleasure on our meeting. I may truly say reflect for the image you presented is mirrored in my life: it roused no motion there.

You asked me to say my prayers, but I never do. Nature, in the commonest instincts is only present with me. All the flame is risen up and the lava has rushed back to fertilize the earth. The sea has retreated for the time within new limits, and the plains dress themselves in short tender green and little flowers. It is as a new born child that the spirit lifts its lids to view thee: hast thou, old magician, a gift and a spell to bestow. When thou wert a child this same was Mother like to thee. be thou angel like to it, in its new hour.

AL (MH: fMS Am 1086 [10:135]). *Addressed:* To / Charles K. Newcomb. / Brook Farm.

936. To Charles K. Newcomb

[n.d.]

Dear Charles,

I thought you would like a copy of Günderode for yourself specially, please accept this from me.[1]

The 5th Symphony is to be given yet once again next Saty eveg; cannot you come down?[2]

Your friend

MARGARET F.

ALS (MH: fMS Am 1086 [10:138]).
1. In 1842 Fuller published her translation of part of Bettina von Arnim's *Die Günderode*.
2. Probably Beethoven's symphony, which began to be performed in Boston in 1841.

937. To Charles K. Newcomb

[n.d.]

How is my dear Charles? When time and the mood permit he must write me at least of outward things how he left Brook farm, whether he had good days at Concord, whether he can tolerate Providence?

Perhaps too he will give me an entrance somehow to the present aspect of the Panorama though I was so dull with his last little key. For I am none the less the dear friend, am I, dear Charles?

AL (MH: fMS Am 1086 [10:144]). *Addressed:* Charles.

938. To Theodore Parker

Saturday morng.

My dear Mr Parker,

Mr Rakemann will be at our^n house this eveg and I depend on seeing you and Mrs P. bringing in your train that lazy man^n Mr Ripley who said he would not walk eight miles for the music and his energetic consort who calls for a friend at six miles' distance to go out with her on horseback.[1] We shall expect you about seven P. M. Yours with regard

S. M. FULLER.

ALS (PHi). *Addressed:* Rev Mr Parker. / Spring St / Roxbury.
at our] at ↑ our ↓
lazy man] lazy ⟨?⟩ man

Theodore Parker, the Unitarian minister at West Roxbury, contributed to the *Dial* when Fuller was editor. He had an often stormy career as a theological controversialist and social reformer.

1. Probably Ludwig Rackemann, who played both violin and piano. He gave concerts in Boston in 1839 and 1840, during which time Fuller often heard him. In 1837 Parker married Lydia Dodge Cabot (1813–80), daughter of John Cabot of Boston (Briggs, *Cabot Family*, 1:643). George Ripley, a Unitarian minister who left his pulpit and later founded Brook Farm, and his wife, Sophia Dana, were friends of Fuller. Ripley published her translation of Eckermann's *Gespräche*.

939. To [Elizabeth Peabody]

[n.d.]

[   ] I think I am very good to have written this long letter. Though 'tis as Swift's cookmaid says "a sad scrawl" and I cannot add as she does in palliation, "My sister Mary she writes better"[1]

Having no "sister Mary" or "Man Booby" to shelter me. But then there is the Universal Mind writing letters; and who cares for family ties in these days? So hoping that some other manifestation of the U. M. will make you amends for the imperfections of its present organ I remain, my dear Miss Peabody, yours in all kindness

S. M. FULLER.

ALfr (CtY). *Addressed:* Miss Elizabeth Peabody / Salem, / Mass.

Elizabeth Palmer Peabody, who preceded Fuller as Bronson Alcott's assistant at the Temple school, owned a bookstore at 12 West Street in Boston, where Fuller gave her "conversations." Peabody became well known for her participation in reform movements.

1. Jonathan Swift's "Mary the Cook-Maid's Letter to Dr. Sheridan": "And now I must go, and get *Saunders* to direct this Letter, / For I write but a sad Scrawl, but my Sister *Marget* she writes better" (*Swift: Poetical Works*, ed. Herbert Davis [London, 1967], p. 164).

940. To Mary Rotch

Thursday morng

My dear Miss Rotch

I will dine with you with pleasure, and pass the afternoon if possible. I have an engagement, but one that I perhaps can postpone
    with great respect yours

S. M. FULLER

ALS (ViU). *Addressed:* Miss Rotch / Tremont House.

Mary Rotch of New Bedford was a member of a prominent Quaker family, several of whom were Fuller's friends.

941. To Sarah Shaw

Wednesday morng

Dear Sarah,

Enclosed is a trifle I owed for omnibus package and postage of a letter. Excuse my troubling thee with it.

I felt, as you perceived, most unwilling to leave your house, but since I am here I find it was very needful, both because they want more "copy" every day, which I should have neglected, if near the woods, and also I had forgotten my Cambridge class which has three more meetings to claim of me.[1]

Yet this brilliant morning I think with desire, of your face to wake me in the morning and Frank's so kind and handsome, and Susy's monkey ways, and all the young uns tumbling head over heels on the bright green grass.[2] Of these luxuries you, no doubt, have your fill, as also of the blossoming wood. Did not you enjoy your drive home that sweet, *sweet* afternoon?

In great haste yrs affecy

MARGARET F.

ALS (MH: bMS Am 1417 [174]). *Addressed:* Mrs Sarah Shaw / West Roxbury.

Sarah Sturgis Shaw, a close friend from childhood, shared Fuller's enthusiasm for George Sand.

1. At this time Fuller was editing the *Dial* and conducting one of her "conversations" for women.

2. Francis George Shaw married Sarah Sturgis in 1835. He was a wealthy socialist who translated George Sand's novels. Their third child, Susanna, had been born in 1839. She married Robert Minturn in 1862 (Roger Faxton Sturgis, ed. *Edward Sturgis of Yarmouth, Massachusetts* [Boston, 1914], p. 3). The other "young uns" were Anna and Robert Gould Shaw.

942. To William Wetmore Story

[n.d.]

To W. W. Story

I take the liberty by this note to offer to your acquaintance, Mr Hart, the "Kentucky Sculptor, whose genius will, I doubt not, inspire you with interest, and to whom your regard might much avail in his short visit to Boston.[1]

S. M. FULLER.

ALS (collection of Gene De Gruson).

1. Joel Tanner Hart (1810–77) was born in Kentucky. He began his career by making busts of Andrew Jackson and General Cassius Clay. Hart moved to Florence in 1849. An inventor and poet, he was a successful if mediocre sculptor. His best-known work is a full statue of Henry Clay (*DAB*).

943. To Caroline Sturgis

[n.d.]

[   ] Have you read Faustina?[1] If not do.

I can buy you here other[n] interesting novels by the Countess Hahn Hahn in German, if you wish. In some respects she seems beyond Sand.

ALfr (MH: bMS Am 1221 [199]). *Addressed:* Miss C. Sturgis / Summer St.
here other] here ↑ other ↓
1. Ida, Gräfin von Hahn-Hahn, published *Gräfin Faustine* in 1841 (*OCGL*).

944. To Caroline Sturgis

Wednesday p. m

dear Caroline,

I am going home to pass this night and tomorrow but think I may come in tomorrow eveg to the concert. If you are out in the eveg will you leave word with some one to let me in as I may come before you. These hearts[n] ease I leave for you.

> Content in purple lustre clad
> Kingly serene and golden glad,
> No demihues of sad[n] contrition
> No pallors of enforced submission
> Give me such hearts ease as this
> And keep awhile the rosy bliss—

M.

ALS (MH: bMS Am 1221 [229]). *Addressed:* Caroline.
hearts] hear⟨s⟩ts
of sad] of ⟨?⟩ sad

945. To Caroline Sturgis

[n.d.]

Thou art a naughty girl to interfere with my plans! I never promised not to print the piece, you only asked me not in case it might be known. There was not any thing to mark you more than your[n] others unless the line

Every stroke I draw—

And I put to it one of my own initials.

The only reason I did not speak to you of it the other day was that I thought you might feel as I do a disgust to your own children which would make it impossible to present them to the public. Why did you not send me the little book. I do hate to have to ask for a thing so many times.

Looking over my bard-box I find this leaf wh I believe belongs to something[n] you have got for my book, so send it.

If H. Hedge lectures *next* Wednesday, I shall stay in that night and to Ellen's next night, if she has her soiree.[1] Let me know befroe hand, if you conveniently can.

AL (MH: bMS Am 1221 [230]). *Addressed:* Miss C. Sturgis / Summer St / Boston.
than your] than ⟨the⟩ ↑ your ↓
to something] to someth⟨g⟩ing

1. Frederic Henry Hedge, then the Unitarian minister at Bangor, Maine, was a prominent Unitarian writer. Ellen is probably Sturgis's sister, Ellen Sturgis Hooper.

946. To Caroline Sturgis

[n.d.]

How was it about that passage in Georgiana's letter? it was not erased; did not George B. ask to see it? he asked me and I said he might take it from you—[1]

I asked Sarah about the impression from her seal. I suppose she has given it to you.[2]

I meant to ask you *not* to take May Cameron for the western book; did you? or have you my copy, let me have it before you go to Naushon[n] I want to copy it into my archive it has stood in that childish hand long enough. If you have copied it, I dont care *much*, but it was one of the things I had rather kept in *my* archive only, as it is one of my milestones, not yet tomb-stones.

Late evening

I have just seen a letter from Anna W to "My dearest Cousin Eliza[3] and sealed with "The fettered Stag." Probably it is used also for notes to the Sedgwicks[4] or "my own sister Mary"[5] O God, O Heaven, O Fate And shall I mention— cetera non desunt We must laugh else the nerves would be too much jarred as the little black boy throws down the porcelain idol!

AL (MH: bMS Am 1221 [231]). *Addressed*: Caroline Sturgis.

to Naushon] to N(?)aushon

1. Georgiana is Georgiana Bruce; George B. may be George Bradford.
2. Sarah is either Sarah Sturgis Shaw or Sarah Clarke.
3. Anna Ward's cousin Eliza was Eliza Hazard (b. 1810), daughter of Thomas Rodman and Margaret Avery Hazard. Eliza married Allan Callom in 1826 (Caroline E. Robinson, *The Hazard Family of Rhode Island, 1635–1894* [Boston, 1895], p. 118).
4. The Sedgwicks were the family of Roderick Sedgwick of New York City.
5. Sister Mary was probably Sam Ward's sister.

947. To Jane F. Tuckerman

[n.d.]

My beloved Child,

I confess I was much disappointed when I first received your letter this evening. I have been quite ill for two or three days, and looked forward to your presence as a restorative; but think not I would have had you act differently; far better is it for me to have my child faithful to duty than even to have her with me; such was the lesson I taught her in a better hour. I am abashed to think how often lately I have found excuses for indolence in the weakness of my body, while now, after solitary communion with my better nature I feel it was weakness of mind, weak fear of depression and solitary conflict. But the Father of our spirits will not long permit a heart fit for worship

> "to seek
> From weak recoils, exemptions weak,
> After false Gods to go astray,
> Deck altars vile with garlands gay etc"

This voice has reached me, and I trust the postponement of your visit will give me space to nerve myself to what strength I should, so that, when we do meet, I shall rejoice that you did not come to help or soothe me, for I shall have helped and soothed myself. Indeed, I would not so willingly that you should see my short-comings, as have you know that they exist. Pray that I may never lose sight of my vocation, that I may not make ill health a plea for sloth and cowardice; pray that, whenever I do, I may be punished more swiftly than this time, by a sadness as deep as now— [   ]

MsCfr (MH: fMS Am 1086 [Works, 1:97–99]). Published in *WNC*, pp. 364–65.

948. To Anna B. Ward?

[n.d.]

[   ] You have put to me that case which puzzles more than almost any in this strange world. The case of a man of good intentions, with natural powers sufficient to carry them out, who after having through great part of a life lived the best he knew, and in the world's eye, lived admirably well, suddenly wakes to a consciousness of the Soul's true aims. He finds that he has been a good son, husband and father, an adroit man of business, respected by all around him without ever having advanced one step in the life of the Soul. His object has not been the development of his immortal being, nor has this been developed. All he has done bears upon the present[n] life only, and even[n] that in a very poor and limited way, since no deep fountain of intellect or[n] feeling has ever been unsealed for him. Now that his eyes are opened he sees what communion is possible; what incorruptible riches may be accumulated by the man of true wisdom. But why is the hour of clear vision so late deferred! He cannot blame himself for his previous blindness. His eyes were holden that he saw not. He lived as well as he knew how. And now that he would fain give himself up to the new oracle in his bosom, and to[n] the inspirations of Nature, all his old habits, all his previous connexions are unpropitious. He is bound by a thousand chains which press on him so as to leave no moment free. And perhaps it seems to him that, were he free, he should but feel the more forlorn. He sees the charm and nobleness of this new life, but knows not how to live it. It is an element to which his mental frame has not been trained. He knows not what to do today and tomorrow, how to stay by himself, nor how to meet others, how to act nor how to rest. Looking on others who chose the[n] path which now invites him at an age when their characters were yet plastic and the world more freely opened before them, he deems them favored children, and cries in almost despairing sadness, Why, O Father of Spirits, didst thou not earlier enlighten me[n] also. Why was I not led gently by the hand in the days of my youth?

And what wouldst[n] couldst thou reply?— Much, much, dear Anna, were this my friend whom I could see so often that the circumstances would be my text. For no subject has more engaged my thought, no difficulty is more frequently met. But now on this poor sheet I can only give you the clue to what I should say.

In the first place the depth of the despair must be caused by the mistaken idea that this our present life is all the time allotted to man for the education of his nature for that state of consummation which is called heaven. Were it seen that this present is only one little link in the long chain of probations, were it felt that the Divine Justice is pledged to give the aspirations of the soul all the time they require for their fulfilment, were it seen that disease, old age and death are circumstances which can never touch the eternal youth of the Spirit, that, though the "plant man" grows more or less fair in hue and stature according to the soil in which it is planted, yet the principle which is the life of the plant will not be defeated but must scatter its seeds again and again till it does at last come to perfect flower, then would he who is pausing to despair realize that a new choice can *never* be too late, that false steps made in ignorance can never be counted by the All-Wise, and trial though a moment's delay against conviction is of incalculable weight, the *mistakes* of forty years are but as dust on the balance[n] held by an unerring hand. Despair is for time, Hope for eternity.

Then he who looks at all the working of the grand principle of compensation which holds all nature in equipoise cannot long remain as stranger to the meaning of the beautiful parable of the prodigal son, and the joy over finding the one last piece of silver.[1] It is no arbitrary kindness, no generosity of the ruling powers which causes that there be more joy in heaven over the one that returns than over ninety and nine that never strayed. It is the inevitable working of a[n] spiritual law that he who has been groping in darkness must feel the light most keenly, best knows how to[n] prize it,—he who has long been exiled from the truth siezes it with the most earnest grasp, lives in it with the deepest joy. It was after descending to the very pit of sorrow that our elder brother was permitted to ascend to the father, who perchance said to the Angels who had always dwelt about[n] the throne: Ye are always with me and all that I have is yours, but *this* is my son.

He has been into a far country, but could not there abide, and[n] has returned. But if any one say "I know not how to return" I should still use words from the same record Let him arise and[n] go to his Father. Let him put his soul into that state of simple, fervent desire for Truth alone, Truth for its own sake which is Prayer and not only the sight of Truth but the way to make it living shall be shown. Obstacles insuperable to the intellect of any adviser shall melt away like frost work before a ray from the celestial Sun. The Father may hide his face for a time till the earnestness of the supplicant child be proved but he is not far from any that seek and when he does resolve to make a revelation will show not only the *what* but the *how.* And none else can advise or aid the seeking soul except by just observation on some matter of detail.

In this path as in the downward one 'tis the first step that describes the whole. One sacrifice of the temporal for the eternal day is the grain of mustard seed which may give[n] birth to a tree large enough to make a home for the sweetest singing birds.[2] One moment of deep truth in life, of choosing not merely honesty but purity may leaven the whole mass.

Dearest Anna I have but begun to write yet I must pause for this little hour is all I could steal from manifold interruptions. It would seem it was not intended I should do this little thing for thee so many causes have worked together to prevent. But, in writing what I have, I have shown my wish I know not if it be the least what you wish, but is true, no doubt, so far as it goes. I have not time to look at it and can only grieve if thou art disappointed. [   ]

ALfr (MH: fMS Am 1086 [Box A]); MsCfr (MH: fMS Am 1086 [Works, 3:333–43]). Published in part in *Life Without and Life Within,* ed. Arthur B. Fuller (Boston, 1860), pp. 344–47.

The contents suggest Anna Barker Ward as the recipient, but she might be another Anna.
upon the present] upon ⟨human⟩ ↑ the present ↓
and even] and ↑ even ↓
intellect or] intellect ⟨and⟩ or
and to] and ↑ to ↓
chose the] chose ⟨at an earlier age⟩ the
enlighten me] enlighten m⟨y⟩e
what wouldst] what ↑ wouldst ↓
the balance] the ⟨?⟩ balance
of a] of ⟨the⟩ ↑ a ↓
how to] how ⟨h⟩ to
dwelt about] dwelt ⟨with him⟩ about
abide, and] abide, ⟨but⟩ ↑ and ↓
arise and] arise an⟨g⟩d
may give] may ⟨noursih⟩ give

1. Luke 15:11–32.

2. Matt. 13:31–32: "The kingdom of heaven is like to a grain of mustard seed, which a man took, and sowed in his field: Which indeed is the least of all seeds: but when it is grown, it is the greatest among herbs, and becometh a tree, so that the birds of the air come and lodge in the branches thereof." Cf. Mark 4:31–32 and Luke 13:19.

949. To Julia Ward

[n.d.]

[   ] I part from this poem with great regret, and, so far as I am concerned, wish very much that it may be published that I may keep it by me. I think I should frequently recur to it.

It is the record of an era of genuine inspiration— of days when the soul lay in the light, when the spiritual harmonies were clearly apprehended and great religious symbols reanimated with their original meaning. Its numbers have the fullness and sweetness of young love, young life. Its gifts were great and demand the service of a long day's work to requite and to interpret them.

I can hardly realize that the Julia Ward I have seen has lived this life. It has not yet pervaded her whole being, though I can recal something of it in the steady light of her eye. May she become all attempered and ennobled by this music! I saw, in[n] her, taste, the capacity for genius, and the almost delicacy of passionate feeling, but caught no glimpse at the time of this higher mood.

It will always be valuable to me to have seen[n] that the church even now can have an influence so real, and that its rites and signs still bear their mystic significance to the willing sense. I had thought only those who had turned their backs upon the church could see in it a text for pure worship.

I think, however, this can only be spiritually apprehended by those of a[n] spiritual experience and that to a superficial reader nothing might be seen in the poem[n] except the technics of Trinitarianism. But, were I the singer! this would content me well.

I admire the feeling of the prophetic spirit of the Old Testament as much as that of the purity and infinite love of Jesus. The parts all please me in various ways. One has a Bunyan-like simplicity, others a soaring sweetness. The music of all is penetrating, "Preaching"— "Woman"— and "The Beauty of Holiness" are rich in thought— Shall such a mind ever swerve from its balance?

There are slight inaccuracies.

Fire is used in several places as a word of two syllables. The rhythm requiring fi-er.

and Much is forgiven to who loveth much which, to be grammatical should be

him who loveth much—

or give an objective in some way to the to."

I am sorry to write such a scrawl, but constant writing spoils my hand just now, and I have no time for elegance. Looking at the neat copy of Miss Ward, I would neatly copy this, did time permit, so much is my emulation fired! If she publishes I would not have her omit the 4 lines about the "lonely room" The personal interest with which they stamp that part is slight and delicate.

If the poem be not published I hope it will be lent me again one of these "long simmer days"

S. MARGARET FULLER.

I know of many persons in my own circle to whom I think the poem would be specially grateful.

ALfrS (MCR-S: MC 272 [23]). Published in part in Laura E. Richards and Maude Howe Elliott, *Julia Ward Howe, 1819–1910* (Boston, 1916), 1:69.

Julia Ward (later Julia Ward Howe) had met Fuller in 1839 and attended some of the conversations (Deborah Pickman Clifford, *Mine Eyes Have Seen the Glory* [Boston, 1979], p. 49; *Letters of MF*, 2:72).

saw, in] saw, ⟨?⟩ in
to have seen] to ⟨see⟩ ↑ have seen ↓
of a] of ⟨inc⟩ a
seen in the poem] seen ↑ in the poem ↓
the to.] the ⟨who⟩ ↑ to ↓ .

950. To ?

[n.d.]

When we were hearing H. D and Mr Angier so much, I wrote these two letters which accompany— I lent them to Amelia—she did not say any-thing I had expected— She showed them to N. P. W.[1] who only thought they were "capital" I dont think that was true but on rereading them the other day the same *peculiar* train of thought was suggested I am desirous to know whether you will think any of the same things so I got Lizzy to copy them— You heard all the songs; but I suppose I must not hope to hear the corresponding words from any one.—

Return them when read. It was just before we went to Andover that they were written and this is a good place for the list.—

J F Clarke Dr to S. M Fuller, journal of a tour to the White Hills— translation from Korner trans from Schiller ie Thekla's Geister Stimme[2]

Aphorisms from—

Recd payment—

ALfr (CtY).

The Yale library identifies the recipient as Elizabeth Peabody, but the people Fuller names were all part of the group that Fuller and James Clarke knew in the 1820s and 1830s. They were not Peabody's intimates. The manuscript may not be a letter.

1. H. D. is probably Helen Davis. Mr Angier is Joseph Angier, a Harvard classmate of James Clarke and William Channing. Amelia is Amelia Greenwood. N. P. W. is Nathaniel Parker Willis (1806–67), poet, essayist, and journalist. From 1829 to 1831 he edited the Boston *American Monthly Magazine*. Later he was associated with the *New-York Mirror* (DAB). Lizzie is perhaps Elizabeth Wells Randall.

2. Schiller's poem "Thekla: Eine Geisterstimme" (*Schillers Werke*, 1:173).

951. To ?

[n.d.]

[   ] I will copy from my journal a little prayer made on first seeing this August moon in the inauspicous way.

O waxing moon— Shed influence mild,
Loved August moon— grieve not thy child

I must perforce follow thee— Demon of my nativity,
But oh succor me— angel of my futurity.
My genius hover near.— Drive away these thoughts of fear
If I indeed be all alone,— cherish the more thy daughter lone
Make the woman all thine own.

Let the man defend
Till this strife and dark doubt end.

> Make me purer
> Stronger surer.
> O let not deadly fear
> Creep so very near.
> Centipede and Scorpion
> So near thy daughter's pillow lone
> Send thy dove to brood
> Over her shadowy solitude.
>
> There must be love
> Below, around, above
> Let the great mind
> Untiring rush to find
> Steadfast stand to bind
> Till the soft heart the needed peace may find.

I will now conclude our whole meeting by the verse I wrote last spring on Sunday night. That day had had its showers & how have they purified the air This is the posy for the days and weeks, too[n] I think.

> Blest be this day, the bell
> That tolled its death
> Came with no knell
> But new life's heavenly breath.

In the moonlit garden at Newport you said; "It is three years since we were[n] here before. Will the next three years do as much for us? And shall we be friends as we are now or *better?*"— Those three years are past [   ]

ALfr (MB: Ms. Am. 1450 [140]).
weeks, too] weeks, ↑ too ↓
we were] we ⟨h⟩ were

952. To ?

[n.d.]

[   ] If such relations do not strike deep root and create permanent interests, what can? Love is no nobler than friendship, no more

worthy of permanent life; but it searches deeper and drinks more life-blood. To me it seems the man or woman who can become indifferent to those they have loved, can hardly be depended on for reality in any thing. [   ]

MsCfr (MB: Ms. Am. 1450 [174]).

953. To ?

[n.d.]

[   ] Though art but a rough and blurred sketch of the Phoenix,— of the Poet, yet refuse to be aught else and the true beauty shall yet glow out in fulness of life. [   ]

ALfr (MCR-S: A/F)

954. To ?

Saturday ev

How true your aversion to my notes,— As true your [re]citation[?]. Good or bad it was well to write them for they relieved my mind. The great law is to reproduce in some way all that has seemed worthy to command our thoughts.

All literature, all art, even these works of M. Angelo are nothing but notes more or less significant on *that* text.

—Yet our souls in cases where they have been led near to the perception of this divine, will resent *subdividing* criticism.

About Titian, Leonardo &c what do I know? correct any blunders you see;— where I have so little knowledge many of course drop from my pen. If I revised any thing of this sort, however, you may be sure I should have the good sense to blot out any words about which I was not certain, for I have enough of certainty to know where I am in the dark—

About speaking positively, I cannot help it; my feelings are so determined and vehement. Yet on this subject I have no right, my field of observation has been so narrow. If I had fineness of instinct it might be ex pede Hercules, but with me a great deal of comparison and analysis is needed to give the dignity of certainty. In literature, indeed, I feel that I well understand ways and means; can allow for obstacles and appreciate success. Here I can only know what I am made to feel, and though I perceive the identity of principles between literature and the arts, am as yet quite subjective as to the picture where I can weigh in golden scales the poem that tells the same thought. Yet, I think, with proper opportunity, here also I should not be the poor critic of detail, but enter into the soul of the maker and reread the spell by which he called the magic shapes into his circle.

MsCfr (MH: fMS Am 1086 [Box A]).

955. To ?

[n.d.]

Your Schiller has already given me great pleasure. I have been reading the "Revolt in the Netherlands" with intense interest and have reflected much upon it.[1] The volumes are numbered in my little bookcase, and as the eye runs over them I thank the friendly heart that put all this genius and passion within my power. Blessed to be the hour in which you lent me "Bigelow's Elements"—[2] I have studied the Architecture attentively till I feel quite mistress of it all. But I want more engravings, [Vitruvius,] Magna Grecia, the [Ionian] Antiquities &c.[3] Meanwhile I have got out all our tours in Italy. Forsyth, a book I always loved much, I have reread with increased pleasure, by this new light.[4] Goethe too studied architecture while in Italy. So his books are full of interesting information; and Madame de Stael, though not deep is tasteful.[5]

MsCfr (MH: fMS Am 1086 [Works, 3:359]). Published in *Memoirs*, 1:148–49.
Two bracketed words are added from the Memoirs *version.*
1. *Geschichte des Abfalls der vereinigten Niederlande von der spanischen Regierung* (Leipzig, 1788) won Schiller a professorship in history at Jena.

2. Jacob Bigelow (1786–1879) published his *Elements of Technology* in 1829. A graduate of Harvard in 1806, Bigelow received his medical degree from Pennsylvania and became the first American to study the flora of the northeastern United States. He taught medicine at Harvard for forty years and was a founder of Mount Auburn Cemetery in Cambridge (*DAB*).

3. Vitruvius Pollio, a Roman architect, wrote *De architectura*.

4. Joseph Forsyth, *Remarks on Antiquities, Arts, and Letters during an Excursion in Italy* (London, 1813). Forsyth (1763–1815) had traveled in Italy in 1802 and 1803 and was imprisoned by the French as he returned to Scotland. He wrote his *Remarks*, his only work, while a prisoner. It was one of a number of travel books that Fuller recommended to a friend in 1844 and of which she wrote in the *Tribune:* "No one who seeks *mere* amusement need try the book, but one who wanted aid in forming taste, or to be stimulated to a higher point of view and more accuracy and to delicacy in observation than contents the crowd will find a preceptor and a friend in Forsyth" (*DNB*; *Letters of MF*, 3:171; *New-York Tribune*, 18 December 1845).

5. Her references are to Goethe's *Italienische Reise* and Mme. de Staël's novel *Corinne; ou, L'Italie.*

956. To ?

[n.d.]

American History: Seriously my mind is regenerating as to my country, for I am beginning to appreciate the United States and its great men. The violent antipathies the result of an exaggerated love for, shall I call it by so big a name as the "Poetry of being" and the natural distaste arising from being forced to hear the conversation of half bred men, all whose petty feelings were roused to awkward life by the paltry game of local politicks, are yielding to reason and calmer Knowledge. Had I but been educated in the Knowledge of such men as Jefferson, Franklin, Rush:— I have learned now to know them particularly.

And I rejoice if only because my Father and I can have so much in common on this topick. All my other pursuits have led me away from him; here he has much information and ripe judgement. But better still I hope to feel no more that sometimes despairing, sometimes insolently, contemptuous, feeling of incongeniality with my time and place. Who knows but some proper and attainable object of pursuit may present itself to the cleared eye.

At any rate wisdom is good if it brings neither bliss nor glory.—

MsCfr (MH: fMS Am 1086 [Works, 3:359–61]). Published in *Memoirs*, 1:149.

957. To ?

[n.d.]

[   ] Mrs. Hemans Miss Landon Miss Jewsbury and other flattered poetesses[1] mourn over womans lot as something peculiar, since I see so many trying to replace the living rose of female youth and grace," by its tawdry artificial of" charm and sentiment at a later day or ceasing to be ornaments sink into battered utensils," since foolish men are abused as old women, since" when left unsustained by man she is so liable to sink into a forlorn old maid instead of rising into an independent existence I must think a better state is craved.— I must resist the argument of the ages, and think the ballad of the matron with the child on one arm and the gun on the other, and Goethe's saying that the noble woman is she who if her husband dies can be a father to the children bespeak the nature of the coming era.

It is not true that we shall always be ready for emergencies because our aspiration is high We must have a reserve of strength ready for occasions The blade must be severely tempered to cut as a true Damascene.

I would like to express what I meant about doing drudgery of our own free will, but I see I am writing more than time will permit of my reading and will wait for another opportunity.

I see no need of womens having political rights to stimulate their energies, when they have all the lite and art scarcely touched yet.— But for the comfort and independence of their lives they many need protection of property and a wider choice of lucrative professions.

a revoir— my theme gar zu reichhaltig.[2]

"Feminity raging",— the lioness roused to defend her cubs,—More violent, *because* unusual, because incalculable to the subject is passion here!

ALfr (MHarF).
May be a journal fragment.
youth and grace,] youth ↑ and grace, ↓
artifical of] artificial ⟨in⟩ of
battered utensils,] battered ⟨utensils⟩ utensils,
women, since] women, ⟨since the male observor says there is inferno for wo⟩ since
1. Fuller names three English women of letters: Felicia Dorothea Hemans, Letitia Elizabeth Landon (1802–38), and Maria Jane Jewsbury (1800–1833). Fuller was fond of Hemans' poetry, which was widely read in the 1830s; beginning in 1820, Landon, who wrote under the initials L. E. L., published a large quantity of sentimental poetry and several novels. Jewsbury, who often wrote for the *Athenaeum*, dedicated her *Lays of Leisure Hours* (1829) to Hemans (*DNB*).
2. "Quite too extensive."

958. To?

[n.d.]

The world turns round and round, and you too must needs be negligent and capricious. You have not answered my note; you have not given me what I asked. You do not come here. Do not you act so,— it is the drop too much. The world seems not only turning but tottering, when my kind friend plays such a part.

ELfr, from *Memoirs*, 1:79.

959. To ?

[n.d.]

You need not have delayed your answer so long; why not at once answer the question I asked? Faith is not natural to me; for the love I feel to others is not in the idleness of poverty, nor can I persist in believing the best, merely to save myself pain, or keep a leaning place for the weary heart. But I should believe you, because I have seen that your feelings are strong and constant; they have never disappointed me, when closely scanned.

ELfr, from *Memoirs*, 1:79.

960. To ?

[n.d.]

I think, since you have seen so much of my character, that you must be sensible that any reserves with those whom I call my friends, do not arise from duplicity, but an instinctive feeling that I could not be understood. I can truly say that I wish no one to overrate me; undeserved regard could give me no pleasure; nor will I consent to practise charlatanism, either in friendship or anything else.

ELfr, from *Memoirs*, 1:84.

961. To ?

[n.d.]

You ought not to think I show a want of generous confidence, if I sometimes try the ground on which I tread, to see if perchance it may return the echoes of hollowness.

ELfr, from *Memoirs*, 1:84.

962. To ?

[n.d.]

Do not cease to respect me as formerly. It seems to me that I have reached the "parting of the ways" in my life, and all the knowledge which I have toiled to gain only serves to show me the disadvantages of each. None of those who think themselves my friends can aid me; each, careless, takes the path to which present convenience impels; and all would smile or stare, could they know the aching and measureless wishes, the sad apprehensiveness, which makes me pause and strain my almost hopeless gaze to the distance. What wonder if my present conduct should be mottled by selfishness and incertitude? Perhaps you, who *can* make your views certain, cannot comprehend me; though you showed me last night a penetration which did not flow from sympathy. But this I may say— though the glad light of hope and ambitious confidence, which has vitalized my mind, should be extinguished forever, I will not in life act a mean, ungenerous, or useless part. Therefore, let not a slight thing lessen your respect for me. If you feel as much pain as I do, when obliged to diminish my respect for any person, you will be glad of this assurance. I hope you will not think this note in the style of a French novel.

ELfr, from *Memoirs*, 1:84–85.

963. To ?

[n.d.]

I want words to express the singularity of all my past relations; yet let me try.

From a very early age I have felt that I was not born to the common womanly lot. I knew I should never find a being who could keep the key of my character; that there would be none on whom I could always lean, from whom I could always learn; that I should be a pilgrim and sojourner on earth, and that the birds and foxes would be surer of a place to lay the head than I.[1] You understand me, of course; such beings can only find their homes in hearts. All material luxuries, all the arrangements of society, are mere conveniences to them.

This thought, all whose bearings I did not, indeed, understand, affected me sometimes with sadness, sometimes with pride. I mourned that I never should have a thorough experience of life, never know the full riches of my being; I was proud that I was to test myself in the sternest way, that I was always to return to myself, to be my own priest, pupil, parent, child, husband, and wife. All this I did not understand as I do now; but this destiny of the thinker, and (shall I dare to say it?) of the poetic priestess, sibylline, dwelling in the cave, or amid the Lybian sands, lay yet enfolded in my mind. Accordingly, I did not look on any of the persons, brought into relation with me, with common womanly eyes.

Yet, as my character is, after all, still more feminine than masculine, it would sometimes happen that I put more emotion into a state than I myself knew. I really was capable of attachment, though it never seemed so till the hour of separation. And if a connexion was torn up by the roots, the soil of my existence showed an unsightly wound, which long refused to clothe itself in verdure.

With regard to yourself, I was to you all that I wished to be. I knew that I reigned in your thoughts in my own way. And I also lived with you more truly and freely than with any other person. We were truly friends, but it was not friends as men are friends to one another, or as brother and sister. There was, also, that pleasure, which may, perhaps, be termed conjugal, of finding oneself in an alien nature. Is there any tinge of love in this? Possibly! At least, in comparing it with my relation to [   ], I find *that* was strictly fraternal. I valued him for himself. I did not care for an influence over him, and was perfectly willing to have one or fifty rivals in his heart. [   ]

I think I may say, I never loved. I but see my possible life reflected on the clouds. As in a glass darkly, I have seen what I might feel as child, wife, mother, but I have never really approached the close relations of life. A sister I have truly been to many,— a brother to more,— a fostering nurse to, oh how many! The bridal hour of many a spirit, when first it was wed, I have shared, but said adieu before the wine was poured out at the banquet. And there is one I always love in my poetic hour, as the lily looks up to the star from amid the waters; and another whom I visit as the bee visits the flower, when I crave sympathy. Yet those who live would scarcely consider that I am among the living,— and I am isolated, as you say.

My dear [   ], all is well; all has helped me to decipher the great poem of the universe. I can hardly describe to you the happiness which floods my solitary hours. My actual life is yet much clogged and impeded, but I have at last got me an oratory, where I can retire and pray. With your letter, vanished a last regret. You did not act or think unworthily. It is enough. As to the cessation of our confidential intercourse, circumstances must have accomplished that long ago; my only grief was that you should do it with your own free will, and for reasons that I thought unworthy. I long to honor you, to be honored by you. Now we will have free and noble thoughts of one another, and all that is best of our friendship shall remain.

ELfr, from *Memoirs*, 1:98–101. Published in part in Miller, pp. 29–31.

Charles Capper argues on the basis of its contents that this letter was written in 1839 to George Davis (Capper, *Margaret Fuller*, pp. 287–89).

1. Matt. 8:20: "The foxes have holes, and the birds of the air have nests; but the Son of man hath not where to lay his head."

964. To ?

[n.d.]

I don't like Goethe so well as Schiller now. I mean, I am not so happy in reading him. That perfect wisdom and *merciless* nature seems cold, after those seducing pictures of forms more beautiful than truth. Nathless, I should like to read the second part of Goethe's Memoirs, if you do not use it now.[1]

ELfr, from *Memoirs*, 1:117.

1. Probably Fuller wants the second part (books 6–10) of *Aus meinem Leben: Dichtung und Wahrheit*, which describes Goethe's youth to the time he met Herder (1762–70) (*OCGL*).

965. To ?

[n.d.]

The moon tempted me out, and I set forth for a house at no great distance. The beloved south-west was blowing; the heavens were flooded with light, which could not diminish the tremulously pure radiance of the evening star; the air was full of spring sounds, and sweet spring odors came up from the earth. I felt that happy sort of feeling, as if the soul's pinions were budding. My mind was full of poetic thoughts, and nature's song of promise was chanting in my heart.

But what a change when I entered that human dwelling! I will try to give you an impression of what you, I fancy, have never come in contact with. The little room—they have but one—contains a bed, a table, and some old chairs. A single stick of wood burns in the fireplace. It is not needed now, but those who sit near it have long ceased to know what spring is. They are all frost. Everything is old and faded, but at the same time as clean and carefully mended as possible. For all they know of pleasure is to get strength to sweep those few boards, and mend those old spreads and curtains. That sort of self-respect they have, and it is all of pride their many years of poor-tith has left them.

And there they sit,—mother and daughter! In the mother, ninety years have quenched every thought and every feeling, except as imbecile interest about her daughter, and the sort of self-respect I just spoke of. Husband, sons, strength, health, house and lands, all are gone. And yet these losses have not had power to bow that palsied head to the grave. Morning by morning she rises without a hope, night by night she lies down vacant or apathetic; and the utmost use she can make of the day is to totter three or four times across the floor by the assistance of her staff. Yet, though we wonder that she is still permitted to cumber the ground, joyless and weary, "the tomb of her dead self."[1] we look at this dry leaf, and think how green it once was, and how the birds sung to it in its summer day.

But can we think of spring, or summer, or anything joyous or really life-like, when we look at the daughter?—that bloodless effigy of humanity, whose care is to eke out this miserable existence by means of the occasional doles of those who know how faithful and good a child she has been to that decrepit creature; who thinks herself happy if she can be well enough, by hours of patient toil, to perform those menial services which they both require; whose talk is of the price of pounds of sugar, and ounces of tea, and yards of flannel; whose only intellectual resource is hearing five or six verses of the Bible read every day,—"my poor head," she says, "cannot bear any more;" and whose only hope is the death to which she has been so slowly and wearily advancing, through many years like this.

The saddest part is, that she does *not wish* for death. She clings to this sordid existence. Her soul is now so habitually enwrapt in the meanest cares, that if she were to be lifted two or three steps upward, she would not know what to do with life; how, then, shall she soar to the celestial heights? Yet she ought; for she has ever been good, and her narrow and crushing duties have been performed with a self-sacrificing constancy, which I, for one, could never hope to equal.

While I listened to her,—and I often think it good for me to listen to her patiently,—the expressions you used in your letter, about "drudgery," occurred to me. I remember the time when I, too, deified the "soul's impulses." It is a noble worship; but, if we do not aid it by a just though limited interpretation of what "Ought" means, it will degenerate into idolatry. For a time it was so with me, and I am not yet good enough to love the *Ought*.

Then I came again into the open air, and saw those resplendent orbs moving so silently, and thought that they were perhaps tenanted, not only by beings in whom I can see the germ of a possible angel, but by myriads like this poor creature, in whom that germ is, so far as we can see, blighted entirely, I could not help saying, "O my Father! Thou, whom we are told art all Power, and also all Love, how canst Thou suffer such even transient specks on the transparence of Thy creation? These grub-like lives, undignified even by passion,—these life-long quenchings of the spark divine,—why dost Thou suffer them? Is not Thy paternal benevolence impatient till such films be dissipated?"

Such questionings once had power to move my spirit deeply; now, they but shade my mind for an instant. I have faith in a glorious explanation, that shall make manifest perfect justice and perfect wisdom.

ELfr, from *Memoirs*, 1:161–64.

1. Fuller slightly misquotes Shelley's 1816 poem "The Sunset":

> The tomb of thy dead self
> Which one vexed ghost inhabits, night and day,
> Is all, lost child, that now remains of thee!

(*Complete Poetical Works of Shelley*, p. 580)

966. To ?

[n.d.]

Tell [   ] that I read "Titan" by myself, in the afternoons and evenings of about three weeks.[1] She need not be afraid to undertake it. Difficulties of detail may, perhaps, not be entirely conquered without a master or a good commentary, but she could enjoy all that is most valuable alone. I should be very unwilling to read it with a person of narrow or unrefined mind; for it is a noble work, and fit to raise a reader into that high serene of thought where pedants cannot enter.

ELfr, from *Memoirs*, 1:169 –70.

1. Johann Paul Friedrich Richter, writing under the name Jean Paul, published his novel *Titan* from 1800 to 1803.

967. To ?

[n.d.]

You question me as to the nature of the benefits conferred upon me by Mr. E.'s preaching. I answer, that his influence has been more beneficial to me than that of any American, and that from him I first learned what is meant by an inward life. Many other springs have since fed the stream of living waters, but he first opened the fountain. That the "mind is its own place," was a dead phrase to me, till he cast light upon my mind. Several of his sermons stand apart in memory, like landmarks of my spiritual history. It would take a volume to tell what this one influence did for me. But perhaps I shall some time see that it was best for me to be forced to help myself.

Elfr, from *Memoirs*, 1:194–95.

968. To ?

[n.d.]

Some remarks which I made last night trouble me, and I cannot fix my attention upon other things till I have qualified them. I suffered myself to speak in too unmeasured terms, and my expressions were fitted to bring into discredit the religious instruction which has been given me, or which I have sought.

I do not think "all men are born for the purpose of unfolding beautiful ideas;" for the vocation of many is evidently the culture of affections by deeds of kindness. But I do think that the vocations of men and women differ, and that those who are forced to act out of their sphere are shorn of inward and outward brightness.

For myself, I wish to say, that, if I am in a mood of darkness and despondency, I nevertheless consider such a mood unworthy of a Christian, or indeed of any one who believes in the immortality of the soul. No one, who had steady faith in this and in the goodness of God, could be otherwise than cheerful. I reverence the serenity of a truly religious mind so much, that I think, if I live, I may some time attain to it.

Although I do not believe in a Special Providence regulating outward events, and could not reconcile such a belief with what I have seen of life, I do not the less believe in the paternal government of a Deity. That He should visit the souls of those who seek Him seems to me the nobler way to conceive of his influence. And if there were not some error in my way of seeking, I do not believe I should suffer from languor or deadness on spiritual subjects, at the time when I have most need to feel myself at home there. To find this error is my earnest wish; and perhaps I am now travelling to that end, though by a thorny road. It is a mortification to find so much yet to do; for at one time the scheme of things seemed so clear, that, with Cromwell, I might say, "I was once in grace." With my mind I prize high objects as much as then; it is my heart which is cold. And sometimes I fear that the necessity of urging them on those under my care dulls my sense of their beauty. It is so hard to prevent one's feelings from evaporating in words.

ELfr, from *Memoirs*, 1:195–96.

969. To ?

[n.d.]

"The faint sickness of a wounded heart."[1] How frequently do these words of Beckford recur to my mind! His prayer, imperfect as it is, says more to me than many a purer aspiration. It breathes such an experience of impassioned anguish. He had everything,—health, personal advantages, almost boundless wealth, genius, exquisite taste, culture; he could, in some way, express his whole being. Yet well-nigh he sank beneath the sickness of the wounded heart; and solitude, "country of the unhappy," was all he craved at last.

Goethe, too, says he has known, in all his active, wise, and honored life, no four weeks of happiness. This teaches me on the other side; for, like Goethe, I have never given way to my feelings, but have lived active, thoughtful, seeking to be wise. Yet I have long days and weeks of heartache; and at those times, though I am busy every moment, and cultivate every pleasant feeling, and look always upwards to the pure ideal region, yet this ache is like a bodily wound, whose pain haunts even when it is not attended to, and disturbs the dreams of the patient who has fallen asleep from exhaustion.

There is a German in Boston, who has a wound in his breast, received in battle long ago. It never troubles him, except when he sings, and then, if he gives out his voice with much expression, it opens, and cannot, for a long time, be stanched again. So with me: when I rise into one of those rapturous moods of thought, such as I had a day or two since, my wound opens again, and all I can do is to be patient, and let it take its own time to skin over. I see it will never do more. Some time ago I thought the barb was fairly out; but no, the fragments rankle there still, and will, while there is any earth attached to my spirit. Is it not because, in my pride, I held the mantle close, and let the weapon, which some friendly physician might have extracted, splinter in the wound?

ELfr, from *Memoirs*, 1:196–97.

1. The unidentified quotation probably comes from William Beckford's *Vathek*, a work Fuller admired.

970. To ?

[n.d.]

It is not in the way of tenderness that I love [   ]. I prize her always; and this is all the love some natures ever know. And I also feel that I may always expect she will be with me. I delight to picture to myself certain persons translated, illuminated. There are a few in whom I see occasionally the future being piercing, promising,—whom I can strip of all that masks their temporary relations, and elevate to their natural position. Sometimes I have not known these persons intimately,—oftener I have; for it is only in the deepest hours that this light is likely to break out. But some of those I have best befriended I cannot thus portray, and very few men I can. It does not depend at all on the beauty of their forms, at present; it is in the eye and the smile, that the hope shines through. I can see exactly how [   ] will look: not like this angel in the paper; she will not bring flowers, but a living coal, to the lips of the singer; her eyes will not burn as now with smothered fires, they will be ever deeper, and glow more intensely; her cheek will be smooth, but marble pale; her gestures nobly free, but few.

ELfr, from *Memoirs*, 1:206–7.

971. To ?

[n.d.]

As to the Daemonical, I know not that I can say to you anything more precise than you find from Goethe.[1] There are no precise terms for such thoughts. The word *instinctive* indicates their existence. I intimated it in the little piece on the Drachenfels. It may be best understood, perhaps, by a symbol. As the sun shines from the serene heavens, dispelling noxious exhalations, and calling forth exquisite thoughts on the surface of earth in the shape of shrub or flower, so gnome-like works the fire within the hidden caverns and secret veins of earth, fashioning existences which have a longer share in time, perhaps, because they are not immortal in thought. Love, beauty, wisdom, goodness are intelligent, but this power moves only to seize its prey. It is not necessarily either malignant or the reverse, but it has no scope beyond demonstrating its existence. When conscious, self-asserting, it becomes (as power working for its own sake, unwilling to acknowledge love for its superior, must) the devil. That is the legend of Lucifer, the star that would not own its centre. Yet, while it is unconscious, it is not devilish, only daemoniac. In nature, we trace it in all volcanic workings, in a boding position of lights, in whispers of the wind, which has no pedigree; in deceitful invitations of the water, in the sullen rock, which never shall find a voice, and in the shapes of all those beings who go about seeking what they may devour. We speak of a mystery, a dread; we shudder, but we approach still nearer, and a part of our nature listens, sometimes answers to this influence, which, if not indestructible, is at least indissolubly linked with the existence of matter.

In genius, and in character, it works, as you say, instinctively; it refuses to be analyzed by the understanding, and is most of all inaccessible to the person who posseses it. We can only say, I have it, he has it. You have seen it often in the eyes of those Italian faces you like. It is most obvious in the eye. As we look on such eyes, we think on the tiger, the serpent, beings who lurk, glide, fascinate, mysteriously control. For it is occult by its nature, and if it could meet you on the highway, and be familiarly known as an acquaintance, could not exist. The angels of light do not love, yet they do not insist on exterminating it.

It has given rise to the fables of wizard, enchantress, and the like; these beings are scarcely good, yet not necessarily bad. Power tempts them. They draw their skills from the dead, because their being is coeval with that of matter, and matter is the mother of death.

ELfr, from *Memoirs*, 1:225–26.

1. A reference to Goethe's definition in book 20 of *Dichtung und Wahrheit*: "something which manifests itself only in contradictions, and which, therefore, could not be comprehended under any idea, still less under one word. . . . All that limits us it seemed to penetrate; it seemed to sport at will with the necessary elements of our existence; it contradicted time and expanded space. In the impossible alone did it appear to find pleasure, while it rejected the possible with contempt" (*The Autobiography of Johann Wolfgang von Goethe*, trans. John Oxenford [New York, 1969], 2:423).

972. To ?

[n.d.]

To-day, on reading over some of the sonnets of Michel Angelo, I felt them more than usual. I know not why I have not read them thus before, except that the beauty was pointed out to me at first by another, instead of my coming unexpectedly upon it of myself. All the great writers, all the persons who have been dear to me, I have found and chosen; they have not been proposed to me. My intimacy with them came upon me as natural eras, unexpected and thrice dear. Thus I have appreciated, but not been able to feel, Michel Angelo as a poet.

It is a singular fact in my mental history, that while I understand the principles and construction of language much better than formerly, I cannot read so well *less langues méridionales*. I suppose it is that I am less *méridionale* myself. I understand the genius of the north better than I did.

ELfr, from *Memoirs*, 1:242.

973. To ?

[n.d.]

What a vulgarity there seems in this writing for the multitude! We know not yet, have not made ourselves known to a single soul, and shall we address those still more unknown? Shall we multiply our connections, and thus make them still more superficial?

I would go into the crowd, and meet men for the day, to help them for the day, but for that intercourse which most becomes us. Pericles, Anaxagoras, Aspasia, Cleone, is circle wide enough for me.[1] I should think all the resources of my nature, and all the tribute it could enforce from external nature, none too much to furnish the banquet for this circle.

But where to find fit, though few, representatives for all we value in humanity?[2] Where obtain those golden keys to the secret treasure-chambers of the soul? No samples are perfect. We must look abroad into the wide circle, to seek a little here, and a little there, to make up our company. And is not the "prent book" a good beacon-light to tell where we wait the bark?— a reputation, the means of entering the Olympic game, where Pindar may perchance be encountered?[3]

So it seems the mind must reveal its secret; must reproduce. And I have no castle, and no natural circle, in which I might live, like the wise Makaria, observing my kindred the stars, and gradually enriching my archives. Makaria here must go abroad, or the stars would hide their light, and the archive remain a blank.[4]

For all the tides of life that flow within me, I am dumb and ineffectual, when it comes to casting my thought into a form. No old one suits me. If I could invent one, it seems to me the pleasure of creation would make it possible for me to write. What shall I do, dear friend? I want force to be either a genius or a character. One should be either private or public. I love best to be a woman; but womanhood is at

143

present too straitly-bounded to give me scope. At hours, I live truly as a woman; at others, I should stifle; as, on the other hand, I should palsy, when I would play the artist.

ELfr, from *Memoirs*, 1:296–97.

1. Probably a reference to Walter Savage Landor's *Pericles and Aspasia*, a favorite work of Fuller's, in which these four characters conduct a series of fictional conversations.

2. Fuller alludes to Milton's well-known invocation in bk. VII of *Paradise Lost*: "Still govern thou my song, / Urania, and fit audience find, though few" (Milton, *Complete Poetical Works*, 341).

3. Pindar (518–438 B.C.) wrote a number of Epinicians, poetic hymns to victory in athletic contests (*Oxford Classical Dictionary*, ed. N. G. L. Hammond and H. H. Scullard [Oxford, 1970]).

4. Makaria is Hersilia's aunt in Goethe's *Wilhelm Meisters Wanderjahre*.

974. To ?

[n.d.]

What I want, the word I crave, I do not expect to hear from the lips of man. I do not wish to be, I do not wish to have, a *mediator*; yet I cannot help wishing, when I am with you, that some tones of the longed-for music could be vibrating in the air around us. But I will not be impatient again; for, though I am but as I am, I like not to feel the eyes I have loved averted.

ELfr, from *Memoirs*, 1:311.

975. To ?

[n.d.]

This afternoon we met Mr. [   ] in his wood; and he sat down and told us the story of his life, his courtship, and painted the portraits of his father and mother with most amusing naivete. He says: — "How do you think I offered myself? I never had told Miss [   ] that I loved her; never told her she was handsome; and I went to her, and said, 'Miss [   ], I've come to offer myself; but first I'll give you my character. I'm very poor; you'll have to work: I'm very cross and irascible; you'll have everything to bear: and I've liked many other pretty girls. Now what do you say?' and she said, 'I'll have you:' and she's been everything to me.

My mother was a Calvinist, very strict, but she was always reading 'Abelard and Eloisa,' and crying over it.[1] At sixteen, I said to her: 'Mother, you've brought me up well; you've kept me strict. Why don't I feel that regeneration they talk of? why an't I one of the elect?' And she talked to me about the potter using his clay as he pleased; and I said: 'Mother, God is not a potter: He's a perfect being; and he can't treat the vessels he makes, anyhow, but with perfect justice, or he's no God. So I'm no Calvinist.'"

ELfr, from *Memoirs*, 1:314.

1. Probably the edition of *Letters of Abelard and Heloise*, trans. John Hughes (London, 1713), on which Pope based his "Eloïsa to Abelard." Hughes's work went through many editions, all of which add Pope's poem after 1775. Sometimes Heloise becomes Eloisa.

976. To ?

[n.d.]

[   ] has infinite grace and shading in her character: a springing and tender fancy, a Madonna depth of meditative softness, and a purity which has been unstained, and keeps her dignified even in the most unfavorable circumstances. She was born for the love and ornament of life. I can scarcely forbear weeping sometimes, when I look on her, and think what happiness and beauty she might have conferred. She is as yet all unconscious of herself, and she rather dreads being with me, because I make her too conscious. She was on the point, at [   ] of telling me all she knew of herself; but I saw she dreaded, while she wished, that I should give a local habitation and a name[1] to what lay undefined, floating before her, the phantom of her destiny; or rather lead her to give it, for she always approaches a tragical clearness when talking with me.

ELfr, from *Memoirs*, 1:314–15.

1. From Shakespeare's *Midsummer Night's Dream*, when Theseus describes poetry's power:

> And as imagination bodies forth
> The forms of things unknown, the poet's pen
> Turns them to shapes, and gives to aery nothing
> A local habitation and a name. (V.i.14–17)

977. To ?

[n.d.]

You know how, when the leadings of my life found their interpretation, I longed to share my joy with those I prized most; for I felt that if they could but understand the past we should meet entirely. They received me, some more, some less, according to the degree of intimacy between our natures. But now I have done with the past, and again move forward. The path looks more difficult, but I am better able to bear its trials. We shall have much communion, even if not in the deepest places. I feel no need of isolation, but only of temperance in thought and speech, that the essence may not evaporate in words, but grow plenteous within. The Life will give me to my own. I am not yet so worthy to love as some others are, because my manifold nature is not yet harmonized enough to be faithful, and I begin to see how much it was the want of a pure music in me that has made the good doubt me. Yet have I been true to the best light I had, and if I am so now much will be given.

During my last weeks of solitude I was very happy, and all that had troubled me became clearer. The angel was not weary of waiting for Gunhilde, till she had unravelled her mesh of thought, and seeds of mercy, of purification, were planted in the breast.[1] Whatever the past has been, I feel that I have always been reading on and on, and that the Soul of all souls has been patient in love to mine. New assurances were given me, that if I would be faithful and humble, there was no experience that would not tell its heavenly errand. If shadows have fallen, already they give way to a fairer if more tempered light; and for the present I am so happy that the spirit kneels.

Life is richly worth living, with its continual revelations of mighty woe, yet infinite hope; and I take it to my breast. Amid these scenes of beauty, all that is little, foreign, unworthy, vanishes like a dream. So shall it be some time amidst the Everlasting Beauty, when true joy shall begin and never cease.

ELfr, from *Memoirs*, 2:99–100.

1. The legend tells of Gunhild, a nun who was seduced by her confessor and then fled her convent. After being abandoned, she makes a hard journey back, knocks on the door, and begs permission to return, only to find that the sisters have not missed her in her absence. An angel took her place so that no one would know that she was gone. Fuller undoubtedly got the story from Karl Simrock, *Rheinsagen, aus dem Munde des Volks und deutscher Dichter* (Bonn, 1836), for she reviewed the 1841 reissue in her "Romaic and Rhine Ballads," *Dial* 3 (October 1842): 137:80, where she translated a portion of the ballad (pp. 146–47).

978. To ?

[n.d.]

Do you believe our prayers avail for one another? and that happiness is good for the soul? Pray, then, for me, that I may have a little peace,— some green and flowery spot, 'mid which my thoughts may rest; yet not upon fallacy, but only upon something genuine. I am deeply homesick, yet where is that home? If not on earth, why should we look to heaven? I would fain truly live wherever I must abide, and bear with full energy on my lot, whatever it is. He, who alone knoweth, will affirm that I have tried to work whole-hearted from an earnest faith. Yet my hand is often languid, and my heart is slow. I would be gone; but whither? I know not; if I cannot make this spot of ground yield the corn and roses, famine must be my lot forever and ever, surely.

ELfr, from *Memoirs*, 2:104–5

979. To ?

[n.d.]

Forget, if you can, all of petulant or overstrained that may have displeased you in me, and commend me in your prayers to my best self. When, in the solitude of the spirit, comes upon you some air from the distance, a breath of aspiration, of faith, of pure tenderness, then believe that the Power which has guided me so faithfully, emboldens my thoughts to frame a prayer for you.

ELfr, from *Memoirs*, 2:107.

980. To ?

[n.d.]

I ought, I know, to have laid aside my own cares and griefs, been on the alert for intelligence that would gratify you, and written letters such as would have been of use and given pleasure to my wise, tender, ever faithful friend. But no; I first intruded on your happiness with my sorrowful epistles, and then, because you did not seem to understand my position, with sullen petulance I resolved to write no more. Nay, worse; I tried to harden my heart against you, and felt, "If you cannot be all, you shall be nothing."

It was a bad omen that I lost the locket you gave me, which I had constantly worn. Had that been daily before my eyes, to remind me of all your worth,— of the generosity with which you, a ripe and wise character, received me to the privileges of equal friendship; of the sincerity with which you reproved and the love with which you pardoned my faults; of how much you taught me, and bore with from me,—it would have softened the flint of my heart, and I should have relaxed from my isolation.

How shall I apologize for feelings which I now recognize as having been so cold, so bitter and unjust? I can only say I have suffered greatly, till the tone of my spirits seems destroyed. Since I have been at leisure to realize how very ill I have been, under what constant pain and many annoyances I have kept myself upright, and how, if I have not done my work, I have learned my lesson to the end, I should be inclined to excuse myself for every fault, except this neglect and ingratitude against friends. Yet, if you can forgive, I will try to forgive myself, and I do think I shall never so deeply sin again.

ELfr, from *Memoirs*, 2:109–10.

981. To ?

[n.d.]

I read with great interest the papers you left with me. The picture and the emotions suggested are genuine. The youthful figure, no doubt, stands portress at the gate of Infinite Beauty; yet I would say to one I loved as I do you, do not waste these emotions, nor the occasions which excite them. There is danger of prodigality,— of lavishing the best treasures of the breast on objects that cannot be the permanent ones. It is true, that whatever thought is awakened in the mind becomes truly ours; but it is a great happiness to owe these influences to a cause so proportioned to our strength as to grow with it. I say this merely because I fear that the virginity of heart which I believe essential to feeling a real love, in all its force and purity, may be endangered by too careless excursions into the realms of fancy.

ELfr, from *Memoirs*, 2:127.

982. To ?

[n.d.]

It is told us, we should pray, "lead us not into temptation;" and I agree. Yet I think it cannot be, that, with a good disposition, and the means you have had to form your mind and discern a higher standard, your conduct or happiness can be so dependent on circumstances, as you seem to think. I never advised your taking a course which would blunt your finer powers and I do not believe that winning the means of pecuniary independence need do so. I have not found that it does, in my own case, placed at much greater disadvantage than you are. I have never considered, either, that there was any misfortune in your lot. Health, good abilities, and a well-placed youth, form a union of advantages possessed by few, and which leaves you little excuse for fault or failure. And so to your better genius and the instruction of the One Wise, I commend you.

ELfr, from *Memoirs*, 2:127–28.

983. To ?

[n.d.]

There is almost too much of bitter mixed in the cup of life. You say religion is a mere sentiment with you, and that if you are disappointed in your first, your very first hopes and plans, you do not know whether you shall be able to act well. I do not myself see how a reflecting soul can endure the passage through life, except by confidence in a Power that must at last order all things right, and the resolution that it shall not be our own fault if we are not happy,—that we will resolutely deserve to be happy. There are many bright glimpses in life, many still hours; much worthy toil, some deep and noble joys; but, then, there are so many, and such long, intervals, when we are kept from all we want, and must perish but for such thoughts.

ELfr, from *Memoirs*, 2:129.

984. To ?

[n.d.]

It gave me great pleasure to get your last letter, for these little impromptu effusions are the genuine letters. I rejoice that man and nature seem harmonious to you, and that the heart beats in unison with the voices of Spring. May all that is manly, sincere, and pure, in your wishes, be realized! Obliged to live myself without the sanctuary of the central relations, yet feeling I must still not despair, nor fail to profit by the precious gifts of life, while "leaning upon our Father's hand," I still rejoice, if any one can, in the true temper, and with well-founded hopes, secure a greater completeness of earthly existence. This fortune is as likely to be yours, as any one's I know. It seems to me dangerous, however, to meddle with the future. I never lay my hand on it to grasp it with impunity.

Of late I have often thought of you with strong yearnings of affection and desire to see you. It would seem to me, also, that I had not devoted myself to you enough, if I were not conscious that by any more attention to the absent than I have paid, I should have missed the needed instructions from the present. And I feel that any bond of true value will endure necessary neglect.

ELfr, from *Memoirs*, 2:128–29.

985. To ?

[n.d.]

You need not fear, dear [   ], my doing anything to chill you. I am only too glad of the pure happiness you so sweetly describe. I well understand what you say of its invigorating you for every enterprise. I was always sure it would be so with me,— that resigned, I could do well, but happy I could do excellently. Happiness must, with the well-born, expand the generous affections towards all men, and invigorate one to deserve what the gods have given.

ELfr, from *Memoirs*, 2:129–30.

986. To ?

[n.d.]

You wish, dear [   ], that I was not obliged to toil and spin, but could live, for a while, like the lilies.[1] I wish so, too, for life has fatigued me, my strength is little, and the present state of my mind demands repose and refreshment, that it may ripen some fruit worthy of the long and deep experiences through which I have passed. I do not regret that I have shared the labors and cares of the suffering million, and have acquired a feeling sense of the conditions under which the Divine has appointed the development of the human. Yet, if our family affairs could now be so arranged, that I might be tolerably tranquil for the next six or eight years, I should go out of life better satisfied with the page I have turned in it, than I shall if I must still toil on. A noble career is yet before me, if I can be unimpeded by cares. I have given almost all my young energies to personal relations; but, at present, I feel inclined to impel the general stream of thought. Let my nearest friends also wish that I should now take share in more public life.

ELfr, from *Memoirs*, 2:131.
Written to one of her brothers.
1. Matt. 6:28.

987. To ?

[n.d.]

He was as premature as myself at thirteen—[1] a man in the range of his thoughts, analyzing motives and explaining principles, when he ought to have been playing at cricket or hunting in the woods. All his characteristics wore brilliant hues: he was very witty, and I owe to him the great obligation of being the only person who has excited me to frequent and boundless gayety. In later days— for my intimacy with him lasted many years— he became the feeder of my intellect. He delighted to ransack the history of a nation, of an art or a science, and bring to me all the particulars. Telling them, fixed them in his own memory, which was the most tenacious and ready I have every known; he enjoyed my clear perception as to their relative value, and I classified them in my own way.

ELfr, from *Collections of the Maine Historical Society*, 8 (1881): 442.
1. George T. Davis.

APPENDIX
Newly Discovered Letters

988. To George T. Davis

Friday eveg. Decr 19th 1829.—

After dating this I stopped to read Willis's two pieces in his last number which came home tonight; he has half a dozen ideas; *such* ideas—[1] I *will* admire him notwithstanding his cloak, patronizing airs to the daughters of *highly respectable families*, and his devotion to the Misses Cain—I do wish I could send you the Magazine but my father has not read it.

And now to answer the letter which pleased me so much—I shall always be glad to have you come to me when saddened.— The Melancholick does not misbecome you (I do not now allude to your *letter*) The lights of your character are *wintry*; they are generally inspiriting— and life-giving, but, if perpetual, would *glare* too much on the tired sense; one likes sometimes a cloudy day with its damp and warmer breath— its gentle down-looking shades. Sadness in some is intolerably ungraceful and oppressive, its affects one like a cold rainy day in June or September when[n] all pleasure departs with the Sun every thing seems out of place and irrelative to the time; the clouds are fog, the atmosphere leaden— but 'tis not so with you— Dont think this mere rhodomontade;[n] my ideas are very good I assure you; and, if you are not convinced that they are so, I shall explain myself more fully in a future letter.

I am glad you think about Aurora Raby.[2] Do Mr Norton and the Men of Edinburgh say he knew nothing, saw nothing in the female character but childish vanity or infatuate tenderness?[3] Show me a Sonnetteer who could feel like him, could tint so softly those eye-rivetting miniatures. You know I have told you— no! perhaps you forget for you did not seem interested[n] what I once thought of my Elizabeth in relation to this sketch of Aurora—[4] also of that most exquisite *copy* from a too rare model, De Lisle's Rosamond, (which could not have been a *creation*; no mind can compound such an one[n] from elements of knowledge or observation; 'tis too stilly unique.)[5] These women have *tenderness*, refined and subdued by that imagination which gives to minds like theirs a sense of the Central Good, The truly Beautiful, from which it leads so many of the less pure; In their souls is no passion, *therefore* no Eloquence, yet how lovely! to hold communion with the half shrinking, half unconscious silence of such beings! I was deceived by E's style of face, or rather she has now a second nature. I think to see her a charming woman but not like Aurora— she is a garden rose with many companions of similar nature though of unequal fragrance— Aurora is like a flower in the glowing desert, which, asking not the companionship of streams, the protecting shade of more majestick plants, nor the fostering nurture of man grows into full beauty from the mere force of that vitality originally given it. Even now when I look at E's face, never *glowing* but often *so radiant* I think of Aurora; E's eyes have such an *in-look* that to be sure results from her imperfect vision, but I loved to think, (when others complained of the want of response in her countenance) that her soul was too in-dwelling, too much in love with its own thoughts of beauty to leap to her eyes at the call of every voice, the query of every idly curious eye. But I will not tire my cousin; I dont think you like to hear me talk on thus.

I will tell why I said your brother loved you truly—[6] I went into his shop a few days after your departure. He came forward and began to talk of you; I casually mentioned your having no fire in your room; this, being a discomfort he could perfectly understand seemed to make him very uneasy; he spoke of it again and again and at last said he would go to Franklin and see about it the very first day he possibly could; and this[n] though I think he was somewhat mortified and disappointed at your not having [   ]

ALfr (MCR-S: MC 351 [Box 19, folder 5]). Published in part in *Memoirs*, 1:80, and *Letters of MF*, 1:158.

September when] September ↑ when ↓
mere rhodomontade;] mere rhodomonta(g)de;
forget for you did not seem interested] forget ↑ for you did not seem interested ↓
compound such an one] compound ↑ such an one ↓
and this] and ⟨all⟩ this

1. Nathaniel Parker Willis had edited the *Token* and was from April 1829 to mid-1831 the editor of the *American Monthly*, published in Boston. Fuller's reference to "two pieces" is puzzling, for none was signed, and Willis undoubtedly wrote more than two. She would have reason to assume that "The Editor's Table" was his, but nothing in it or in other essays corresponds to her comments to Davis.

2. Aurora Raby is a young woman in Byron's *Don Juan:*

> a certain fair and fairy one,
> Of the best class, and better than her class,—
> Aurora Raby, a young star who shone
> O'er life, too sweet an image for such glass,
> A lovely being, scarcely form'd or moulded,
> A Rose with all its sweetest leaves yet folded.

(*Byron's John Juan: A Variorum Edition*, ed. Truman Guy Steffan and Willis W. Pratt [Austin, 1957], 3:475)

3. Andrews Norton was a faculty member at the divinity school in Cambridge who was known for his conservative position on literature and theology. His presence and authority were much on the minds of Fuller and her friends as they began to champion German literature, especially Goethe, whom Norton detested. Of Byron, Norton had written: "There is a pestilential atmosphere about the ruins of such a mind. The great injury likely to result from his writings, consists in the circumstance, that a man of

George T. Davis. Courtesy of the Harvard University Archives.

powers so extraordinary, should have enlisted himself without shame in the cause of evil; that he should have presented himself before the world to avow his contempt of decency, his depravity, and his impiety" ("Lord Byron's Character and Writings," *North American Review* 21 [October 1825]: 359). The "men of Edinburgh" were Francis Jeffrey, Sydney Smith, and Francis Horner, who had begun the *Edinburgh Review* in 1802.

4. Elizabeth Randall, who knew both Davis and James Clarke, his Harvard classmate.

5. Elizabeth Caroline Grey (1798–1869) published *De Lisle; or, The Distrustful Man* in 1828. Lady Rosamond Trevannon, a most estimable woman, marries the hero, Hubert De Lisle, and becomes the focus for his neurotic distrust. Fuller remembered it well enough to recommend it to Caroline Sturgis in 1838 (Virginia Blain, Patricia Clements, and Isobel Grundy, *The Feminist Companion to Literature in English* [New Haven, 1990]; *Letters of MF*, 1:323).

6. Wendell Davis (1776–1830) married Caroline Willmans Smith, daughter of Ralph Smith of Roxbury, in 1802. Davis graduated from Harvard in 1796 and became a lawyer. He served in the Massachusetts Senate with Timothy Fuller and was later sheriff of Barnstable County (*Massachusetts Register*, 1815; Harvard archives; *CC*, 8 September 1802). Davis had three sons, Wendell Bayard (1803–27), George Thomas, and John Thornton Kirkland (b. 1818). Wendell Bayard graduated from Harvard in 1823 and entered the divinity school but died while a student. His youngest brother then took the name Wendell Thornton. His Harvard classmates (1838) included James Rusell Lowell and William Wetmore Story. In 1841, Thornton Davis married Maria Louisa Russell, sister of George's wife (Harvard archives; *Memorial Biographies of the New England Historic Genealogical Society* [Boston, 1880], 1:141; *CC*, 8 September 1802; William T. Davis, *Ancient Landmarks of Plymouth*, 2d ed. [Boston, 1899], pp. 82–83). In a letter to her father in 1835, Fuller says she saw "a good deal of your former ward Thornton Davis" (*Letters of MF*, 1:230).

989. To George T. Davis

Boston 29th Decr. 1829.—

My dear Cousin,

Samuel called last night to give me your letter he seemed in great glee; I found myself shaking hands with him to my great astonishment. Pray tell me about his "liaison". Mrs Greenwood thinks him one of the handsomest youths that ever crossed her threshold and Ann says "though he has not so *intellectual an expression* as George yet he *is* handsome, *so* handsome and *such* a goodhumored, kind laugh"[1] And today I received the Leonard Woods letter which is *fine*, over which I have meditated and shall meditate, perhaps answer it fully by and by.—[2]

I am in Amelia's room writing at one coin du fee[?] on[n] her very bad little writing desk (when I go home I shall know how to prize our good table) She occupies the other corner; her head bent over "Reginald Dalton" which she has just begun and which makes her laugh every three moments;[3] 'Tis past noon, I hope we shall have this eveg to ourselves. This morng was beautifully soft and sunny. A. and I went out to walk, met M. Davis, told her "I had a note from you to

Helen but had left it at Mr Greenwood's and had no way to send it before H. Eustis shd go to C."—[4] "could not she call at Mr G's and get it? I could tell her where I'd left it." "No! impossible;— she'd only come to town to prepare for the Quadrille party, *must* go out immediately" Well, I told her, I would send it soon as possible. We walked together as far as Miss Oliver's where she stopped, began again about the note said they shd come in town Thursday, but could not call then; finally she decided to ask Mrs Minot to send for it—[5] When I came home this eveg, I found she had called and taken it notwithstanding her haste. Oh! how miserably dispirited she seemed— I heard she said at Mrs Blake's party that she and Margaret Fuller were great friends!! How delightful!—

I passed an hour and a half very happily[n] at Pendleton's looking over not *glancing at* engravings with Amelia and Sarah Clarke.[6] I found two designs which filled my mind with thoughts— which I will not now prate about.— We went last night to Labassie's;[7] I did not enjoy it the least; but few children danced and the actors on the scene were the most common-place of common-place juveniles. I believe I never before happened on an assemblage to me so entirely unexciting— not even his Lordship there to observe on; Madame Labassie was not there; nobody waltzed but those two Brazilians, the Misses Fretre— although I was half-sorry I went for I've enjoyed myself so highly of late whenever I've been out and *this* evening has marred the entireness of my feelings of pleasure.— I have not seen James for more than a week he called here to see me last Saturday but I was out. I hope he will be at E's tomorrow eveg she has a little party.[8] Ben Winslow walked with me today he was arrayed in a cloak with those long tassels and yellow lining I believe; I thought his drapery became him pretty well but the more fastidious Amelia says he looks frightfully. "*Maria*" saw Ben at church and was struck by his "*fine countenance*" she made divers inquiries concerning his manner, character and disposition thereupon—[9] I dined at E's today; Almira had been there she *defends* J. C. Park and is not ashamed, says *she* believes he married because he *loved* and that there was no constraint about the matter;—[10] and, if so was he not magnanimous to set aside all considerations of vanity and interest in behalf of Her, the Chosen of his heart?!!—

I will tell you about Lovelace.[11] His character in the book is shown out to the eye gradually and with great skill; if you were not one able and accustomed to allow for the varieties, the apparent incongruities of character I should not dare to sketch to you from a final survey. Lovelace's character is based on the love of power and the spirit of enterprize. He is hard of heart from excessive indulgence of these qualities but not wantonly cruel from love of excitement. He combines the greatest apparent versatility of manner with the greatest real consistency in conduct. No impulse of the moment, no temporary lure could lead him to an act of vulgar villainy; his tastes are too refined; indeed he has all the refinement that man can have without virtue or generosity. His temperament is one of violent passions but his Pride can always command them— aye, even in the bitterness of all that is truly death loss of all he best loved, failure in what he most desired But no!— I cannot depict his character thus, no pencil could throw such *expression* into a single sketch. I was charmed in the book with the first views of Lovelace Eloquent, witty, brave, profligate I thought no more than his companions, and only more Marque from the strong individual cast of his every act. He seemed to hold in such light regard the very *admiration* of all others to look so proudly on every manifestation of his strength as if his conscious Soul told that never on aught he met in life could his full power be exerted, nor could any mind but his own appreciate that character which could never on any occasion be fully called into action. Such being my first feelings my heart strove as if in life against a true knowledge of his character, reluctantly and line by line I knew it, and only on full conviction could I look calmly on it— Then I *detested* and *pardoned* him— How imperfectly does this pen express what I have felt and thought; I imagined I could do it when I began. The resemblance to you which I mentioned is in his levity, nay! brilliant vivacity and airy self-possession under circumstances of the greatest apparent difficulty, doubt and mortification. I allude particularly to his interview with Hickman, and his visit to poor Clarissa's last asylum from which she flies to avoid him. And this conduct of Lovelace is not a mere effort of will but flows naturally from parts of his character apparently least calculated to combine[n] to such a result. And there are analogies though not likenesses between the stimulants to such action in your character and his. But I dont think I can let you know what I think till we meet unless I were to treat the subject in a more regular way—

Adieu. Ann has come home and seems dying to talk. I hope to hear again from you this week.

M.

Ann sends her love.— she says she hopes "your eye wont glance over this circumstance" with *such* a soul-sent giggle!

:

ALS (MCR-S: MCR 351 [Box 19, folder 5]). *Addressed:* Mr George T. Davis. / Franklin. / Mass. *Postmark:* Boston Dec 31 MS. *Endorsed:* S. M. Fuller. ⟨Cambridge⟩ ↑ Boston ↓ / Dec. 29 1829.

du fee[?] on] du fee[?] ⟨?⟩on
very happily] very ⟨?⟩ happily
to combine] to ⟨produce⟩ combine

1. Mary Langdon married William Pitt Greenwood in 1796. Fuller was an intimate of the family in her childhood. Ann is Angelina Greenwood.

2. Leonard Woods, Jr. (1807–78), son of a conservative theologian, was born in West Newbury and graduated from Union College in 1827 and from the Andover Theological Seminary in 1830. He became a minister in New York City and then was president of Bowdoin College from 1839 to 1866. The elder Woods and Timothy Fuller were long-time friends (*DAB*).

3. Amelia is Amelia Greenwood. John Gibson Lockhart published *Reginald Dalton* in 1823.

4. More of Fuller's friends: Margaret and Helen Davis (no relation to George) were the daughters of Daniel and Louisa Freeman Davis. H. Eustis is Henry Lawrence Eustis (1819–85), a member of the Lowell-Story set, son of Abraham and Rebecca Sprague Eustis. After his graduation from Harvard (1838) and from West Point (1842) and a stint in the army, Eustis became an engineer and then a professor at Harvard. He returned to the army to serve in the Civil War (*DAB*).

5. William Minot (1783–1873), a Boston lawyer, married Louisa Davis (1788–1858), sister of Helen and Margaret Davis, on 29 July 1810. She was the daughter of the solicitor general of Massachusetts, Daniel Davis, and Louisa Freeman, the sister of Dr. James Freeman. Louisa Minot was a painter and writer who was interested in social reform (James Jackson Minot, *Ancestors and Descendants of George Richards Minot, 1758–1802* [n.p., 1936], pp. 17–19).

6. John B. Pendleton (1798–1866) and his brother, William S. Pendleton (1795–1879), founded a lithographic printing firm in Boston in 1825. The first such firm in the United States, it was very popular (*DAB; Brian Pendleton and His Descendants, 1599–1910*, comp. Everett Hall Pendleton [n.p., 1910], p. 750). Sarah Ann Clarke, James Clarke's sister, was an artist who studied with Washington Allston.

7. In 1822 Claude Labasse of Paris married R. K. Overy in Boston (*CC*, 1 May 1822).

8. James is James Freeman Clarke; E. is probably Elizabeth Randall.

9. Benjamin Pollard Winslow (1810–79), a Harvard classmate of Davis and James Clarke (class of 1829), married Mary Timmins Quincy Hill in 1832 and became a businessman in later life (Harvard archives; *CC*, 29 December 1832). Maria is probably Maria Randall, Elizabeth's sister.

10. Almira Penniman was another friend from Fuller's childhood. John Cochran Park, a lawyer and the son of Fuller's Boston schoolmaster, married Mary F. Moore on 23 November 1829 (*CC*, 28 November 1829).

11. Robert Lovelace is the principal male character in Samuel Richardson's *Clarissa* (London, 1748).

990. To George T. Davis

Cambridge. 23d Jany. 1830

My dear Cousin,

You profess yourself satisfied with my religious opinions—[1] Yet most persons would consider them as amounting to what you deprecate believing, even "temporarily," ie, Deism. I do not myself consider them in this light, because I do not *disbelieve* or even *carelessly set aside* Revelation; I merely remain in ignorance of the Christian Revelation because I do not feel it suited to me at present. And the reason you yourself have given; "The philosophers" you say "appealed to the intellect,— Christ to the sympathies"— And these sympathies I do not wish to foster— Shall I quicken the heart to a sense of its wants when I can so ill supply those of the mind?— I shall write no formal answer to what you say, but any-thing that occurs to you will be welcome interesting to me. And sometimes I shall speak. At any rate I like to have your thoughts by me in their own garb and colors— I am too apt to retain only impressions from a conversation.— I thought there was *much* in your views of Leonard Wood's character, though indeed you did seem to have measured him rather by the standard of personal comparison than by that of perfection.ⁿ This is natural enough!— But there is great beauty and truth in what you say— "Too intellectual to be sympathizing" And I was struck too by what you say of the acceptance in which Heaven holds generous faith.— I have read Leonard Woods'sⁿ letter often and cannot but think of his prophetick fear that half stimulating contact might produce that sameness in the intellectual world, never to be dreaded in the material.

I believe I understand about Mr Wilde;[2] I hope you will tell me a great deal when you come back. James did sketch a little but not with spirit.— In truth I did not know when I began how exhausted I was. I have taken a long walk the first for a fortnight, paid two decent visits, and one at Mrs Higginson's very long and most pleasantly exciting—[3] Then my Journal does exhaust me. I felt charmed by the image presented by Neal in Miller's obituary;[4] ie Miller seeing his life for months, the substance of his existence, his present Soul whelmed in the vasty deep when others but wondered at his grief in loving his thick logbook. I thought to put my soul *without* me too— and began to keep a Journal this year in *fearless sincerity*. It is my very life in all its moods and tenses, strength and folly, beauty and deformity. But the habit of keeping it gives an aching intensity to my thoughts. In pursuing this Record I feel all the pains and fascinations of the most intimate confidential intercourse without its sweetness, its composing and sustaining influences. But I shall keep it through the year unless I find it goes nigh to break my heart or turn my brain— Tis indeed a most fascinating employ and the return to *any* common employment is generally highly distasteful to me. I felt greatly inclined to write to you this eveg but I must defer the rest till tomorrow. I have just read a letter from Marian Marshall to Amelia; she seems *good* and happy Amelia is reading Brown's novels.[5] If I get excited writing tomorrow I should forget these little items. Marian inquires after you; she has met a "James Clarke man" now.

Sunday eveg— I have been reading the foregoing two pages— and far from thinking them most "excellent" they seem to me very very dull— but I am at present excited and hope your receptive feelings will be more propitious. You will be pleased to hear that I have been most happy. Henry Hedge came for me about four oclock this afternoon and I went with him home to his father's whence I have just returned.[6] And I never can feel more perfect enjoyment from any one's conversation. I return satisfied on many points and shall feel the pleasurable effects of the conversation for weeks. I feel as if I had taken into my mind his new metaphysicks, experience new beautiful things he has seen and known, and new beautiful imaginings. There was no one there and Mrs [Hedge] after observing "that Henry and Margaret thought themselves such high geniuses that nobody could get up to or comprehend them" was so kind as to interfere no further. But what did I mean to tell *you*? Oh! I asked Henry "whether, if he had not chosen the profession of a Christian Divine, he should not have contented his youth with Natural religion and remained ignorant of Christianity."— He said he should have waived the subject to later years probably, because he had an impression that Christianity appealed rather to the sympathies than the intellect; but he was mistaken, that he had found in this religion a home for theories cherished before, nearly all of novel or peculiar that he had added, with the most beautifully profound views of life.— I thought you might like to hear his opinion of this.— Ah! What pleasure to meet with such a daring yet realizing mind as his!— But the fine things which I heard and the also fine things which I myself said, thought, and shall think shall be inscribed on the pages of my journal since I cannot keep my records in "hearts" as you do. However my memoranda shall be always with me and at my command. I doubt your being as well assured of yours.— Talking of hearts La belle I fancy is submitting the well filled leaves of hers to the comprehending eye of Mr Hutchinson who is reported to have said "that he had for the first time found an echo to his feelings in those of Miss Fay"—[7] You see I persist in giving you les nouvelles de vos amies despite your *remarks*. This letter is hardly worth sending and scarcely legible for I hold the paper in one hand and write with the other, however, be merciful for the sake of your cousin

M.

ALS (MCR-S: MC 351 [Box 19, folder 5]). *Addressed:* Mr. George T. Davis. / Franklin / Mass. *Postmark:* Boston Jan [*illegible*]. *Endorsed:* S. M. Fuller. Cambridge / Jan. 23rd. 1830.

of perfection] of ⟨reflection⟩ perfection
Leonard Woods's] Leonard Wood's'⟨s⟩

1. Fuller had summarized her religious opinions for Davis in an earlier letter (*Letters of MF*, 1:158–59).

2. Whom Fuller names is not clear, though he could be James Wilde (1812–87), who graduated from Harvard in 1832 and became a doctor (Harvard archives).

3. Probably Louisa Storrow Higginson, wife of Stephen Higginson of Cambridge, whose home Fuller often visited. They were the parents of Thomas Wentworth Higginson, Fuller's biographer and Emily Dickinson's champion.

4. James William Miller published the *Boston Literary Gazette* but had merged it with John Neal's *Yankee*. An opium addict, Miller went to the West Indies, where he died in 1829. Neal wrote his obituary in *The Yankee; and Boston Literary Gazette*, n.s. 7 (December 1829): 298–303. A journal that Miller had kept in London was unfortunately lost on his return trip. Neal called it "the living truth of what De Quincey had portrayed or tried to portray with the pencil of untruth in the celebrated Opium-Eater: that every wild vision of his heart, every strange colour and shape of his fiery and bewildered imagination had a place there" (p. 300). John Neal was a writer and editor from Maine. Later he published Fuller's story "Lost and Won" in the *New England Galaxy*.

5. Charles Brockden Brown.

6. Frederic Henry Hedge, who graduated from the divinity school in 1828, was at this time minister of the West Cambridge church. His father, Levi Hedge, was the professor of natural religion and moral philosophy at Harvard.

7. Harriet Howard Fay, however, married William Hardy Greenough in 1831. She was the daughter of Judge Samuel Prescott Phillips Fay of Cambridge.

991. To James F. Clarke

Saturday afternoon
[27 March 1830]

My Cousin,

I thank you for your note. Ten minutes before I received it[n] I scarcely thought that any thing again would make my stifled heart throb so warm a pulse of pleasure— Excuse my cold doubt, my selfish arrogance— you will when I tell you that this experiment has before had much uniform results; those who professed to seek my friendship, and whom indeed I have often truly loved, have always learned to content themselves with that inequality in the connexion which I have never striven to veil.[1] Indeed I have thought myself more valued and better beloved because the sympathy, the interest were all on my side— True! such regard could never flatter my pride nor gratify my affections since it was paid not to myself, but to the need they had of me; still it was dear and pleasing as it has given me an opportunity of knowing and serving several lovely characters; and I cannot see that there is any-thing else for me to do on earth. And I should rejoice to cultivate generosity since (see that *since*) affections gentler and more sympathetick are denied me.

I would have been a true friend to you; ever-ready to solace your pains and partake your joy as far as possible. Yet I cannot but rejoice that I have met a person who could discriminate and reject a[n] proffer of this sort— Two years ago I should have ventured to proffer you friendship indeed, on seeing such an instance of pride in you; but I have gone through a sad process of feeling since; and those emotions so necessarily repressed have lost their simplicity, their ardent beauty. *Then* there was nothing I might not have disclosed to a person capable of comprehending, had I ever seen such an one! now there are many voices of the soul which I imperiously silence. This results not from any particular circumstance or event but from a gradual ascertaining of realities.

I cannot promise you any limitless confidence, but I *can* promise that no timid caution, no haughty dread shall prevent my telling you the truth of my thoughts on any subject we may have in common. Will this satisfy you? Oh let it; suffer me to know you.

I write with an unsteady hand perhaps incoherently; but I was very eager to answer you as soon as I was able. Farewell— your cousin

M.

P S. No other cousin or friend of any style is to see this note.

ALS (MHi). Published in part in *Memoirs*, 1:66–68; Chevigny, pp. 102–3; and *Letters of MF*, 1:162–63. *Addressed:* Mr J. F. Clarke.

Fuller here answers a letter from Clarke of the same day (Letters of JFC, *pp. 11–12*).
received it] received ↑ it ↓
reject a] reject ⟨?⟩ a

1. Clarke had written: "I should have been happy in going further with you than with all before, but there must be an answering store" of emotional honesty (*Letters of JFC*, p. 12).

992. To James F. Clarke

Saturday Eveg. May 1st 1830.

My dear Cousin James,

The holy moon and many-toned wind of this night woo to a vigil at the open window; a half satisfied interest urges me to live, love, and *perish*!! in the noble, wronged heart of Basil;[1] my Journal, which lies before me, tempts to follow out and interpret the as-yet-only-half-understood musings of the past week; Letter-writing compared with any of these things takes the ungracious resemblance of a *duty*. I have, natheless, after a two hours reverie to[n] which this resolve and its preliminaries have formed excellent warp, determined to sacrifice this hallowed time to you. Oh Man of Genius and Feeling,—but I beg you to consider it as a proof of friendship nearly unprecedented in experience of the person who now scribbleth on to you.— Thank you for your letters.—

It did not in the least surprize me that you found it impossible at the time to avail yourself of the confidential privileges I had invested you with; On the contrary I only wonder that we should ever after such gage given and received, (not by a look or tone, but by *letter*), hold any frank communication. Preparations are good in life, prologues ruinous. I felt this even before I *sent* my note; but could not persuade myself to consign an impulse so embodied to oblivion from any consideration of expediency.

You "particularly long for a general view of the Elizabeth affair."[2] The statement of my *views* shall be *general* and *concise*. I really respect you too much and think experience too valuable to persons capable of it ever to concern myself about the *results* for you. I see no present good you receive except gratifying your tastes in presence or absence in contemplating or heightening the charms of a lovely object. As to harm you are not a person to be bowed down by your affections and if you *feel* your being enervated I presume you will conquer or die. *You* need a present type of the Beautiful to kindle Fancy withal and I see not why E. should not suffice for years; seeing her as you do.

I think you will be more and more satisfied with Godwin.[3] He has fully lived the double existence of man and he casts the reflexes on[n] his magick mirror from a height whence[n] no object in life's panorama can cause one throb of delirious hope or gasping ambition. At any rate you may if you study him know all he has to tell. He is quite free from vanity and ca[   ] not miserly any of his treasures from the [   ] posterity.

—My pen is too, too bad neither mon pere nor Eugene up to mend it. For, you must know, I cannot make pens; perhaps some ungracious persons would add "nor do any one thing useful in the 'varsal world"

—My sentiments remain unchanged. Your eloquence has touched my soul; Your manliness commanded my respect. Can I ever forget it?

I am sensible that this letter will disappoint you— it could not be otherwise. Perhaps you will be better satisfied one day; though for that I may not vouch. Adieu my friend.

M.

ALS (MHi). Published in part in *Memoirs*, 1:68–69, 110, and *Letters of MF*, 1:165–66. *Addressed:* Mr. James F. Clarke. / Cambridge. *Endorsed:* May 1 1830.

reverie to] reverie ⟨b⟩to
reflexes on] reflexes ⟨fr⟩ on
height whence] height whe⟨?⟩nce

1. A reference to the anonymous *Basil Barrington and His Friends* (London, 1830).

2. Clarke had made his request in his letter of 11 April 1830 (*Letters of JFC*, p. 14). He was at this time in love with Elizabeth Randall.

3. In his letter, Clarke had described his reactions to William Godwin's novel *Mandeville: A Tale of the Seventeenth Century in England* (Edinburgh, 1817).

993. To James F. Clarke

Cambridge 7th May 1830.

Dear Cousin James,

I am about to essay expressing to you tho[se] fancies about your character and situation which you so resolu[   ] imagine worth your knowing—[1] They will be entirely useless to you [   ] regards action. But you say you wish to be *roused* to thought [   ] fear you will not receive even this benefit.— That which, hints [   ] in the glow of conversation, might have acted strongly on your mind will now strike you as idealess and leave your thoughts unagitated— 'Tis always so after expecting anything of this kind, be it what it may, not *answering* expectation it disappoints— But here as elsewhere the fault was mine and I will rather sacrifice my vanity than leave you fancying yourself deprived of something valuable.

I have greatly wished to see among us such a person of Geniu[s] as the nineteenth century can afford— ie. one who has tasted in the morning of existence the extremes of good and ill both imaginative and real— I had imagined a person endowed by nature with that acute sense to Beauty (ie Harmony or Truth) and that vast capacity of desire which give soul to love and ambition.— I had wished this person might grow up to manhood *alone* (but not *alone in crowds*) I would have placed him in a situation so retired, so obscure, that he would quietly but without bitter sense of isolation stand[n] apart from all surrounding[n] him; I would have had [   ] on steadily feeding his mind with congenial lore, hopefully confident [   ] he only nourished his existence into perfect life. Fate would [   ]tting season furnish an atmosphere and orbit meet for his [   ] thing and exercise; I wished that he might adore not fear the bright phantoms

167

of his mind's creation and believe them [   ] the shadows of external things to be met with hereafter. [   ]ter this steady intellectual growth had brought his [p]owers to manhood so far as the ideal can do it, I wished [t]his being might be launched into the world of realities [h]is heart glowing with the ardor of an immortal towards [p]erfection; his eyes searching every-where to behold it; I wished [h]e might collect into one burning point those withering palsy[in]g convictions which in the ordinary routine of things so gradually pervade the soul; That he might suffer in brief space agonies of disappointment commensurate with his unpreparedness and confidence. And I thought thus thrown back on the representing, pictorial resources I supposed him originally to possess; With such material— And the need he must feel of using it, Such a man would suddenly dilate into a thing of Pride, Power, and Glory— A centre round which asking, aimless hearts might rally— A man fitted to act as interpreter to the one tale of many-languaged ages!

What words are these! Perhaps you will feel as if I sought but for "the longest and strongest"— Yet to my ear they do but faintly describe the imagined powers of such [   ]

—I knew I could not write about it save in this one st[   ] and 'twas therefore I spoke of seeming "vagaries"— But thin[k] what you will!— There was something in the unshrinkin[g] confidence with which you now and then pursued with all your strength the flying footsteps of Truth; in your putting by vanities confessedly dear to you; in your incapaci[ty] to be happy without some *imaginative* love in whose atmosphere your Fancy might breathe and plume herself that made me think you might have been the Being I wished to see;— I grieved for your premature yet parti[cular] experience; I regretted that your mind should be squander[ed] on petty objects whose elusion could teach you no new or strengthening lesson— I sorrowed that your affections should be daily wasted in modes which would probably unfit you forever for feeling those in which the whole existence takes part; affections— the offspring not of *fancy* but of strong admiration.

If you do not understand how I apply this to what you said of Louisa, I will sometime tell you—² But I flatter myself you will— Yet I shall not be surprized if all this excites no feeling of reality in you; I have thought ever since the moment that I unwarily mentioned the subject to you that this would probably be the case— I have decided to fulfil my promise *now* for reasons [wh]ich you will see in a letter which I shall write you [in t]wo or three days; perhaps sooner if I can.

M.

ALS (MHi). Published in part in *Memoirs*, 1:69–70; Miller, pp. 28–29; and *Letters of MF*, 1:166–67. *Addressed:* Mr James F. Clarke. / Cambridge. *Endorsed:* May 7th 1830.

isolation stand] isolation ⟨?⟩ stand
all surrounding] all surround⟨?⟩ing

1. In his letter of 11 April 1830 Clarke had said: "I may as well make a full confession. I was afraid you overrated me. For though I always felt myself possessed of powers, yet I knew that many years would pass before they could be unfolded so as to be felt by men" (*Letters of JFC*, p. 15).

2. Louisa Hickman, Clarke's cousin whom he had loved, married Samuel J. Smith in November 1828.

994. To James F. Clarke

Cambridge Oct 25th 1830.

I hear you are sick, my dear James and remembering how you wrote to me when left in that forlorn estate I feel strongly[n] impelled to copy from then; Throughout our acquaintance I acted out every ungentle impulse careless of consistency or the thoughts of others; why should I fear to err on the other side? I do feel a worthless emotion of friendship for you at this moment; I will express it; you will perhaps have learned to know what such things mean from me; And, if the inappropriateness shock you, just suppose yourself rereading[n] a letter dated six months back.

I envy you your fever *really* (not as young ladies talk of the delights of riding in coal carts, seeing vulgar intoxication &c) but really because I should like one myself just now; I feel a senseless happiness to which such an interval of bodily ill would lend new spring. For you, I wish you would condense your sufferings into a week if possible for Mother is to have a party full of "background, real Martin, at which I wish your presence. Do get well and come all rejuvenated to speculate on the drolleries and dulnesses of others or patronize their budding virtues— I was sorry you did not come again to Lynn. Mr and Mrs B,— are prepared to receive you as the Man of Ross.[1] I was very happy but Elschen ached as to her head, eyes, ears, side, and feet; she could not eat for heat nor sleep for cold nor walk out for East-wind nor stay in for oppression; in short her state was one of "squalid wretchedness[2] 'Twas perfectly droll to see her stand gazing for the first time on the waves as they broke on the shore; her eyes fixed in rapt enthusiasm on the overwhelming dash, break, boom &c while with both hands she held her red-cloak tight over her mouth lest that insidious East should seize the time to invade the soul's frail dwelling.

169

We passed some hours at Marblehead very delightfully. I had no idea of such a unique English place being situate in Yankee-land. Then near-sighted Elschen and my no *less hapless* self scrambled over the rocks far, *far* behind our laughing, shouting, lynx eyed cronies who mercilessly exhorted us to jump and run, (as it seemed to us), into the very arms of the vasty deep

However we did reach them at last and sat above a "Spouting Horn" wh might vie with Nahant seeing the tide rise and moralizing as humanity *will* by the waterside on life &c Then we saw some" *active!* sea-gulls and a whirr[ing] which emulated them. Dont I discover what Lord Nat would call a beautiful vein of rich descriptiveness?[3] Ah! I *should* shine viva voce!!! I wish" twere etiquette for me to pay you a visit. I *can* appear "a ministering angel on such occasions; you must take my word for this since you can have no chance of forming an opinion. I shall expect an account of your delirium— that being a favorite modern subject and both you and myself true disciples of the nineteenth century. But do not shatter your constitution; only suffer enough to feel the zest of recovery. There are two beautiful works which I would recommend to your perusal during convalescence "The Vestal" "A Tale by Dr Gray" and "Pride and Prejudice" by Miss—[4] Adieu

M.

PS. Make my best respects to your grandfather if you dont think he would disapprove my writing which *Mrs* Freeman certainly would.[5]

ALS (MHi).
feel strongly] feel ⟨?⟩ strongly
yourself rereading] yourself ↑ re ↓ reading
saw some] saw so⟨?⟩me
I wish] I ⟨should⟩ ↑ wish ↓

1. Fuller described her visit with David and Almira Barlow, who lived in Lynn, in her letter to Amelia Greenwood, 17 October 1830 (*Letters of MF*, 1:169–70). John Kyrle (1637–1724), the Man of Ross, was known for his good works and for his ability to make peace between angry neighbors. Pope memorialized him in his third "Moral Epistle" (*DNB*).
2. Elschen is Elizabeth Randall.
3. Lord Nat is N. P. Willis.
4. Thomas Gray, *The Vestal; or, A Tale of Pompeii* (Boston, 1830), and Jane Austen, *Pride and Prejudice* (London, 1813). Gray (1803–49) graduated from Harvard in 1823, became a doctor in Roxbury, and married Mary Turrell Fales in 1834 (Harvard archives; *CC*, 17 September 1834).
5. Rev. James Freeman and his wife, Martha Curtis Clarke Freeman.

995. To James F. Clarke

Cambridge 26th Octr 1830
Deux heures apres midi!!

Dear James,

I had anticipated your wish and sent a note for you to George early this morning but he, always an "unchancy" youth, had mounted and set forth, I fear, to Newton;[1] I did not tell him that I wished to write; *so* as[n] you may not get that epistle for many days I will write[n] another for which nótre Polly says *some* gentleman is to call. Now, my dear James, you must not let this sickness[n] "wear your heart away" You must husband[n] its energies to battle with the ills of sentiment. Employ your hours in inventing an anti Barber system of Elocution; see how stout the Dr's heart is, he never brooded as you do. Emulate him and rise from your bed blest in the self-sufficiency of virtuous industry. Suppose you write an imaginary tour round your sick chamber in the Irving method full of *sweet fancyings* of its tenants, the reveries of the furniture &c[2]

Wednesday morning— I was interrupted in my course of suppositions— We *did* go to Nahant but it rained before we arrived so 'twas impossible to walk about; I did not admire the sea so much as in the glad, transparent light of the morning; now 'twas troubled without being majestick; and sky and sea suffused with one sullen, boding hue. I like the strength with which a wave breaks on the land its insidious stealth of approach and proud collected break. But that aimless strife and tossing nowise delights me. I cannot write any more now for I am tremendously hurried and shall be in Boston when *the* gentleman carries. I think I'll send this patchwork scrawl though George says you had my other yesterday on that economical principle of "not missing an opportunity." Adieu! Be blest! and get well!—

M.

ALS (MHi). *Addressed:* Mr James F. Clarke. / Newton. / politeness of an unknown / gentleman.

so as] *so* ↑ as ↓
will write] will ⟨un⟩ write
this sickness] this si⟨?⟩ckness
must husband] must h⟨?⟩usband

1. Clarke was at the Freeman home in Newton. George is George Davis.

2. Probably Fuller remembers the "Family Reliques" chapter of Irving's *Bracebridge Hall* (1822), though Geoffrey Crayon begins *Tales of a Traveller* with his boredom as an ill traveler confined to his room in Germany.

996. To James F. Clarke

Thursday eveg—ⁿ
[28 October 1830]

You are finely composed, my friend, about your views of life; I presume you have given me in your letter those "half dozen bright ideas" which illumed the lucid intervals of your fever—

As to the pursuit of Fame as an end I think you are very right.[1] In other days the love of Fame was but a noble, ardent love of sympathy men had time to feel, and reverence waited on renown. The celebrity of today is not more transient than itsⁿ flush and radiance are shorn of glory. Some portion of notoriety is desirable as a garb wherein one may confront the world and sheltered from its ruder breath dig and delve for real treasures.— I shall be glad if you abandon Love for the present.[2] When you *have* hoarded your treasures you will again feel the want of someone to partake them. What you have felt has answered every purpose in aiding to form your character. Many must love very early or never. The associations of youthful pleasure are necessary in common and unimaginativeⁿ minds to beautify an attachment Without some such redeeming point they would become sordid. Their love has its birth in dependence and its being in habit. But a strong and feeling mind must try many experiments and the love of its[?] maturity is not the need of sympathy but the joy of admiring. But the lights and shades of your character will harmonize more fairly as your sun approaches the meridian. I do not think you are now capable of feeling or inspiring a constant and ardent attachment. But your character will poise itself Those oblique and eccentrick movements now necessary to its progress shall be regulated the checks taken off your manners and the consummated truth be made manifest to all well-opened eyes inⁿ general and to some one soft dewy pair in particular Accomplish yourself my dear James, for the world here and beyond and in due time the taste for tête a tête dinners &c &c will steal upon your well warmed and lighted heart. You have now but flowers and fruit to lay on the altar of your household gods gems and frankincense will be expected when you shall consecrate a shrine for your own proper sacrifice. The Deities of Love and Peace must be conciliated by dear-bought and far-sought offerings. Your "young affections have run to waste and watered a desert" whence sprung "weeds of dark luxuriance tares of haste"ⁿ You must restrain their flow till you have built a fountain of pure and polished marble.

There *is* an idea in all this which I trust you will be able to disentangle—I am glad you did not Martinize last night;[3] if your feelings were such; An evil and perverse fate has indeed pursued your fathers family but "the longest lane will have a turning, the most vehement flood an ebb."[4]

You see I pity you no more than you do me! We shall at last believe ourselves enviable and Tuckerize every-think into the solution "Whatever is, is right"[5] A dogma which fortunately for human improvement can never be taught by any thing save Experience.—

I too am beginning to lay aside that infantine habit of making general reflections Une chose gagnée certainement!!

AL (MHi). *Endorsed*: Nov 1, 183⟨1⟩0

"Thursday" could be either 28 October or 4 November. Not only does the endorsement suggest the former, this letter is part of a series—some dated, some undated—that Fuller and Clarke exchanged the last week of October 1830. On Monday, 25 October, Fuller wrote inviting Clarke to her mother's party, which was probably held that week. The night of the party (Wednesday, the 27th), Clarke sent a response, which Fuller answered in this letter dated "Thursday eveg." She wrote again on "Friday eveg" to talk of dreams. Clarke answered (Monday, 1 November) and Fuller responded on 2 November. Thus this letter was written on 28 October and the following one on the 29th.

than its] than ⟨?⟩ its
and unimaginative] and unimaginati⟨?⟩ve
eyes in] eyes ⟨an⟩ in
of haste"] *Here Fuller made an* x *and wrote along the side*: "Blackness and ashes", Miltons apples; on such unsavory aliment we live to Knowledge. *She refers to* Paradise Lost, *bk. X, where Satan and his minions, now turned into serpents, feed on the dead sea fruit:*

> *fondly thinking to allay*
> *Their appetite with gust, instead of fruit*
> *Chewed bitter ashes, which th' offended taste*
> *With spattering noise rejected.*

(*Milton,* Complete Poetical Works, *p. 411*)

1. In his letter to Fuller, Clarke acknowledged that Milton and Joanna Baillie speak well of fame, but he went on to say that "the love of fame is a vanity which can never foster any really noble fruits. I give up fame therefore, except such a kind as is an instrument in carving out a man's fortune" (*Letters of JFC*, p. 25). Their text is Milton's "Lycidas":

> Fame is the spur that the clear spirit doth raise
> (That last infirmity of noble mind)
> To scorn delights, and live laborious days.

(Milton, *Complete Poetical Works*, p. 144)

2. Clarke had said: "I think too, Margaret dear, that I must give up Love," and then went on: "I doubt the possibility of any one's really loving me. I am too suspicious; I have too little confidence" (p. 26).

3. In his letter, Clarke had quoted from the scholar Martin in Voltaire's *Candide*; thus their talk about "Martinizing."

4. In 1829 the Clarke family was impoverished when the chemical factory that Clarke's father had built was destroyed by fire. Her quotation is unidentified.

5. Fuller quotes the best-known line from the closing of Pope's *Essay on Man*; the entire passage would have been relevant:

> Thou wert my guide, philosopher, and friend?
> That urg'd by thee, I turn'd the tuneful art

From sounds to things, from fancy to the heart;
For Wit's false mirror held up Nature's light;
Shew'd erring Pride, whatever is, is right;
That Reason, Passion, answer one great aim;
That true Self-Love and Social are the same;
That Virtue only makes our Bliss below;
And all our Knowledge is, ourselves to know.

(*The Poems of Alexander Pope*, ed. John Butt et al. [New Haven, 1951], 3:166)

997. To James F. Clarke

Friday eveg—
[29 October 1830]

Dear James,

That faithless swain never took my note. I was sorry and mean to send it yet though of no great worth for I cant bear to have any thing lost. 'Tis the most superb moonlight and I am oppressed by the most deadly melancholy. If I am not in my own heart perfectly happy the moonlight troubles me as much as even it did Lord N's skating hero.[1] The "beauties of nature" never could console me for any ill. I like to vivify them from myself. I do not believe any one finds peace from their contemplation. How can we? if bright, Nature jars, if clouded, she sadly analogizes with the troubled soul.— I do hope that at this moment you are either calmly asleep or reading some good book or listening to some kind and interesting friend; not looking into the beautiful vague of the sky for an answer to some idle question! I had last night a horrid dream. I have often undergone in the visions of night the anguish of bereavement or hope deferred and I have some-times[n] thought that at those times I learned to read strange secrets in the hearts of others which real life never made familiar to my own. This might account for my understanding so well and sympathizing so little. And some have believed that the soul lives most in sleep— But last night I suffered from mean jealousies and ceaseless suspicions of I know not what ill— At last I was in a room with a person whom I felt that I loved very much but whose face I could not see. I believe I urged or tempted this person to look up a chimney. I heard two loud reports quick one after the other; this person exclaimed "God Almighty" in a voice of the utmost anguish and horror, and seemed about to fall back into my arms when I awoke. I realized on the instant that I was no longer asleep but those sounds still rung in my ears and have haunted me all day.— Now what do you think of this dream?— Oh Jean Jacques the second. I think it may vie with the Haven dream; dont you? I shall certainly look out and twist something that happens into an interpretation— One feels mighty self-complacent at being the subject of such sublime intimations.—

And now that I've written all this which you will think mighty foolish I am very bright again. I dont know how[n] it is; there is a zest in telling things to unsuitable persons. I could not have said a word to those who would have heard with such delight and wondering credulity! Did you ever hear of a journal of dreams which Dr Holly kept?[2] I wonder what has become of it.— How *do* you do?— I fancy you did not like my first note or you would have answered it. If you dont give some sign this time, I shall forbear. I hear you are better; *will* you be well next

M.—

ALS (MHi). *Addressed:* Mr James F. Clarke. / Newton. *Endorsed:* Nov 1. 1830.
have sometimes] have some ⟨?⟩times
know how] know ↑how↓

1. Lord N is N. P. Willis, but his piece is unidentified.
2. Horace Holley (1781–1827) graduated from Yale in 1803. He was the minister of the Hollis Street Church in Boston from 1809 to 1818, when he became the president of Transylvania University (*DAB*).

998. To James F. Clarke

Tuesday eveg 2d Novr 1830[n]

How much your letter gratified me, dear James! There is a coherence and energy about it which pleases my taste. I understand and am amused by those scintillations which delight George so greatly, but such cross[?] lights are easily cast by the disdainful and embittered spirits of these days. A fixed and reasoned enthusiasm such as you here display is now much more rare; indeed! the only source of the romanesque on which we can draw!— Your generous confidence touches my heart—[1] I will not wrong it by professions and promises, whose folly, indeed, the past has shewn. Could I again wound you, I should evince something worse than caprice! Enough! That night-scene made me laugh, and smile, and sigh; Louisa is the most softly romantick character I have known. I was at first almost distressed by some instances which Sarah Whittier told me of her early dispositions.

At first I misinterpreted but afterwards felt there was loveliness in their folly.—[2]

The realization of hope which you describe *I* have never known except in *day*-dreams— All that I can recollect of the night presents detached scenes, sometimes ludicrous, sometimes distorted and terrible— Sometimes sanctified by ineffable tenderness. And I never felt this in a dream save to persons with whom I have a genuine magnetick[n] affinity. Waking I walk in delusion; I seek and fancy qualities in those I meet which they cannot possess. I force myself to esteem[n] many, to appreciate good-qualities which never roused one *answering* thrill amid my sensibilities. But in sleep Time and circumstance being unheeded, the interested blindness which springs from them vanishes and the liberated soul feels its nature and distinguishes its[n] allies.

Mrs Farrar, who is deeply conversant with these subjects, bases her[n] religion in a great measure upon them. It is enchanting to talk with her about them, there is holy beauty in the very boldness of her belief. She resolves both dreams and presentiments into that necessity of imaginative supremacy which you very clearly and beautifully discussed. She carries it several steps further; but I have an idea that I gave you an account of several remarkable circumstances which had happened to her. I have not formed a fixed opinion on the subject but I delight to hear what others think.— Me Roland, the most reasonable and clear minded of women tells this story in her memoirs.

"My mother had suffered more than a year from a suffocating disease in the head of which the physicians could not guess the cause. After having vainly tried different remedies; they confessed she had best trust to exercise and good country air. We determined on passing Pentcost at Mendon. On the morning appointed for our departure I did not wake as early as usual, a painful slumber oppressed me, checkered by sinister dreams. I dreamt we returned to Paris by water through the perils of a storm; when we wished to land, a corpse lay in our way; though[n] frozen with affright at this spectacle, I would have examined its lineaments, when my mother's sweet voice awakened me as she moved me on the bed. I was enchanted at seeing her as if she had saved me from something dreadful, and embraced her with the utmost tenderness. My mother seemed much better for the journey. I had promised to visit Agatha at the convent. My mother had intended accompanying me; but found herself a little fatigued. I would have given up the visit but she insisted on my going with Nurse and taking a turn in the Jardin du Roi before my return.

I staid but a few moments with Agatha. "Why in such haste" says she "is any one in waiting?" "no" but I would hasten back to mamma"— Why! you said she was well." "Yes, nor does she expect me. I dont know what torments me; I must see her" While I spoke my heart swelled in spite of reason.— I left Agatha with an air so singular that she begged me to send her a note next day. I hastened home though Nurse wished much to walk in the Jardin du Roi" She returned only to find her mother in the agonies of death.[3]

Me Roland seems disposed to resolve this by animal magnetism. Her theory is beautifully expressed and if you would like to see it I will send it you— There is something very fascinating in that belief that in proportion as we are fondly attached to any person we may become gifted with the power of foresight with regard to them. Just so Mrs Farrar believes that as we are more or less faithful to our true selves the spirit of prophecy will speak in the heart more or less— Would it not be lovely to think that in proportion as the ardor, purity, and clearsightedness of love are[n] magnified you might hope to take place of a guardian angel to the beloved.

I lend implicit faith to this recital of Me Roland's. She is a person of singularly cool, reasoning mind. She had shaken off a thousand fetters of prejudice and stood erect in a modest dignity truly remarkable. Why should we then deny her the nobler superstition which she had philosophically adopted?

Father is reading aloud the foreign news. There is a noble stir in the world; let us hope that soon the eye ear and heart shall talk busily to the mind and all that is morbid and stagnant pass away.—[4] This wicked pen has dragged my letter all into blots but I cannot write another—disregard appearances mon ami!

Wednesday morng

I was obliged to stop short last night being unable to shut my ears to the wild profusion of noises some angry, some jocular which suddenly[n] rose up in our usually quiet sitting-room. But today I have a few moments to myself. I would ask. Why, if imagination occupies the hours of sleep in extending and fortifying her dominion does she so instantly resign her sceptre when the eyes unclose to reality? You suppose the Soul to be then in its truest and best estate *clairvoyant*, reconciling, and discriminating to a wonderful degree. Yet how instantly does the light of day recal our common and meaner interests. Loves, so inferior! and pains unworthy an immortal throng instantly on the soul. Is it so natural to us to stoop We cannot endure to have a *reverie* rudely broken, one hours experience of *passion* will make common life distasteful for months. But how lightly and forgettingly we resign the pleasure of Dreamland.

AL (MHi). *Addressed:* To / Mr James F. Clarke, / now lying grievously sick at— / his grandfathers dwelling in Newton— / by the hands of a soi-disant, ci-devant friend. *Endorsed:* Nov 1 1830.

1830] *Elizabeth Randall wrote on the wrapper:* Poor James! may Hygeia prepare you for the party next week, & may your fine barber, the fever, *keep* your hair in its present exquisite curl. Elschen, on her passage—
    genuine magnetick] genuine m⟨g⟩agnetick
    to esteem] to ⟨?⟩ esteem
    distinguishes its] distinguishes ↑ its ↓
    bases her] bases ⟨?⟩ her
    way; though] way; th⟨r⟩ough
    love are] love ⟨in⟩ are
    which suddenly] which ⟨?⟩suddenly

1. Clarke closed his letter by saying, "I can trust in you. I dread no caprices" (*Letters of JFC*, p. 22).

2. Clarke used his letter to elaborate a theory of dreams and to describe several he had had, including one that began as a comic visitation and ended with the appearance of Louisa Hickman. Sarah Williams Whittier was Fuller's cousin, whom she often saw in her girlhood.

3. Fuller found the episode in Jean Marie Roland de La Platière's *Mémoires de Madame Roland*, in the section that concludes with her mother's death (*Mémoires de Madame Roland* [Paris, 1823], 1:216–17).

4. The *Boston Daily Advertiser* for this date contained stories on an insurrection in St. Petersburg, a revolt in Dresden against the king of Saxony, a revolt in Vienna, and disorders in Brussels.

999. To James F. Clarke

Wednesday eveg 18th Jany 1831

My dear cousin James,

I dont know why I hesitated so long about writing to you. For I can say very little; because you are still ignorant of a fact on which and by which my observations are at once grounded and proved true; I had half-hoped[n] you had discovered the existence of this fact. Since it is not so I cannot with any propriety hint at its nature.[1]

Yet I will endeavor to satisfy you— Elizabeth's conduct was not "systematick" that is to say, she did *not* reason with herself and lay down a *plan* for her conduct with regard to you. Her conduct was in each instance the spontaneous expression of impulses, which were however invariable in their action. After seeing you a process of this kind would always ensue— "I am sorry I am not happier[n] in James's society; how he has left me dissatisfied and pained. I admire some things in him I do not nor never shall love him; but why should I pain him?" After this half compunctious fit there was an[n] invariable revulsion of argument of this sort— "James does not really love *me*; if he *did*, if he loved me understandingly, he would read the language of my actions at once! He could not be interested and engaged when I am wearied and sad;" his pain would be too great; no! 'tis a phantom that he loves! Why should I by grateful patience continue the illusion? let him see me petulant and weary as I feel, and this film must be brushed from his eyes"— These" pros and cons would pass after every interview when her mind was not engrossed by some more powerful interest.

I regretted intercepting your letter because I think E. might have understood it better than a conversation during which she suffered so much— I looked upon you at that time as a man infatuated, and thought your fever must work itself off and that your pains would not be lessened by such sympathy as she could offer. I thought letter would lead to" letter and interview to interview. I think now it might have satisfied your mind to have sent that letter and that you would never again have imagined her ignorant of your feelings and acting in unconsciousness. I cannot in a letter enumerate the incidents which led me to either conclusion; but if ever you feel inclined I will tell you all of them. Perhaps a calm" unshrinking examination of the past may aid your future steps and prevent much of that anguish of misconstruction to which your fervency of soul and proud mauvaise honte of manner make you *peculiarly* subject where you best merit to be truly read.

For your other question "why I think you utterly uncongenial?" I can only answer at present— Elizabeth's lively and" flexible fancy requires continual food from the looks and actions of those she loves, nor could she warmly love any one who spoke to her in words alone and never *led* on her fancy—" But I cannot explain myself more fully I think I shall prepare a memoir of the past with full length portraits in reverse of yourself and E. but this I could not give you except in a certain contingency to whose occurrence I must not at present look.

In the mean-while be of good cheer, my excellent cousin. Most happy for you was it that E. could not be deceived into loving you. Of this I feel assured as ever. Your affections have *not* been wasted or consumed they will rise from these ashes fairer and brighter than ever— And that every painful experiment may lead you as much nearer Truth as this has done is the best wish my sincere affection has to offer you The beauty of Error is indeed great and her charms irresistible to the long protracted" youth of genius but I do believe that in Truth" alone can we hope to clasp the living form of Love. May your next Morgana lead you to a still" more elevated region![2]

affectionately your friend and cousin

MARGARET F.

My wretched near-sighted hand writing looks more awkward and unseemly than usual. Excuse it; I am very cold and headachy and cant do any thing properly; but had resolved to write to-night—

ALS (MHi).
half-hoped] half-⟨?⟩hoped
not happier] not happ⟨?⟩ier
was an] was ⟨it⟩ an
and sad;] and s⟨?⟩ad;
eyes"— These] eyes"— ⟨This⟩ These
would lead to] would ↑ lead to ↓
a calm] a ca⟨m⟩lm
lively and] lively an⟨y⟩d
her fancy—] her f⟨?⟩ancy—
long protracted] long p⟨o⟩rotra⟨?⟩cted
in Truth] in ⟨?⟩ Truth
a still] a ↑ still ↓

1. Fuller had intercepted a letter that Clarke wrote Elizabeth Randall. In his of 10 January to Fuller, he said: "You said you were sorry that you had prevented my explanatory letter from being given to her. Why are you sorry? You gave it as your final opinion that there were no sympathies between us, and that we were altogether unsuited to each other. Can you explain a little?" (*Letters of JFC*, p. 30).

2. Fuller probably refers to the fairy Morgane who appears in *Perceforest*, a fourteenth-century French prose romance.

1000. To James F. Clarke

[11 February 1831]

"I'll gang, I'll gang, Lord William, she said For ye've left me nae ither guide."[1]

And I may say so to you, my cousin, inasmuch as I have no way to answer your very kind and polite invite save by coming into town. Had you awaited my decision, I believe I should have contented myself with a *lecture* by way of evening amusement, being very desirous to[n] inform myself tonight respecting tomorrow's eclipse,[2] that I might not meet that delightful incident as an *entire* stranger and still more because my hon. papa (who little knows that when I leave home tis but to *vary* the *scene* of drudging my fingers with needles and my head with ideas) (well! This *is* a sentence; I always had supposed my style to be clear and concise; where was I) oh?) my papa coming home last night full of the anticipation of folding to his heart his long-lost daughter M. met her on the threshold just departing to that scene of *riot* and heartless dissipation a *levee*; and on the occasion gave vent to some expressions of disappointment and anguish which cut me to the heart. True! they did not prevent my going out *when I was dressed*, but they *would* have prevented my *dressing* to go out tonight (*especially* as there is nobody at home to fix my hair) tonight could I have let you know— Oh dear! I *must* come to the point. The state of things is this— My mamma is dining in town at this moment. She was to have come out in the stage; I will ride to her in a sleigh wherein she may ride out and if she will dress my hair; I will thereafter come to your house where I will have left this note on my way to Avon Place. But as to *conversation*,— I shall expect you to protect me from having a word of French spoken to me it would frighten me; I am too sensitive and enthusiastick to converse in any foreign tongue— "But there is something more," to use your own lucid form of connection; I am obliged by your mother and sister's politeness but believe I shall stay[n] the *night* with Elizabeth.

Now my dear James; dont you ever write a note again without giving a person a chance to answer it— And let me tell you I expect a little more ceremony even from you, mon ami, *bien*-connu— Is that French? No, yes, no matter— In English let me say— read Lamb and never more subscribe *"Yours &c!* to your
affectionate cousin

M.

ALS (MHi). *Addressed:* Mr James F. Clarke— *Endorsed:* Feb 11th 1831.
desirous to] desirous ⟨firstly and mostly⟩ to
shall stay] shall ⟨pass⟩ ↑ stay ↓

1. Fuller quotes from "The Douglas Tragedy":

> "O chuse, O chuse, Lady Marg'ret," he said,
> "O whether will ye gang or bide?"—
> "I'll gang, I'll gang, Lord William," she said,
> "For you have left me no other guide."—

Scott published the ballad in his *Minstrelsy of the Scottish Border* (*The Poetical Works of Sir Walter Scott, Bart.* [Edinburgh, 1880], 3:7).

2. Dr. Enoch Hale (1790–1848) was to lecture to Boston's Society for the Diffusion of Useful Knowledge on the almost total solar eclipse that was to occur on Saturday, 12 February 1831 (*Boston Daily Advertiser*, 12 February 1831).

1001. To James F. Clarke

Tuesday eveg—
[11 October 1831][n]

My dear Cousin,

I was very sorry to fail to my engagement yesterday but the rain prevented my walking out of town and I was obliged to bide[n] my Father's time. If you feel inclined to pour the lore of the Foreign Review into my desiring ear on Thursday afternoon, I will be at home and disengaged.[1] Tomorrow I go to Miss[n] Coolidge's wedding for no good purpose except to see Elizabeth shine in a new pearl set and big tortoise-shell comb.[2] I do not delight in the prospect of my eveg for sundry reasons but it cannot be *dis*agreeable except my entrée. have not answered your note I perceive. I like the Sonnet, not *as* a Sonnet however, so far from displaying[n] a single thought distinctly elaborated twas a fragment from a train of thoughts and not clearly expressed. Expliquez[?] moi "The soul of Each"— Does my Cousin believe that stately trees, pensive flowery &c have their souls. Is that your philosophy?[3]

—And if that[n] is the thing to be expressed it is a fault poetie[?] to talk of "new-spread wings"— I like to see the word Life used in its true sense and the last lines use—[n] tres belles or beaux according as the French word may be.[4] I am as bad at remembering du and de as Milord Byron but dont tell; you know all my reputation is for learning

—Perhaps you may think I ought to feel your Sonnet too much to criticize but you should remember you steeled me against it by such cheating, making me turn the page for one to my own eyebrow. I dare-say you will not-a-bit the-less send me the next; especially when I pronounce yours, though decidedly inferior to Petrarch, quite equal to S. T. Coleridge's

I poetize the events of my daily life!—[5] I! who can scarcely persuade myself that one of my emotions is worthy of a tear— and scarce respect the thoughts which produce so little sufficiently[n] to write them in my journal. I should die of humiliation at the end of a sonnet. Besides mine are *well spent days*. This for instances. Five livelong hours of it consumed in a visit to a dress-maker and sewing for my honored mamma. Two in studying Tacitus and reading French[n] with my beloved brother. My pleasures (the others were duties so called) reading Voltaire hearing the great trees rattle paying a visit at Mrs Channings[6] and looking at the new wood-box. I have not classed these in the proper order certainly. The wood box is *most* poetical I think of all![n]

—I hope it is not true that Dr Freeman is ill?— At E.s I read that tangled phantasm of passionate folly, Glenarvon, from beginning to end, and made some new remarks on that mist of hallucination and bewildered cunning the Dr's mind.[7] You did not come to hear Kathleen; it was as well, the evening was not magnetick (NB.) (I shall never explain what I mean by this)— I am swallowing by gasps that *cauldrony*? beverage of selfish passion and morbid taste the letters of Mlle Lespinasse[8] It is good for me— How odious is the abandonment of passion such as this unshaded by pride or delicacy, unhallowed by religion— A selfish crabing, only every[n] sound of enjoyment stifled to cherish this burning thirst. Yet the picture so minute in its touches is true as death— I should not like Delphine now—[9] I read a quantity of Allemagne in town but could not find Werner.—[10] Is your quotation from Richter or whom?—[11] "Pensive flowers," have flowers characteristicks in your eyes? When people talk so about them I always think if they are conscious how they must detest us! no wonder they wither near us. Douze heures sonnés I thought it was proper for me to write at midnight too!

If you have not seen Mr Alston's new picture should you not be charmed to go with me? I hear tis seeable at Miss Scollays for some days to come.[12] Farewell! your faithful friend

MARGARET F.

ALS (MHi). Published in part in *Memoirs*, 1:110–11.

Because this letter answers Clarke's of Thursday, 6 October, it was probably written on Tuesday, 11 October.

to bide] to ⟨wait⟩ bide
to Miss] to ⟨?⟩ Miss
from displaying] from ⟨?⟩ displaying
if that] if ⟨w⟩ that
lines use—] lines ⟨?⟩ use—
little sufficiently] little suffi⟨?⟩ciently
reading French] reading ⟨f⟩French
The wood box is *most* poetical I think of all!] ↑ The wood box is *most* poetical I think of all! ↓
only every] ↑ only ↓ every

1. Clarke had offered "to come and read the other number of the *Foreign* to you tomorrow" (*Letters of JFC*, p. 32).

2. Elizabeth Storer Coolidge (b. 1798) married George Merrill of Philadelphia in Newburyport (Newburyport VR; *CC*, 29 October 1831).

3. In his poem, Clark had said: "Why dost thou feel, my soul, this warm emotion / Raised by these stately trees and pensive flowers?" and then followed his question by the assertion that "The plant decays, the beast, yea man must die, / The soul of each moves onward, a new sphere / Receives it with its new spread wings" (*Letters of JFC*, p. 31).

4. "The bud of life in me has partly blown, / In them less opened, yet like that in me."

5. Clarke had said that he thought "it would beautify our lives if we would poetize the most romantic event or feeling of each day for each other."

6. Probably Susan Higginson Channing, William Henry Channing's mother.

7. In *Glenarvon* (London, 1816), Lady Caroline Lamb wrote a fictional account of her affair with Byron.

8. Julie-Jeanne-Éléonore de Lespinasse (1732–76) established a salon in Paris. Her love letters to the comte de Guibert were published as *Lettres de Mademoiselle de Lespinasse, écrites depuis l'année 1773, jusqu'à l'année 1776* (Paris, 1809).

9. Fuller was thoroughly familiar with the works of Anne-Louise-Germaine Necker, Madame de Staël. Her novel *Delphine* was published in 1802. Her book on Germany, *De l'Allemagne*, was published in 1810.

183

10. Zacharias Werner (1768–1823), an important Romantic dramatist, had visited Mme de Staël about the time he wrote his best-known play, *Der vierundzwanzigste Februar* (*OCGL*).

11. Clarke closed his letter with a quoted prose paragraph that began, "Nobody is so lonely in the world as an atheist" (*Letters of JFC*, p. 32).

12. Allston painted *Spalatro's Vision of the Bloody Hand* (based on Ann Radcliffe's *The Italian*) for Hugh Swinton Ball of South Carolina. In October, Allston objected to the exhibition at Scollay's, saying that the picture might be damaged (*The Correspondence of Washington Allston*, ed. Nathalia Wright [Lexington, Ky., 1993], pp. 296–97, 303). Catherine Scollay (1783–1863) was the daughter of William and Catherine Whitwell Scollay of Boston (*Bostonian Society Publications* 5 [1908]: 52).

1002. To James F. Clarke

[November 1831][n]

I asked that I might know what to think— I was sure what I felt. T'is not probable I shall have any return of the sensations imparted by your manner the days of the Soley's party[1] the note and the funeral— but if I do I shall speak them, you will say no and *I shall believe you.* So if you think of this at all let it be for your own sake and whether that be best, I shall not pretend to decide— Every thinking feeling being should decide within itself[n] its own way: and means— but there can never be harm in friends throwing across their light though it may be coloured &c All helps "mental culture". I hope you will feel that I am sincerely your friend

M.

ALS (MHi). *Addressed:* Mr James F. Clarke. *Endorsed:* Nov 1831.
Dated by the endorsement.
within itself] within ⟨g⟩itself

1. Fuller often visited the family of John and Rebecca Soley of Charlestown. Their daughter Mary had been Fuller's schoolmate at Miss Prescott's school in Groton.

1003. To James F. Clarke

[26 January 1832][n]

My dear Friend,
I thank you for showing me the letters— Your brother's is excellently written I wish you would go and speak next Tuesday in favor of

your friend— why should not you speak at *our* Lyceum?— Mr G. Chapman "distinguished himself" last eveg.[1]

All that relates to George must be interesting to me— though I never voluntarily think of him now—[2] The apparent selfishness and caprice of his conduct have shaken my faith— but not destroyed my hope— That hope, if I who have so mistaken others, may dare to think I know myself, was never selfish— It is painful to lose the friend whose knowledge and converse mingled so intimately with the growth of my mind, the only friend to whom I was all truth and frankness, seeking nothing but equal truth and frankness in return— But this evil may be borne— the hard, the lasting evil was to learn to distrust my own heart and lose all faith in my power of knowing others—

In this letter I see again that peculiar pride, that contempt of the forms and shews of goodness— that fixed resolve to be any-thing but "like unto these Pharisees" which were to my eye such happy omens— Yet how strangely distorted are all his views! The daily influence of his intercourse[n] with me was like the breath he drew, it has become a part of him— can he escape from himself?— Would he be unlike all other mortals? his feelings are as false as those of Alcibiades—[3] and of his also vanity is the spring— He influenced me and helped form me to what I am? others shall succeed him?— shall I be ashamed to owe any-thing to friendship? but why do I talk— for nothing can be more false than such ideas of independence— a child could confute them by defining the term *human being*— He will gradually work his way into light— if too late for[n] our friendship— not, I trust, too late for his own peace and honorable well being— I never insisted on being the instrument of good to him— I practised no little arts, no! not to effect the good of the friend I loved!— I have prayed to Heaven (surely we are sincere when doing that) to guide him in the best path for him, howsoever far from me that path might lead— The lesson I have learned, the severe chastisement my eager selfishness has received may make me a more useful friend, a more efficient aid to others than I could be to him— Yet I hope I shall not be denied the consolation of knowing surely one day that all which appeared *evil* in the companion of happy years was but *error*.

Your letter, like many others of yours, satisfied me except by renewing the wish that I could see *more* entirely and constantly into your mind than I do— I have written because I cannot talk so in midst of a family circle— Farewell my friend—

M. F.

P S. You ought to show *me* the verses— you have promised a dozen[n] times— I wish you would give me back the letter I wrote last autumn after H. Davis's party— I *must* burn it— George's resolve to "come as a hero or come not at all"—has disgusted me with all *that*— Dont read it over before you bring it.

ALS (MHi). Published in part in *Memoirs*, 1:83–84, and *Letters of MF*, 1:175–76. *Endorsed:* Jan 26th, 1832.

Dated by the endorsement.
his intercourse] his ⟨societ⟩ intercourse
late for] late ⟨into⟩ for
a dozen] a ⟨?⟩dozen

1. George Chapman (1809–34) graduated from Harvard in 1828 and from the divinity school in Cambridge in 1831. He preached in the Cambridge area until 1832, when he went to the West as a missionary. Upon his return to New England in 1833, Chapman was ordained at Framingham. Six months later he died of consumption (Harvard archives).
2. George Davis.
3. The Athenian Alcibiades switched his allegiance to Sparta and then back to Athens.

1004. To James F. Clarke

7th August 1832.

Dear James,

Where are you, and what doing? and *why* dont you come here? I feel quite lost; it is so long since I have talked myself— To see so many acquaintances, to talk so many words and never tell my mind completely on any subject. To say so many things which do not seem *called out* makes me feel strangely *vague* and *moveable.*—

'Tis true the time is probably near when I must live alone to all intents and purposes— separate entirely my acting from my thinking world, take care of my ideas without aid (c'est a dire[n] except from the "illustrious dead") answer my own questions, correct my own feelings and do all that "hard work" for myself— How tiresome 'tis to find out all one's self-delusion— I thought myself so very independant because I could conceal *some* feelings at will and did not need the *same* excitement as other young characters did— And I am not independant nor never shall be while I can get any-body to minister to me. But I shall go where there is never a spirit to come if I call ever so loudly— But I dont wish to anticipate the time when stones and running brooks shall be my only companions— and I wish to talk with you now about the *Germans*

I have not got any-body to speak to that does not talk commonplace— And I wish to talk about such an uncommon person— About Novalis!—[1] a wondrous youth— and who has only written *one volume*. That is pleasant! I feel as if I could pursue my natural mode with him, get acquainted, then make my mind easy in the belief that I know all that is to be known. And he died at twenty-nine, and as with Korner your feelings may be single, you will never be called upon to share his experience and compare his future feelings with his present.[2] And his life was so full and so still.

—Then it is a relief after feeling the immense superiority of Goethe. It seems to me as if the mind of Goethe had embraced the universe— I have felt that so much lately in reading his lyric poems— I am enchanted while I read; he comprehends every[n] feeling I ever had so perfectly, expresses it so beautifully, but when[n] I shut the book, it seems as if I had lost my personal identity— All my feelings linked with such an immense variety that belong to beings I had thought so different. What can I bring? There is no answer in my mind except "It is so" or "It will be so" or "No[n] doubt such and such feel so"— Yet while my judgement becomes daily more tolerant towards others the same attracting and repelling work is going on in my feelings. But I persevere in reading the great sage some part of every day, hoping the time will come when I shall not feel so overwhelmed and leave off this habit of wishing to grasp the whole and be content to learn a little every-day as becomes so mere a pupil. But now the one-sidedness, imperfection and glow of a mind like Novalis's seem refreshingly human to me. I have wished fifty times to write some letters giving an account first of his very pretty life and then of his one volume as I re-read it chapter by chapter— If you will pretend to be very much interested perhaps I will get a better pen and write them to you. But you know I must have people interested that I may speak. And I wish to ask you, now I think of it whether you feel as I expect people to feel about the *tasteless want of reserve* exhibited in my hand-writing.[3] I see I shall never improve— Now though I sat down with the best resolves I have written this letter just as usual. And so in my journal and even extract-books If I were a princess I would have a secretary and never write another line— I always fancy whoever reads this hand-writing must see all my faults. And I dont like to have them seen without my consent.—

I called on *Miss Smith* when in town but forgot to ask about your letter in proper times. Mark this— Amelia was charmed with your visit which you thought such a failure— "Such is the nature of social intercourse" Did you ever receive my invite for[n] that Sunday eveg to meet Helen[4] It is well you did not come. She was very angry with me again and probably you might have come in for a share— So much thunder and lightning is rather fatiguing— I dont think I shall venture near her soon

Mr Henry has returned to Cambridge and many other little things have happened which I cant take the trouble to write—[5] Miss Woodward told me she had lately[n] seen and liked you very much "Indeed she had always been interested in you on account of your family &c" Did you like *her*?— Have you seen Elizh— She is well and divides her time between hard piano practice and the study of *Johnson* and Mrs *Chapone!*—[6]

This is a sad blotting half-sheet I have taken, but I shall send this whole scrawl. I feel so much more natural since I began to write that I dare say I have nothing more to tell you and you need not come here. But write if you have encountered any-thing new or pretty. I must not expect die Grosse und Schöne.— With love to Sarah if she be with you yours

M.

ALS (MHi). Published in part in *Memoirs*, 1:118–19, 119–20, and *Letters of MF*, 1:177, 178.

aid (c'est a dire] aid ↑ (c'est a dire ↓
comprehends every] comprehends ⟨?⟩every
but when] but ⟨while⟩ ↑ when ↓
or "No] or "⟨n⟩No
invite for] invite ↑ for ↓
had lately] had ↑ lately ↓

1. Fuller appears to have discovered the poetry of Friedrich, Freiherr von Hardenberg, known as Novalis.

2. Karl Theodor Körner was a poet and playwright.

3. Clarke replied: "I do not know what you mean by *tasteless want of reserve*, except that your hand-writing has an individual character. It is not the writing master's hand, to be sure. It may be that ladies should not have an individual autograph, but I can not see why not" (*Letters of JFC*, p. 34).

4. Helen Davis.

5. Probably Caleb Sprague Henry (1804–84), a Congregational minister who later became an Episcopalian. Between churches at this time, Henry had been minister at Greenfield (where he undoubtedly knew George Davis). He later held church and academic positions in New York City. Henry was a prolific author and a peace advocate (*DAB*).

6. Which of the works of Samuel Johnson (1709–84) Elizabeth Randall read is not known; she probably had been reading Hester Chapone's *Letters on the Improvement of the Mind, Addressed to a Young Lady* (London, 1773), her best-known work. Hester Mulso (1727–1801), who married an attorney named Chapone in 1760, was a writer whose letters and poetry drew the attention of Johnson and Richardson (*DNB*).

1005. To James F. Clarke

[mid-August? 1832][n]

Dear James,

I send you the close of my translation which I would like to have you read— I have left out some of the Harp's Swedenborgian remarks; I found it so difficult to English them—[1] I send you also Körner's letter in this book I have turned down the leaf at the place and hope you will be able to decypher it— Return the book in a few days 'tis one of those which I compose my mind to rest withal after coming home from parties— Also two of your German books— It pains one to part with Ottilia—[2] I wish we could learn books as we do pieces of musick and repeat them in the author's order when taking a solitary walk. But now if I set out with an Ottilia this wicked fairy Associations conjures up such crowd's of less lovely companions that I often cease to feel the influence of the Elect One. If you have translated more from Hermann and Dorothea, will you send it me? If I see Elizh tomorrow may I read your sermon to her?— Here are the Cornlaw Rhymes![3] I went to the Levee last night and discovered a "genuine man" in Edmund[n] Quincy at least he said "I *possess my soul in patience*"!!![4] And he looked as if he might use the *last* word.— There is a leaf[?] which went astray somehow from the record[n] of the day which was *not* like my Thanksgiving.— What a business letter this is! I am obliged to rebuke my pupils between every sentence for all their little natural ways which surely go to prove the accuracy of Tiecks proposition that all[n] Krieg is natural to *man*

M.

ALS (MHi). Published in part in *Memoirs*, 1:117. *Addressed:* Mr Clarke.

Dated on the assumption that her reference to Novalis was written shortly after her initial comment on his writing in the preceding letter.

in Edmund] in ⟨the⟩ Edmund
the record] the re⟨?⟩cord
that all] that ↑ all ↓

1. Fuller may refer to one of the "Harfenspieler" poems in Goethe's *Wilhelm Meisters Lehrjahre*.

2. One of the main characters in Goethe's *Die Wahlverwandtschaften*.

3. Ebenezer Elliott (1781–1849) was a successful businessman devoted to radical politics and writing. Of his several volumes of verse, the best known was *Corn Law Rhymes* (London, 1831), poems that displayed his hatred for the laws that regulated the import and export of grain. The laws were designed to ensure a supply of cheap grainstuffs for the population but were often the cause of high prices paid by the poor and working classes (*DNB*).

4. Edmund Quincy had graduated from Harvard in 1827, two years before Clarke. He later became a reformer and abolitionist.

1006. To James F. Clarke

[24 August 1832]

[   ] If I believed you had been keeping your German journal daily for me I should blush at my own remissness, but I daresay you have been interrupted— I have had no time lately to feel a need of writing to you about German.— I have thought of you every-day however and sometimes often in the day and was very glad to get your letter which I shall answer in person.

I have suspended Novalis for more than a week because I have had the other two volumes of Körner (including to my great delight his life) and was obliged to return them next Monday.[1] Perhaps I shall talk to you about Korner but need not write; he charms me and has become a fixed star in the heaven of my thought, but I understand all that he excites perfectly— I felt very *new* about Novalis— "The good Novalis" you call him after Mr Carlisle—[2] He is indeed *good*, most enlightened yet most pure Every link of his experience framed (no! *beaten!*) from the tried gold.

I have read *thoroughly* (that is to say according to my present Ich) only two of his pieces— "Die Lehrlinge zu Sais" and Heinrich von Ofterdingen— From the former I have only brought away piecemeal impressions,[n] but the plan and treatment of the latter, I believe I understand. It describes the development of poetry in a mind, and with this several other developments are connected— I think I shall tell you all I know about it some quiet time after your return but if not will certainly keep a Novalis journal for you some favorable season when I live regularly for a fortnight.

I have had many visitors ripping up my time, some of them most "lingering unloved guests" Of *these* I, will not speak.— Leonard has *called*—[3] but most alas! I was not at home— Miss E. Peabody made me a two hours visit this morng and I have passed the whole aft. with Dr Follen and the Miss Cabots.[4] I shall be styled soon in common parlance "*fine*" and you will be "proud of me"

I have seen George and had a long talk with him— But will say nothing till I have finished seeing him. He has gone to Taunton for a day or two but will be here next week.

Little Flagg has made Amelia into a picture which looks very Wordsworthian.[5]

I have scribbled these slight remarks during a most animated shower— how the sun is about to burst forth in glory I must go into the garden to see it set— When you come back I hope you will show me the comet.[6] I have dreamt of it but cannot find it— I will leave this open— perhaps I may wish to write more— Today is 24th August— I am feeling very happy.—

ALfr (MHi). Published in part in *Memoirs*, 1:120–21, and *Letters of MF*, 1:178–79.

piecemeal impressions,] piecemeal impr⟨e⟩essions,

1. Which edition Fuller read is not known. There were by then five four-volume editions of Körner's works.

2. In the July 1829 issue of *The Foreign Review and Continental Miscellany*, Carlyle had published "Novalis," his review of the Tieck-Schlegel edition of *Novalis Schriften*.

3. Leonard Woods, Jr.

4. Charles Follen (1796–1840) was a German émigré who became the first professor of German at Harvard (*DAB*). He married Eliza Lee Cabot, whose sisters were Mary Clarke Cabot (1786–1846) and Susan Copley Cabot (1794–1861), daughters of Samuel and Sally Barrett Cabot (Briggs, *Cabot Family*, pp. 227–28).

5. George Whiting Flagg (1816–97), a nephew of Washington Allston, was a painter. Fuller may, however, refer to his brother, Jared Bradley Flagg (1820–99), who also became a painter (*DAB*).

6. A periodical comet discovered in 1826 returned in late summer 1832. It was visible to the unaided eye by mid-October (*Times* [London], 4 and 26 September 1832).

1007. To James F. Clarke

[ca. September 1832][n]

1st.—

I think this is true and that it would be better if none but descriptive or epick poems were allowed to the pupil— When the feelings are developed[n] by the little rencounters[n] of life. the pupil will find out for himself[n] their haunts of musical sympathy— If he should be obliged to talk to the moon, trees &c a-while first, thus making his own poetry, the delay will do no harm. *My* pupil shall learn musick *before* poetry, but shall not be fostered on either. This "partial experience" causes at last a tone of sarcastick langour. II. This thought is pretty, but one me semble there is a defect in the expression— The pictorial effect on the minds eye is confused and disagreeable.— I suppose you like the "ladder" better[n] than the "pinions" I *think* I do for people in general.— I *feel* that the pinions would suit me better than this economical ladder. But then again I *think* I will be content. III— I have no remarks to make about this— I should think it might be popular; it is a very consoling, reconciling way of interpreting the universe. T'is the spirit of Novalis's Lehrling zu Sais which I have just been reading— I *feel* as if I could believe it; if ever I leave my Sais and act out my feelings I will say what I think of the result— But it has always *seemed* to my *mind* that human spirits wanted something[n] definite and, as such, imperfect to cling to, and that only when[n] thus supported can they[n] act energetically. IV.— You should not repeat this affectation so frequently. V— "Philosophy!"— If metaphysical philosophy[n] be meant here— I do not know the Kantites but sich as Goethe and— Tieck give the senses their place, I think, ministring to and acting from the Soul and never to be lightly deemed of by her Essence-ship,[n] but still her servants only, (in a right state of things) and evidently *usurpers* when paramount, however prolonged and imperious their sway. "All-comprehending philosophy"? Is not that religion?— Must not all philosophy be eclectick.??— VI— Is very pretty and true. VII. No doubt we ought to be more ready to listen to those who are profoundly convinced of the truth and universal utility of their codes— This selecting opinions to gratify tastes is an insult to the heart, sure to be revenged sooner or later. IX— Perhaps no man can directly convert another without leaving his individuality— But the sight of a being so confident of his ground as to be unwilling to move is very enticing to the seeking soul, lost in an unspeakable labyrinth of doubts fears and conjectures. Will not such an one have many voluntary disciples? X. Yes XI— Very probable. XII. What is an Apothegm, if this be one?— It is a very well expressed opinion— Are Apothegms merely detached thoughts? XIII What is the distinction made between all these Ideals? Here is a feeling which I understand but I want the sister thought more precisely expressed. XIV. You believe all these things and yet maintain that the nineteenth century gives hopes of the perfectibility of man here below,— that hedging and ditching is better than planting and watering.

"The radical unity of nature" that is that nature is vivified by one spirit.

As to the recipie for preserving individuality of character, I never yet have met with one which satisfied me— Novalis makes his Lehrling listen to a number of sich till

"Der Lehrling hört mit Bangigkeit die sich kreuzenden Stimmen— Es scheint ihm jede Recht zu haben, und eine sonderbare Verwirrung bemachtigt sich seines Gemüths"—[1] And 'tis so with me— Each seems to me to have something right, for the mind which has felt how hard it is to preserve individuality has made one step towards it, and its thoughts on the subject merit attention— But nothing I have ever seen comes up to my wishes—

"Study the ancients and great moderns"— It does seem to me that the disciple's place and mood is more favorable than the usual one of the Censor passing judgement on the varied productions of many ordinary[n] minds just according to what he is— Yet most *active* minds are formed thus, and the other way lies greater chance of "slothful admiration," than generous emulation— But it is more intensifying.

—If you intend to succeed as a preacher beware of such phrases as this "The universal poet rests on the philosopher" VIII— This I understand perfectly and believe to be true— But how— *how* is it to be done?— If I could ascertain this much I should be satisfied—

I doubt not that one means of getting right is the refusing to speak what one is not sure one knows— I used to think, as well learn by one sort of mistakes as another, speaking whatever[n] comes into your mind makes it more definite, you can look steadily at[n] it; then throw it away or keep it as seems fit. But this mode of proceeding dulls the moral sense and whatever does that hurts the character more than it benefits the mind.

I believe I will write no more— I have taken no pains to think, but merely wrote down what struck me after reading yours— I am sensible that most of my thoughts are very shallow on these and all other topicks. I am merely quick to perceive; there is nothing profound, searching or creative in my mind— I have suffered all the evil influences of my day.

And thus I like this mode of learning— Another person brings all the thoughts— I pass judgement, choose and clap at pleasure

—Conversation is my natural element. I need[n] to be called out and never think alone without imagining some companion.— Whether this be nature or the force of circumstances I know not; it is my habit and bespeaks a second-rate mind.

Do you really believe there is any-thing "all comprehending" but religion?— Are not these distinctions imaginary? Must not the philosophy of every mind or set of minds be a system suited to guide them and give a home where they can bring materials among which to accept, reject, and shape at pleasure. Novalis calls those who harbour these ideas "unbelievers"— but hard names make no difference— He says with disdain "to *such*, philosophy is only a system which will spare them the trouble of reflecting"—[n] Now this is just my case— I *do* want a system which shall suffice to my character and in whose applications I shall have faith— I do not wish to *reflect* always, if reflecting must be always about one's identity, whether "*ich*" am the true ich &c— I wish to arrive at that point where I can trust myself and leave off saying "it seems to me" and boldly feel it *is* so *to me*, my character has got its natural regulator, my heart beats, my lips speak truth. I can walk alone, or offer my arm to a friend, or if I lean on another, it is not the debility of sickness but only wayside weariness— This is the philosophy *I* want— This much would satisfy me.— Then Novalis says

"Philosophy is the art of discovering the place of truth in every encountered event and circumstance; to attune all relations to truth.—

Philosophy is peculiarly homesickness— an overmastering desire to be at home"—[2]

I think so— but what is there *all-comprehending*, eternally conscious about that?

What I write seems so imperfect

—How I sympathize with Coleridge— vide ap. XIV.[n] It is wonderful that he ever wrote[n] a line—[3] No crisis— no eros— always drawn onwards— Shelley was all eros.— How full! how bright would have been his final conviction!

ALfr (MHi). Published in part in *Memoirs*, 1:107, 123, and *Letters of MF*, 1:182. Addressed: Mr. James F. Clarke.

Very likely this is Fuller's response to the sermon Clarke sent her in September 1832 (Letters of JFC, p. 34). *It may be a letter-journal of the type they favored.*
are developed] are de⟨p⟩veloped
little rencounters] little renco⟨ntr⟩unters
for himself] for hi⟨?⟩mself
"ladder" better] "ladder" ⟨?⟩better
wanted something] wanted somet⟨im⟩hing
that only when] that ↑ only when ↓
can they] can ⟨it⟩ ↑ they ↓
metaphysical philosophy] metaphysical philosop⟨y⟩hy
her Essence-ship,] her ⟨e⟩Essence-ship,
many ordinary] many ↑ ordinary ↓
speaking whatever] speaking ⟨an⟩ whatever
steadily at] steadily ↑ at ↓
I need] I ⟨?⟩need
of reflecting"—] of reflecti⟨o⟩ng"—
Coleridge— vide ap. XIV.] Coleridge— ↑ vide ap. XIV. ↓
ever wrote] ever wr⟨?⟩ote

1. From Novalis, *Die Lehrlinge zu Sais*: "Anxiously, the novice listened to the crisscrossing voices. Each seemed to him right, and a strange confusion overcame his spirit" (*The Novices of Sais*, trans. Ralph Manheim [New York, 1949], p. 51).

2. From Novalis, *Fragmente und Studien*, 9:566: "Die Philosophie ist eigentlich Heimweh—Trieb überall zu Hause zu sein" (*Novalis Schriften*, ed. Paul Kluckhohn [Leipzig, n.d.], 3:162).

3. Fuller refers to *Aids to Reflections*, probably to Aphorism XIV of the "Introductory Aphorisms": "In our present state, it is little less than impossible that the affections should be kept constant to an object which gives no employment to the understanding, and yet cannot be made manifest to the senses. The exercise of the reasoning and reflecting powers, increasing insight, and enlarging views, are requisite to keep alive the substantial faith in the heart" (Samuel Taylor Coleridge, *Aids to Reflections*, ed. Henry Nelson Coleridge [Port Washington, N.Y., 1971], p. 73).

1008. To James F. Clarke

Tuesday morn—
[November 1832][n]

Dear James,

I was half-sorry that I was not chez moi to see you last night— I felt so very— *very* bright— twas pity you should not have had the benefit thereof. I dont believe I shall be so much so again for *weeks*.— And was sadly checked on my return by a note from Elizh informing me that I cannot celebrate my Thanksgiving with *her* for the man who will not tell stories except when i'the vein hight W. Wells is coming with all his family to monopolize the cheer.[1] This is mighty disagreeable I have passed this day with Elizh so long— I cannot think of any one else I shall wish to be[n] with I think I shall feel[n] quite orphaned when the day comes— Now I think of it I will answer a note you sent me a fortnight since for I feel as if I wished to put a refusal and a protest on record— "Portraits"— I never again intend to be in "*such bad taste*" as to show any subject his or her face belimned and beoiled at a single sitting.[2] If I ever again *do* sketch to any lady or gentleman my ideas of her or his peculiarities such remarks shall be quite involuntary, flashing out in the heat of discourse.— I will not again be deliberately personal— *Why?* you may guess and, if you cannot, must remain in ignorance.—

I suppose you were not in jest in your predictions about the tomes I am to hurl down *on* the "foreheads" of the hapless Publick. (Is *that* grammatical?)—[3]

I know not whether to grieve that you too should think me fit for nothing but to write books or to feel flattered at the[n] high opinion you seem to entertain of my powers after such ample opportunity for observing all my weakness— I have generally supposed that people who spoke of me thus were dazzled by a superficial brilliancy[n] of expression which I am some times[n] excited into. But you have had it in your power to see perfectly the want of depth and accuracy, the ceaseless fluctuation of my mind— Still you think this— I can only say that if I ever do fulfil your prediction it will be indeed "against my will" and I am sure I shall never be happy

—Whether I was born to write I cannot tell but my bias towards the living and practical dates from my first consciousness and all I have known of women authors' mental history has but deepened the impression

—But I feel too variously on this subject to hope to be understood— I have often told you that I had two souls and they seem to

195

roll over one another in the most incomprehensible way— All my tastes and wishes point one way and I seem forced the other— But it skills not talking about this— I have felt lately as if I could resign myself to the stream of events and take the day at its due worth. It is at such times that I can learn— But I fear, *I fear* that I shall see my vocation too darkly to accomplish any-thing of consequence here below— if it[n] be as you think I shall surely resist conviction till the last moment.

Adieu, my kind friend— And no more of self for a long time I think except *incidentally.* But[n] I wished to speak *formally* on this subject—

very truly yours

M.

I forgot. Will you get from the library the 12th Vol Tieck and read 9th Scene 2d Act, and be amused.[4] Perhaps you may think it worth translating— I had not time before I sent it back.

ALS (MHi). *Addressed:* Mr James F. Clarke.

Dated by the reference to the approaching Thanksgiving holiday. The estimate of 1832 is based on Clarke's reference to her letter "two years since" that Fuller wrote on 18 January 1831.

to be] to ⟨f⟩be
shall feel] shall ⟨then⟩ feel
at the] at ⟨h⟩ the
superficial brilliancy] superficial ⟨?⟩ brilliancy
some times] some⟨what⟩ ↑ times ↓
if it] if ⟨if⟩ it
incidentally. But] *incidentally.* ⟨T⟩But

1. Fuller's reference is unclear, but W. Wells is probably a member of Mrs. Randall's family, for she was the daughter of Thomas and Hannah Adams Wells.

2. In an undated letter, Clarke recalled the playful vow she made in January 1831 to "prepare a memoir of the past with full length portraits in reverse of yourself and E." by asking: "What became of the portraits you were to draw some two years since of Elizabeth and myself?" (*Letters of JFC*, p. 35).

3. In the same letter, Clarke had urged her to write: "Margaret, you are destined to be an author. I shall yet see you wholly against your will and drawn by circumstances, become the founder of an American literature!"

4. Which edition of Tieck she describes is not clear.

1009. To James F. Clarke

[April 1833][n]

My dear Friend,
I cannot sufficiently regret that I did not read your Article while you were here that I might have talked with you about it— It is so excel-

lent, so able so satisfactory that I cannot endure the thought of its dying with me. I never have seen any-thing of yours written one half as well— Here is indeed the difference between the overflowing of mind and "intellectual effort"— The parts of the subject are treated fully, clearly and in proper sequence— the style is at once energetick and graceful the illustrations few but apt and definite.— What you say of the uses of ridicule, of[n] the distinction between extravagance and enthusiasm I like particularly. To make a criticism[n] or two just to season all this (and yet you know I cant be styled a *friendly* critick) "Mr Carlyle is a man of genius therefore" his style is not simple &c Goethe himself is the highest instance how consistent are the utmost delicacy of definition and individuality of expression with perfect simplicity of style. You give your meaning fully but would be open to attack here from the evil-disposed.[1]

Mrs Hemans's poetry could not force its way where there was not strong predisposition &c[2] I should think your remarks went to prove that *no* poetry could. You do not mention Wordsworth as one of the moral popular poets He may be styled popular in the best sense as he has exercised so much sway over the leading English minds— but is indeed not so with the young and ardent who are the Poet's natural audience.

The article is bold and I am not a sage counsellor— I cannot well judge what effect any-thing is like to produce on a New-England pub-lick with which I have nothing in common. But having acknowledged this I will say I think I should venture to publish it— You may incur some odium and the attack which would not have offended Goethe or Scott probably will offend Mr Norton. But enfin, you are a man also now, you understand this subject far better than he does and I cannot think that what pays such homage to truth is in reality irreverent to any one

—I therefore send the article if you do not decide to publish please give it back to me and if you *do*, give me one of the printed copies if possible.

Adieu, yours ever

MARGARET F.

ALS (MHi). *Addressed:* Mr. J. F. Clarke.

Dated by reference to Clarke's article on Goethe, which, according to his "Journal of Myself," he sent to the New England Magazine *in April 1833 (MHi). The editor accepted it for the June number, but, as Clarke told Fuller between 7 and 17 May, he declined to publish the article* (Habich, "JFC's 1833 Letter-journal," p. 53.) *The date of this letter thus could be early May.*
ridicule, of] ridicule, ⟨?⟩ of
a criticism] a criti⟨s⟩cism

1. On 23 April Clarke wrote in his letter-journal: "The day spent chiefly in finishing and transcribing a reply to Norton's article. I have some misgivings about it. It will make him very angry. I scratched out & mollified many angular expressions, but I could not for the life of me avoid being rather personal. I have always suspected that I had a vile tendency to polemics that would get me into trouble. I imagine the Prof. taking up the article, & saying What in THUNDER is this???!" (Habich, "JFC's 1833 Letter-journal," p. 48).

2. Many editions of the poems of Felicia Dorothea Hemans were available to Fuller, including one edited by Andrews Norton.

1010.   To James F. Clarke

Monday Eveg.
[ca. 22 April 1833][n]

Dear James,

I am obliged to go tomorrow morng without seeing Juliet or Belvidere or any pretty thing— Console me by writing about any beautiful realities you may encounter for I am going to a very sad *one*— But all will be bright I hope when the blossom hangs on the bough and then — you will come. Send me the journal and I will send you Tasso when I have finished it.[1] E has given me 2 lessons on the guitar and I am er case to sing— "Far from my thoughts vain / world begone" to mine own accompaniment

—I cannot write with Sarah's soft pencil adieu my friend—

M.

ALS (MHi). *Addressed:* Mr J. F. Clarke. *Endorsed:* Early in 1833—going to Groton. / 1832–33.
Dated by her reference to the translation of Tasso.

1. Fuller was completing a translation of Goethe's *Tasso*, which was not published until after her death.

1011.   To James F. Clarke

Groton 3d May 1833.—

My dear Friend,

I did not receive your "prendre congé" package until last eveg when on my return from Boston I found it lying on my table side-dished[n] by two letters from Eliz. and Anna Higginson.[1] Such a society to be collected round me in my little apartment at Groton in holiday dresses too, all three so courteous, soft bright, and easily entertained— Is this solitude?— I expected to see you in Boston but suppose you had some good reason either of fact or feeling for not coming— I did not care to see you in that (to me) most anti-imaginative and unloved city— But if you had come intended to propose a walk to Amelia's new home— but as you did not, read Plato with Eliz— instead— That morng[n] and no doubt he was a more profitable companion than either you or A and talked on topicks of as much interest as you could have done

—I think the verses beautiful— Opening your note and seeing that a page or two began with capital letters, I turned to that first and while reading them believed them to be translated from Schiller—

—I think you are wrong in applying your artistical ideas to occasional[n] poetry[2] An epick, a drama must have a fixed form in the mind of the Poet from[n] the first; and copious draughts of ambrosia[n] quaffed in the "heaven of thought" soft fanning[n] gales and bright light from the outward world give muscle and bloom (c'est a dire give life) to this skeleton, but all occasional poems must be moods and can a mood have a form fixed and perfect more than the wave of the sea. But perhaps I do not fully understand you— As to the balancing you know my *feelings*, but they are not *opinions*— There is no objection to your balancing; if the plan can fascinate you so; that shows you have need of trying an experiment which will probably teach you *much because* you feel the need of trying one— You are taking up these things just as I am forced to lay them down— perhaps my being *forced* to do so you would consider an argument in favour of balancing. My weary soul sickens at experiment or[n] system, but how great their delights to one to whom their combination is new!— I read great part of your journal last night with my eye and my heart not with my mind.[3] when this also has been brought to bear on your "transition state" I may be said to have read "attentively" and you shall have the result— I should indeed like to have[n] you keep your journal *to* me and write every evening—[4] I cannot promise to do the same because 1st my life is (as far as I can judge) singularly outward at present and I have no *need* to express my feelings— Now this may change in a day— an hour—but I do not *know* that it will and *therefore* cannot promise. IIdly I have much duty work to do at present, so much which, if not contrary to my inclinations, has no regard to them, that I do not like to bind myself to a friend in any-way— I would have my friendship's perfe[ct] freedom. But I will write when I feel like it and I dare-say that will be often— Do not regard what I do but fancy me all you wish.

—I saw Miss Kemble as I read your journal—[5] it is very strange to me to see a person who interests me and feel satisfied— But she was rather the end than the beginning of a train of thought— You ask me how I like my new home— I like it because[n] I can walk out of[n] or into it and never think of a prison— I have got some splendid far blue hills to look at and it does not hurt me now to think of distant things— I extend my arms and utter forth apostrophes beginning with Oh that!— no longer— I know my poverty but have no tickets in the lottery to make me anxious and all things are bearable except suspense and remorse— I have nearly finished the third act of Tasso— I could get through the *play*[n] in three days but have no time to write except in the eveg— I have read no German except Faust which I take every sunny noon to a wood about a quarter of a mile from the house and the birds and wind rustling their long-stepping feet over the thick carpet of last year's dried oak-leaves do their best to make me feel at home. The *appletrees* will soon be in full blossom and then I shall expect you— I will show you a "sweet pretty" drive along the banks of the river and take you to the wood where I read Faust.— But you have given Miss Kemble your translation of Geschwister and passed me by.[6] It is not right to neglect a friend for a stranger however talented and graceful— I will not give you a copy of *my* next work.

Adieu— I could write a much longer letter if I waited till we send to Eugene, but I think you must wish to hear from me therefore adapt this to[n] the post— I do not talk of Arthur, you perceive but I should if I sent you a *Journal*.[7]

As ever yours

M.

ALS (MHi). Published in part in *Memoirs*, 1:121, and *Letters of MF*, 1:181. *Addressed:* Mr. James F. Clarke. / Cambridge / Mass.—*Postmark:* Groton Ms / May 4.
   table side-dished] table ⟨i⟩ side-dished
   instead— That morng] instead— ↑ That morng ↓
   to occasional] to ⟨an⟩ occasional
   form in the mind of the Poet from] form ↑ in the mind of the Poet ↓ ⟨at⟩ from
   of ambrosia] of am⟨r⟩brosia
   soft fanning] soft ↑ fanning ↓
   experiment or] experiment ⟨?⟩or
   to have] to ↑ have ↓
   like it because] like ↑ it ↓ ⟨?⟩ because
   out of] out ↑ of ↓
   through the *play*] through ⟨it⟩ ↑ the *play* ↓
   this to] this ⟨letter⟩ to

1. Clarke had sent Fuller a letter that included a poem titled "Pour prendre congé" (*Letters of JFC*, p. 39), written on the occasion of the Fuller family's move from Cambridge to Groton. It was the custom to announce one's departure by leaving a card at friends' homes with P.P.C. ("pour prendre congé," literally to take leave) written on the left corner (Ivor H. Evans, *Brewer's Dictionary of Phrase and Fable* [New York, 1959]). Ann Storrow Higginson (1809–92) was the daughter of Stephen and Louisa Storrow Higginson (Thomas Wentworth Higginson, *Descendants of the Reverend Francis Higginson* [n.p., 1910], pp. 28–29).

2. About one of his own poems, Clarke said: "Poetry should have a form, fixed because perfect" (*Letters of JFC*, p. 40).

3. Fuller had apparently received. twelve pages of Clarke's journal (see Habich, "JFC's 1833 Letter-journal," pp. 48–52). After receiving this letter from Fuller, he wrote more (Habich, pp. 52–54).

4. Clarke had said: "I think of making my correspondence with you my only journal this term. I will tell you what I do every day. Will you do the same for me?" (*Letters of JFC*, p. 39).

5. Frances Anne Kemble, the English actress and author, had begun a very successful American tour in 1832 (*DAB*). She performed in Boston from 16 April to 17 May 1833. Clarke described for Fuller the reaction of a friend to Kemble's Juliet: "He thought her acting finer than that of any female he had ever seen" (Habich, "JFC's 1833 Letter-journal," pp. 55, 49).

6. Clarke apparently had his translation of Goethe's play *Die Geschwister* privately printed. He donated twenty copies for the fair held by the New-England Institution for the Education of the Blind (Habich, "JFC's 1833 Letter-journal," pp. 51, 55).

7. Arthur Fuller had suffered a severe eye injury in April when a servant accidentally hit him with a piece of wood. Clarke had opened his letter with words of sympathy for the Fullers (*Letters of MF*, 1:180; *Letters of JFC*, p. 38).

1012. To James F. Clarke

Monday June 3d [1833] a
beauteous day war[m]
brilliant and mild

My dear Friend

I part with Plato with regret: I could have wished to "enchant myself" as Socrates would say with him some days longer.— Eutyphron is excellent. 'Tis the best specimen I have ever seen of that mode of convincing— There is one passage in which Socrates, as it were aside (since the remark is quite a way from the consciousness of Eutyphron) declares qui il aimerait incomparablement mieux des principes fixes et inébranlables a l'habilite de Dedale avec les tresors de Tantale—[1] I delight to hear such things from those whose lives have given the *right* to say them. For 'tis not always true what Lessing says and I myself once thought

"F. Bon was fur Tugenden spricht er denn? Minna. Er spricht von keiner; denn ihn fehlt keine.[2] For the mouth[n] sometimes talketh virtue from the overflowing of the heart as well as love, anger &c.

Criton I have only read once but like it I have not got it in my head tho' so clearly as the others

The Apology I deem only remarkable for the noble tone of sentiment and beautiful calmness.

I was much affected by Phaedon but think the argument weak in many respects— The nature of abstract ideas is clearly set forth: but there is no justice in reasoning from their existence that our souls have lived previous to our present state since it was as easy for a Deity to create at once the idea of beauty within us as the sense which brings to the soul intelligence that it exists in some outward shape— He does not clearly show his opinion of what the soul *is*, whether eternal *as* the Deity, created *by* the Deity or how. In his answer to Simmias he takes advantage of the general meaning of the words harmony discord &c— The soul might be a result without being a harmony— But I think too many things to write and some I have not had time to examine. I shall have it again sometime: meanwhile I can think over parts and often say to myself beautiful, noble, and use this as one of *my* enchantments. One other remark— Socrates says death produces life, and life death. I think this as fallacious as to say that the *absence of light modifies light*.

I return Lessing— I could hardly get through Miss Sampson E. Gaelotti is good in the same way as Minna.[3] Well-conceived and sustained characters, interesting situations but never that profound knowledge of human nature, those minute beauties and delicate, verifying traits which lead on so in the writings of some authors who may be nameless. I think him easily fathomed, strong, but not deep.

You will be glad to hear that Elizabeth is much revived already by change of air and scene. She brought me a graceful note from Sarah which I shall answer soon Mr and Mrs Barlow are coming here today.— Farewell. I have been writing all the morning and my hand aches; but if I can I shall get ready your trans. to send with a few marks which you of course will adopt or not as you think proper.— As Ever

M.

ALS (MHi). Published in part in *Memoirs*, 1:116–17, 121, and *Letters of MF*, 1:183–84. *Addressed:* Mr. James F. Clarke. *Endorsed:* June 3 1833.

the mouth] the ⟨?⟩ mouth

1. Fuller comments here on Plato's "Euthyphro," Lessing's *Minna von Barnhelm*, and Plato's "Crito," "Apology," and "Phaedo." She quotes from "Euthyphro": "that he

would love fixed and immovable principles incomparably more than the competence of Daedalus together with the treasures of Tantalus" (*The Works of Plato*, trans. Benjamin Jowett [New York, n.d.], 3:79).

2. Fuller quotes from *Minna*, act 2, scene 1, when Minna responds to a question posed by her maid: "Of what virtues does he talk, then?" She answers: "He talks of none, for he is wanting in none" (Brander Matthews, ed., *Great Plays* [New York, 1901], p. 208).

3. Both Fuller and Clarke were reading Lessing's dramas: *Miss Sara Sampson, Minna von Barnhelm*, and *Emilia Galotti*.

1013.   To James F. Clarke

Friday morng June.
[14? June 1833]ⁿ

Dear James,

I have not written nor shall I now write an answer to your journal, because *I* do not feelⁿ like it; my thoughts have been so dissipated by continual talking and running in and out since Mr and Mrs Barlow and the R's have been here.[1] So I shall only say what is necessary now and be more diffuse some days hence.

I was not sensible Tasso stood in need so very much of correction I know nothing about Anapests &c[2] I believe we have no book which could instruct me: Have the goodness to supply a word whenever you see it has been unintentionally omitted: I will myself retrench and harmonize the redundant lines: I did however intend the use of such lines as "where Petrarch found a home and Ariosto models"—[3] I do not know whether they are according to rule and should be obliged to hunt for my authorities: but they are frequent not only in Shakspeare but other dramatists I think I shall retain them but can tell better after I have read the passages aloud. If any part is copied let me have it to correct: And Elizh says she will copy part if you can send it while she *is here*. This is the loveliest day— So warm!— And a thunder shower last night has freshened and purified the air. We are going out on the river this aftn under Mr Dana's protection.[4] Father is quite positive we shall be drowned and E. has dreamed a dream and feels a foreboding that "something dreadful will happen today." I keep thinking of Ottilia's last boating expeditionⁿ but natheless we are going.[5] *Write as if nothing had happened* do not be vexed by the meagr[ene]ss of this the spirit will prompt me to write a proper answer to you soon. If any more corrections occur, do not fail to send them "you see how much I expect from you"— I am vexed that Mr

203

Angier will not come I shall feel dissatisfied if he goes home without my having seen him.—

AL (MHi). *Addressed:* Mr. J. F. Clarke. *Endorsed:* No 1.

Dated on the supposition that this letter and the next went in the mail together and that they were answered by Clarke in his of Friday, 21 June.

not feel] not ⟨any⟩ feel

Ottilia's last boating expedition] Ottilia's ↑ last ↓ boating ↑ expedition ↓

1. The R's are the Randall sisters.

2. In a lengthy commentary on Fuller's translation, Clarke had made suggestions about her inept versification: "As to the versification, you take freedoms which may be allowable, but which I do not remember to have met with before in English blank verse." After several examples, he continued, "'Circumstance' is an anapest, I suppose. I should like to have you give me your ideas on this subject. I recollect hearing my Grandfather blame Byron's blank verse for his liberal use of dactyles and anapests" (*Letters of JFC*, pp. 43–44).

3. Clarke quoted three lines of her translation:

> Chance scatters again what she alone collected
> Of Wisdom and free thought while still
> Where Petrarch found a home and Ariosto models

and then said: "Omit the last word and is it not still a complete line?" (*Letters of JFC*, p. 44).

4. Samuel Dana, the Fullers' neighbor, from whom the Fullers bought their Groton farm.

5. In Goethe's *Die Wahlverwandtschaften* Eduard and Charlotte fall in love with two visitors, a young Hauptmann and Ottilie, a young woman. Despite the twin love affairs, Charlotte conceives a child by Eduard. He departs for the wars in despair, leaving the woman alone. Late in the novel Ottilie accidentally drowns the baby when she drops it over the side of her boat.

1014. To James F. Clarke

[ca. 17? June 1833][n]

[   ] The person who was to have taken the accompanying meagre note forgot to call— thus I have recd your little note pas Eugene— I am sorry you cannot finish your trans. I am not *quite* sure I shall wait for you for I do not think you will find the West a region favorable to such exploits and I doubt when you become more interested in the American outward world you will care less for the German world.[1] And since there is no hurry I can copy Tasso myself; so send it— 'Tis well that you have met with some romance in real life; but I do not understand.

I am not quite so well as when you were[n] here; but the dissipation of thought and feeling which hurts my mental health does good to E.

She is better, she is sometimes even gay and I think even such a new scene as this which if it" presents nothing to fascinate her feelings yet brings nothing to irritate them or to revive images" of past sadness would exhaust the vein of bitter and cynical feeling. Were it so I feel sure that I could submit to pass months with her thus; yet— you wrote to me of your inconsistencies now hear mine I have been so barbarous so false to the wishes of my heart and the intent of my mind as to have" been twice very angry with her and to express my feelings in a tone of most sarcastick violence and without regard to time or place— *This* is my "tenderness" thought I to myself. These passions came upon me so unexpectedly I seemed to myself so calm, so just, I can never be sure that I shall not sin again precisely in the same way— I made it up to Lizzy but for myself— James you were inconsistent, imprudent when you gave vent to anger which you could never *act* out, but what shall we say to such trespass against the spirit of a sacred trust, such weak indulgence of feeling as mine!—

We went out in the boat, a poor leaky nutshell but we were all *delighted Belinda happy.*[2] A radiant sunset, the river perfectly still, we glided down so gently, the girls singing sweet songs and when night came on the perfect" harmony of blue black and french gray the reflection of the shrubs and the thinly veiled stars conveying the feelings of purity and fixedness— The eye was filled, the mind gently stirred, the heart calmed.

Write something more about the pictures" I like "unripe" as well or better than" mature thoughts;[3] I often think if writing and talking people could act sincerely on St Pierres declaration "that his thoughts were unfinished but that if other minds should" by his endeavor be aided to superior conceptions he should be satisfied" I for one should not be malcontent— Pour moi, a Shelley *stirs* my mind more than a Milton and I'd rather be excited to think than have my tastes gratified— Besides I think your descriptions vie with Peter Lockhart's though I dont love paying such compliments.[4] I have read sundry books and *one* beautiful bit of poesy by— Mrs Hemans

> "Ay I did weep
> Kind heavens how I did weep."

But more of these things hereafter.— Send your poesy I pray you if you have or write any more; here I sit in the company of these beautiful hills all ready to read it—

When I look up at E. it seems wicked to be writing to you that her visit made me fell less well. You will never breathe it. I would not have her know it for worlds but the comments she makes on every thing do sometimes oercloud my courage of soul and her visit has brought me into a closeness of contact with the townspeople that seems to my taste morbid or otherwise profaning or at least un*nun*like; But I am not a nun and I feel it now about Eugene and I would ask a favor of you on the subject so very, very near my heart. He has no part I presume for the coming Exhibition as he writes nothing about it an[d] this time the parts must be given out. Now this I do not understand. I am sure he has faithfully if not ardently applied to his studies: and his habits have been so regular. Will you without speaking to him on the subject inquire about his standing and let me know frankly the result—[5] If he had got a part I daresay Father would have let him keep the Lieutenancy— I feel mightily dejected by his disappointment but can do nothing— Most willingly would I learn his lessons in Entsagung for him. I am used to it and he has already had a pretty number of the petty kind, but it is in this instance impossible. Let me hear [f]rom you as soon as possible about [thi]s and other matters.

Faithfully yours

MARGARET F.

AlfrS (MHi)
Dated by Fuller's reference to Clarke's letter of 14 June [1833] (Letters of JFC, p. 41).
you were] you ⟨are⟩ were
if it] if ⟨it⟩ it
revive images] revive ⟨former⟩ images
to have] to ⟨le⟩ have
the perfect] the ⟨b⟩ perfect
the pictures] the pi⟨t⟩ctures
better than] better ⟨a⟩than
minds should] minds ⟨?⟩should

1. On 14 June, Clarke told Fuller that he did "not have time to continue" his translation of Schiller's *Die Jungfrau von Orleans* (*Letters of JFC*, p. 41). He had already made his decision to leave Boston to become a minister in Kentucky.

2. Elizabeth Randall's sister Belinda.

3. After describing his reactions to several paintings in his letter written in the first week of June, Clarke concluded: "And thus I have been led to give you my unripe ideas. You must excuse me if a more thorough study places me on another point of view" (*Letters of JFC*, p. 48).

4. Fuller probably refers to John Gibson Lockhart, who wrote *Peter's Letters to His Kinsfolk* in 1819.

5. Clarke responded with news that Andrew Preston Peabody said that Eugene's "chance of a part was small—that his recitations in some departments were rather good (he specified Latin and Greek), but in others, poor. He said that in composition and modern languages his rank was quite low—in the last he had received no mark for the three last recitations" (*Letters of JFC*, pp. 50–51). The exhibition was held on 29 April 1834. Eugene and Hiram Wellington gave "A Conference: 'The Comparative Influence of Literary and Political Institutions, in Forming Individual Character.'" At the graduation of 27 August 1834, there were 26 parts for the 52 members of the class. Eugene

Fuller did not receive one. On 14 July he was directed by the faculty to study Whately's *Rhetoric* during vacation, sit for an examination on the Saturday preceding graduation, and pass the exam as a condition for graduation (Harvard archives).

1015. To James F. Clarke

Monday eveg 1/4 past
nine
[24 June 1833][n]

My dear Friend,

The intelligence you send me about Eugene afflicts me greatly I thought my expectations about him were so moderate. I had laid their foundations in such intimate knowledge, I could not be disappointed— Will you write tomorrow about it by the man who brings this— I am the more surprized on account of the *branches* in which he is spoken of as deficient. He has studied no modern language except French. I taught him almost all he knows in that myself; to my certain knowledge, he must be better acquainted with it than most students and he has several times been complimented on his proficiency. Two of his themes have been "paralleled" not long since. His comfort for many years, his means of success which to a mind like his is necessary depend on his college rank. But I will not trouble you with this, only let me know the result of your examination of the college books.

Thanks for the corrections. I shall improve by them.[1]

Have had a letter from Mrs Farrar in which she tells me Mrs Robinson[2] was charmed with you and another from A. Higginson who mentions having invited you to a stroll to Mt Auburn by which she intends "to commemorate the summer" Pray give notes thereon; it *must* have been amusing.

Elizh grows better daily and *I* am better now. I am not sure but my bad feelings were attributable chiefly[n] to a feverish cold which had been poisoning my system with each new breath more and more for a fortnight. I have given the fever its congi after 36 hours confinement to the bed and a quantity of horrible beverages, but I have the cold still yet am much happier and am gradually getting subdued to consider health a blessing. To give you an idea of E's improvement she said Sunday, after some reflection, that she was not *sure* it would be best for me to go into a consumption, *this* summer. She would not have said that a month since. She bids me tell you that she has serious thoughts of joining the Shakers and now she bids me tell you that she

207

did *not* bid me tell you any such thing or any thing else; no! not any thing else but something else. This message is all her own I assure you she has really shown originality here"

You know which of us has nonsense to spare." This last is all repetition, I know. Excuse us gay beings for filling up your valuable time which must be particularly engaged just at present with this somewhat superfluous matter not to say stuff." What a dear little hand. I wish I could write so, but my little finger aches desperately and puts a stop to ineffectual attempts at rivalry. For I have been writing all day.

Adieu! will you call this a charming letter? Seriously I am yours

M.

ALS (MHi). *Addressed:* Mr James F. Clarke. / Cambridge.
Dated from Clarke's letter of Friday, 21 June, which Fuller here answers (Letters of JFC, *pp.* 50–51).
attributable chiefly] attributable ↑ chiefly ↓
here] *Here Elizabeth Randall wrote:* It is all Margaret's nonsense—
spare.] *Here Elizabeth Randall wrote:* So of course, you will not hesitate as to who is the author of the above message.
stuff.] *Here Elizabeth Randall wrote:* Ridiculous insinuation! "Wherever Miss E. is, there is nonsense" I suppose she would say—
1. Clarke commented on the syntax of her *Tasso:* "We read this, expecting the verb to follow the adjectives; you mean it to be understood before them" (*Letters of JFC,* p. 51).
2. Therese Albertine Louise van Jakob Robinson, a linguist who knew Goethe, had emigrated with her husband to the United States. Under the pen name Talvi she published *Volkslieder der Serben* (Halle, 1825) and translated John Pickering's *Über die indianischen Sprachen Amerikas* (Leipzig, 1834). Clarke described his meeting with her in a recent letter to Fuller, who met Robinson in September (*Letters of JFC,* p. 47; *Letters of MF,* 1:208).

1016. To James F. Clarke

Groton 27th July 1833

My dear Friend,

I wish to write to you so vehemently that I must— *must* do it, albeit quite contrary to my judgement for I was vexed at the coldness with which you expressed a hope of hearing soon from me and thought in my heart you should not so very soon. But I cannot wait any longer I am so desirous to sympathize with you in success— oh how delightful to feel that good is visibly descending on *one* of my friends— they have all been so disappointed and tortured that I have often felt as if blight had fallen on all connected with me and even with you,

James.— I was prepared to see you never estimated as you deserved, to see the results of all your efforts imperfect and only to be consoled by the feeling that there was nobleness in them which would bear its blossom and fruit but leider, not in your time But what I now hear from all quarters convinces me that it will not be so— my friend, shall himself reap the reward of his faithful endeavor of his "generous seeking"— I hear from all quarters, praises of your performances of late but particy at the late examination All are agreed about that and I perceive that both in matter and manner you were[n] thought to take preceden[ce] of one whose energy of mind and character my own feelin[   ] had tested and who would, I believed, make a pro[   ] impression wherever he should feel sufficiently inte[   ] to attempt it."[n] But I perceive the impression you produced was far more distinct, entire, and satisfactory— Even Mr Barlow who, naturally enough has always shown disinclination to acknowledge that "you were much" made haste to express to me the altered state of his convictions. He spoke with great warmth of the feelings with which you had inspired him although he said looking at me with a comick expression he "knew he was making me feel altogether too grand about my cousin." I attached more importance to his expression of feeling than to any of the many which have reached me because I know he is a man who has not the slightest natural sympathy with you; no production of yours could have reached his mind through the *affinities.*—[1]

And you are gone— and you will prosper— you will improve daily— It is well— just what I wished and yet I regret your departure[n] surprisingly. I am not just where I have so often wished to be— I am alone— inasmuch as the communication I can have with any human being must be fragmentary and imperfect— it is impossible that any whom I know now should have [a]ccess at will to my confidence— I shall not have profound [i]ntellectual sympathy with any one— I feel my situation [n]ow profoundly but calmly— Two years ago when I began [   ] realize all I must do for myself or be lost, I could [   ] think of it a moment without anguish— I thought I never never could see this day with composure. Yet I have often wished for it and most of all when borne beyond myself I have related to you some page of feeling and you would hear me with cold gravity, then rise and leave me. O how I hated that impulse which showed me a slave for I gave my heart's blood unpaid—a child—an infant still, for I sinned against my own conviction and violated my character.

But I have no such feeling now for it seems right to commemorate the breaking up of our intimacy by speaking frankly what is in my mind at this time.— We must I think be both of us quite grown up now. The wor[ld] receives you as a man— and I feel as if my characte[r] had taken its tone and as if there might be ornaments added and wealth accumulated there or the reverse but as if the fabrick was now shaped into proportion and its altar dedicated.

I longed (may I say it without irreverence) to give you my *blessing* when you departed— to express the nature of my hopes and expectations for you, in appropriate words[n] to compress all I had ever thought and felt towards you in the retrospect of a few hours. But your manner repressed me and it was well I believe for a thousand of those things styled extravagances in this working day world were in my head to do.

Now that I have lost you I think of you constantly and if you were near enough should certainly write for you the journal I refused to keep three or four months ago— I believe I have spoken to you of the imaginary conversations I love to hold with the living and dead. Yesterday I took Hood's and Pinkney's poems and Miss Martineau on Scott into the wood.[2] I passed three or four hours there reading passages[n] from them and conversing with you about it. I assure you your talk was fine. At least you delivered a long tirade about colouring in reference to the beautiful light which was shimmering across the wood. I was much pleased with your ideas. At last a bird flew past me and I laughed to perceive that I am still myself. I have talked with you also about two chapters in a book called "Saturday Evening" by the author of Histy of Enthusiasm. If you have ever met with it send your real ideas; the two chapters are "The Recluse" and "The few noble."[3] I expect the dose of Cambridge I am to take in the autumn will dispel all these wild [f]ancies— Sometimes I feel so wild and free— I mourn [ ]at I was not brought up in this solitude. I must [   ] have been greatly blest and good or greatly wretched. Now mediocrity has got and will keep me. I have a great mind to cross my letter throughout[n] as it is going so far though you *did* say you would not be bribed to read such an one as Elizabeth's. But perhaps you *could* not read it. Adieu— yet stay one word. I thought I perceived in your manner such a feeling as I had when I came here. A wish to forget the old and press forward to the new— to surrender the whole mind to a new impression till one had tried its influence— One of those natural ugly George Davis feelings. They *are* outwardly ugly but they are natural therefore right—[n] If you were here you would half shake your head in a provoking manner and say "I dont understand you" with a look which seems to add "False feeling I doubt." What I would say is if you wish not to write, if you do not wish to break in on the entireness of your first impressions by communicating them do not— do not; wait till the spirit prompts— Let us be free in friendship [   ] world confines us close enough in all else— And now Adieu.

28th— I have read over this letter and I^n find its style and arrangement by no means *perfect*. But I feel so much more at ease since I have written that I am resolved to send it— I have a strange liking for sending you these foolishly frank uninterpreted letters I believe I spend all my practical faith of the sentimental sort on you.

AL (MHi). *Addressed:* Revd. James F. Clarke. / Louisville, / Kentucky. *Postmark:* Groton Ms / July 29. *Endorsed:* July 29 S. M. F. (No 1. Ky.).
you were] you ⟨a⟩ were
to attempt it.] to ⟨show himself—⟩ ↑ attempt it. ↓
your departure] your ⟨absence⟩ ↑ departure ↓
appropriate words] appropriate ↑ words ↓
reading passages] reading ⟨their⟩ passages
letter throughout] letter ⟨throughout⟩ throughout
therefore right—] therefore ⟨?⟩ right—
and I] and ↑ I ↓

1. Clarke had just left for his new position in Louisville. In response to this praise of his abilities, he told Fuller of the failure of the sermon he had just preached: "In the midst of my sermon yesterday half a dozen women got up and walked out. And the whole congregation did not amount to thirty, and I was convinced from first to last that my words were falling like water on a rock" (*Letters of JFC,* p. 57).

2. Fuller probably read Thomas Hood's *Whims and Oddities in Prose and Verse* (London, 1826) or his *Plea of the Midsummer Fairies* (London, 1827). Edward Coote Pinkney (1802–28) was the son of William Pinkney, one of the diplomats who adjusted claims with Great Britain under the Jay Treaty. The younger Pinkney was a naval officer and editor; his *Poems* appeared in 1825 (*DAB*). Harriet Martineau published her "Characteristics of the Genius of Scott" in the December 1832 and January 1833 issues of *Tait's Edinburgh Magazine.*

3. Isaac Taylor, a lay theologian who wrote *A Natural History of Enthusiasm* in 1829, published *Saturday Evening* (London, 1832) anonymously. The topic of "The Recluse" is "add to godliness, brotherly kindness," in which Taylor says "there is, perhaps, no order of sentiment which reason cannot approve, and which Christianity condemns, that more strongly recommends itself as innocent and excellent, than that of a secluded meditative piety" (p. 188). "The Few Noble" defines the paradox of Christian nobility even though "the most conspicuous or notable praise of Christianity is its fitness to benefit the undistinguished mass of mankind." Taylor acknowledges that "here and there is found one who admits the religion of heaven in its own manner, and imbibes its sublimity and beauty without detriment" (pp. 339, 342).

1017. To James F. Clarke

Groton 17th August 1833

Dear James,

I received your Marietta letter some days since but deferred answering hoping to hear from you first at Louisville— Having located you and got some expression of sentiment in answer to mine sent some three weeks since I thought I should like writing to you better— For my feeling towards my corres— was expressed by a lady who was here this aftn when my mother pressed her to come some day and take tea "With pleasure Madam when you and Miss Fⁿ have been at *our house.*" But a lingering of vanity or as you would call it Faith makes me believe you must be wishing to hear from me and the letter will be so *long* going—

One or two iotas before I get carried away by my feelings!— I wish you not to pay the postage of your letters— do you pay for mine and I will for yours— That is much the most simple way of adjusting such matters— Then address to Miss Fuller care Hon T. Fuller and not to my father for me as before—

What does James mean when he talks of "feeling dull in crossing the mountains?"[1] And what sort of *dull*— Never use the word.

I have been living a very unindividual life— My morngs are passed in instructing the children— This I do very thoroughly as far as I go— I have the satisfaction to perceive that they make some progress and have inspired some desire to excel— [*illegible*]! how I used to feel when I heard these phrases used about any body. I have been sewing till my spirit is faint from inanition— If weaving has any [ten]dency to inspire poetical thoughts it must be something in the nature of the motion— All other sitting-still occupations are chilling and cramping— I have read nothing (to signify) except Goethe's Campagne in Frankreich— Have you looked through it and do you remember his intercourse with the Wertherian Plessing—[2] That tale pained me exceedingly— We cry Help— help and there is no Help— in man at least.— How often I have thought if I could see Goethe and tell him my state of mind he would support and guide me— he would be able to understand— he would show me how to ruleⁿ circumstances instead of being ruled by them and above all he would not have been so sure that all would be for the best without our anⁿ effort to act out the oracles he would have wished to see me what Nature intended— but his conduct to Plessing and Ochlenschlager shows that to him also an appeal would have been vain![3]

My brothers have been here dashing about and enjoying every thing to the fulness of animal spirits— I went about with them a great deal— had a juvenile party and played blindman's buff and forfeits till twelve o'clock at night— Also I have given Eugene a lesson daily in German and I think when he goes back he may laugh Dr Follen to scorn— but what skills it? I have now sounded his spirit through— he is a sweet youth— may perhaps be a good and happy man— but he has no ambition I shall never have the pleasure of feeling enthusiastically about him and here also must dispense with a future. Charles Emerson is engaged—to Elizabeth Hoare— very excellent![4] The connexion proves that *he has* a heart and she has one which must have ached unless filled by some large object; it is not of the class which possess such contractile powers.— I dont know whether you heard of Wm Russell's engagement— I confess I did not think the lovely Anna could have been forgotten so soon

Sunday 18th I wish I'd had this pen when I began— I've blotted my letter even worse than you did yours. I was interrupted yesty by a visit[n] from a demoiselle whose mode of being seems peculiar. Mr Farley is a "rising" lawyer he has a pretty house, a good looking wife and three little daughters; the eldest aged sev[en] Miss Rice (my visitor and Mrs F's sister)[n] lives with them—[5] Mr F earns for his children— Mrs F. sews for them and otherwise takes care of their physique— Miss R of their minds and she has got these two little beings into such drill that the youngest a child not quite six years old is reading Virgil and can write a tolerably good hand of the childish sort. She says this little creature studies hard four[n] hours per diem 5 days in the week. They live quite secluded Miss Rice appears to have no society and no pleasures except that of reading Latin Authors in the evegs with Mr Farley— And thus has she passed six years of her life— I should think her five or six and twenty, sh[e] dresses gaily has a fresh colour, and a bright, cheerful, though not handsome countenance— If Mr Farley was a man of captivating manners or brilliant talents I could understand his persuading her to pass her youth in this manner but nothing can be more earthy and sensual than the expression of his countenance. He called here the other day and gave me an account of his system of education which he confessed he considered as an experiment. He is making himself as completely responsible for his children as Rousseau would have been for his Emilias for he and his coadjutor Miss R. may be said to bar out all foreign influences from them—[6] I doubt whether the result prove a happy one— The rural publick every whit as malicious and gossiping as a city one have not scrupled to whisper certain calumnies against Mr F. and Miss Rice which I utterly disbelieve as they might naturally be suggested in this envious world by the singularity of their mode of living, because I do not believe any man will give his daughters into the care of a woman whom he does not respect and thirdly and mostly because the parties having heard these slanderous reports calmly and absolutely disregard them— Still I should like to know what Miss Rice proposes to herself in life— I suppose I might find out for she seeks my acquaintance apparently because she thinks me learned but I grow too indifferent now-a-days to develope people that are neither beautiful nor heroick.

Elizabeth has been passing two or three weeks at Newport— Her letters to me have of late expressed more resignation and hopefulness— But W. Pickering has now returned to Boston and the sight of him may have power to re-open the springs of bitterness— George D. sent me a message about your success Mr Angier has notified me that he is coming hither this week but I fancy tis more moonshine. Many *old* Cambridge people have visited me this ten days last in passing among others Charles Stuart.[7] This youth was well-dressed, in high spirits, seemed to think himself getting on finely in the world and that it was not so bad to have the bitter before the sweet— He is about to become coeditor with Lord N. P. Willis!—[8] Time is indeed a leveller if not a comforter.

I am well aware, my friend that this is a miserable, commonplace journalizing letter— I dont believe I shall write another such but when I began I fancied myself i'the finest mood— I intended[n] to have given you some ideas suggested by the Shaker worship which I saw for the first time last Sunday[n] but cannot now.— Let me hear from you something of the outward life, but *more* of the inward— Farewell— as ever yours

MARGARET F.

P. S. Say whether you dislike reading *crossed* letters.[9] I have a great many questions to ask you but wait hoping you will answer without having heard them and supposing you would prefer my being somewhat egotistical.

ALS (MHi). Published in part in *Memoirs*, 1:122, and *Letters of MF*, 1:181–82. Addressed: Revd. James ⟨I⟩ F. Clarke. / Louisville, / Kentucky.— *Postmark:* Groton Ms / Augt 19th. *Endorsed:* S. M. F. Aug 19. No 2 Ky.
you and Miss F] you ↑ and Miss F ↓
to rule] to ⟨master⟩ ↑ rule ↓
our an] our ⟨?⟩ an
a visit] a ⟨letter⟩ visit
visitor and Mrs F's sister)] visitor ↑ and Mrs F's sister ↓)
hard four] hard ⟨?⟩ four
I intended] I ⟨f⟩ intended
last Sunday] last ⟨s⟩Sunday

1. "Four days spent in crossing the mountains to Wheeling," said Clarke in his letter of 31 July, "made me quite dull again, notwithstanding the excitement of stage accidents, a pleasant Baltimore girl for a companion to Cumberland, and the horrible jolting of the National Road" (*Letters of JFC*, p. 56). When he answered this Fuller letter on 9 September, Clarke said: "The journey, the prospect before me, the novelty aroused me, the chain which I dragged after me, uncoiling at each remove, the thought that I *ought* to think and feel a great deal, united together in shutting up my mind" (*Letters of JFC*, p. 59).

2. Goethe's *Campagne in Frankreich 1792* was published as part 5 of *Aus meinem Leben*. Friedrich Viktor Plessing had corresponded with Goethe.

3. Adam Gottlob Oehlenschlager was a Danish author.

4. Charles Emerson, Waldo's younger brother, died before he could marry Elizabeth Hoar, who became one of Fuller's closest friends.

5. George Frederick Farley, who had moved to Groton in 1832, graduated from Harvard in 1816 and was admitted to the bar in 1820. In 1823, he married Lucy Rice (1799–1854), daughter of John and Lucy Hubbard Rice of Ashby. Fuller appears to mistake the daughters, for the Farleys had only two, Mary and Sarah. Farley was a gifted lawyer whose oratory often ran to sarcasm. Mrs. Farley's sister is unidentified (Groton VR; *Groton Historical Series*, 2:325; Davis, *Suffolk County*, 1:358).

6. Rousseau's *Émile* (1762) described his views on an ideal education of Émile and Sophie, his fictional children. One of Rousseau's ideas was that education of the young should avoid books, moral reasoning, and appeals to authority.

7. Charles Stuart (1811–80) graduated from Harvard in 1830 and later became a lawyer. He was known for his ability to compose Latin and Greek verses (Harvard archives; *1830. H.U. Memoirs* [Boston, 1886]).

8. N. P. Willis, an editor (with George P. Morris and Theodore S. Fay) of the *New-York Mirror*, was then in Europe, sending back articles to the paper. Stuart's name did not appear among the list of editors, though he may have been working for the *Mirror*.

9. In reply, Clarke said: "Like my letters crossed? Yes, best one, cross and recross them until they resemble a darned place in a stocking. . . . I will emulate Champollion for the sake of having one more of your thoughts to ponder and appropriate" (*Letters of JFC*, p. 59).

1018. To James F. Clarke

Groton 30th August *1833*

Having just rode home with the Revd C.— Babbidge I think I must be in a frame of mind well suited to converse with the Revd J. Clarke—[1] For I could not but smile to perceive from several little items how fully one Revd may sympathize with another even at the distance of 12 hundred miles— Verily there is no escaping from the dust and weariness and burden of this state of seclusion— "Free"?— Vain thought!— There is no freedom save in the hope of a better existence?— And in believing this I trust I do not sin against thy creed O Schiller.

"Degrade yourself in my eyes"—[2] why should you think it probable— possible?— I wish to see you with your feelings *controlled* but not *subdued*. Is it possible that the present circumstances should *not* give you a heart-ache?[n] But it is well— it is best that you should know the extent of the evil at first. I doubt not you will be enabled to overcome at last the difficulties of your situation for the spirit in which you encounter them cannot be in vain.

Something has knocked at my heart every day and bid me write to you and yet I did not wish to visit you as I was in such a state of vegetative calmness— My fingers have been busy, my eyes wide open but my mind has been so still, my feelings seemed sunk down so deep— I almost believed I should never hope nor fear perhaps never *think* again. So I have delayed fancying[n] that it was seed-time, and that by and by some fruits and blossoms would spring up fit to send to a friend at such a distance. But no such June-time has come and now I write because I feel slightly sad this evening and because I wish to hear from you again before I go to Cambridge.

Three or four afternoons I have passed very happily at my beloved haunt in the wood reading Goethe's "second residence in Rome"—[3] your pencilmarks show that you have been before me. I shut the book each time with an earnest desire to live as he did— always to have some engrossing object of pursuit— I do sympathize deeply with a mind in that state. While mine is being used up by ounces I wish pailfulls might be poured into it— I am dejected and uneasy when I see no results from my daily existence but I am suffocated and lost when I have not the bright feeling of progression.

Why can I not write more to-night— I do not know— I feel very friendly towards you— But every-word seems egotistical or too trifling to send so far— Oh faut attendre Demain peut-etre.[4]

31st Evening—

I have just returned from a sweet walk. A thundershower had purified the air into perfection and retired over the hills just in time to embellish the setting sun and rising moon with the variegated companies of clouds which lingered behind.

The air is full of autumn, the insects of the season are chaunting their melancholy bodings and the red and yellow garlands are getting ready to crest her "languid downfal of hair" withal—[5] For the first time these things have no power to affect me— I gl[   ] around the eye of observation and *see* the s[   ] for the first time— I used to feel very painfu[   ] Spring and Autumn the crisis-times of the year. The influences of the first could wake no answering harmony in my soul which assimilated too profoundly— with those of the latter— 'Tis not so now— but *why* I wot na yet.

This aftn I have been reading a memoir of J. H. Payne Poor fellow!—[6] All biographies (Scott's, Goethes, Korner's, Madame Rolands— and— some dozens more excepted)[n] make me sick at heart and make it hard to realize that there is a Heaven. (I have nowadays the consolation of thinking it would not be so if Goethe had the writing of them. *He* would let us see the cui bono—) But in this case such a brilliant dawn and such a gray afterday of baffled efforts stifled ardor— talents wasted on ignoble objects— And forced to return without "fame or fortune at last after having vowed he would not— poor— poor Howard!

I see the translation[n] works of Korner advertised as in the press who 'tis by I cannot guess but dont expect[n] it will be good.[7] Even

Shelley could not transfuse the eager etherial spirit of Korner into reflective hackneyed English— Also Characteristicks of Goethe by Sarah Austin[8] Which book I shall peruse when I go *down* below as the people here say.— There are some German scholars in N. York. The Knickerbocker contains some quite good trans. from Faustus with copious quotations from and warm praises of our friend Mr Carlisle's "abominations" as Mr Norton calls them[9] After all you did not give Mr N your answer.[10] By *after* all I mean maugre your promise to that effect. "I don't like some things about the Clarkes. There are many trans. in the N York Mirror from Lessing Herder and Richter— I should like to know who these German people are.[11]

When you next write do describe your locale a little that I may feel on equal terms in writing to you. If I hear from you by tomorrow's mail I shall add a few words— Excuse my comparing you with Mr Babbidge under whatever circumstances I suppose you would say and believe me as ever yours

MARGARET F.

Sunday 1st Sept— I am as much disappointed in not hearing from you today as if I'd had any particular reason to expect it. I am much dissatisfied with this letter. Notwithstanding its expression and air I was thinking not of myself but you while writing and was affected as you would have wished by yours. Which had you rather that I should journalize often at eveg such thoughts and affairs as have engrossed me during the day in which case my letters will be motley and not very consistent in tone or only now and then when I am in an earnest mood. Repondez s'il vous plait.

ALS (MHi). Published in part in *Memoirs*, 1:121–22. *Addressed:* Revd James F. Clarke. / Louisville. / Kentucky. *Postmark:* Groton Ms Sept— 2. *Endorsed:* S. M. F. Sept 2 / (No 3 Ky.).
a heart-ache?] a ⟨head⟩ heart-ache?
delayed fancying] delayed ⟨hoping⟩ ↑ fancying ↓ *Fuller then wrote in the right margin*: the obliterated word would flatly contradict my thoughts Mere words these words.
more excepted)] more ex⟨?⟩cepted)
the translation] the ↑ translation ↓
dont expect] dont ⟨?⟩ expect

1. Charles Babbidge (1806–98), who graduated from Harvard in 1828, was ordained on 13 February 1833 at Pepperell, where he remained for 65 years. In 1839 Babbidge married Eliza Ann Bancroft (1808–93), daughter of Luther and Anna Bancroft (*Heralds*, 3:8–10; Margaret J. Bancroft, "Bancroft Family," typescript NEHGS, p. 100).

2. In his letter of 12 August, Clarke concluded a gloomy summary of his Kentucky life by saying: "I wonder how this letter will strike you. Will it degrade me in your eyes? If it does, so be it" (*Letters of JFC*, p. 58). A month later, on 13 September, he admitted that he was "acquiring the Kentucky style of oratory, and am credibly informed that I am gaining fast on the good graces of the people" (*Letters of JFC*, p. 63).

3. *Zweiter römischer Aufenthalt vom Juni 1787 bis April 1788*, part 3 of *Die italienische Reise*, was published in 1829. The Italian stay rejuvenated Goethe and stimulated him to a new creative level (*OCGL*).

4. Oh, wait for tomorrow, maybe.

5. From the concluding stanza of Hood's "Ode: Autumn," in which Autumn is personified:

> O go and sit with her, and be o'ershaded
> Under the languid downfal of her hair:
> She wears a coronal of flowers faded
> Upon her forehead, and a face of care;—

(*Selected Poems of Thomas Hood*, p. 46)

6. Theodore Sedgwick Fay's *Sketch of the Life of John Howard Payne* (Boston, 1833) had first been published in the *Boston Evening Gazette*. Among other troubles, Payne had lost a large amount of money when he leased the Sadler's Wells theater. Fay notes that Payne had not wanted to return to the United States because "he was reluctant to shew himself, after so many years, not quite so well off as when he went away" (p. 17). The final indignity came when the Boston benefit organized for his support was sparsely attended.

7. Fuller probably saw advertisements for *The Life and Writings of Carl Theodor Körner (Written by his Father), with Selections from his Poems, Tales, &c*, trans. G. F. Richardson (Philadelphia, 1833).

8. In *Characteristics of Goethe: From the German of Falk, von Müller, &c* (London, 1833) Sarah Austin translated comments made about Goethe by his contemporaries.

9. "Horae Germanicae" appeared in the January 1833 and February 1833 issues of *The Knickerbocker*. The essay closes with almost three pages of quotation from Carlyle's "Goethe's *Works*," *Foreign Quarterly Review* 10 (August 1832). The *Knickerbocker* author (perhaps Charles Fenno Hoffman) says that "the general scope of the poem and [Faust and Mephistopheles] are admirably touched on." Carlyle, he continues, is "a writer whose Germanized tastes and habits of thought, give a peculiar zest and interest to his eloquent contributions" (p. 84). Andrews Norton had attacked Goethe and his admirers in his "Recent Publications Concerning Goethe," *Select Journal of Foreign Periodical Literature* 1 (April 1833): 250–93. He used Carlyle as a representative of a school whose "writers speak forth only mysteries and oracles, and this, often in language as obscure and barbarous, as that in which the ancient mysteries and oracles were involved," whose aim is to "sweep away all old notions of philosophy, morals, and religion" (p. 260).

10. Clarke sent the essay to *The New-England Magazine* but then had second thoughts. Seven days later he confided that the piece arrived too late for the May number but that the editor, Joseph T. Buckingham, would publish it in June. Clark lost his nerve and withdrew the essay, saying to Fuller: "It is not my affair, my business, to engage in a strife about Goethe" (Habich, "JFC's 1833 Letter-journal," p. 53).

11. Beginning in June, the *Mirror* published seven abstracts under such titles as "Fables from the German of Herder" and "Scraps from the German of Jean Paul." The issue for 1 June had an entire story, "The Rock of Hans Heiling," by Theodore Körner.

1019. To James F. Clarke

Boston.
Sunday Eveg 21st
Sept. [1833][n]

I must write to you this evening, my dear friend, I feel so very blessed. I am in a really Sabbath state of feeling and I wish to converse a few moments with James who is very ungrateful if he has not been thinking of *me*.

I have been this aftn with your mother Sarah and Elizabeth to hear William[n] Channing preach at Mr Emerson's (I hate writing the name out in this familiar manner but after a minute's pondering Mr— seems prim and affected.)[1] Some things he said about Faith made me think of you— and I wished you had been there to hear words which you would so fully have[n] understood— That many did appreciate them I doubt— Your friend has his trials *here* worse perhaps than yours as he is[n] among expecting friends— His *manner* is very generally unsound[?] and his matter not received with any enthusiasm by the carping religionists of our sect. Believe me you have chosen wisely in going where you may[n] have opportunity to form your manner *freely.*— Yes freely— for the indifference you meet may distress you but cannot modify your opinions.—

Yet I wish I could see you tonight— you *must* write. I recal what I said— I wish to hear from you extremely— I fear too from your silence that you do not like my letters— They *were bad,* but I don't *like* to have you think so—

Sarah has given you the items of Amelia's engagement.[2] She has a *George* after all but most unlike the other. She is so happy tis impossible not to sympathize with her.

Elizabeth has written to you of which I am glad— W. Pickering has very unjustifiably renewed his visits and attention— yet I hope it will end well.— I am going to stay with Mrs Farrar next week. She speaks with much warmth of you.— I have a great deal to say to you but the want of response on your part checks me. Adieu be blessed—

M.

ALS (MHi). *Addressed:* Mr. James F. Clarke. *Endorsed:* (No 4. Ky.).

Since the contents clearly place this letter in 1833, Fuller probably misdated it by one day. Sunday was the 22d.

hear William] hear ⟨M⟩William
fully have] fully ⟨un⟩ have
he is] he ⟨has⟩ is
you may] you ⟨would⟩ ↑ may ↓

1. Emerson had resigned his pulpit at Boston's Second Church in September 1832 and the parish had not yet selected his successor. William Henry Channing did not receive that call, or one from Brattle Street, where he preached on 20 October (*Letters of MF,* 1:195).

2. Amelia Greenwood was engaged to Dr. George Bartlett, whom she married in November 1834.

1020. To Anne Warren Weston

Friday aftn.
[October? 1833?]ⁿ

My dear Miss Weston

I dined out of town yesterday and did not receive your note till it was too late to answer it.— Today I had intended to come and take tea with you but I find myself so extremely fatigued and the weather is so unpropitious that I hope you will excuse me especially as I could not have staid in the evening. Perhaps you and your sisters will come to Groton this summer and I shall be able to see you at leisure—[1] At all events I shall be in Boston ere long on my way to or from N. York and will, if possible call on you—

With regards to your sisters yours sincerely

S. M. FULLER.

ALS (MB: Ms. A. 92. Vol. 14, p. 83). *Addressed:* Miss Anne Weston.

Anne Warren Weston (1812–90) was the third child of Warren and Nancy Bates Weston of Boston (George Walter Chamberlain, *History of Weymouth, Massachusetts* [Boston, 1923], 4:729).

Dated by the reference to a trip to New York, which occurred at the end of October 1833.

1. Her sisters were Maria (who became a prominent abolitionist), Caroline (1808–82), and Deborah (b. 1814).

1021. To James F. Clarke

Boston 7th Oct 1833.

My dear Friend,

I received your two good letters[1] at Cambridge where I have been passing these ten days last past.—ⁿ

As to Amelia's engagement I ought not to say much about it— You were right in supposing I was not a confidante in the matter, nor do I regret it!—[2] Amelia seems perfectly happy— I confess Dr. B. does not seem to me such a finishing portion as I should wish to see a friend of mine supplied withal. But perhaps I am wrong when she is so blest I cannot bear to think it all delusion. So I stand and wait hoping to discover many charms and fine traits in thisⁿ [*illegible*]. This is profoundly confidential between us.

I saw Mr. Elliott frequently and think him a marvellous proper youth— He talked of you with an affectionate enthusiasm which gratified me. Mr. Osgood too was eloquent in your praise—[3] Mrs. Farrar made many inquiries and I read her proper excerpts from your letters—

I was very happy in Mrs Farrar's house— There all goes on in harmonious gentle movement. She was so kind, so entertaining— *he* so sweet, so bright— I saw all the people I used to know but as my pulse[n] doth now more healthfully keep time I find myself better able to enjoy them after their own fashions than in former days— Helen Davis made a party for me and invited your sister and Elizabeth R. to meet me!! Mrs Farrar, Mrs Devens, and Miss Ware had also their soirées—[4] saw Henry Hedge several times to some effect— I had one quite good talk with Mr Ware about Miss Martineau—[5] one with Mr Palfrey about Mr Robbins (who is likely to have Brattle St and is pronounced to have many virtues and *no* faults— of manner.)[6] Mr Felton lent me his Flaxmans which I drew in at the eyes with unfeigned delight) Did you know Flaxman was a Swedenborgian, and did you guess it from his angels?—[7]

One pleasant day I passed at Mr T. Lee's in Brookline.[8] Twas the loveliest day and I enjoyed every-thing. Mr Bancroft dined there, talked much, earnestly, and well— Of Wilhelm Meister he spoke with a reverent desire to do justice, but could not keep to the true standard— His tastes kept getting in the way.[9]

Mr Lee (who pleased me much) is a Realist of the first water and was brought out in bold relief relief by the opposing lights of Mr Farrar and Mr Bancroft.

I recommend to your attention a review of Goethe in the last Edinburgh—[n] It is so very candid the reasonings are so free and so just.[10] You will observe that the writer is repelled by those sides of G's character with which *you* have the closest affinity.— Ah I am too tired I am going to Cambridge to *drink* honied what?[n] from the lips of Hon E. Everett—[11] *Sip* I should have said— If I am awake when I return shall then finish.

8th Octr. Morng. I was in very good spirits when I wrot[e] last night but this morng my attention has been forcibly recalled to some painful domestick circumstances I must write to you, dear friend, for you are the only one I have on earth young enough to sympathize with me and firm in faith enough to sustain me.

O pray for me— Hard as has been the part I have[n] had to act, far more so than you ever knew; it is like to become much more difficult. Pray that I may go through all with cheerful spirit and unbroken faith— that any talents with which Heaven has endowed me may be ripened to their due perfection and not utterly wasted in fruitless

Chandler Robbins. Courtesy of the Harvard University Archives.

struggles with difficulties which I cannot overcome. Pray that I may deserve to feel self-complacency— If I could only have that!—

I think I am less happy in many respects than you but particularly in this. You can speak freely to me of all your circumstances and feelings can you not?— It is not possible for me to be so profoundly frank with[?] any earthly friend. Thus my heart has no proper home only can prefer some of its visiting-places to others and with deep regret I realize that I have at length entered upon the concentrating stage of life— It was not time; I had been too sadly cramped— I had not learned enough and must always remain imperfect. But so it is and now I must be as painfully seeking for the centre of my orbit as I was formerly to "wander into the vague" with which you used to reproach me. Enough! I am glad I have been able to say so much.

You know that Elizabeth is going with your mother to Georgia. I am very glad. William P. keeps coming here and making appeals to her feelings. But it is good for her to see that he can act thus without any serious intent. She must regard him in his true light sometime though she cannot now prevail on herself to condemn him. She is delighted at the thought of change. I have read your Robert Hall piece and like it much—[12] Send me a sermon if you have opportunity— I heard a beautiful one from Mr Ware on "religion considered as a restraint and as an excitement.— You will *need* the skill of Champollion to decipher this—[13] By the way, if I can be free and serene enough these winter months which I am to pass in seclusion at Groton I shall read many books about Egypt.!— Mrs Farrar has given me Schiller's works— I was delighted, after all I think I can get more intimate with my dead than with my living friends— Yet I should like to see you and have not been able to supply your place as yet— Adieu—

M.

E. wishes you not to pay the postage of your letters, for the rest see No 2 my Louisville corres— with some additional fuss of her own about "fears tis improper to speak of it at all'"[n] &c—

ALS (MHi). Published in part in *Memoirs*, 1:122. *Addressed:* Revd James F. Clarke. / Louisville. / Kentucky. *Endorsed:* S. M. F. Oct 7th 1833 MF / (No 5. Ky.).

past.—] past. ⟨I⟩—
traits in this] traits ⟨?⟩ in this ⟨St⟩
my pulse] my pu⟨s⟩lse
last Edinburgh—] last Edin⟨g⟩burgh—
to *drink* honied what?] to *drink* ⟨?⟩ ↑ honied what? ↓
I have] I ↑ have ↓
it at all"] it ↑ at all" ↓

1. Clarke had written on 9 and 13 September (*Letters of JFC*, pp. 59–63).

2. Having not yet received Fuller's previous letter, Clarke wrote on 13 September: "You don't tell me anything about Amelia's engagement to Dr. Bartlett. I should like to hear about [it]. I think when my sisters get engaged I ought to know the why and wherefore. Who is this youth who aspires to lead away an enthusiast and blue?" (*Letters of JFC*, p. 62).

3. Fuller mentions two of Clarke's friends who also became clergymen: William Greenleaf Eliot finally settled in St. Louis, where he founded Washington University. Samuel Osgood was a Unitarian minister for several years before he became an Episcopal priest. Both Eliot and Osgood worked with Clarke to establish *The Western Messenger*.

4. Mrs. Devens is either Jane Caroline Lithgow (1795–1874), who in 1815 married Richard Devens (1784–1847), or her sister, Mary Lithgow (1797–1848), who married Charles Devens (1791–1876) in 1819. Jane Devens lived in Charlestown; Mary Devens lived in Boston (William Dawson Bridge, *Genealogy of the John Bridge Family in America, 1632–1924* [Cambridge, 1924], pp. 429–31). Which of the nineteen children of the Rev. Henry Ware, Sr., Fuller met is not known.

5. Henry Ware, Jr. (1794–1843), graduated from Harvard in 1812, was ordained in 1817 at Boston's Second Church (where he later took Emerson as his junior minister), and became Professor of Pulpit Eloquence and Pastoral Care at Harvard in 1829. Ware traveled in Europe from April 1829 to August 1830, during which time he met Wordsworth, Southey, and other writers (*DAB; Heralds*, 2:227–28). Fuller was probably reading Harriet Martineau's pamphlets on political economy.

6. John Gorham Palfrey (1796–1881) had been the minister at Brattle Street from 1818 to 1831, when he left the pulpit to join the Harvard faculty. Palfrey edited the *North American Review* from 1835 to 1843, served one congressional term (1847–49), and wrote an influential history of New England (*DAB*). The gossip was wrong, for Chandler Robbins became Emerson's successor when he was ordained at Second Church on 4 December 1833. Brattle Street continued without a permanent minister until Samuel Kirkland Lothrop was installed in June 1834. Lothrop (1804–86) graduated from Harvard in 1825, attended the divinity school in Cambridge, and was ordained at Dover, New Hampshire, in 1829. That year he married Mary Lyman Buckminster, the sister of the Rev. Joseph Buckminster. Lothrop, who followed Edward Everett and John Gorham Palfrey at Brattle Street, served the church until its demise in 1876. A theological conservative, Lothrop specially disliked Emerson's writing (*Heralds*, 3:224–28).

7. Cornelius Felton (1807–62) graduated from Harvard in 1827. He was professor of Greek from 1832 to 1860, when he became president of the university (*DAB*). John Flaxman was an English engraver whose work Fuller had long admired. In 1784 he joined the Theosophical Society, a group founded to promote Swedenborg's writings. Although not officially a Swedenborgian, he read the Swede's works and made engravings based on them (David Irwin, *John Flaxman, 1755–1826* [London, 1979], pp. 116–18).

8. Thomas Lee (1779–1867) was a wealthy businessman who devoted himself to landscape gardening and philanthropy. In 1827 he married Eliza Buckminster, an author and Fuller's distant relative (*NEHGR* 76 [1922]: 206).

9. After his graduation from Harvard in 1817, George Bancroft studied and traveled in Europe, where he met Goethe on several occasions. Bancroft had taught at the Round Hill School in Northampton, where he still lived while writing the first volumes of his *History of the United States* (*DAB*). In November 1834 Bancroft provoked Fuller into her newspaper letter opposing his view of Brutus.

10. Wrote William Empson, "Faust, before Goethe took it up, was an old worn-out tapestry painting. We admire as much as any one, not only the more than original brightness which he has given to the colours, but the skill with which he has breathed over its leading figures a poetical and living interest which they never before possessed" (*Edinburgh Review* 57 [April 1833]: 141).

11. Already having been the minister of Brattle Street and Harvard's professor of

Greek, Edward Everett was approaching the end of his decade of service as the U.S. representative for Middlesex district. He was the most accomplished orator of his generation.

12. In his review of *The Works of Robert Hall* (*Christian Examiner* 28 [September 1833]: 1–7), Clarke appealed to "those who delight in studying every manifestation of human greatness and generosity," a topic that informs much of the correspondence between Clarke and Fuller (p. 2). Robert Hall (1764–1831), an English Baptist clergyman, was the subject of Clarke's address at Harvard on Visiting Day, July 1833.

13. Jean-François Champollion, who first deciphered the Rosetta Stone, had died on 4 March of the previous year.

1022. To James F. Clarke

30th Octr[n]
1833.

"She was not fair, nor full of grace,
    Nor crowned with thought or aught beside.
No wealth had she, of mind or face,
    To win our love, or raise our pride;
No lover's thought her cheek did touch;
    No poet's dream was 'round her thrown;
And yet we miss her— ah, too much,
    Now— she hath flown!
We miss her when the morning calls,
    As one that mingled in our mirth;
We miss her when the evening falls,—
    A trifle wanted on the earth!
Some fancy small or noble thought
    Is checked 'ere to its blossom grown;[n]
Some chain is broken that we wrought.
    Now— she hath flown!
No solid good, nor hope defined,
    Is marred now she hath sunk in night.
And yet the strong immortal Mind
    Is stopped in its triumphant flight!
Perhaps some grain lost to its sphere
    Might cast the great Sun from his throne;
For all we know is— 'She was here,'
    And— "She hath flown.—"[n]

I have copied these stanzas for you in the faint hope that you may like them— I am afraid you will not better[n] than I did your Jeanie or Mary Morrison (which was it) I found them in a volume of songs and other poems bearing[n] on its title page the primrose and crocus name of Barry Cornwall,[1] though among them I found "the Admiral's return" "Gomarra" and others attributed in your Blackwood to Motherwell.[2] There is a quaint simplicity in the expression of these half-defined thoughts, an[n] absence of inference and analysis, which remind me of the beloved Charles Lamb whom twenty grains of enthusiasm, combined with his humour and pathos would have vivified into a poet— as it is, he has never written any poetry except Hester— "The old familiar faces" and "Rosamund"[3]

Hazlitt's Lectures have lately come within my ken Pray read if you can get them— They are eloquent and discriminating[n] even when unjust. The satire is very keen and vehement. Read the critiques of[n] Scott and Campbell particularly and let me know what you think of them.[4]

I rejoice to inform you that it is not *our* Mr Carlyle who has been so unauthentick as to fancy himself inspired in this nineteenth century. Mr Emerson found him living with his lovely wife![n] in happy literary seclusion.[5] He is much prejudiced against the Americans on the score of their want of Reverence.[n]

I have taken the liberty to show your answer to Mr Norton to Mr and Mrs Farrar.[6] They are mightily edified thereby and wish in turn to benefit those slightly Germanized characters Dr and Mrs Follen

I gave leave— You are not vexed?— By the way is not the article mine? You gave it to me once. But Sarah claims it.

I have been reading the papers on Shelley in the New Monthly[n] which you gave me an account of and am, as usual, annoyed by approaching a poet on his prosaick side.—[7] Do you remember an article on Brougham as the "Man of the Time"—[8] This has charmed me, especially [the] passage on the reasons why Men of genius fail in their first attempts in large assemblies—

We are waiting as patiently as we can for Mr Crocker to get ready for N York— I feel as if I for one could not go but that is because I am accustomed to petty disappointments— If I *do* go I will finish this letter *there*.

New York 6th Novr. 1833.

I think you will like to hear a little from us here. This is our third day— E. seems pretty happy and your Mother too, though now and then she pronounces it *hor*rid with very prolonged emphasis on the first syllable that she should be thus separated from all her children. "And it takes so much time to think of them all before I go to sleep." And then she drops a tear or two.— I believe I should love her if we were together long enough— Her innocence, and naiveté generosity of disposition are winning my heart.

I begin to feel in high spirits already. Even this little change of scene has been infinitely good for me. You have not forgotten the lovely Anna.[9] I see her considerably much. E. and I were at a party there, and heard Count Brigham sing Hood's "I remember" in the most airy manner.[10]

Probably I shall write you a long letter when I return to Boston. Pour le present Adieu.

AL (MHi). *Addressed:* Revd. James F. Clarke./ Louisville. / Kentucky. *Postmark:* New York Nov 7. *Endorsed:* (Ky. No 6.).

30th Octr] 30th ⟨Nov⟩ ↑ Octr ↓
blossom grown;] blossom ⟨brought⟩ grown;
hath flown.—"] *In the margin opposite the poem, Fuller wrote:* I think there is exquisite felicity of expression here.
not better] not ⟨like them⟩ better
other poems bearing] other ⟨?⟩poems ⟨p⟩bearing
thoughts, an] thoughts, ⟨whi⟩ an
and discriminating] and ⟨very⟩ discriminating
the critiques of] the ↑ critiques o⟨n⟩f ↓
living with his lovely wife!] living ↑ with his lovely wife! ↓
of Reverence.] of ⟨?⟩ Reverence.
Shelley in the New Monthly] Shelley ↑ in the New Monthly ↓

1. Bryan Waller Procter (1787–1874) published plays and poems under the name Barry Cornwall. Friend of Hunt, Lamb, and Hazlitt, Procter published no poetry after his 1832 *English Songs, and Other Small Verses,* the volume Fuller probably read (*DNB*).

2. William Motherwell was a Scottish poet and editor. John Wilson (writing under the name Christopher North) reviewed Motherwell in *Blackwood's* 33 (April 1833): 668–81, but he did not discuss any of Barry Cornwall's poems. For Fuller's comments on the Motherwell article, see *Letters of MF,* 1:187.

3. Charles Lamb (1775–1834) is now better known for his essays and criticism than for his poetry. "The Old Familiar Faces" and *A Tale of Rosamund Gray and Old Blind Margaret* were published in 1798; "Hester" appeared in 1803 (*DNB*).

4. Fuller was mistaken, for *The Spirit of the Age* (London, 1825) was a collection of essays, not lectures. Typical of Hazlitt's acerbic comment on Scott is his observation that "Sir Walter would make a bad hand of a description of the *Millennium,* unless he could lay the scene in Scotland five hundred years ago, and then he would want facts and worm-eaten parchments to support his drooping style." In his essay that combines judgments on Campbell and Crabbe, Hazlitt unstintingly praises the former but concludes that "if Mr. Crabbe's writings do not add greatly to the store of entertaining and delightful fiction, yet they will remain, 'as a thorn in the side of poetry,' perhaps for a century to come!" (*The Complete Works of William Hazlitt,* ed. P. P. Howe [London and Toronto, 1932], 11:58, 169).

5. Emerson visited Thomas and Jane Carlyle at Craigenputtock on 26 August 1833: "There he has his wife a most accomplished & agreeable woman. Truth & peace & faith dwell with them & beautify them. I never saw more amiableness than is in his countenance" (*JMN,* 4:219–20). Emerson arrived in New York on 7 October (Rusk, *Letters of RWE,* 1:396).

6. Clarke had sent Fuller his essay that attacked Norton (Habich, "JFC's 1833 Letter-journal," p. 53).

7. "The History of Percy Bysshe Shelley's Expulsion from Oxford," *New Monthly Magazine and Literary Journal* 38 (1833): 17–29.

8. Bulwer's "Lord Brougham: The Man of the Time," *New Monthly Magazine and Literary Journal* 32 (December 1831): 507–22. Henry Peter Brougham (1778–1868), Baron Brougham and Vaux, had been a prolific writer for the *Edinburgh Review* and

controversialist for antislavery causes. After a short career in law, Brougham was sent to Parliament, where he helped pass the Reform Bill. In 1830 he became lord chancellor (*DNB*). Bulwer said that Brougham's first speech in Commons "added to the innumerable instances of what are called 'failures,' in men of ability, who for some time mistake the taste of their audience. . . . The ordinary error which a man of superior mind commits is that of at first assuming the station, and speaking with the tone of those who, though no more than his equals in mind, hold a different position from himself in an assembly where they have grown into respect" (pp. 510–11).

9. Anna Barker later married Samuel Gray Ward.

10. Count Brigham is unidentified, but his song was set to Hood's "I Remember, I Remember," first published in *Friendship's Offering* for 1826 and then in *The Plea of the Midsummer Fairies.*

1023. To James F. Clarke

Novr 26th 1833.

My dear Friend,

I thought four days ago when I received your letter that I would not write to you any more. But Sarah tempted me tonight to write "a note only a note by Clinton"[1] She seemed to wish so much to pour out wealth of letters from Clinton's pockets that I could not resist. I shall not answer your letter now—[2] I do not clearly comprehend the tone of it— However as you say, though coldly, that you are "mine as ever" I shall address you as my dear, kind friend always; if not perfectly sympathizing with my feelings yet almost always comprehending my thoughts, and oh *so* different from the apparently ossified human beings whom I meet—You see I have the grace to say *appar*ently.

And yet I will answer one part of your letter though I will not tell you much that I have thought about it— Do not fear being so "terribly outward"[3] Is it not what you have so long asked— and for the want of quick sensibility tell me how should it be otherwise. Must not our feelings sink down deep— *deep* when the bark which bore the rich freight is stripped of all its sails by a rough gale from the seeming beauteous coast on which we were seeking to land them. But trust the prophecy of one who has as good a title as any Sybil to utter oracles to other hearts; some reflux of the tide will cast them on some shore of palms and fragrance where no breath can tell of the black waves which once closed over them. So much for the Souvenir style!— I had a very fine time in New York— It was to me a "moon-lit *ocean*"" I saw Elizabeth beginning to be happier— and felt sure that change was doing and would do her good. I saw many pretty things; the prettiest Titian's Bella Donna (about whom I shall write a novel) and Anna B—[4] I went through the second chapter of my acquaintance with this "fairy-like musick" very happily. I made some amusing acquaintance, heard wealth of good stories, and collected quantities of those most desirable articles new ideas. But I shall not tell you about it, for in comparison with your new world this slight interlude in my ancient and honorable existence would seem flat and unprofitable.[5]

I went this afternoon with Sarah and Eugene to see Medora—[6] I am too sorry that you are not here on her account.— I was not however affected as many are— I was first awed by the spiritual presence and then enchanted by beauty. I have no pathetick associations with death. No link rivetted in my heart chains me to that afterworld which as yet I have sighed for more in mind than heart.

Sarah said to me in a low voice "She looks like one whose heart would break at once, she could not wait to suffer much" I answered by[n] some of Byron's lines about the "pure porcelain" but I believe she did not recognize them— Probably Don Juan has been omitted in her Education[7]

I shall send you the description of some other pictures I saw in N York if you wish.— One trait struck me— A young gentleman who went to hear Mr Eastburn with us—[8] (There was the loveliest church musick it wide-oped Elizabeth's heart) said to me when we came out "I always like to hear sermons on this subject. We cannot be too frequently reminded of the danger of merging the past and future in the present. Here[n] is indeed our greatest danger." When I said that mine and that of most persons whom I knew was the opposite he thought I spoke in irony and seemed to have been as much troubled by his selfunconsciousness as some of us have been by our selfconsciousness— Your cousin J. M'Kesson made me his confidante— I was about to be flattered but next day he paid the same compliment to E— I like him however.

Bennett Forbes is engaged to Rose Smith.[9]

I was at Cambridge some days since. Mrs Farrar was writing to you she told me. Mr Elliott was there but I did not enjoy seeing him at all. I seemed to exercise a petrifying influence. Mrs. F. complained that he was not half so agreeable in my society—[n] This I thought ungrateful in your disciple inasmuch as I was the means of establishing[n] him there. George Davis is in town and has paid me several visits. He came one evening with Harriet R.—[10] They talked much about you [   ] of course.— She was rather empressée toward me w[   ] I thought capricious— N' importe.[n] I am going ho[me] tomorrow—

Home—

James— What should you think of my coming to th[e] West[n] and teaching a school— I wish to earn money to go to Italy— Not quite yet— My children want me at present— But by and by would this be a feasible plan?

I shall not give Ellen your George Davis message.[11] Her head is giddy enough already— She has g[ot] one admirer of the name of Clarke which at the impulsive age of 13 is quite enough to impede her progress in French more than is like to prove agreeable or convenient to her governess.

I am very silly to send you all this *stuff* in return for your unfriendly good-for-nothing letter. Adieu— tis eleven P. M.[n] and I've a novel to finish— Village Belles—[12] much superior to Goethe— O much I assure you— "As ever yours"

M.

ALS (MHi). *Addressed:* Mr James F. Clarke— / Louisville / Kentucky— / Mr M'Kesson.

in New] in ⟨n⟩New
saw Elizabeth] saw Eliza⟨th⟩beth
answered by] answered ⟨in⟩ by
present. Here] present. ⟨It⟩ Here
agreeable in my society—] agreeable ⟨when I was there⟩ ↑ in my society ↓ —
of establishing] of es⟨?⟩tablishing
N' importe.] N' im⟨?⟩porte.
th[e] West] th[e] ⟨w⟩West
eleven P. M.] eleven ⟨?⟩P. M.

1. George Clinton McKesson (1809–51), son of Judge John (1772–1829) and Sarah Hull McKesson (1783–1810), was Clarke's cousin (Weygant, *Hull Family in America*, p. 509).

2. In his letter of 12 November, Clarke bitterly recalled his love for Elizabeth Randall and omitted Fuller's name from a paragraph describing his best friends.

3. Clarke had said: "For the last four months I have felt horribly outward. I seem to be destitute of a soul. At least I cannot trace, as erst, its pulsations and throbs and shootings. I wonder whether I am to continue thus mechanical long. Is it necessary to success and usefulness? (*Letters of JFC*, p. 64).

4. It is not clear which picture Fuller saw. She may refer to Titian's *La Bella* (1536). Anna B. is Anna Barker.

5. Fuller echoes *Hamlet*, I.ii.133–34: "How [weary], stale, flat and unprofitable / Seem to me all the uses of this world!"

6. Horatio Greenough had agreed to carve a figure inspired by the dead Medora of Byron's "The Corsair" for Robert Gilmor, Jr., a Baltimore merchant patron of the arts. The sculpture, Greenough's first nude, went on display at Harding's Gallery on 24 October (Crane, *White Silence*, pp. 54–57; Nathalia Wright, ed., *Letters of Horatio Greenough, American Sculptor* [Madison, Wis., 1972], pp. 190–91).

7. Fuller probably quotes from stanza 11 of Canto 4 of *Don Juan*

> The Heart—which may be broken: happy they!
> Thrice fortunate! who of that fragile mould,
> The precious porcelain of human clay,
>   Break with the first fall: they can ne'er behold
> The long year linked with heavy day on day,
>   And all which must be borne, and never told.

(*The Works of Lord Byron*, ed. Ernest Hartley Coleridge [London, 1903]: 6:186)

8. Manton Eastburn (1801–72) was born in England but educated at Columbia and the General Protestant Episcopal Theological Seminary. He was ordained in the Episcopal priesthood in 1822, became the assistant rector of Christ Church, and then rector of the Church of the Ascension, where Fuller probably heard him. Eastburn was later the bishop of Massachusetts (*National Cyclopedia*).

9. Robert Bennett Forbes married Rose Green Smith in January 1834 (*CC*, 25 January 1834). Forbes (1804–89) became a China merchant and ship owner (*DAB*).

10. Harriet Russell, whom Davis married.

11. Clarke had said: "Assure [your sister] Ellen that my affection for her is yet undiminished by time or absence, and that as yet I have instituted no flirtation with any Kentucky damsel" (*Letters of JFC*, p. 66).

12. [Anne Manning], *Village Belles* (London, 1833). Like Fuller, Manning (1807–79) was highly educated and fluent in several languages. *Village Belles* was the first of her many novels (*DNB*).

1024. To James F. Clarke

24th Dec 1833.
Groton.—

Do you remember a conversation we had[n] in the garden one starlight evening last summer about the incalculable power which outward circumstances have over the character— You would not sympathize in the regrets I expressed that mine had not been formed amid scenes and persons of nobleness and beauty eager[n] passions and dignified events instead of those secret trials and petty conflicts which make my transition state so hateful to my memory and my tastes— You then professed the faith which I resigned with such anguish, the faith which a Schiller could never attain, the faith in the power of human will; and I was struck as I have often been before by the varied ways in which we are all led round and round the same circle at what ever point we begin. "Faith in human will!" "Circumstances so little power" yet in every letter you talk to me of the power of circumstances. You tell me how changed you are— Every one of your letters is different from the one preceding and all so altered from your former self. All very good!— Quite right since circumstances are now favorable to you. I, for one, could never regret your getting away from the "Atlantick ways of thinking for a long time even though you leave me behind with other *Eastern* things—[1] such as Goethe for instance! For are you not leaving all our old ground and do you not apologize to me for all your letters?— Why do you apologize?— I think I know you very— very well considering that we are both human and have the gift of concealing our thoughts with words— Nay further!— I do not believe you will be able to become any thing which

I cannot understand. I know I can sympathize with all who feel and think from a Dryfesdale up to a — Max Piccolomini.[2] You say you are become a machine, if so I shall expect to find you a grand, high-pressure, wave-compelling one— to require plenty of fuel (and who more fit than I to feed the intellectual burner with pine chips?— Was I not born to fill the ear of some Frederick or Czar Peter with information and suggestions on which he might reflect and act) (O what a parenthesis!— never— never shall I concoct a letter or aught else into decent style)— But I think I was saying that you must be a steam engine and move some majestick fabrick at the rate of 50 miles an hour along the broad waters of the 19th century.[3] None of your *pendulum*[n] machines for me! I should to be sure turn away my head if I should hear you *tick* and mark the quarters of hours— but the bang and whizz of a good large life-Endangerer would be musick to mine ears! O no! sure there is no danger of your requiring to be set down *quite on a level* kept in a *still place* and would up every eight-days— O no— no— you are not one of that numerous company "Who live[n] and die,

> Eat, drink, wake, sleep between,
> Walk, talk like clock-work too,
> So pass in order due over the scene.
> To whom the Past— *is* past
> The future— nothing yet &c—

But we must all be machines— you shall be a steam engine— George shall be a mill— with extensive water privileges— And I will be a spinning Jenny—[n] no upon second thoughts I will not be a machine— I will be an instrument not to be confided to vulgar hands, for instance a chisel to polish marble— or— a whetstone to sharpen steel!![4]

Did you not ask me for a "glorious document".— Truth and heros for ages?—

If you could guess how alone I am "and now I am alone"— Wolfe![5] W. had Mary's sainted spirit looking down and not only approving but sympathizing with his pure thoughts and excellent actions. Pour moi, All my stock is getting into consuls and will never produce one per cent unless foreign affairs should raise them in market in a way not to be expected.

I have been at home a month playing Margaret Good child with some success. All that time my Father has not once seemed dissatisfied with me.

I perceive that vagrant genius M'Kesson has not yet delivered my letter— Since then I am in love— I make you my confidant I am in Love[n] with Lucius M. Sargent[6] I know you will say 'tis wrong to cherish hopeless passions but what says Schiller? Liebe

Kennt der allein der ohne Hoffnung liebt, "*what* Nonsense"[7] seriously he is the only "delightful" person I have seen for a long time do you know him?— My child Belinda is with me now looking like a primrose untimely blighted.[8] Mother is trying to nurse her but fears she is too late. I hope better things I am more and more convinced that Mother is a "piece of an angel—

Dear James you will receive this about new years time can you feel like writing a hymn or devotional exercise for me and send it— I think I must feel much pleasure from it. Faithfully your

MARGARET F.

ALS (MHi). Published in part in *Memoirs*, 1:85–86, and *Letters of MF*, 1:192–93. *Addressed:* Revd James F. Clarke / Louisville. / Kentucky. *Postmark:* Groton Ms / Dec 25. *Endorsed:* S. M. F./ on machines &c / 1833 Sarah M. Fuller/ Dec 25.

we had] we h⟨e⟩ad
beauty eager] beauty ⟨Ea⟩ eager
your *pendulum*] your *pendu⟨?⟩lum*
"Who live] "Who l⟨?⟩ive
spinning Jenny—] spinning ⟨?⟩Jenny—
in Love] in ⟨l⟩Love

1. In his letter, Clarke said: "New England and its thoughts are becoming foreign to me. I see no review—no books—and plunged in this sea of Western life, I hardly care to keep up my acquaintance with Atlantic ways of thinking" (*Letters of JFC*, p. 67).

2. Jasper Dryfesdale is the revengeful steward in Scott's *Abbot;* Max Piccolomini appears in Schiller's *Piccolomini* and *Wallensteins Tod.*

3. When he answered Fuller, Clarke said: "Nothing can be more unlike a steamboat or steam engine than my present way of getting along" (*Letters of JFC*, p. 70).

4. In his letter of 9 September Clarke said: "Indeed, without the blessing of your confidence and intimacy I should have a very machine-like feeling, in going about my works" (*Letters of JFC*, p. 61).

5. Fuller refers to two poems by Charles Wolfe, both titled "Song." The first is a lament for a dead lover named Mary, from which Fuller quotes:

> While e'en thy chill, bleak corse I have,
> Thou seemest still mine own;
> But there I lay thee in the grave—
> And I am now alone!

The second poem has Mary's spirit addressing the poet: "Go, forget me—why should sorrow / O'er that brow a shadow fling?" (*The Burial of Sir John Moore and Other Poems* [New York, 1979], pp. 4–5). Charles Wolfe (1791–1823) was an Irish cleric who wrote poetry. His best-known work is "The burial of Sir John Moore" (*DNB*).

6. Lucius Manlius Sargent (1786–1867) studied at Harvard and was admitted to the bar, though he did not take up a lawyer's career. A prolific writer, Sargent became one of New England's best-known temperance advocates (*DAB*).

7. From Schiller's *Don Carlos*, II.viii.1893–94: "He alone knows love who loves without hope" (Dalbiac, *Dictionary of Quotations*, p. 235).

8. Belinda Randall.

1025.   To James F. Clarke

Groton iv Jany 1834.

My dear friend, I have just been attempting a wee bit sermon on one of your texts— When you come I dare-say I shall have a string to show you which you will compare with yours and generously flatter me that only the difference of discipline could occasion such dissimilar results.

—I dare-say you will think so— I am well pleased that you found such friends in Cincinnati.[1] I am *not* sorry that you find none such in Louisville.— I am glad that Tracy Howe succeeds— Tis proof of the Goetherian principle that all sorts of stones may find places in the grand fabrick of society—[2] I am sure T. H. cannot be a fair polished corner-stone anywhere.— By the way you say in one letter, "I found the more I acted, the less I understood of Goethe and German lyricks" Not I presume because you find your principia falsified in life but because you have not peace and leisure to reflect so deeply as you were wont, since I find you recurring to the renunciation system with such glee.—[3] "Timothy Flint stems the nineteenth century" what does thee mean?—[4]

You have no right to be vexed with me for scolding you— Please remember *I* have long said: I said when you parted from me here that I did expect[n] our friendship to terminate— You answered, "Have faith. Do not believe that what has been must be again" and I then said as I do now "Tis not in my power— my trust is broken forever" You know how reluctant I was to believe it possible that the friendship between myself and George[n] could meet its fate so suddenly— I had been so open, so honorable, so truly myself—The intimacy had been so long, so constant— I though myself appreciated by that person— Since he could leave aside my esteem, since he could willingly forfeit the attachment of the only person on earth who knew him thoroughly I could never confide again in an attachment founded on similar causes— Pardon me, dear friend, I grieve to check your generous enthusiasm. As yours is so was mine I know your feelings; the person who can blight such forever is not enviable. No morbid selfishness, no worldly-mindedness on my party, God willing, shall ever come to chill your fairest feelings—I will never be to[n] you as George is to me a walking memento mori— haunting your day-dreams— But a second shock to my faith and my pride were not bearable— Not I must be prepared, steeled against the assaults of fate— 'Tis not that I think you capable under any circumstances of selfishness— I know your heart, dear James, it is not *that* I distrust. But your path and mine will gradually diverge and an intimacy, so intellectual, so unimaginative suffers from absence and in lessening soon ceases to be any-thing— Such an infidel am I so thorough a convert to the power of circumstances that I expected that our intimacy would terminate when I left Cambridge— Its continuing to subsist is a matter of surprize to me— And I expected ere this you would have found some Hersilia or sichlike to console you for losing your Natalia—[5] See, my friend, I am three and twenty. I believe in love and friendship— but I cannot but see that circumstances have appalling power and that those links which are not riveted by situation,[n] by interest (I mean not merely worldly interest but the instinct of self-preservation) may be lightly broken by a chance touch— I speak not in misanthropy I believe

Die Zeit ist schlecht, doch gibt's noch grosse Herzen[6]

And that yours, my friend is one of them. Surely I may be pardoned for arriving at the same result with the chivalrous "gift of the Gods." I cannot endure to be one of those shallow beings who can never get beyond the primer of experience who are[n] ever saying—

Ich habe geglaubet; *nun glaub' ich erst recht,*
Und geht es auch wunderliche, geht es auch schlecht
Ich bleibe im glaubigen Orden.[7]

Yet when you write— write freely and if I dont like what you say let me say so— I have ever been frank as if I expected to be intimate with you good threescore years and ten— I am sure we shall always esteem each other— I have that much faith. Sarah is all that you say— I love her and have a great mind to write

Pray send me sketches of Messrs Perkins and Cranch and let me know whether the latter is that softly looking swain—[8] I saw in Cambridge[n] with Mr Elliott.— Your critiques both on Hamilton and Bulwer are very good—[9] Both belong to the large class who can discover the False— but in the former tis accident, in the latter principle. Happy are those who can also display the True— Bulwer may possibly arrive at that dignity but I doubt it. He is very much in earnest.— As ever yours

S. M. Fuller

Lucy Ashman is about to open a school in Cambridge—[10] Mr Edes you perhaps may have seen has left his people.[11] Chandler Robbins has done one unpopular thing already.

ALS (MHi). Published in part in *Memoirs*, 1:82. *Addressed:* Rev. James F Clarke— / Louisville— / Kentucky— *Postmark:* Groton Ms / Jan ⟨2⟩ 6. *Endorsed:* S. M. Fuller / Jan 6. (Ky. No 9).

did expect] did ex⟨?⟩pect
and George] and ⟨g⟩George
be to] be ⟨as⟩ to
by situation,] by si⟨?⟩tuation,
who are] who ⟨?⟩are
in Cambridge] in Ca⟨r⟩mbridge

1. Clarke had exchanged pulpits with Ephraim Peabody. In his letter of 19 December, he mentioned James Perkins, Edward Cranch, Tracy Howe, and Timothy Flint (*Letters of JFC*, p. 69).

2. Uriah Tracy Howe (1811–88), son of Samuel and Susan Tracy Howe, had lived in Northampton, Massachusetts. He became a lawyer in Cincinnati. On 21 September 1835 he married Sarah Templeman Coolidge (1814–74), daughter of Charles and Mehitable Templeman Coolidge of Boston (Howe, *Howe Genealogies*, p. 295; Emma Downing Coolidge, *Descendants of John and Mary Coolidge of Watertown, Massachusetts, 1630* [Boston, 1930], p. 355).

3. Said Clarke in his letter: "I found that the more I *acted* here, the less I understood of German and Goethe's lyrics. So I gave them up, and think I must be content with the ideas I have at present for I shall never get any more" (*Letters of JFC*, p. 65).

4. Clarke's words were "Timothy Flint I also saw much of; he swims boldly against the stream of the 19th century, but is too sensitive to have any influence" (*Letters of JFC*, p. 69). Timothy Flint (1780–1840), born near North Reading, Massachusetts, graduated from Harvard in 1800. A minister who had been a missionary in the Mississippi valley, he turned to literature after 1826 (*DAB*).

5. Hersilia is one of Wilhelm Meister's correspondents in *Wilhelm Meisters Wanderjahre;* Natalia is his "amazon," whom he loves in the *Lehrjahre* but must leave to undertake his travels.

6. Fuller alters a line from Theodore Körner's "Der Dreiklang des Lebens": "Die Zeit ist schlect, doch gibt's noch grosse Seelen" (The times are bad, yet great souls still exist). She substitutes "hearts" for "souls" (Dalbiac, *Dictionary of Quotations*, p. 118).

7. Fuller quotes here from the second stanza of Goethe's "Gewohnt, Getan":

> Ich habe geglaubet, nun glaub ich erst recht!
> Und geht es auch wunderlich, geht es auch schlecht,
> Ich bleibe beim gläubigen Orden.

(*Sämtliche Werke*, 1:88)
Frederick Braun translates the passage:

> I have believed, *now I believe all the more,*
> And even if things go strangely, even if they go wrong,
> I will remain in the ranks of the believing.

(Frederick Augustus Braun, *Margaret Fuller and Goethe* [New York, 1910], p. 86)

8. James Handasyd Perkins (1810–49) was a lawyer, minister, and writer. Edward Pope Cranch (1809–92), the brother of Christopher Pearse Cranch, was a Cincinnati lawyer (Habich, "Annotated List," pp. 173, 177).

9. In his letter of 12 November, Clarke was sharply critical of Thomas Hamilton, an Englishman who wrote *Men and Manners in America* (Edinburgh, 1833). "How I dislike the travels of a mere man of taste, like that. Refined, good tastes are his, doubtless, but why take them abroad—such things belong only to home" (*Letters of JFC*, p. 64). In December, he wrote on Bulwer's *England and the English* (London, 1833). "How sadly apparent does Bulwer's lack of principles of thought become when he leaves off describing facts and attempts at causes. His thoughts are impulses, without consequence or dependa" (*Letters of JFC*, p. 69).

10. Lucy Hooker Ashmun (1797?–1836), daughter of Senator Eli Porter Ashmun, lived in Cambridge (CVR).

11. Henry Edes (1808–81), son of Rev. Henry Edes, graduated from Brown in 1828 and from the divinity school in Cambridge in 1831, when be became minister of the First Parish of Canton. On 28 October 1833 he left the church (Daniel Huntoon, *History of the Town of Canton* [Cambridge, 1893], p. 562).

1026. To James F. Clarke

Groton 7th Feby 1834,—

My dear Friend,

I do not like to put off writing any longer for I belie[ve] a month has passed since my last, and yet somehow 'tis easier t[o] write to others— I compose letters to you almost every day, but they dont seem worth sending so far and are not committe[d] to paper— I wait and wait for some peculiarly pleasant mood and at last write haphazard. I hope I shall make up from fullness of soul when I see you, and that time no longer seems very distant—[n] Apres tout, this writing is mighty dead— O for my dear old Greeks who talked every-thing— no[t] to shine as in the Parisian saloons but to learn, to teach, to vent the heart, to clear the mind. A gnome or sprite is perpetu[ally] haunting me in the shape of a huge pen which calls on my reluctant fingers to grasp it— I never feel a momentary p[   ] sure in its company and disgust crowns the results— Happy dear James to whom this persecuting sprite[n] is ever a freer fairy, softening and harmonizing your mental physiogno[my.] So should it be with the child of the nineteenth century disciple of the new era— he who is to interpret Kant's philosophy to Uncle Sam's utilitarian family.

But why do I talk thus? Not see the use of Metaphysicks—[1] Moderate portion taken at stated intervals I hold to [be] of much use as discipline of the faculties— I only object [to] them as having an absorbing and antiproductive tend[ency.] But 'tis not always[n] so— may not be with you— Wait till y[ou] are two years older before you decide that tis your vocatio[n.] Time enough at six[n] and twenty to form yourself into a metaphysical philosopher— The brain does not easily g[   ] too dry for *that*— Happy you in these ideas which give you a tendency to optimism. May you become a p[ros]elyte to that consoling faith— I shall neer be able to f[ollow] but shall look after you with envious eyes.

As to metaphysicks mine is rather a prejudice than an opinio[n]

237

adopted at an absurdly early[n] age, when I sought, and sought [   ]hile and, not finding what I wanted, retired believing [the]re was nothing in it which would lead us beyond our [pr]esent "state of seclusion." For the rest you know I think [the]re is no choice in human pursuits except in their [va]rious degrees of liberalizing the mind, as[n] fostering [t]he generous and religious affections.— When we talked [f]ormerly on these subjects you seemed to believe that [a] "pure ray of white light" was to be found on this path [a]nd such belief[n] as I said leads to optimism— But if [y]ou do as you express it now think of your metaphysics [m]erely as "new forms for thought" and *therefore* important [   ]ncur; some one must shape these new moulds for the [m]inds of each new generation; if this be your[n] genuine vocation [my] friend your appropriate craft for the body or mind?[n] politick— bon!

—So! you thought yourself bound in conscience to tell [me] you were not yet a great man at the West—[2] But I do not [de]spair yet— I perceived before that you were not satisfied [   ]e not your letters been very outward— Has any one breathed [   ] bright satisfaction of fulfilled hope and rewarded [eff]ort. You enjoyed writing to me from Cincinnati because [yo]u had there been happy— I shall always see somewhat [of y]our feelings— I say no more we have often argued the point [   ]ntire communicativeness— But do not think I can [   ]eve for your not succeeding as I[n] should for some I love [   ] not apprehend that temporary[n] failure will freeze your [ab]ilities or shake your confidence in yourself as it [   ]ght— *mine.*— And you say you are free— Free to speak and think— A year of freedom; much gained at all events.— ["mem]orable circumstances" I repeat the phrase.—

[A r]everend man of our parish and his wife discover [   ]ked prediliction towards me; they have been frequently [   ] and the other day I was seduced into spending the day [with] them and think I may in[n] time approximate to a friendship [wit]h them; I find much to displease me in the manners of both— [He] is very ugly and awkward, as much so as Mr Willard[3] of Cambri[dge,] with a peculiar *good* sort of a drawl and rather a declam[atory] *style of* conversation— But he is well read and loves litera[ture] better than any-thing— he is also sincerely desirous to perfo[rm] the duties of his station and, without officiousness, to enligh[ten] others upon theirs— His wife a ruddy-cheeked, blue eyed Philina sort of person, high animal spirits, some talent but her gayety is not graceful and she uses many famili[ar] cant phrases, a practise I cant abide, except in the young beautiful and fashionable— I have another playmat[e] Miss Weston a little bit of a girl, with short hair and pantalets who has taken charge of the children of a well *propertyed* widower in our neighborhood, very little to the satisfaction of the Groton spinsters. She has considerable character,[n] and still more cultivation— likes Coleridge and sich and comes to talk th[em] over with me— But I have *not time* to go to her much and th[at] woman must have uncommon charms or powers who cou[ld] lead me into a new intimacy— I have turned over that leaf [for] the present

When you return you[n] will find me an uncommonly well informed young woman— I spend every leisure hour in stopp[ing] up gaps in my education— I am determined I will not get absorbed in any-thing new till I shall have gone through a fixed plan of survey and repair— But ah! I have disc[overed] already so many unthought of fissures and yawning chasms, no wonder the poor soul catches cold— Such absence of the po[wer] of concentration, such want of mental discipline, and just enough smattering of every-thing to show me my app[   ] wants and palsy all my plans— My mind, I believe, ha[s] some natural power, but now can only act in acquisiti[on] and suggestion— "No system"! you will say— I am inclined [to] agree with the seemingly ill-natured assertion of the Ed. revie[w] that a well taught schoolboy of 16 possessed more thorough knowl[edge] of [   ] than the most accomplished woman— I am not an accom[pl]ished woman; yet I cannot but feel with Me Roland that [c]omparing myself with the herd je[n] vaux rien—

[Yo]u have never yet answered me about the schoolmistress plan—[4] [Pe]rhaps you considered it a mere chimera! 'twas not so— I cannot [ye]t give up my beloved plans of travel and I can think of [no] other way of fulfilling them.[n] I could not indeed leave home [   ]t at present; indeed I am not sure that Father would [conse]nt at all, but I should like to know what is in my [   ]r. But speak not of it defeated wishes are ridiculous— [Egot]ism— egotism! I set you a fine example— What a rich [   ]d I have— what an affectionate heart! I dispatched two letters [longe]r than this today to Anna Barker and Elizabeth— By the [way,] E. is *very* happy. I have for the first time in my life recd [fro]m her a letter perfectly healthful in tone and free from [   ]

[I] like your aunt Campbell much.[5] [*illegible*] Jones has been fighting a duel said to be about M. Marshall but as I do not know the particulars from any authentick personage I forbear giving them to you.—[6]

Pardon the fearful array of long words which bristle oer this letter and remember that I have of late conversed rather with books than men.

AL (MHi). Published in part in *Memoirs*, 1:107, 123–24, and *Letters of MF*, 1:179. *Addressed:* Revd James F. Clarke. / Louisville. / Kentucky. *Postmark:* Groton Ms / Feb 8. *Endorsed:* S. M. Fuller / Feb 8th. (No 10. Ky letters.).

very distant—] very dista⟨?⟩nt—
persecuting sprite] persecuting ⟨p⟩ sprite
not always] not ⟨any⟩always
at six] at ⟨?⟩six
absurdly early] absurdly ↑ early ↓
mind, as] mind, ⟨&⟩ as
such belief] such beli⟨?⟩ef
be your] be ⟨?⟩ your
body or mind?] body ↑ or mind? ↓
as I] as ⟨if⟩ I
that temporary] that ↑ temporary ↓
may in] may ⟨?⟩ in
considerable character,] considerable c⟨?⟩haracter,
return you] return ⟨I⟩ you
herd je] herd ⟨?⟩ je
them] *Here Fuller marked the passage with an X and wrote at the end of the letter*: I perceive in rereading I [have] not expressed my meaning— I wish to earn pence by [tea]ching and wearing cotton gowns and living on bread and water here and after to use them in Italy!!—

1. In an undated letter, Clarke said: "I know you will not feel the force of what I have been saying because you do not see the use of metaphysics, nor do you believe in the melioration of the human condition. You object to metaphysics that they say old things in new forms" (*Letters of JFC*, p. 72).

2. As he did often, Clarke began his letter with a catalog of his failures: "I like the West, but the West does not like me" (p. 70).

3. Sidney Willard was professor of Hebrew and Oriental languages at Harvard from 1807 to 1831.

4. In answer to her second request, Clarke said: "This Western country is a wild country and I would advise no female friend of mine to come to it in any capacity which would bring her into such collision with the natives as you would be as a teacher. The only place fit for your purpose is Cincinnati." He thought "teaching in Kentucky intolerable, on account of the utter disrespect and lawlessness of the children here" (*Letters of JFC*, p. 73).

5. Clarke's aunt Maria Hull (1788–1845) married Edward F. Campbell (1786–1861) in 1815. After graduation from Harvard, Campbell became a lawyer and then a planter in Augusta, Georgia (Weygant, *Hull Family in America*, p. 511). It was the Campbells whom Mrs. Clarke was then visiting.

6. Helen Davis described a duel that Jones (a soldier from North Carolina) fought with Robert C. Hooper over Marian Marshall: "We have had a famous duel this week, & as these bloody affairs are not common with us, it has excited much attention." Jones struck Hooper and called him a coward and a liar. Hooper responded by knocking down Jones. A meeting was arranged, but Daniel Parkman, the deputy sheriff, caught them and prevented the duel. On 31 January the men met in Pawtucket, Rhode Island, and Jones was slightly wounded. He fled to Canada after the grand jury indicted the two and their seconds on 12 February (Helen Davis to James F. Clarke, 2 February 1834, MH; *Boston Evening Transcript*, 1 February 1834; *Boston Daily Advertiser*, 13 February 1834).

1027. To James F. Clarke

Groton 17th April 1834

My dear friend,

Although I did not deserve it,[n] I have been somewhat disappointed at not receiving a letter from you for so long a time. I have not felt like writing but I wished to hear nor did I suppose James would be punctilious with me— But I will not imitate the modern Griselda and begin to scold when I am myself to blame; I suppose you have not felt like writing either— any-thing but sermons.—

Spring has come and I shall see you soon.— If I could pour into your mind all the ideas which have passed through mine— you would be well entertained I think for three or four days. But no hour will receive aught beyond its own appropriate wealth— you will talk to me a great deal I hope— If I am not frank towards you the cause will be the old one— want of self-complacency— Thanks for your information about the school— My circumstances since I wrote last are so modified as to make it doubtful whether I shall be able to act on the plan. One difficulty is my Mother's present state of health. This excellent woman and beloved friend has of late been subject to violent illnesses of a sort which require great attention. Unless her health should improve I ought not to leave her and assume such a responsibility that I could not return if she wanted me.— I have spoken to her (though not to my Father) of the plan and observe she regards it with great aversion. But all may be changed again before you come— will you then, dear James, on your return, if you can with propriety, ascertain what sort of a situation I would have, what compensation for such an undertaking (horrible I confess to my imagination.) &c— I mean merely by leading questions to such persons as may know, I could not expect any thing further in such a vague state of things— But I should like to have some defined plan to which I may turn if circumstance (O unspiritual deity, I must again call thee) should render[n] it desirable.

Eugene urges me to request yet another favor. Pardon me indeed it is very disagreeable to me to use "gli amici del cuore" in these worldly ways— But my affection for him carries it. He thinks you are well acquainted with a certain James Sullivan Dwight now at Meadville P.A.[1] E. has fixed his eye and heart considerably on a school in which said J. S. D is established and which he is to leave at Commencement. J. S. D.'s father has promised to write to him and make interest that Eugene should be his successor. But E. dreads lest *my* father should not have expressed his wishes to Dr D. with sufficient urgency because he apparently does not think the salary large enough. Will it be consistent with your convenience and— conscience to write and second the application by a favorable word in behalf of Eugene—

I know you will share my pleasure at Eugene having a part for Exhibition and being heir presumptive to one for Commencement not high indeed— but his having one at all saves my heart from a thousand ills and removes a deep shade from his future fortunes.

I am glad to have got over this part of my letter— Money— Money— root of all evil— how much have I not suffered already from things connected with its absence or[n] superfluity. A *money talk* always makes me wish to shuffle off this mortal coil more than anything—[2] How ever; it is hardly proper for a lady to talk to a gentleman on such topics even between you and me, who have always been more bluntly Citoyen and Citoyenne to one another than two young persons brought up in *tolerably* polished society ever were—[3] I never felt that I could be quite free here— and I should like you in a week's space or so to burn these first two pages of my letter.

You asked me a number of questions in your last as to our former acquaintance— I have probably been more absolutely separated from them than yourself— though not for so long a season. Five months now have I been at home with no amusement except "Beschaftigung" which though I cannot truly say it "nie ermattet" yet I may say that it "der Seele sturm beschwört." I should have no objection however to a few touches from Freundschaft leise zarte hand"—[4] I am going to Boston the latter part of next month there to mee[t] Elizabeth.— Amelia continues "perfectly happy" Angy in agreeable excitement—[5] Mrs Farrar busy as usual and in harmony with the universe. (By the way did you ever answer her half-letter? I never heard.) Nobody has been worse to me than Sarah. Who has written me only one ugly little note. But you know all about *her*. I have *not* seen R. W. Emerson. How should I? But I hear he is preaching at Hingham and elsewhere *with vast applause*—[6] You[n] see that Mr Lothrop has got Brattle street, instead of Mr Channing or yourself— a circumstance which does not tend to restore *my* harmony with the *American* part of the universe. I am at present engaged in surveying the level on which the publick mind is poised— I no longer lie in wait for the tragedy and comedy of life— the rules of its *prose* engage my attention— I talk incessantly with common-place people, full of intense curiosity to ascertain the process by which materials apparently so jarring and incapable of classification get united into that strange whole the American publick. (Observe I have read all Jefferson's letters—[7] North Americans, daily papers &c without end) H. Hedge seems to be weaving his Kantians into the American system in a tolerably happy manner— vide last Christn Examiner

Revr of Everett's phi Beta oration—[8] A Unitarian named Brownson preached here a week or two since on a similar subject, many of whose opinions reminded me of you, particy his ardent admiration for the Apostle Paul.[9] He belonged to the French sect of St Simonians; do you know aught about them?—[10] You will be pleased to hear that I have begun to read my bible con amore— I have learned what I wanted. I tried writing sermons but found it not at all in my way— I could only write reveries— I have however preserved one or two that I may show you what strange work I made of it— I am just beginning to feel how much I have to say to you— and have no more room— I feel strangely confiding though we have had no intercourse for so long and what says friend Bulwer that sentimental oracle—

> Ah could we to ourselves betroth
> *One* heart a very shade of ours
> Would time alone not alter both
> The creatures of the hours.—

You will not praise me for pretty writing this time The next shall be better— Yours as Ever

M.

Is C. M'Kesson still with you— I do not like my friend with the short hair and pantalets so well as I did for reasons which would probably recommend her to *him*.

ALS (MHi). Published in part in *Memoirs*, 1:124. *Addressed:* Revd James F. Clarke. / Louisville / Kentucky. *Postmark:* Groton Ms / April 18. *Endorsed:* S. M. Fuller Ap 18 / Ans. (Ky letter no 11).
deserve it,] deserve ↑ it, ↓
should render] should re⟨?⟩nder
absence or] absence ⟨?⟩or
applause— You] *applause*— ⟨I⟩You

1. John Sullivan Dwight, son of Dr. John Dwight, a Boston physician, graduated from Harvard in 1832 and pursued an interest in German literature. He published Fuller's German translations in his 1839 edition of *Select Minor Poems, Translated from the German of Goethe and Schiller*. Dwight graduated from the divinity school in 1836 and was ordained at Northampton but left the ministry. In later years he became a prominent Boston music critic (*DAB*). In his reply of 6 May, Clarke said that he did not know Dwight or Harm Jan Huidekoper, with whom Dwight was living and who later became Clarke's father-in-law (*Letters of JFC*, p. 76). Apparently Eugene did not go to Meadville.
2. *Hamlet*, III.1.63–67:

> To die, to sleep—
> To sleep, perchance to dream—ay, there's the rub,
> For in that sleep of death what dreams may come,
> When we have shuffled off this mortal coil,
> Must give us pause.

3. Clarke tried to reassure her: "All this is vastly disagreeable, I grant, but let us do it philosophically, since it is inevitable" (p. 77).

4. Fuller quotes from two stanzas of Schiller's "Die Ideale":

> Und du, die gern sich mit ihr gattet,
> Wie sie der Seele Sturm beschwört,
> Beschäftigung, die nie ermattet,
> Die langsam schafft, doch nie zerstört.
>
> Employment too, thy loving neighbour,
> Who quells the bosom's rising storms;
> Who ne'er grow weary of her labour,
> And ne'er destroys, though slow she forms.

The closing phrase comes from the previous stanza: "Thou, Friendship, of all guides the fairest" (*Schillers Werke*, 1:70; Nathan Haskell Dole, ed., *Poetical Works of Friedrich Schiller*, trans. E. P. Arnold-Forster [Boston, 1902], pp. 40–41).

5. Angelina Greenwood, Amelia's sister.

6. Emerson had preached at Dr. Channing's Federal Street Church the previous Sunday. The Sunday before that, on 6 April, he was in three Boston pulpits: New North, Hollis Street, and Friend Street. Hingham is not on the list for 1834 (*The Complete Sermons of Ralph Waldo Emerson*, ed. Albert J. von Frank [Columbia, Mo., 1992], 4:11).

7. Fuller had read *Memoir, Correspondence, and Miscellanies, from the Papers of Thomas Jefferson*, ed. Thomas Jefferson Randolph. First published in 1829, it had been often reprinted.

8. Edward Everett delivered the Phi Beta Kappa address to the Yale chapter on 20 August 1833. Hedge reviewed the published address, "The Progress of Society," in *The Christian Examiner* of March 1834.

9. Orestes Brownson began in Universalism and moved through Unitarianism on his way toward Catholicism. He had been recently an independent minister in Ithaca, New York, but left there to become the Unitarian minister at Walpole, New Hampshire. He frequently came to the Boston area, where he met Dr. Channing and George Ripley. The month after this letter was written, Brownson became the Unitarian minister in Canton, Mrs. Fuller's hometown (Arthur M. Schlesinger, Jr., *Orestes A. Brownson: A Pilgrim's Progress* [Boston, 1939], pp. 27–31).

10. Claude-Henri de Rouvroy, comte de Saint-Simon, founded French socialism. His works connected a theory of social change based on class conflict with a political system of an elite hierarchy of talent. Finally, Saint-Simon developed a system of Christian ethics shorn of theology. Brownson was reading deeply in Benjamin Constant, Victor Cousin, and Saint-Simon, especially his *Nouveau Christianisme* (ibid, pp. 32–34; *The Encyclopedia of Philosophy*, ed. Paul Edwards [New York, 1967], 7:275–76).

1028. To James F. Clarke

Groton 13th Novr 1834.

My dear Friend,

This is Amelia's wedding-day and as I cannot be present with her I think I must console myself by a little chat with you— Tis somewhat singular, of four marriages which[n] have taken place within a month from out the circle of my ci-devant intimates— J Hillard's— G.

Davis's, Amelia's and M. Soley's—[1] I should have been present only at the latter, and that from preference, though that preference did not arise from superior warmth of affection towards M. S.— I truly enjoyed her marriage— She was a fair sight to behold— something so radiant as must live ever in my memory— Thus though I had no sympathy with her feelings yet I understood perfectly and was not distasted by them and I knew the game with her could not be a very losing one— She had not staked so deeply that it could go fatally against her.

I had rather a pretty note from H. Russell inviting me to her wedding— I should have[n] liked much to have attended it for many reasons as this was not possible— I wrote a note which, I flattered myself, was neat and appropriate— This has in turn elicited a reply interesting from what you style in your Nahant verses "childlike trust" in which she begs me to tell her what I know of *James*— I have not yet responded. I had a partic account of the marriage but will not send one as I suppose you are furnished by Sarah. George Hillard is setting out upon wedded life in a very moderate wise-like manner as regards the needful economies—[n] They are to live with Mr Gannett, who I should think, would be as little constraint and interruption as any person good or bad.[2]

You ask me to give you an account of Amelia's affairs— I do not yet know Dr B.— He is not a man, according to A, to be known through his intellects but through his affections. All her thoughts now revolve round one centre— She is entirely absorbed and perfectly happy "My parlour in Green St and the study[n] George has built close by" are inviting to her eye as could be the fabled palaces of Vathek with all their perfumed gardens—[3] All the relations are pleased and no human being displeased— The consequences time will unfold— As to Amelia I think she will prove much such a woman as her "Mother was before her— And a very good thing too!—

Our family—? My Father is in better health— better spirits and likes living here— My Mother seems at present quite well. She has many fatiguing and sordid tasks to perform— but she goes through them with a cheerful spirit— If she continues thus and this sort of life do not seem likely to destroy her, a part of the painful weight that has lain upon my mind will be removed. Brother Eugene has been keeping a school in the country but has not found it very profitable and is now about to enter col[one]l Storrow of Virginia's family for a year as a private tutor—[4] I shall thus lose his society for a-while— I hope the change may be for his good and that more extended knowledge of the world may deeply grave in his mind the necessity for a steady and

honorable ambition— This *may* be and on[n] the other hand my knowledge of this always-to-be loved brother's character makes me forsee
much ill which may arise from absence of the checks he receives under
the parent roof— For either I am prepared— He has tenderness of
heart, some principle, much refinement of feeling and good capacity,
and if he lives obscure or go astray— I cannot think it will be my fault—

Brother William is still in the West Indies—[5] I have no plans which
reach into the future— and in those for the disposal of my time I am
controlled by others— For the next fortnight I must make the preparations for Eugene's going— Afterwards I am to take *all* the children— (I have one under my care at present) and, if I can make
arrangements that suit me, several stranger damsels who crave to
learn foreign[n] tongues, Who wish to know the Latin for E pluribus
unum and to be able to translate French and Italian quotations in the
novels they may have occasion to peruse— Such hours as can [be]
spared from these fascinating pursuits and the sister employment of
needlework I shall devote to[n] a plan of study which I have marked out
for myself which includes a certain portion of history, some theology,
and several German and Italian works—[6] I have besides one or two
literary plans to (attempts on) which I shall give any free bright hours
which may fall to my lot— I feel altogether much more courageous
and resolute than I did last winter— I accomplished all I proposed
these [   ] so far as my own efforts went— probably I shall do the
same now— I have several invites for the following summer, but as
none takes me to Europe or even to Niagara I do not fix my mind at
all on them— Indeed I was very happy at Newport but another summer some very pleasant circumstances will be much changed I love
Anna passing well; a delightful harmony reigned between us—[n] we
were surprizingly near and I am sure dear to each other—[7] and it is a
real grief to me that I must live so far from the light of those sweet
eyes— Most of her family too I liked or loved. I have now egotized as
you requested and shall in future be less *subjective* in my style— Your
letter was very agreeable to me Its tone was one of unpremeditated
frankness; that is all I wish— Indeed I know I should have been sad
in the world without you, but I could have borne it— God grant we
can continue friends. But

> Leider Kann man nichts versprechen
> Was die Herzen widerspricht.[8]

Write to me about your *Barbers and Poles*! your Keatses and your
Clintons your Sunday school and your sermons, your few pleasures

and many plagues, your high hopes and drear misgivings,[9] Some of your verses too, will you not?[n] I urge nothing but shall be interested in all— And I will receive with a spirit, if less pure less pious than your own yet still loving what is good and bright, still true to the *"original standard"* and sincere against all things and against itself— aye feeling[n] any-thing better than to live the rootless echo of the past, cloaking one's poverty of soul with words— Not that I deprecate the common traffick on life's publick mart but in friendship I will not do it— nor bear it.— But as this perhaps seems mere rhodomontade to you believe me now

Sincerely yours

M. F.

ALS (MHi). *Addressed:* Revd James F. Clarke. / Louisville. / Kentucky. *Postmark:* Groton Ms / Nov 14. *Endorsed:* S. M. Fuller Nov 14 1834 / Ans. (KY Letter 14).

marriages which] marriages ⟨?⟩ which
should have] should ↑ have ↓
needful economies—] needful e⟨?⟩conomies ⟨of life⟩—
the study] the st⟨y⟩udy
and on] and ⟨on⟩ on
learn foreign] learn foreig⟨?⟩n
devote to] devote ⟨the⟩ to
between us—] between ⟨?⟩ us—
misgivings, Some of your verses too, will you not?] misgivings, ↑ Some of your verses too, will you not? ↓
aye feeling] aye ↑ feeling ↓

1. Amelia Greenwood married George Bartlett; George Hillard married Susan Tracy Howe (1808–79), daughter of Judge Samuel Howe (and sister of Tracy Howe), on 27 October (*CC*, 29 October 1834; Howe, *Howe Genealogies*, p. 175); George Davis and Harriet Russell married on 16 October (*CC*, 18 October 1834). Mary Soley married William Bradford DeWolfe on 22 October (*CC*, 29 October 1834).

2. George Hillard had only recently established his law practice with Charles Sumner. Ezra Stiles Gannett was the assistant minister for Dr. William Ellery Channing, whom he succeeded at the Federal Street Church in 1842. Gannett was later a founder and president of the American Unitarian Association.

3. *Vathek: An Arabian Tale*, written in French by William Beckford, was published in English in 1786.

4. Samuel Appleton Storrow, formerly a judge advocate in the army, had a plantation at Culpeper, Virginia.

5. William Henry Fuller became a businessman and settled in Cincinnati.

6. Fuller was at this time corresponding with Frederic Henry Hedge about her theological studies (*Letters of MF*, 1:211–14).

7. Anna Barker.

8. From Goethe's "Abschied":

> Zu lieblich ists, ein Wort zu brechen,
> Zu schwer die wohlerkannte Pflicht,
> Und leider kann man nichts versprechen,
> Was unserm Herzen widerspricht. (*Sämtliche Werke*, 1:46)

9. Fuller puns on the news Clarke had sent her of Horace Barbour, a friend in Kentucky, and the family of Casimir Mackiewiez, a Polish (actually Lithuanian) family that had emigrated to the Midwest (*Letters of JFC*, p. 80). Clarke had become a friend of George Keats, the poet's brother. In reply to Fuller's query, Clarke said that Barbour had gone to Mobile, that "my Poles do not behave themselves very well," and that "Geo. Keats is one of the best men in the world" (*Letters of JFC*, p. 82). Clinton is Clinton McKesson.

1029. To James F. Clarke

Groton 8th Jany 1835.—

My dear Friend,

Your two letters were[n] valuable Christmas and N year's presents but I could not answer them earlier—[1] For yr first do you think you shall remain at the West after balancing again and again the arguments between that wild region and our well rubbed one. Apropos— this extract from a letter recd from H. Hedge some time since. "I had the other day a letter[n] from J. F. Clarke and a delightful one it was. I have great hopes of that young man though I am somewhat disappointed in the direction of his powers. I had hoped (perhaps unwisely) that he would be a preacher to the cultivated and refined; it is those who most need a physician for they are the most diseased; but his ambition seems to be for the popular. No matter if he will but be a faithful interpreter of the high and the spiritual. Why should I care to whom he is sent or thinks himself sent."[2]

I fear I shall be disappointed of Sarah's visit this winter and always— It *is* a disappointment.

You misunderstood me or I expressed myself ill about Harriet[n] Davis. She did not ask me about your character she asked me what I was hearing from you now[3]—I omitted answering her letter for some time being firstly ill and secondly engrossed with or by Eugene for several weeks previous to his leaving us and she is now revenging herself by equal neglect.—

A kind deed of George's towards one very dear to me has led me to think that you are nearer the truth in your estimate of his character than I in mine and that he is not selfish and unfeeling as I have supposed— This much I ought to say— time will settle the matter fully—

I have been deeply grieved by the death of a young man here— William Austin—[4] I dont know that you are at all acquainted with him— I have seen him often since we lived here— he was engaged to a young lady in the neighbourhood— The engagement was very disinterested on his part; she belonged to a family who have suffered great misfortunes— They were once rich and are now very poor— they lost[n] their eldest daughter three or four years since, a lovely young woman, and[n] their third is a miserable invalid, their fourth— her mind is almost destroyed by epilepsy— three little boys they can ill afford to educate and clothe— W. A boarded in the family while in college and became attached to the second daughter a girl neither beautiful or talented, but he loved her with romantick devotion— He has made great extertions to get lucre for her sake— after graduating he kept school two years at a thousand a year and the necessary application undermined his health— he was attacked by a cough and obliged to leave his school— but he seemed to get better; he had gained many[n] excellent friends and had no difficulty in getting ten pupils at two hundred a year, a respectable income and he hoped very soon to take his beloved from a home of sordid tasks and constant petty distresses to his own heart[h] and board— he was also to take one of her little brothers and educate him— but death has marred all these schemes of well earned happiness and usefulness and withdrawn the last prop from a falling house. The cough returned, sleep and appetite failed he could not bear to leave his pupils lest he should disappoint their parents;— when at last he was forced to come[n] here for a while to recove[r] his strength and spirits in the society of [her] with whom his heart was at home he was already in a lung fever which soon changed into the[n] fatal typhus and last night when he died I felt as if it were a thing even by me hardly to be borne— I was not his friend but he was one of those blameless beings on whose active intelligence, steady worth, modesty and gentleness the mind of a mere acquaintance may love to dwell— And oh the poor girl he has left behind— her only earthly hope withdrawn while so many cumber the ground— She has at least had the consolation of being with him constantly to the last— His illness has been of the beautiful kind— he has been some days delirious, talking incessantly repeating fragments of poetry and passages from elegant authors or talking tenderly of those he was leaving unawares— all the overflowings of his perturbed mind pure and sweet— Excuse me for writing so much about it— I would not defer this letter and could not well write about anything else. You, my friend were a stranger to him but Death is interesting to us all I fear you will hardly be able to read it. I might conclude with the childish distich—

My pen is poor (for my dear Eugene is absent.
My ink is pale (for I cannot keep it from freezing this
intense cold weather.

My love for you
Will never fail (*I hope*

But grown up people dont accept such excuses for defects in Form—

M.

ALS (MHi). *Addressed:* Revd James F. Clarke. / Louisville. / Kentucky. *Postmark:* Groton Ms / Jany 9. *Endorsed:* S. M. Fuller 8th Jan / 1835—
letters were] letters ⟨?⟩were
day a letter] day ↑ a letter ↓
about Harriet] about H. ↑ arriet ↓
they lost] they ⟨?⟩ lost
woman, and] woman, ↑ and ↓
gained many] gained ⟨th⟩ many
he was forced to come] he ↑ was forced to ↓ c⟨a⟩ome
into the] into ⟨?⟩ the

1. Clarke wrote in November and again on 15 December 1834 (*Letters of JFC*, pp. 82–87).

2. Hedge wrote Fuller on 17 November 1834 (MH-AH bMS 384/1 [15]). Clarke, in reply to Fuller, asked her to solicit manuscripts from Hedge for the soon-to-be-formed *Western Messenger* (*Letters of JFC*, pp. 88–90).

3. Clarke had responded to Fuller's comment: "It is odd that Harriet should write to you about my character. I have not offered myself as her servant" (*Letters of JFC*, p. 84).

4. William Austin (1811–35) graduated from Harvard in 1831. He was the son of William Austin (1778–1841), the author of the popular tale "Peter Rugg, the Missing Man" (Thomas Bellows Wyman, *The Genealogies and Estates of Charlestown* [Boston, 1879], p. 33).

1030. To James F. Clarke

[Groton, 1 February 1835][n]

[   ]had been there.[1]

A voice of uncommon compass and beauty never sharp in its highest or rough and husky in its lowest tones— A perfect enunciation; every syllable round and energetick though his manner was the one I love best very rapid and full of eager climaxes. Earnestness in every part sometimes impassioned earnestness a sort of "dear friends believe, *pray* believe— I love you and you *must* believe as I do" expression Even in the argumentative parts— I felt as I have so often done before if I were a man decidedly the gift I would choose should be that of eloquence— That power of forcing the vital currents of thousands of human hearts into *one* current by the constraining power of that most delicate instrument the voice is *so* intense— Yes I would prefer it to a more[n] extensive fame, a more permanent influence—

Did I describe to you my feelings on hearing Mr Everett's eulogy—[2] on la Fayette[n] No I did not for that was when we had quarrelled and while I was staying at Mrs Farrar's with Anna Barker and Mr Dewey—[3] singular constellation. That was exquisite— The old hackneyed story— not a new anecdote, not a single reflection of any value— but the manner, the manner— the delicate inflections[n] of voice, the elegant and appropriate gestures the sense of beauty produced by the whole which thrilled alike the most gentle Anna and the most ungentle Margaret to tears flowing from a deeper and a purer source than[n] that which answers to Pathos.— This was fine but I prefer the Thompson manner. Then there is Mr Webster's unlike either simple grandeur, nobler, more impressive less captivating— I have heard few fine speakers— I wish I could hear a thousand I never have heard you say what sort you liked best will you tell me? I think I admire or rather *feel* Mr Taylor's style of eloquence less than most persons. I suppose because I have less simplicity and less tenderness.[4]

Are you vexed by my keeping the six vols of your Goethe— I read him very little either I have so little time— many things to do at home my three children and three pupils besides whom I instruct for hire Yes James, I am beginning to serve my apprenticeship to the world in good earnest— We shall see how it will end yet Earning *money*— think of that.— Tis but a little but 'tis a beginning. I shall be a professional character yet— But my children come on finely verily I think I have done them much good if some future gardener do not root it all up— I do not believe you will ever get three human beings at a time into better order than I have them— By the way— I have always thought all that was said about the anti religious tendency of a classical education all nonsense and old[n] wives' tales— But their puzzles about Virgil's notions of heaven and virtue and his gracefully described gods and goddesses have led me to alter my opinion and I suspect from reminiscences of my own mental history that if all governors dont think the same tis from want of that intimate knowledge of their pupils minds which I naturally possess— I really find it difficult to keep their *morale* steady and am inclined to think many of my own skeptical suffering[s] are traceable to this source. I well remember what reflections arose in my childish[n] mind from a comparison of the Hebrew history where every moral obliquity is shown out with such naiveté and the Greek history full of sparkling deeds and brilliant sayings and their gods and goddesses, the types of beauty and power with the dazzling veil of flowery language and poetical imagery cast over their vices and failings But to return to Goethe What do you consider to have been his religious opinions?— I speak seriously— give me a definite answer which I may compare with my own ideas— I am deeply interested in the Old testament— I have read Jahn's histy of the Hebrew commonwealth that I may be able to connect and understand all the disjointed parts—[5] I am now reading the O.T. in my old German copy. (thinking it would seem more fresh in a foreign tongue) with the assistance of Eichhorn and Jahn's archaeology—[n] whether I shall persevere no one knows—[6] Life grows scantier, employments accumulate I feel less and less confidence in my powers. You, dear James, speak of "catching my onward spirit" and I know this from you is not meant ironically but I think your progress is vast compared with mine— Sometimes I doubt whether I make any, whether I am not merely giving up one thing for another— Certainly I do not learn or think so fast as I once did But I *must* stop; this is the thirteenth page I have written this evening— If you do not think my letter worth half a dollar you must sell it at auction for what you can get. But if you do— think it worth the half-dollar[n] I have a proposal to make I will if you please write to you the *first* of every month if you will write on the *16th* beginning with this— We shall thus have time to receive one another's letters and write once a month which is more than we have done of late— Eugene and I write to one another once a fortnight on stated days and like it— I used to hate regular arrangements but I have become quite a creature of routine— If you agree write this coming 16th— I feel as if only *begun* to write to you— Shall not sign the letter lest you should decide to *sell* it.

ALfr (MHi). Published in part in *Memoirs*, 1:124–26, and *Letters of MF*, 1:218–19. *Addressed:* Revd J. F. Clarke / Louisville / Kentucky. *Postmark:* Groton Ms / Feb 2. *Endorsed:* Answered March 16.

This fragment is the conclusion of letter 104 (Letters of MF, *1:219–21*).
to a more] to ⟨to⟩ a ⟨a⟩ more
eulogy— on la Fayette] eulogy— ↑ on la Fayette ↓
delicate inflections] delicate infl⟨?⟩ections
source than] source ⟨from⟩ than
and old] and ⟨w⟩ old
my childish] my ↑ childish ↓
Jahn's archaeology—] Jahn's archae⟨l⟩ology—
do— think it worth the half-dollar] do— ↑ think it worth the half-dollar ↓

1. George Thompson, the English abolitionist, had spoken in Groton on 15 January.
2. Everett delivered the eulogy on 6 September 1834.
3. Orville Dewey, who had been the Unitarian minister at New Bedford, became minister at the Church of the Messiah in New York City in November 1835.
4. Edward Thompson Taylor (1793–1871), minister at Boston's Seaman's Bethel, was acclaimed for his preaching style. Melville modeled Father Mapple on Taylor (*DAB*).
5. Fuller was corresponding with Hedge on these topics (*Letters of MF*, 1:215–16, 223–24). Calvin Stowe translated *Jahn's History of the Hebrew Commonwealth* in 1828.

6. Fuller also read Johann Gottfried Eichhorn's *Einleitung ins alte Testament*. Since she uses the English title for Jahn's *Archaeology*, she may have read Thomas C. Upham's *Jahn's Biblical Archaeology* (Andover, 1823), which had subsequent editions in 1827 and 1832. Upham's work was a translation of Johann Jahn's Latin *Archaeoligia biblica* (Vienna, 1814). Fuller, however, may have read his *Biblische Archäologie* (Vienna, 1796–1802).

1031. To James F. Clarke

Groton 29th March
1835,

My dear James,

I received your Cincinnati letter 19[n] days from date and one today in 13 days— What is the reason your letters are often so long on the road? I have sometimes thought you must delay putting them in the post— I will answer first your first *"favour"*

I am much pleased with your plans of a periodical; it was just what I wished you to do now—[1] I am too ignorant of the people you have to deal[n] with to make any useful suggestions. I have written to H. Hedge and will so to Mrs Farrar in your behalf, but the former is in all the agonies of suspense[n] as to whether he shall banish himself to Bangor or starve on the Editorship of the Christian Examiner, and the latter is deeply engaged making her husband happy and writing the Life of William Penn—[2] As to myself I think you jeer me— do you suppose[n] I keep on hand "bundles" of articles all ready for the Western[n] Examiner?—[3] I am however doing my best to comply with your[n] request and shall send you by the first opportunity— Imprimis a slight thing on the "Last days of Pompeii— I have been excited to write this by the many (to my mind) foolish remarks I hear constantly on the subject and by a vulgar bit of abuse copied from *Cobbett!* into the Xn register. I would like to have it published by way of venting my feelings, but, if, as I think very probably, the views do not suit you, do not use the[n] piece out of complaisance for me but return it and at some future day I shall probably take it as my basis and expand my ideas into better form.[4] 2d. On[n] the biographies of Revd Geo. Crabbe and Miss Moore— As they are much read I thought this might suit you— 3d On Philip van Artevelde; not yet found time to write it but have all in my head—[5] The drama has occupied much of my attention and I would like to take a general survey of Goethe's Schiller's, Alfieri's Manzoni's, Miss Baillie's and Coleridge's with reference to this one, so much admired. I should endeavour to condense but fear I might make an article too long for you as your *main* object is not *literary*. I wish however to write it and give a fixed shape to some ideas I *think* not altogether common-place— My own favourite project since I began seriously to entertain any of the sort is six historical tragedies of which I have the plans of three quite perfect. However the attempts I have made on them have served to show me the vast difference betwixt conception and execution yet I am, though[n] abashed, not altogether discouraged—[6] My next favorite plan is a series of tales illustrative of Hebrew history— The proper junctures have occurred to me during[n] my late studies on the historical books of the O.T. This task however requires[n] a thorough and imbuing knowledge of the Hebrew manners and spirit, with a chastened energy of imagination which I am as yet far from possessing. But if I should be permitted peace and time to follow out my ideas I have hopes—

Perhaps it is a weakness to confide to you embryo designs which never may glow into life or mock me by their failure but if I die and leave no trace I confide in you to let my fond aspirations perish with me.—[n]

So much for your first although there was one topick which if you had not resolutely marked me as the "friend of your *mind*" only I might have responded to.— For your second favour I do not know whether to be most obliged by your answering my questions (what novel attention) or pleased by your manly candour. My really dear James, has any of my talk about, ambition glory and "all that truck" (to use our Editorial friend's phrase)[n] ever led you to mistake me so far as to make you nervous when you talk to me of want of success— I cannot but think so from the resolute manner in which you now and then make one of these avowals. I have the most firm faith that your active mind and warm love of truth can not fail eventual[n] success. I am well content to bide your time. I only hope you will not stay in the West longer than your own mind says is good for yourself and others from false ideas of consistency of purpose.[7] As to your poetry (which I shall impatiently expect trusting you, maugre all your broken promises) I cannot answer you better than in the words of Uhland with whom H. Hedge (once more my benefactor) has made me acquainted

> "Nicht an wenig stolze Namen
> Ist die Liederkunst gebannt—
> Deines vollen Herzen's triebe
>   Gib sie keck im Klange frei,
> Säuselndwandle deine Liebe.
> Donnernd uns dein Zorn vorbei!

Singst du nicht dein ganzes Leben
Sing' doch in der Jugend's drang
Nur im Bluthenmond erheben
Nachtigallen ihren Sang.

Kann man's nicht in Bucher binden
Was die Stunden dir verleihn
Gib ein fliegend Blatt den Winden
Muntre Jugend hascht es ein.[8]

I suppose you have heard all about Mr R. W. Emerson's engage-ment.[9] But of that, and Reinhard and the study of Greek and the Channing's tour to Europe I have left myself no room to speak—[10] I have written very ill because my hand is hurt. I shall send Dr Lieber's poem to Sarah with the other things—[11]

M. F.

ALS (MHi). Published in part in *Memoirs*, 1:126–27, and *Letters of MF*, 1:229. Ad-dressed: Revd James F. Clarke. / Louisville / Kentucky. *Postmark:* Boston Mar 31. En-dorsed: Ky 1⟨8⟩7.

letter 19] letter 1⟨?⟩9
to deal] to ⟨?⟩ ⟨?⟩deal
of suspense] of suspen⟨c⟩se
you suppose] you s⟨?⟩uppose
the Western] the ⟨Chris⟩ Western
with your] with ⟨my⟩ your
use the] use ⟨it⟩ the
2d. On] 2d. O⟨?⟩n
execution yet I am, though] execution ↑ yet ↓ I am, ⟨?⟩ though
me during] me ⟨a⟩ during
however requires] however ⟨a⟩ requires
with me.—] with ⟨you⟩ me.—
truck" (to use our Editorial friend's phrase)] truck" ↑ (to use our Editorial friend's phrase) ↓
fail eventual] fail ↑ eventual ↓

1. In his letter of 20 February, Clarke told Fuller of his plans for the *Western Exam-iner:* "We mean to make this a first rate affair, and to combine literature and other miscellaneous matters with religious discussions. I mean it to have a Western air and spirit, a free and unshackled spirit and form, as far as may be" (*Letters of JFC*, p. 88). There already being a *Western Examiner* (and it an atheist publication), Clarke and his associates changed the name to the *Western Messenger* (Habich, *Transcendentalism and the "Western Messenger,"* pp. 55–56).

2. She wrote Hedge the day before this letter to Clarke (*Letters of MF*, 1:228). Clarke wrote that from Eliza Farrar he wanted "an article on Divine Influences, for I think with Fichte that Transcendentalism and Spirituality can be made perfectly intel-ligible to any simple, untrampled minds" (*Letters of JFC*, p. 89).

3. Wrote Clarke: "I wish you to help me by writing on topics of religion, morals, literature, art, or anything *you* feel to be worth writing about. Will you not send to Sarah a bundle of good long (or good short) articles to be forwarded to me" (*Letters of JFC*, p. 88).

4. The *Christian Register* of 21 March 1835 contained a paragraph from an unnamed source in which William Cobbett attacked Bulwer, "whose desultory and heterogenous essays can serve no other earthly purpose than those of making ignorance stare, idleness fall asleep, and encourage emptiness and conceit in the indulgence of contempt for everything civil or political that is more than six months old or that is not, like the Bourbon police, imported from some country that our wise fore fathers taught their sons to despise." In August of the same year Fuller, who admired Bulwer's work, published a review of his *Last Days of Pompeii* in the *Western Messenger*.

5. Her review of George Crabbe's biography of his father and of William Roberts, *Memoirs of the Life and Correspondence of Mrs. Hannah More*, appeared in the June 1835 *Messenger;* her "Philip Van Artevelde" appeared in December.

6. Fuller apparently wrote four tragedies, at least two of which were based on the life of Guastavus II Adolphus, king of Sweden (*Letters of MF*, 1:229n).

7. In his letter of 16 March, Clarke had said, "Am I going to stay in the West always? Sarah writes me that *you* say I am not—pour moi, I know nothing about it" (*Letters of JFC*, p. 90).

8. Fuller quotes portions of four stanzas of Uhland's "Freie Kunst." The full stanzas are:

> Nicht an wenig stolze Namen
> Ist die Liederkunst gebannt;
> Ausgestreuet ist der Samen
> Über alles deutsche Land.
>
> Deines vollen Herzens Triebe,
> Gib sie keck im Klange frei!
> Säuselnd wandle deine Liebe,
> Donnernd uns dein Zorn vorbei!
>
> Singst du nicht dein ganzes Leben,
> Sing doch in der Jugend Drang!
> Nur im Blütenmond erheben
> Nachtigallen ihren Sang.
>
> Kann man's nicht in Bücher binden,
> Was die Stunden dir verleihn:
> Gib ein fliegend Blatt den Winden!
> Muntre Jugend hascht es ein.

Margarete Münsterberg's translation:

> Nay, this art doth not belong
> To a small and haughty band;
> Scattered are the seeds of song
> All about the German land.
>
> Music set thy passions free
> From the heart's confining cage;
> Let thy love like murmurs be,
> And like thunder-storm thy rage!
>
> Singest thou not all thy days,
> Joy of youth should make thee sing.
> Nightingales pour forth their lays
> In the blooming months of spring!
>
> Though in books they hold not fast
> What the hour to thee imparts,
> Leaves unto the breezes cast,
> To be seized by youthful hearts!

(Ludwig Uhland, *Werke* [Frankfurt, 1983], 1:37; Kuno F. Ranke, ed., *The German Classics* [New York, 1913], 5:221–22])

9. Emerson became engaged to Lydia Jackson on 30 January 1835 (Ralph L. Rusk, *The Life of Ralph Waldo Emerson* [New York, 1949], p. 211).

10. On 1 February Fuller had asked Clarke if he had read *Memoirs and Confessions of Francis Volkmar Reinhard* (*Letters of MF*, 1:219). Clarke answered on 16 March: "I read his Memoirs a few months since; some things about them I liked, but the general impression was not so pleasant with me as it appears to have been with you. I studied it more for his mind than his character; perhaps that was the reason" (*Letters of JFC*, p. 89). Among other topics, Clarke said that he studied "perhaps three or four" hours a day and that Greek was one of his subjects. He said that William Henry Channing and his family were to go to Europe "because they are disappointed in Wm's not being so popular a preacher as they expected" (*Letters of JFC*, p. 90).

11. On February 20, Clarke had asked: "Have you that poem on Niagara of Dr. Lieber's and will you send it to me" (*Letters of JFC*, p. 89).

1032. To James F. Clarke

1st April 1835

I forgot, dear James, to mention in my letter, that Father wishes to take your Examiner. I shall send your prospectus to Mrs Farrar; Groton affords no subscribers. We send to Boston tomorrow and I have not had time to write the Van Artevelde piece, but when it is done, I will send it to Sarah; perhaps the rest of the bundle will wait for it. Be so good as to let me know whether I have confined myself within the proper limits as to space, whether I go deep enough or *too* deep for your purpose (the latter, I think, can hardly be but I dont know *how* "barbarious" your Western morselings are), whether I use too many words, in short *any* faults you may perceive.[1] I used to fancy in my ignorance that if one had any thing in's head, it were as easy to write it out as to talk it out, but I am now satisfied that the art of writing, like all other arts, requires an apprenticeship. I believe I spoke to you about the periodical, the illuminati think of setting up here next year;[2] they intended to ask your assistance but you will be "on your own hook"; by the way can you oldbuckize that phrase for me?—[3] I send this sermon and charge, though old, thinking you may not have seen and may feel interested in them as I did— Observe the dogmatism of Mr Ware about Unitarianism.[4] Do you know F. Kemble attends at Mr Furness church—[5] How goes on Mr Elliott?— I fear he thought me rude at Newport— My breaking my engagement was quite involuntary and will not, I hope, prevent his coming to see me if he is "our way"— in haste yours

M. F.

ALS (MHi). *Addressed:* Rev. J. F. Clarke. *Endorsed:* S. M. F. April 1st 1835 / With articles for Western Branch— Ky letter 1⟨7⟩8.

1. Clarke responded on 12 May: "You ask whether you are *too deep*. Not so, but not distinct enough, not enough of plainness and detail in the setting forth and development of the idea (mind, I always speak of *our* public). The article on Bulwer for example is a sort of comment and illustration of the text from Goethe about True and False. This leading idea is not prominent enough to the reader, too many indications to other trains of thought, springs just touched in passing which commence a firm swell of music and then stop, rich veins of silver partly worked, then left. . . . I think the language too elevated throughout" (*Letters of JFC*, p. 95).

2. On 20 February Hedge wrote Fuller, "Mr. Geo Ripley & myself are intending to establish a periodical of an entirely different character from any now existing a journal of spiritual philosophy in which we are to enlist all the Germano-philosophico-literary talent in the country. . . . It is our desire & strong hope to introduce new elements of thought & to give a new impulse to the mental action of our country" (MH-AH bMS 384/1 [17]). No such journal appeared (until 1840, when the *Dial* was published), thanks in part to the creation of Clarke's *Messenger*.

3. A reference to Jonathan Oldbuck, laird of Monkbarns, the title character in Scott's *Antiquary*.

4. Fuller's reference to a "sermon and charge [to the new minister]" indicates that their occasion was an ordination, but whose is unclear. Both Henry Wares (Sr. and Jr.) were Harvard professors at this time. The son best fits Fuller's description (*DAB; DivCat*).

5. A resident of Philadelphia since her marriage, Fanny Kemble attended the church where William Henry Furness was the minister.

1033. To James F. Clarke

6th April [1835]—

In reading over what I have written my taste is grated by the repetition of epithets and phrases such as beauty, simplicity, distinguished excellence &c— Will you, who can judge coolly from your distance, let me know whether I sin more than others in these respects or whether the fault is in the poverty of language on such topicks?— Tell me whether there is fulness, precision, detail enough. Mrⁿ Barlow said I generalized too much. I wish to know whether I have improved in that particular. The fault is natural when one has talked so much and written so little. I am sure I *can* correct it. Give my any criticisms, no matter how severe, that occur to you. My grand object is improvement.[1]

I ought to apologize for writing out this piece so badly. I fear it will give you trouble. I was very tired and unwell but thought I should have an opportunity to send it and knew my after engagements must prevent my attending to it.

As I observed by the advertisements that every review had its article on Van Artevelde. I chose to compare it with others and give a more brief account of itself than I should have done had the poem been less generally noticed.

I received to day a letter from H. Hedge; He says "I *have* seen the prospectus of the Western Examiner and am selfish enough to regret its appearance. I fear that work will interfere with the success of mine, in the West and especially diminish the amount of contributions I should otherwise receive from Messrs Clarke and Peabody.[2] Pray say to the former of these Gentlemen that all my labour will be required for the Spiritual Enquirer and that so far from helping him I must beg help *from* him. I will however with great pleasure subscribe to the Western Examiner and, if I find it possible write something for it"

Poor H. is very much out of spirits He has accepted[n] a settlement at Bangor for one year—[3] most unwillingly; he feels it not to be the place for him; but with a wife and two children it is impossible to disregard that lower kind of expediency which has to do with Cash. I must hope his fine mind will get some outward help yet.

I received also a sweet letter from Amelia. She says hers is the "happiness that maketh the heart afraid"—[4] I often wish I could show you some of the letters I receive particularly Eugene's which one, a moi, highly amusing— Farewell, my friend.

M F.

The Groton Athenaeum will take your Examiner— Direct to care of Revd C. Robinson, their number unless I write you to the contrary.[5]

ALS (MHi). *Addressed:* Revd J. F. Clarke. *Endorsed:* 18–No 2.

enough. Mr] enough. ⟨Give me my⟩ Mr

has accepted] has ⟨?⟩ accepted

1. In his answer of 12 May, Clarke offered this advice: "When we quote we must say plainly all about it, and communicate the whole idea. But thus we may quote from Plato, or Coleridge, or Goethe, just as safely as from Dr. Channing, Locke, or Walter Scott. There are no prejudices for or against" (*Letters of JFC,* p. 94).

2. Ephraim Peabody (1807–56) graduated from Bowdoin in 1827 and from the divinity school at Cambridge in 1830. Later in that year he was ordained in Cincinnati. With Clarke, Peabody was a force behind the *Messenger.* He later was the Unitarian minister in New Bedford and, from 1846 to his death, at King's Chapel, Boston (*DivCat*).

3. Hedge was the Unitarian minister at Bangor, Maine, from May 1835 until March 1850 (*DivCat*).

4. From Thomas Hood's "Ode to Melancholy":

> The sunniest things throw sternest shade,
> And there is ev'n a happiness
> That makes the heart afraid! (*Selected Poems of Thomas Hood,* p. 51)

5. Charles Robinson was the Unitarian minister at Groton from 1826 until 1838.

1034. To James F. Clarke

Groton 28th April 1835.

My dear James, I am glad you are so punctual since it enables me to be so too— your letter found me last Sunday confined to my bed with a severe indisposition and it was the only Sabba-day thing I had.

I fear you are doing too much just now— Beware, lest by and by when the power of mental effort is very important to yourself and others you should find it exhausted— I should not like to see you with lead in your head like poor Mr Dewey—[1] just when every body was wide awake for you.— If you like my pieces I will write one on Coleridge's Table talk when it comes out—[2] I might be equal to that, though not one of his philosophic works— Why you call me "transcendental" I dont know.[3] I am sure if I am on[e] it is after the fashion of le Bourgeois Gentilhomme.[4] As far as[n] I know myself I am at present "all no how" except on matters of taste— "View of Goethe"—[5] Why dont you write a *Life* of Goethe in 2 vols octo accompanied by criticisms on his works— This vision swims often before mine own eyes, but I know too many are swimming there of the kind and would gladly see this one realized by a friend— If *I* do it— there shall be less eloquence[n] perhaps but more insight than a De Stael.

As to the Hebrew tales I have written the first but cannot now think it worthy your eye— After the agony[n] of so miserably failing to my Ideal is calmed I shall read it and see whether there is sufficient hope of success to encourage my continuing the series— Since you encourage me I would ask— would translations from the modern French novelists take with your reading public— would any Cincinnati publishers buy one of a very clever little fiction called "Cinq-Mars."[6] It would make a thin duodecimo— and, if it took, the healthy might be culled from the incessant productions of that literature and added to ours. My aim is *money*— I want an independent income very much, but I could not venture any thing in which my own pride and feelings are engaged for lucre. But to translating in four modern languages I know myself equal and if I could set some scheme of this kind going it would suit me very well. But with all my aspirations after independence I do not possess sufficient at present to walk into the Boston establishments and ask them to buy my work and I have no friend at once efficient and sympathizing— If I cannot make my pen avail me I must ere long take other means—

You have undoubtedly heard of William Channing's engagement— but perhaps you have long been in his confidence—[7] I was surprized, as I had for more than two years supposed him secretly attached to my friend Miss Barker, and his manner last autumn when he visited us both in Cambridge confirmed that idea. I admired much at that time the cheerfulness with which he spoke of life and its different probations, but my admiration is somewhat diminished now I know that he was at that time so happy in his affections; even the disappointments of a lawful and honorable ambition may be borne when there is this sweetness in the cup— You probably know the lady. I should[n] think her heart must be a fresh fountain; her expression and manner are peculiarly sweet and artless.—[n] And you, dear James, is there no Julia Allen for you, young, innocent, refined, [   ] enough to gratify your tastes and able to appreciate your heart— If that heart had such an home, we should hear no more of "ill regulated feelings" happiness would be the regulator— But I am trespassing on my limits as I am not the amica del cuore— I will talk to you of one who is so to me— Anna Barker— have I ever told you how much I love her?— you know my magnetic power over young women— well! some ten or twelve have been drawn into my sphere since you knew me— to all I have given sympathy and time (more than was agreeable) to her alone— love, confidence warm as if I still knew Disappointment only by name or dark presentiment. The ground we have in common is not extensive, but full of fragrant flowers and wet with gentle dews.— Never could fancy create[n] a being of greater purity grace and softness— Sarah proposed to me to write a novel and make myself a heroine— Whether I might not, with some aid of poetical embellishment, figure in real bloody tragedy I wot not— but if I write a novel I shall take Anna for my heroine.

I am going to Boston tomorrow, yet direct your next here— I shall probably return in time to receive it— Mrs Farrar has been much out of health and "towering" to Washington &c on that account.

Did you ever hear of Henri Heine?— I have seen some extracts from a work of his on[n] modern German belles lettres which are highly amusing.[8] Have been fascinated into reading Richter's Flegel Jahre—[9] and cannot resist the *original* mind when I am with it though not of the kind I naturally like— Hard to get into the stream and harder to get out as somebody in Blackwood said about Rabelais.

AL (MHi). *Addressed:* Revd James F. Clarke / Louisville, / Kentucky. *Postmark:* Groton Ms / April 29. *Endorsed:* S. M. F. May 1st / 1835. Ky 19.

As far as] As f⟨o⟩ar ↑ as ↓
less eloquence] less e⟨?⟩loquence
the agony] the ⟨the⟩ agony
I should] I ⟨th⟩ should
and artless.—] and a⟨t⟩rtless.—

fancy create] fancy ⟨g⟩ create
his on] his ⟨?⟩ on

1. In his letter of 12 April, Clarke gave Fuller a catalog of his activities, which included several lectures in addition to his pastoral duties. A breakdown in 1833 had caused Orville Dewey to resign the New Bedford pulpit and travel to Europe.

2. Apparently Fuller never reviewed *Table Talk* (London, 1835). In his reply on 12 May, Clarke cautioned Fuller to "take notice of that deficiency of the practical understanding which constituted *his* onesidedness in Philosophy, Art, and Life" (*Letters of JFC*, p. 93).

3. Clarke had told Fuller to "be as transcendental as you please; if you express transcendentalism distinctly there is no objection to it drawn from its logical inconsistence with a domineering philosophy" (*Letters of JFC*, p. 91).

4. Molière first wrote and performed *Le Bourgeois Gentilhomme* in 1670. In the play, M. Jourdain, the bourgeois, hires a philosophy master to teach him spelling and the almanac.

5. Clarke had said: "I have received some vols. of Goethe from you and have again been excited by reading them to a *purpose* of undertaking to give my view of him." In reply to Fuller, he said: "I should like to see your '*View of Goethe*, 2 vols. 800, Philadelphia, Carey Lea & Co.—' Send me a copy of it, will you?" (*Letters of JFC*, pp. 92–93, 94).

6. Alfred de Vigny, *Cinq-Mars* (Paris, 1826). Of the novel, Fuller wrote in her 1839 journal: "It is well brought out, figures in good relief, lights well distributed, sentiment high, but nowhere exaggerated, knowledge exact, and the good and bad of human nature painted with that impartiality which becomes a man, and a man of the world." She had her reservations: "It is one of those works which I should consider only excusable as the amusement of leisure hours" (MH). In reply, Clarke said: "I assure you that there is not a reading public on this side of the mountains. I do not think there is at present any publisher in Cincin. who would venture on a Western novel even. But such a translation as you describe would no doubt find a purchaser among the Harpers, etc., who are rivaling each other in snapping at the last new novel" (*Letters of JFC*, p. 94).

7. In 1836 William Henry Channing married Julia Allen of Rondout, New York. In his reply, Clarke said the engagement was a surprise and that there was no "Julia Allen" in his immediate future (*Letters of JFC*, p. 94).

8. Fuller had read excerpts from *Zur Geschichte der neueren schönen Literatur in Deutschland*, which had been published in 1833.

9. Jean Paul's unfinished novel, *Flegeljahre*, was published in 1804–5.

1035. To James F. Clarke

Boston 2d June 1835,

Dear James,

Although my mind be dissipated with over-much babbling and my frame be wearied with over-much walking in a very hot sun I will not break our compact by deferring my monthly epistle.

I received yours on Saturday last just before taking the most delightful ride on horseback— out to *Horn Pond* that unromantically named scene of former days— Oh the day was divine and the whole ride presented a succession of pictures *so* beautiful— the want you complain of would have been satisfied if you could have been there—[1] yet how is this? my friend; you talk of being separated from the contemplation of "wood, sky, &c" I thought nature at least was beautiful and lofty with you Thanks for your critiques on my attempts; I will endeavor to profit by them if I write more for you. Mr Elliott wishes me to write a review of Mr Dewey's new vol, and I intend to do so if I have time to do the subject any-thing like justice but many engagements press upon my anticipation.[2] Do not be sick; if you are often so; tis proof positive that you do too much.

Julia Allen is sister to Mrs Sparks who I grieve to tell you is supposed to be in the last stages of a consumption. I thought you had seen both sisters often.[3]

I have become much more acquainted with William Elliott and now look upon him quite as a friend The purity and brightness of his feelings— his uncommon fairness and modesty of mind I never appreciated before—[4] Boston is delighted with him and I never have seen any one beg with[n] more dignity.

Mr Angier made me a visit the other day and showed considerable originality in expressing his views of the past, present, and future. One or two things he said I think are sufficiently striking to be imparted to you but I have not room for them. He entirely deprecated the idea of his engagement to Miss Rotch, whether in sincerity or not time will show—[5] Most people opine that even if she be not too ambitious to accept him her papa will never consent. Mr H Ware said his ordination was the most beautiful thing of the kind ever seen; all the parts so exquisitely performed. I read Mr Dewey's sermon in manuscript and verily it was superb I should have thought its requisitions[n] would have frightened the new dignitary.[6]

Sarah is going with me to Groton next week— *dear* Sarah. I not only *like* but *love* her now. All the little obstacles to our intercourse have vanished I am no longer too much for her and she, I think is quite frank with me.

I have seen the Greenwoods several times. Amelia is truly happy— her Dr seems if not a highly intellectual, quite a moral being and suits her exactly— while Angy seems as much engrossed by her Richard as she could be by any hero—[7] She is quite as pretty but less funny than formerly.

Sister Ellen has gone out to pass this day at Newton. Mr Elliott wishes us to go too— if *I* do it will be entirely because[n] he wishes it— I feel your absence too sensibly when there to enjoy a visit.

Marsylvia was married yesterday in the Catholic church— Oh how unlike their ceremonies in every respect to the ideas we form from the descriptions of De Stael and Schiller— An awkward[n] coarse-looking priest— no music— a serm[on] muttered over the heads of the parties in a manner so indistinct that no other person could hear one word— I have seldom been more disgusted. Our manner of performing the ceremony has always fallen wofully short of my feelings about it yet is far better than this.

I am sorry your Mother is so restless about your staying at the West— I think she might be easily persuaded to come to you, if you are quite sure it is best for you to stay.

Have been reading lately Mrs Jameson's Visits and Sketches; a brilliant book.[8] Also Miss Martineau's Letters to the deaf, republished in our Xn Register was very gratifying to me I am glad to perceive from your letter to Sarah that you are likely to become acquainted with her—[9] if you do pray write me all about it— Dear James I have been interrupted too often and hurried too much for the good of this letter— Perhaps I shall have much to tell you by and by and yet I know not; tis not always when we have most to tell that tis easiest to do so— I am called to a visitor Adieu—

M.

ALS (MHi). *Addressed:* Revd J. F. Clarke / Louisville. / Kentucky. *Postmark:* Boston Ms / Jun 2.

beg with] beg ⟨?⟩ with
its requisitions] its re⟨g⟩quisitions
entirely because] entirely ⟨w⟩ because
An awkward] An aw⟨?⟩kward

1. In his letter of 12 May, Clarke had lamented that he "knew not how strong the love of beauty was in my heart till I find myself debarred from field, wood, sky, water, mountain forms and hues, and the contemplation of the divine human face and figure" (*Letters of JFC*, p. 94).

2. It was William Eliot, not Fuller, who finally reviewed Dewey's *Discourses on Various Subjects* (New York, 1835) (Habich, "Annotated List," p. 102).

3. Frances Anne Allen (1815?–35), who married Jared Sparks on 16 October 1832, died on 12 July (*DAB; NEHGR*, 20 [1866]: 274; *CC*, 22 July 1835).

4. Fuller had hardly concealed her first impression: "W. Eliot tells me he likes you prodigiously," said Clarke on 14 June, "says you treat him with less contempt than formerly, less like a plaything" (*Letters of JFC*, p. 97).

5. Joseph Angier was Clarke's close friend and Harvard classmate. In 1836 he married Elizabeth Rotch (1815–84), daughter of Joseph and Anne Smith Rotch of New Bedford. Joseph Rotch was Eliza Farrar's cousin (John M. Bullard, *The Rotches* [New Bedford, 1947], p. 413; *DivCat*).

6. Orville Dewey, *On the Preaching of Our Savior* (New Bedford, 1835), delivered at the ordination on 20 May.

7. Angelina Greenwood was engaged to Richard Warren, whom she married in October 1836.

8. Anna Jameson's *Visits and Sketches at Home and Abroad*, published in 1834, helped popularize German culture in England.

9. Harriet Martineau's "Letter to the Deaf" first appeared in *Tait's Edinburgh Magazine* 5 (April 1834): 174–79 and subsequently in the *Christian Register* on 30 May 1835. In his letter to Fuller of 14 June, Clarke described his four-hour visit with Martineau (*Letters of JFC,* p. 96).

1036. To James F. Clarke

Groton 27th June 1835.

Dear James— Your Lexington letter, received three or four days since, was very interesting— I only wished you could have written down the whole four hours of Martineau and copied your letter to her for me.— Your description is much more flattering to my anticipations than any I have heard; particularly as to her personal appearance.[1]

—I doubt whether it is a fact that people must *be fed and clothed before they can be spiritualized* on the contrary I am inclined to think that a degree of starvation, well managed, is favorable to this desired result—[2] Probably I shall see her as I expect to be in Cambridge at that time on return from my journey and Mrs Farrar intends inviting her to stay— but it is not probable I shall become acquainted with her; many will be seeking her and as I have no name nor fame I shall not have much chance.—[3]

On my return— this reminds me I dont think I mentioned this proposed journey in my last, as I was not quite sure, at that time, of going— if I did excuse repetition, but I think I did not— I am going with Mr and Mrs Farrar and several other select individuals to Trenton Falls— Are not you glad?— I who have never seen the North River!— I think I *must* be very happy.[4] (How prettily Dr Lieber mentions your accompanying him there in his tiresome book)[5] I fear I shall miss you as we set out the last week in July— About the time I suppose you will come to Boston. I wish to see you although I fear our intercourse may be as unsatisfactory as that of last year.

Sarah has been giving me ten days and is now gone to Lebanon Springs with Mr and Mrs G. Davis. Now we are really well acquainted and go on finely— S. learned a German lesson with me daily— when I am in Boston I shall give her more, and took many sketches— I conducted her to most of the spots I visited with you and to sundry other verdant solitudes in various styles.

I have not yet recd the Western Examiner and am impatient—

Cannot the numbers which are sent to me have the names of writers prefixed in pencil?

I never felt any-thing resembling "contempt" for Wm Elliott (*there*— I always *shall* spell his name wrong) but I confess I underrated him— You know it is my besetting fault to be too harsh or too enthusiastic in my judgements of character. I see that[n] he has a mind— independent opinions of his own to dignify that sweetness and brightness of temperament which were all I liked in him before. We are quite friends now, I believe. I felt real sorrow when we parted, and *feel*— if the expression may be allowed— affection as well as esteem for him— He will be happy— undoubtedly.

I have made a new acquaintance whom I *think* I should like to become a friend. Mrs Robinson—the German lady—you remember[6] I am surprised you did not talk of her more— she is very brilliant— not in the Fanny Kemble style indeed (by the way I am disappointed Miss Martineau should express so favorable an opinion of a book which quite destroyed my previous interest in its[n] author) and her attainments fill me with envy—[7] I have been reading a work of hers although[n] timeless for ah!— how full this life of lessons in your darling Entsagung— all my plans of study and writing this summer are dashed by the prospect of this delightful journey— all the days must be dedicated to the needle, family &c up to the moment[n] of departure in order to smooth the path and leave mine house in order Just so 'twas last summer— and in the autumn I take the children again— However I think now I shall live down all obstacles in time

R. W. Emerson— the reverend, and I are tottering on the verge of an acquaintance. It must come, by and by, in spite of fate, meanwhile hope is as good as manna if not quite so satisfying as the dainties of Egypt

I am looking out for a suitable person to steal from him your copy of Sartor Resartus, if I succeed you will know it by the greater originality and richness of my letters—[8] Farewell dear James au relire[n] if not au revoir yours very faithfully

M. F.

ALS (MHi). *Addressed:* Revd James F. Clarke. / Louisville / Kentucky. *Postmark:* Groton Ms / June 9. *Endorsed:* Ky letter 4.

see that] see ⟨now⟩ that
in its] in i⟨n⟩ts
hers although] hers alt⟨?⟩hough
the moment] the moment⟨s⟩
au relire] au re⟨?⟩lire

1. In his letter of 14 June, Clarke said of Martineau: "She has positively the sweetest smile I ever saw, and she laughs just like Elizabeth Randall. Her *ear* is the smallest and prettiest I am acquainted with—unfortunately it will ngt hear" (*Letters of JFC*, p. 96).

2. "She is preparing the people for Carlylism," said Clarke, who went on to write the words Fuller here underlines (*Letters of JFC*, p. 96).

3. Fuller did meet Martineau in Cambridge in late 1835 and early 1836.

4. She described her trip in a letter to her parents (*Letters of MF*, 1:232–33).

5. Francis Lieber, *Letters to a Gentleman in Germany* (Philadelphia, 1834), which Clarke favorably reviewed in the first issue of the *Messenger*.

6. Therese Albertine Louise von Jakob Robinson.

7. Kemble's *Journal*, which covered 1 August 1832 to 17 July 1833, had been published in both London and Philadelphia in 1835. Clarke wrote Fuller, "[Miss Martineau] thinks it will exalt her on the whole in the estimation of liberal people" (*Letters of JFC*, p. 96).

8. Carlyle's *Sartor Resartus* begin in the November 1834 *Fraser's*.

1037. To James F. Clarke

Boston 26th July
1835,

My dear James

I should have sent an answer to your last letter but that I supposed it would pass you on the way— I was charmed with the extracts from Miss Martineau's letter.[1] I hope you will make your promise of showing me the whole an exception to your bad habit of forgetting little promises.— May the acquaintance continue and prove a source of enduring pleasure to you!—

I have been all day to hear Mr Furness (of whom more anon) and since my return have been sitting in the parlour in company with your friend—?— Dr Lieber. As I was to him only Miss Fuller, an unmarried female of no mark or likelihood and his head was full of business no progress was made towards acquaintance— we talked on general subjects.[n2]

If I said I had or might have much to tell you I suppose I referred not to outward events but to what had passed in my own mind— much has passed there, but whether I can tell it you or no must be determined by the nature of our meeting— I suppose I shall find you here when I return from my journey I am to set forth Amer. to start[3] tomorrow[n] morning and shall be gone two or three weeks— The Western Messenger has not been sent me and I must wait all that time, before I can read it—[n] didnt thou, my Revd friend, put my name on the subscription list? I confidently expected that thou wouldst— *I am* very impatient and a little vexed—

Affectionately yours

M. F.

ALS (MHi). *Addressed:* Revd J. F. Clarke. *Endorsed:* Ky 22.

subjects.] *Here Fuller marked the page with an* x *and wrote at the end of the sheet:* Perhaps his mind would have been moved towards me if he had known that I read his ⟨?⟩ plan for Girard College quite through yesterday.

forth Amer. to start tomorrow] forth ↑ Amer. to start ↓ tomorrow
read it—] read ↑ it ↓ —

1. Clarke included them in his letter of 24 June (*Letters of JFC*, pp. 97–98).

2. Lieber published his *Constitution and Plan of Education for Girard College for Orphans* (Philadelphia, 1834) in hopes of having it accepted by the Girard Trust, which had $5 million to establish a training school for orphans. Despite the support of such prominent men as Joseph Story, Lieber did not win the commission. The visit Fuller describes came just as he was under intense fire from conservatives in South Carolina, who were opposed to his appointment to the faculty at South Carolina College (Frank Freidel, *Francis Lieber: Nineteenth-Century Liberal* [Baton Rouge, 1947], pp. 105–7, 124–25).

3. Fuller mimics Touchstone's comic definitions in *As You Like It*, V.i.47–54.

1038. To James F. Clarke

Groton,
Sunday 11th Octr 1835,

My dear James,

After you left me the other day I was shocked at the selfishness which could make me forget to renew my questions about the manual labor schools in the west. The poor youth in whose behalf I inquired is, no doubt very sick with hope deferred, and will not know what to do until he hears from me. Will you relieve my mind by writing an answer to those questions immediately?[1]

I forgot[n] to tell you that I had discovered on rereading those letters the meaning of Mr Carlyle's adjective "gigmanic" In a note to one of his papers (I am not sure but it may be to one of the Sartors) he gives as an instance illustrative of the conventional meaning of respectability this little passage at a trial.

Witness "He was a respectable man, Sir."

Counsel "What do you mean by respectable?" Witness. "*He kept a gig.*" And, subsequently, Mr C. was wont to class these *respectable* persons as Gigmen. Hence, probably,[n] Gigmanic.[2]

Your visit was grateful to me (although I could not wish it prolonged, lest it should distract my mind from duties that ought now to be peculiarly sacred)[3] and left a most pleasant impression on my mind. An impression that you will now be able to proceed on your chosen path in a temper, not only firm and courageous, but bright and hopeful. Apropos, I will now copy a little poem of Uhland's which I meant to send you sometime since.

Timothy Fuller. Courtesy of the Harvard University Art Museums.

Rechtfertigung.

Wohl geht der Jugend Sehnen
    Nach manchem schonen Traum,
Mit Ungestum[n] und Thranen
    Sturmt sie die Sterneraum,
Der Himmel hort ihr Flehen
    Und lachelt gnadig: *nein!*
Und lasst vorubergehen
    Den Wunsch[n] zusammt der Pein.

Wenn aber nun vom Scheine
    Das Herz sich abgekehrt,
Und nur das Wechte Reine,
    Das Menschliche begehrt;
Und doch mit allem Streben,
    Kein Zeil erreichen kann:
Da muss man wohl vergeben
    Die Trauer auch dem Mann.[4]

I liked the stanzas you left with me very much, both conception and execution— I wish I could have expressed my affection and regret at parting— but we *may* meet another year as I shall, very probably, feel bound to remain with my mother and family— I wish you would write, not only in answer to this but directly after you arrive at your Western home. Sister Ellen has been quite sick since you were here but is now better, so is Richard and Mother is not yet wearied out. My love to Sarah—

yours faithfully,

MARGARET F.

ALS (MHi). *Addressed:* Revd James F. Clarke / at Dr Freeman's / Newton, / Mass. *Postmark:* Groton Ms / Oct. 12. *Endorsed:* Ky letter 23.

I forgot] I forg⟨e⟩ot
Hence, probably,] Hence, ⟨?⟩ probably,
Mit Ungestum] Mit ⟨u⟩Ungestum
Den Wunsch] De⟨r⟩n Wunsch

1. The Unitarians supported trade schools, but they were not flourishing, as Clarke told Fuller in his letter of 14 October. "The truth I expect," he said, "is that the schools are 'not the thing they were cracked up to be,' as Westerners say" (*Letters of JFC,* p. 106).

2. It was Carlyle's "Diamond Necklace," not *Sartor Resartus,* that played on the image. Carlyle, like others, drew from one of the accounts of the trial of John Thurtell (1794–1824), who committed a notorious murder and who is the "respectable" man of the quotation (*DNB*).

3. Her father died on 1 October, leaving Margaret in charge of the large family.

4. Uhland's poem "Rechtfertigung" was published in 1816. Fuller translated the lines for Eliza Farrar in April 1836:

> Our youthful fancies, idly fired,
>   The fairest visions would embrace;
> These, with impetuous tears desired,
>   Float upward into starry space;
> Heaven, upon the suppliant wild,
>   Smiles down a gracious *No!*—In vain
> The Strife! Yet be consoled, poor child,
>   For the wish passes with the pain.
>
> But when from such idolatry
>   The heart has turned, and wiser grown,
> In earnestness and purity
>   Would make a nobler plan its own,—
> Yet, after all its zeal and care,
>   Must of its chosen aim despair,—
> Some bitter tears may be forgiven
>   By *Man*, at least, *we trust, by Heaven.*

(*Letters of MF*, 1:247–48) In her haste, Fuller omitted all umlauts and wrote *Thranen* for *Tranen*, *Sterneraum* for *Sternenraum*, and *Wechte* for *Echte*.

1039. To James F. Clarke

Groton 6th Decrⁿ 18[35]

My dear James—

You had not received the news of your Grandfather's death when you wrote to me.[1] Judge Dana too who was with me the morng you bade me farewell now lies in this church yard by the side of my Father.[2] Verily the honored elders of the landⁿ are passing away in a crowd and leaving us their parts to play can we do it?— Can you, my friend, fill the place of your independent, candidⁿ and beneficent grandfather. Can I make good to my fellow creatures the loss of my pious, upright and industrious Father. Once I was more presumptuous but now I have attained more accurate ideas of the obstacles to be overcome in life.

To turn from death to so called life Elizhs marriage seems as far off as ever; when it is settled I will let you know.[3] I have not seen Sarah to get the account of your journey. I rejoice to hear you might have loved even though "business did not now permit." I thought those springs could not have beenⁿ dried up by one disappointment. I am sensible that I must in a great measure give you up when ever [you] become more tenderly attached to any other [wo]man, but I trust I can never be so selfish [   ] not, on that account, to wish what seems [n]ecessary to you. You ought to have love, you [w]ould flour-

271

ish so beneath it, and repay [i]t so generously. I am glad to see by this little communication that I am not absolutely barricaded into my cold situation of "friend *of the mind*."[4]

George Davis made me a visit a week or two since, (Harriet remaining in Boston with her friends) We talked much of you and very pleasantly of every-thing yet I saw abundant reason not to regret our being no longer intimate. Our minds no longer harmonize, we take things on a different level— as far as I am concerned our ancient intercourse would have been a hindrance. Yet we can still communicate more closely with one another than either could with the herd.

If the Artevelde piece is printed do, my dear James, have some attention paid to correcting the press.[5] My other pieces were full of blunders from beginning to end. Perhaps my handwriting is responsible for some, but surely not for such as "the love of *Earth* is a healing and renovating principle" (wh[at] a beautiful sentiment!) "stories" for p[   ] and others equally gross and wh would disgrace the cheapest newspaper.[6] Hav[e] seen nothing worthy what I supposed Mr Peabody to be.[7] Who wrote a piece on Mystery signed F. and the whole of wh[ich] is comprized in that phrase of Goethe "open secret".[8] Your articles are much th[e] best there— I intend to remark upon them sometime when 'tis not midnight and I am not writing with this "*awful*" steel pen which prefers dropping the ink to shedding it.

Have sent to Boston for your sermon b[ut] not got it yet.[9]

Dear James you made me when here an offer which I thought too liberal for a moments consideration yet I shall now accept it if you still feel willing to make so great a sacrifice. Will you lend me Goethe for some months, perhaps a year My reason for wanting it, the only one wh could induce me to accept such a favor must be profoundly confidential between us. Miss Martineau encourages me to my Life of Goethe.[10] She thinks the time is ripe, she thinks I can do it. I have confiden[ce in] her judgement for she has knowledge [of] the public mind and cannot be biassed [in]to partially for me by long habits of [   ] time.[11] Whether time and means [w]ill be granted me I cannot tell but [I i]ntend to make the attempt. Now as I mean [n]ot only a memoir but a detailed criticism of his works I ought to have them for[n] sometime and I cannot, at present, afford to buy them. Are you willing to part with your Master for my sake? Indeed I feel very unwilling to ask it, that you should part with the books so long and send them all this way for an End which may never be accomplished My only confidence is I think I would do as much for you— Be in no hurry to send them till a convenient opportunity offers. I shall have plenty of other reading to do for it let alone my winter's task of Eichhorn which I have scarce begun and Titan wh Mr Bokum gave me and wh I am vainly trying to get time to read.[11] When I say I am perfectly confidential I mean that you must not let even Sarah know of my plan.

I have exchanged a letter with H. Davis which will I think place matters on a more amicable footing between us. If I were not almost dead, I would not send you such a horrible looking sheet. But I thought I would put off writing no longer so do excuse

M.

ALS (MHi). *Addressed:* Revd James F. Clarke. / ⟨Louisville⟩ Mobile / ⟨Kentucky⟩ Alabama. *Postmark:* Groton Ms / Dec 7. New Orleans Jan. *Endorsed:* Ky 24.

Decr] *Though Fuller wrote* Novr, *the postmark and the references to the deaths of Freeman and Dana show that the month was December.*

the land] the⟨ir⟩ land
independent, candid] indepen⟨t⟩, ↑ dent ↓ candid
have been] have ⟨could not have⟩ been
of [   ] time.] of [   ] ⟨?⟩ time.
them for] them ↑ for ↓

1. Dr. James Freeman died on 14 November (*DAB*).

2. Samuel Dana, the Fullers' neighbor, died on 20 November (Groton VR). He was a prominent lawyer, a member of the Massachusetts legislature, and chief justice of the circuit court of common pleas.

3. Elizabeth Randall's fiancé was Albert Cumming of Georgia. In reply, Clarke wrote: "I believe I expressed to you my acquiescence in this marriage arising from the belief that it is the only way by which she could be taught that there is not earthly good of any *satisfactory* worth" (*Letters of JFC*, p. 108). Later letters show that the marriage was unhappy.

4. Stung by her comment, Clarke replied: "I never understood why you chose to think yourself 'the friend of my mind' emphatically and exclusively. . . . But surely I have made you the fullest confessions of my *Heart* follies" (*Letters of JFC*, p. 112).

5. Her essay appeared in December, despite the specific order from Clarke and Peabody that it appear in the September issue of the *Messenger* (*Letters of JFC*, pp. 107–8).

6. Clarke replied, "I was as much horrified by the blunders of the press, and scolded more about them than you think necessary to do—especially that *earth* for *truth*, horrid mistake. But poor Peabody was not to blame. He was away in Mass. The Editor pro. tem. was a lawyer, and in love, and full of other business" (*Letters of JFC*, pp. 112–13). Uriah Tracy Howe, the temporary editor, married Sarah Coolidge in September 1835 (Habich, *Transcendentalism and the "Western Messenger,"* p. 62).

7. Ephraim Peabody had an article in every issue of the *Messenger* that year.

8. William Henry Furness, "Mystery in Religion Recognized by Unitarians," *Western Messenger* 1 (October 1835): 284–91 (Habich, "Annotated List," p. 102).

9. *False Witnesses Answered* (Boston, 1835).

10. In reply, Clarke readily agreed to send the books, seconded Martineau's opinion, and defined what sort of book Fuller should write (*Letters of JFC*, p. 113).

11. Late in 1834, Frederic Henry Hedge sent Fuller his copy of Johann Gottfried Eichhorn's *Einleitung ins alte Testament*, which she read in the spring of 1835 (*Letters of MF*, 1:212, 216, 223, 228). Hermann Bokum taught German at Harvard from 1835 to 1838 (Harvard archives).

1040.   To Elizabeth P. Peabody?

[1836?][n]

With regard to what you say about the American Monthly, my answer
is, I would gladly sell some part of my mind for lucre, to get the
command of time; but I will not sell my soul: that is, I am perfectly
willing to take the trouble of writing for money to pay the seamstress;
but I am *not* willing to have what I write mutilated, or what I ought to
say dictated to suit the public taste.[1] You speak of my writing about
Tieck. It is my earnest wish to interpret the German authors of whom
I am most fond to such Americans as are ready to receive. Perhaps
some might sneer at the notion of my becoming a teacher; but where
I love so much, surely I might inspire others to love a little; and I
think this kind of culture would be precisely the counterpoise required by the utilitarian tendencies of our day and place. My very
imperfections may be of value. While enthusiasm is yet fresh, while I
am still a novice, it may be more easy to communicate with those quite
uninitiated, than when I shall have attained to a higher and calmer
state of knowledge. I hope a periodical may arise, by and by, which
may think me worthy to furnish a series of articles on German literature, giving room enough and perfect freedom to say what I please.
In this case, I should wish to devote at least eight numbers to Tieck,
and should use the Garden of Poesy, and my other translations.[2]

I have sometimes thought of translating his Little Red Riding
Hood, for children. If it could be adorned with illustrations, like those
in the "Story without an End," it would make a beautiful little book;
but I do not know that this could be done in Boston. There is much
meaning that children could not take in; but, as they would never
discover this till able to receive the whole, the book corresponds exactly with my notions of what a child's book should be.

I would like to begin the proposed series with a review of Heyne's
letters on German Literature, which afford excellent opportunity for
some preparatory hints.[3] My plans are so undecided for several coming months, that I cannot yet tell whether I shall have the time and
tranquility needed to write out the whole course, though much
tempted by the promise of perfect liberty. I could engage, however, to
furnish at least two articles on Novalis and Körner.[4] I trust you will be
interested in my favorite Körner. Great is my love for both of them.
But I wish to write something which shall not only *be* free from exaggeration, but which shall *seem* so, to those unacquainted with their
works.

I have so much reading to go through with this month, that I have but few hours for correspondents. I have already discussed five volumes in German, two in French, three in English, and not without thought and examination.

ELfr, from *Memoirs*, 1:168–69.

Dated by the reference to her plans for writing. She had written essays on Mackintosh and Heine by the summer of 1836 (Letters of JFC, p. 121). Charles Capper convincingly assigns the letter to Peabody on the basis of her association with the American Monthly *(Capper,* Margaret Fuller, *p. 383n30).*

1. Fuller refers to *The American Monthly Magazine*, for which she wrote while Park Benjamin was editor.

2. Fuller had probably been reading Tieck's *Phantasus* (1812–17) (*OCGL*).

3. Fuller's language suggests she had read *Letters Auxiliary to the History of Modern Polite Literature in Germany*, the 1836 translation by G. W. Haven of Heine's *Zur Geschichte der neueren schönen Literatur in Deutschland* (Leipzig, 1833). She reviewed the English translation in *The American Monthly Magazine*, n.s. 2 (July 1836): 1–13. In the essay she said: "We rejoice to see among us symptoms of a growing interest in German literature, having some time been convinced that this is the very culture we want to counterpoise the natural influences which, amid all our so-called prosperity, are threatening to blight every poetic bud, and turn the American mind into a spiritual spinning jenny, set in motion by no higher impulse than that of utility" (p. 2).

4. Fuller apparently never wrote on Novalis, but James Clarke published her essay on Körner in the *Western Messenger*.

1041. To James F. Clarke

Groton 29th Jany 1836.

Dearest Friend,

I have been passing five weeks in Boston and Cambridge which have done me a great deal of good; I recd your Mississippi letter while there but was too much engaged to write. On returning yesterday I found your beautiful Mobile letter which I must answer first of all the file which stares reproachfully at me— Yes my dear friend, there is indeed a higher sympathy between us—[1] I am no longer without God in the world and in my new feelings of peace I value more all the hearts in which my Father has given me a portion— The clouds of distrust and false pride have rolled off from my mind and in my state of protection I can love and trust in simplicity and fearlessness. Would I could tell you more of the present condition[n] of my being for it is blessed. O pray for me, you who are indeed very good that I may be able to perfect my present development by courageous and wise action. My circumstances are very difficult I am called on for a[n] decision of great importance to me— I seem to approach the crisis of my temporal existence— I am near the parting of the Ways. Since you are not near enough to advise pray for me that I may be neither rash nor cowardly but may be guided into that course which will be for my best good. I cannot but think your effectual fervent prayer will avail me much.— No more of this now!

Yes— Anna Barker is lovely and as you say she loves me much;[2] it is rather sad that so much space should lie between us. Pray tell me in your next with feminine minuteness all you saw and heard of her for I am deeply interested and can get little information. I am quite satisfied about *"friend of the Mind"* now by[n] what you say— I know very well I used to be the friend of the Heart; but you have so often called me by this other name the past year and the tone of your letters has been so cold and repressing that I thought you meant to depose me from my ancient niche. It is all right I see— Yes if you can indeed learn to love any love but that of imagination you will be beloved, fear not— The maiden you describe is not such a phoenix but she may be found and make you happy when found— More of this another time.— Thanks for the Goethe and what you say of what I should do.[3] I will lay[n] it to heart— Write any thing which occurs to you on the subject I dare say I shall fructify thereupon. It is a great work. I hope nobody will steal it from me— I took a dose of Fichte while in C— but it did not do— I could not understand.—[4] Can you recommend me a *good History of Philosophy*. Nobody could, so I have brought home two[n] which are not at all what I want— Tennyman's and Buhle's— both[n] in German. I want something lucid[n] and compendious—[5] I have been reading today the Western Messenger. Your tribute to your grandfather is truly eloquent— and the eloquence is that of both heart and mind.[6] It is a warm and warming outpouring from a most hallowed fount. It gave me much delight— But you must let me scold you for your translations of Goethe I suppose they are just as you first wrote them out and certainly very bad— What vexes me is that as your bits of Schiller are good people will suppose these are equally so. It is a shame to degrade such a very transparent and flexible style into English whose literalness makes it unfaithful. Surely we should consult the idiom of our own language if we want to do justice to a writer who valued form so highly. Then why is it not that Epithalamium better done? How many beautiful ideas marred for want of a proper finish— You *can* do it— those verses you gave me when you were here were done as they ought to be. The Genuine Portrait, though imperfect, is much less so— Do not let living in the West lower your literary while it elevates your moral standard— You cannot be a poet of the first order but your ideas well deserve that you should pay more attention to their *expression*[7]

I have had many happy hours with Miss Martineau. I trust we shall now be dear friends forever— My only fear is that she overrates me as is her wont where she loves. *I shall not be disappointed in her*[n]

I have thought so much about her, perhaps I shall write you a letter on the subject one of these days— I have said only the least bit of what I meant. I have so much to tell that would be interesting to you. I meant to have told you about Wm Channing's Swiss journal which I read and Mr Alston's new picture[8] but there is no room now so farewell from yours affectionately

M. F.

Has Abraham quite recovered?[9]

ALS (MHi). *Addressed:* Revd James F. Clarke. / Louisville. / Kentucky. *Postmark:* Groton Ms / Jany 30. *Endorsed:* Ky 25.

present condition] present ⟨state of⟩ condition
for a] for a⟨n⟩
now by] now ⟨you⟩ by
will lay] will ⟨r⟩ lay
home two] home t⟨?⟩wo
Buhle's— both] Buhle's— bo⟨h⟩th
something lucid] something ⟨L⟩lucid
I shall not be disappointed in her] ↑ *I shall not be disappointed in her* ↓

1. On 7 January, Clarke wrote Fuller: "Your letters make me happier even than they formerly did; their tone is of, it strikes me, a truer confidence than of old. And should it not be so? Do we not know each other better than we did then, for are not our sympathies now those of a higher and purer purpose" (*Letters of JFC*, p. 111).

2. Said Clarke: "I should surely have fallen in love with your beautiful friend Anne Barker, had I stayed much longer in her neighborhood. But that would have been a mistake, for she would never care for me" (*Letters of JFC*, p. 112).

3. Clarke was free with advice: "Aim to make in it and by it a manifestation of those great truths for want of which this age is so weak and sickly. Make it a religious book" (*Letters of JFC*, p. 113).

4. Johann Gottlieb Fichte had published *Das System der Sittenlehre nach den Principien der Wissenschaftslehre* in 1798.

5. Clarke did not answer this letter directly, though he did answer hers of 11 February, in which she asked a similar question. Fuller read Johann Gottlieb Buhle's *Geschichte der neuern Philosophie seit der Epoche wiederherstellung der Wissenschaften*. Wilhelm Gottlieb Tennemann had published *Geschichte der Philosophie* and *Grundriss der Geschichte der Philosophie*.

6. "Character of James Freeman, D.D.," *Western Messenger* 1 (January 1836): 478–87.

7. Clarke had regularly published his translations of German works. The January issue had three Schiller poems and "Book of Ruth. Translated from Goethe's 'Notes and Illustrations to the Western Oriental Divan.'"

8. Channing was at this time traveling in Europe. Washington Allston finished three paintings in 1835: *The Evening Hymn; Landscape, American Scenery;* and *Rosalie*. Fuller here probably refers to the latter, on which she wrote a poem; she sent it to Clarke in

her next letter. *Rosalie* is a half-length figure in which the woman holds a book and touches the chain she wears on her neck (Edgar Preston Richardson, *Washington Allston* [Chicago, 1948], pp. 211–12).

9. Clarke's brother Abraham.

1042. To ?

[ca. 1? February? 1836?][n]

I am having one of my "intense" times, devouring book after book. I never stop a minute, except to talk with mother, having laid all little duties on the shelf for a few days. Among other things, I have twice read through the life of Sir J. Mackintosh; and it has suggested so much to me, that I am very sorry I did not talk it over with you. It is quite gratifying, after my late chagrin, to find Sir James, with all his metaphysical turn, and ardent desire to penetrate it, puzzling so over the German philosophy, and particularly what I was myself troubled about, at Cambridge,— Jacobi's letters to Fichte.[1]

ELfr, from *Memoirs*, 1:164–65.

Dated by the reference to Mackintosh, which Fuller says she read in her letter of 1 February 1836 to George T. Davis.

1. *Jacobi an Fichte* was published in Hamburg in 1799. Mackintosh reported his reading of this work and *Über die Lehre des Spinoza* (Breslau, 1785) on 1 January 1807: "Jacobi is a singular example of the union of metaphysical acuteness with mysticism. . . . His book on Spinoza is most ingenious; and when I read him, I think I understand his results; but when I lay down the book, they escape the grasp of my mind" (*Memoirs of the Life of the Right Honourable Sir James Mackintosh*, ed. Robert James Mackintosh [London, 1835], 1:321).

1043. To George T. Davis

Groton, 1st Feby, 1836—

My dear Cousin,

I received your letter sometime since but was staying in Cambridge at the time and could not conveniently answer it. Since I returned I have read the life of Sir James Mackintosh with great interest. I think few things have ever been written more discriminating or more beautiful than his strictures on the Hindoo character, his portrait of Fox and his second letter to Robert Hall after his recovery from derangement. Do you remember what he says of the want of *brilliancy* in Priestley's moral sentiments:— those remarks, though slight, seem to me to mark the character of his mind more decidedly than any thing in the book.[1] That so much learning, benevolence, and almost unparalleled fairness of mind should be in a great measure lost to the world for want of earnestness of purpose might impel us to attach to the latter attribute as much importance as does the wise uncle in Wilhelm Meister.[2]

As to the trifle I sent you on *the* great question I thought I perceived while in Boston that the time for polishing it was already gone by. It is however valuable to me to have written it, slight as it was, for the interest thus excited has led me to acquire more information from various quarters and I am already considerably enlightened on the subject. No effort is ever utterly lost! I doubt there is nothing in it worthy of reproduction but about this should like your opinion. Perhaps I may solicit your aid on some other occasion since you boast such power over the press!—

I have recd two letters from James lately. One from N. Orleans and one from Mobile!— The latter contains some beautiful passages: if you were here I would read them to you. Have you seen what he has written about his grandfather?— It is a fine tribute.

Your brother I was glad, a few days since, to hear has recovered. Perhaps he is with you now— he seemed to wish it— I saw less of your mother than I had intended.[3]

I am obliged by your and Harriet's invitations to Greenfield.— If it be possible I will fix a time for you to meet me and pass a week or two with you as you propose. But my plans are all painfully undecided. That of my going to Europe is again revived among my friends.[4] If I go it will be in August with Mr and Mrs Farrar and Miss Martineau— and to be with Miss M. while in London, an arrangement equally delightful and profitable to me— All that I could do and see would seem to open up many prospects to me— but[n] then, on the other hand, the moment I return I must maintain myself and you know we women have no profession except marriage, mantua-making and school-keeping. If I can make up my mind that it is [   ] for myself to go, I think matters can be so arranged that it will not eventually be a loss to my Mother and family. I intend to be very wise and deliberate til the last moment; and I rather think I shall not go; staying behind will be such a pretty trial to my fortitude and quite finish my moral education— Indeed at the expense of my intellectual but this last is quite a secondary affair— 'tis said. Oblige me by not speaking of all this— such plans are best never known except by their fulfilment!— I only wish to say that if I do not go to Europe, I may come to Greenfield as this last is somewhat less difficult— Meanwhile, with remembrances to Harriet yours truly

M. F.

ALS (MCR-S: MC 351 [Box 19, folder 5]). Published in part in *Memoirs*, 1:165. *Addressed:* George T. Davis Esq. / Greenfield, / Mass— *Postmark:* Groton Ms Feb 3. *Endorsed:* Margaret Fuller / 1 Feb 1836.

me— but] me— ⟨?⟩ but

1. *Memoirs of the Life of the Right Honourable Sir James Mackintosh*, ed. Robert James Mackintosh (London, 1835). Fuller reviewed the work in *American Monthly Magazine*, n.s. 1 (June 1836): 570–80, where she commented on most of these topics: she quotes a passage in which Mackintosh emphasizes the contradictions in Hindu life, such as "'austerities and self-tortures almost incredible, practised by those who otherwise wallow in gross sensuality'" (p. 577). She omits Fox, but quotes Mackintosh on Priestley: "'Frankness and disinterestedness in the avowal of his opinion were his point of honour. In other respects his morality was more useful than brilliant'" (p. 576).

2. Fuller refers either to Natalia's uncle in *Wilhelm Meisters Lehrjahre* or the uncle of Hersilia and Julieta in the *Wanderjahre*.

3. Davis's brother was Wendell Thornton Davis; their mother was Caroline Willmans Smith Davis.

4. She was unable to go to Europe.

1044. To James F. Clarke

Groton 11th [February 1836][n]

My dear James,

H[o]w I wish you were near me!— [   ] [d]esire for your sympathy but now it seems as i[f you m]ight help me a great deal for my mind is in a prodigious ferment— I have taken this large sheet hoping I may be able to state my difficulties in part and that perhaps your answer may do me good. It is only *perhaps*, for we are too far asunder— I always feel that I cannot now get at you so as to help you much— You [w]rite to me when depressed and before I can answer be of good cheer" and tell you why you should, you have become happy again by your own exertions— But these are mind and not heart difficulties and I fear me I shall be still more harassed by them a month hence.

I have long had a suspicion that no mind can systematize its knowledge and carry on the concentrating processes without some fixed opinions on the subject of metaphysics. But that indisposition [   ]

even dread of the study which you may remember [h]as kept me from meddling with it till lately in meditating on the life of Goethe I thought I must [g]et some idea of theⁿ history of philosophical opin- ion in Germany that I might be able to judge [o]f the influence which it exercised upon his mind. [   ] I can comprehend him every other way [   ] [p]robably interpret him satisfactorily to others [   ]an but get the proper materials)— When [   ] in Cam- bridge I got Fichte and Jacobi— I was [   ] interrupted but some time and earnest [   ] devoted— Fichte I could not under [   ] all though the treatise which I re[   ]d to be popular and [   ]wingen" to conviction— Jac[   ]nd in details [   ] but not in sy[   ] at his mind must have been moul[   ]d with which I ought to be acquain[   ] in or[der] to know him well— Perhaps Spinoza's— Sin[ce] I came home I have been consulting Buhle's and Tennemann's histories of philosophy and dipping into Brown, Stewart, and that class of books.ⁿ But the mass of study wh seems to be required appals me.[1] I have not time even if I had heart for it— There seems so much for me to do that I am almost crushed already when I think of it— Perhaps I shall appear to you like an- other of my sex who asked to have political economy explained to her in two words— but I would fain, my dear friend, have you help me to some kind of royal road if you know of any and I think you may for I know you did not give much time to the subject and yet you appeared to arrive at some sort of satisfaction.[2] What I want is, first, to get a distinc[t] idea of the histy of philosophy merely as a development of mind— I want to be able to make out tables for myself of all the ramifications of schools and the principal masters in each from the Greeks downward— So that I may have it all clear in my mind and know what to [   ] or at least *how* to think when I hear [   ] about Platonists—ⁿ Scholastics— Realists— [Nom]inalists &c &c &c— You will be surprized at [   ] [i]gnorance but I have not even a distin[   ] what Bacon did for the mind— [   ] [ca]n learn this without reading the [   ] Organum—[3] Please define for me the [   ] Scotch Philosophy—ⁿ Tell me *exactly* [   ] meant by *Tran- scendental* and exactly why [   ] is called the *Critical* philosophy—[4] [   ]ow if you can in what particulars Re[in]hold, Schelling and Fichte have modified the doctrines of Kant— If I understand this latter he undertakes to fix the boundaries of speculation— and con- siders Freedom, Immortality, God and our relations to these as *the* topics upon which we exercise what he calls *pure Reason* and which areⁿ entirely beyond the boundaries of under[st]anding.

I *have* supposed I understood all about wh I ask but,ⁿ upon examination, find all my ideas was vag[ue] and confused— I am ardently desirous to learn will you be my teacher?— You see I do not shrin[k] from letting you see the full extent of my ignorance in the hope that you will enlight[en] me.

I wish you would tell me in how far you consider Goethe as united to any philosophic school— I never find him speaking of any-body but Spinoza— but I have hitherto troubled my head very little about these things in reading him— so he may have made many allusions which I have not understood— I wish too you would let me know what you consider definitively his opinion of Christian revelation. I find things on that subject wh appear to me contradictory— [Th]is letter is of great importance to me and I entre[at y]ou to answer it as quickly and fu[lly] as you c[   ] [J]ames, do you still entertain the same [   ] of my literary capacities as formerly—[5] Have [   ] [b]een disappointed in the progress of my min[d] [   ] you think I shall ever be able^n to reproduce [   ]at I know Sometimes I feel very desponding. I [   ]

I have taken to writing sonnets and have produced twenty these last few days— I will send you one I have written on Alston's Rosalie but it is for your own self; you must not put it in your Messenger Perhaps I am vain to think you can like it [we]ll enough—

> Thou gentle offspring of a twilight mood!
> 'Tis not for beauty that we love thee so,
> No passion, no imaginative glow
> Upon thy spell of soft repose obtrude;
> But light-winged thoughts like reveries that brood
> Over the sleeping sense of infancy
> Bring, by the magic of thy harmony,
> An Ideal to us, felt not understood.
> Can words express the hidden sense that dwells
> In the nice adaptation of thy hues?
> Here all the colours Blend but ne'er confuse—
> No contrast bold the painter's secret tells;
> Tis in the perfect finish of the Whole
> We fi[nd] the essence of an Artist's soul.

I should be very happy if [I] could write them well [   ] put [   ] reading [   ] and [   ] think it [   ] be a pleasa[nt] life.

Very affection[   ] yours.

M. F.

Have I ever thanked you for Jeremy Taylor which Sarah gave me in your behalf— I read [   ][6]

ALS (MHi). Published in part in *Memoirs*, 1:127, and *Letters of MF*, 1:244–45. *Addressed:* Revd James F. Clarke, / Louisville, / Kentucky.— *Postmark:* Groton Ms Feb 13. *Endorsed:* Ans. Feb 29th.

Dated by Clarke's reply of 26 February 1836 (Letters of JFC, pp. 113–16).
of the] of ⟨?⟩ the
of books.] of ⟨people⟩ ↑ books ↓ .
about Platonists—] about P⟨h⟩latonists—
Scotch Philosophy—] Scot⟨h⟩ch Philosophy—
and which are] and ↑ which are ↓
all about wh I ask but,] all ⟨these thing⟩ ↑ about wh I ask ↓ but,
be able] be ab⟨?⟩le

1. It is not clear if Fuller ever read Spinoza. Thomas Brown and Dugald Stewart were leaders of the Scottish school of common-sense philosophy. She had read Brown's *Lectures on the Philosophy of the Human Mind* in 1825 (*Letters of MF*, 1:151).

2. Clarke recommended Cousin's *Criticism on Locke*, translated "by Mr. Henry" (*Letters of JFC*, p. 115). The work was *Elements of Psychology; Included in a Critical Examination of Locke's Essay on the Human Understanding*, trans. C. S. Henry (Hartford, 1834).

3. Fuller sought help from others. In a letter to Eliza Farrar on 17 March, she said that she had begun Bacon's *Novum Organum* and thanked Professor Farrar for the loan of Herschel's *Preliminary Discourse on the Study of Natural Philosophy* (*Letters of MF*, 1:246).

4. Clarke said: "I give you Kant's answer. 'I call all knowledge *Transcendental* which is everywhere occupied, not with the objects themselves, but with our means of knowing them, so far as they can be known *a priori*'" (*Letters of JFC*, pp. 115–16).

5. Clarke wrote: "I think your fault in writing is a want of unity, arising from the leading idea being swallowed up in the host of subservient ones. You ought to fix definitely and deeply the one leading characteristic of Goethe's mind and let this be illustrated through and by the whole life" (*Letters of JFC*, p. 116).

6. Jeremy Taylor (1613–67), an English divine, wrote several volumes of religious commentary, sermons, and verse. Among his best-known works are *A Discourse of the Liberty of Prophesying* (1646), *The Rule and Exercises of Holy Living* (1650), and *The Rule and Exercises of Holy Dying* (1651). Which of his works Fuller mentions is unknown (*DNB*).

1045.   To James F. Clarke

Groton 14th March [1836]—

My dear James—

I had begun a letter to you which I intended shd fill the whole of this immense sheet but just as I had got to the end of a long paragraph it would have puzzled you sadly to understand I, in the impatience of my movements, threw a penful of ink over it— I took this as a kind of monition, that I had best not proceed and indeed on reading it over I found my thin attempt was useless, unless I could write a volume, and I fancy that in this case half (of the sheet) may be better than the whole Your letter, which I had looked for impatiently, was what I wished and I trust your sympathy will not grow cold and that I shall have the rest in a day or two—

After I had cast the burthen of my cares upon you I rested and read Petrarch for a day or two— But that could not last— I had begun what Coleridge calls "taking stock" and was forced to proceed— He says few persons ever did this faithfully without being dissatisfied[n] with the result and lowering their estimate of their supposed riches— With me it has ended in the most humiliating sense of poverty— and only just pride enough is left to keep your poor friend off the parish— As it is I have already asked alms of several[n] besides yourself but though they all have given what they had it has by no means answered my purpose and I have laid their gifts aside with my other hoards which gleamed so fairy bright and are now, in the hour of trial, turned into mere *state-stones*— I am not sure that even if[n] I do find the philosopher's stone I shall be able to transmute them into the gold they looked so like formerly— James— do you understand me?— *I* now comprehend all *your* former processes of which I had at the time such imperfect notions.— It will be long before I can give a distinct and, at[n] the same time, concise account of my present state— I believe it is a great Era— I am thinking now— really thinking, I believe; certainly it seems as if I had never done so before— If it does not kill me, something will come of it— I had not patience to wait for your letter and had already answered a good many of my questions by the help of books— It is[n] however very valuable to me— write everything that occurs to you and let me have it— Why are you not here— How much you might do for me— how much more rapid this process would be— how much less I should suffer if I could talk it out— It would do you good too for never was my mind so active and its subjects are God— the universe— Immor*tality.* But shall I be fit for anything till I have absolutely re-educated myself— Am I— can I make myself fit to write an account of half a century of the Existence of one of the Master Spirits of this world?— It seems as if I had been very arrogant to dare to think it— yet will I not shrink back from what I have undertaken— Even by failure I shall learn much—[1]

How incoherent all this seems— Perhaps I can say more after getting your next letter; you must write to me very often now— as I shall to you— you asked my to send you my attempts at poetry— I will give you a bit in every letter till you "cry Hold Enough" Here is a nondescript— Have I told you how in the days now past when I could go from strength to strength without any fortress of my own I have loved Titan and the Flegel Jahre— I suppose not; I have told you so little of my large experience of books and nature and human creatures these three years past. Nor will these tell you much except my magnetism.

> *Richter—*
>
> Poet of Nature— Gentlest of the Wise!
> Most airy of the fanciful— most keen
>   Of satirists!— Thy thoughts like butterflies
> Still near the sweetest-scented flowers have been.
>   With Titian's colours, thou canst Sunset paint—
> With Raphaels dignity, celestial love,—
>   With Hogarth's touch minute each vulgar [   ]
> Of meanness and hypocrisy reprove.—
>   Canst to devotion's highest flight sublim[e]
> Exalt the mind of tenderest pathos' art,
> Dissolve in purifying tears the heart,
>   Or bid it, shuddering, recoil at crime.
> The fond illusions of the youth and maid,
>   At which so many world-formed sages sneer;
> When by thy altar-lighted torch displayed
>   Our natural religion can appear.—
> All things in thee tend to one polar star
>   Magnetic all thy influences are!—

Some readers murmur at the want of system in Richter's writings
>   A labyrinth— a flowery wilderness!
>   Some in thy "Slipboxes" and "Honey Moons"
>   Complain of— Want of *order* I confess
>   But not of system in its highest sense—
> Who asks a guiding clue through this wide mind
>   In love of Nature the most sure will find.—
>   In tropic climes live like the tropic birds
> Where'er a spice-fraught grove may tempt thy stay
>   Nor be by caves of colder climes disturbed
> No frost the summer's bloom will drive away.
> Nature's wide temple and the azure dome
>   Have plan enough for the quick spirit's home.

In these rude affairs I can never express a thought distinctly and but a miserably small portion of what I feel. I often think if I had been only gifted to express adequately what I feel in verse I would have asked no more of fate. But I see I shall have to be thankful if I can be fit for any task— Will you send me a copy of that piece I gave you about a thunder-storm. Dont forget it for I mean to make a journal out of these effusions and have no other record of that mood wh was as intense as my present one though I suppose that piece could give no idea of it to any one but myself.—

Since I wrote to you last I have the letter from Anna Barker to wh your postscript is affixed. She likes you very much and I am glad you had those days to scan so fair a page of living poesy— She is quite happy in her convent— In the height of the Philosophy fever I have been staying ten days at Lowell with a very agreeable woman—[2] I made some pleasant new acquaintances and among others in some degree that of the wittiest of men, Dr Dana—[3] who lent me the Novum Organum its ain-sell— I saw Mr Osgood there several times— he talks of going to Cincinnati— will he be a good helper to you?—[4] Write dear Friend about the inward life to yours always

M—

ALS (MHi). Published in part in *Memoirs*, 1:127–28, 147–48. *Addressed:* Revd James F. Clarke. / Louisville. / Kentucky. *Postmark:* Groton Ms / March 14. *Endorsed:* Ky 27.

being dissatisfied] being di(i)ssatisfied
of several] of sever⟨l⟩al
even if] even ↑ if ↓
and, at] and, ⟨?⟩ at
It is] It ⟨h⟩is

1. Full of his own plans for the *Western Messenger* and his parish, Clarke all but ignored her: "I am charmed with the philosophical tumult into which your head is thrown" (*Letters of JFC*, p. 117).

2. Probably Temperance Horton Colburn, with whom Fuller occasionally stayed.

3. Samuel Luther Dana (1795–1868) graduated from Harvard in 1813 and took the M.D. degree in 1818. A chemist for the Merrimac Manufacturing company in Lowell, he wrote several scientific papers (*Dana Family*, p. 365).

4. Osgood went to the West in March (Habich, *Transcendentalism and the "Western Messenger*," p. 175).

1046. To James F. Clarke

Groton 19th April 1836—

Dear Friend,

Your letter imparted to me a pure satisfaction; the heart seemed to speak in it without reserve— Sometimes it seems as if you had a feeling of pride which stood between you and me, or some other feeling!— 'Tis but a film— yet sufficient to prevent you from radiating much heat upon my earth-bound state.

Who is the imaginative love. Give name and date!—[1] I am shocked to perceive you think I am *writing* the life of Goethe— No! indeed! I shall need a great deal of preparation before I can have it clear in my head.— I have taken a great many notes but I shall not begin to write it till it all lies mapped out before me. I have no materials for ten years of his life— from the time he went to Weimar up to the Italn journey— Besides! I wish to see the books that have been written about him in Germany by friend or foe— I wish to look at the matter from all sides— New lights are constantly dawning upon me and I think it possible I shall come out far enough from the Carlyle view perhaps[n] from yours and will distaste you which will trouble me.[2]

In a brief, but seemingly, calm and authentic notice of Goethe's life which I met with in an English publication the other day I find it stated that his son was illegitimate, that he lived out of wedlock with the mother for twenty years and only married her on acct of the son as late as 1806— I confess this has greatly pained and troubled me— I had no idea that the mighty "Indifferentist" went so far with his experimentalizing in *real life*. I had not supposed he *"was"* all he *"writ,"* and have always maintained that stories which have been told me as coming from Dr Follen which represented him as a man of licentious life could not be true because he was living at a court whose outward morality, at least, must be pure under the auspices of a princess like the Grand duchess Amelia.— In the same publication many, not agreeable, hints are thrown out respecting those very ten[n] years which I know so little about.[3]

How am I to get the information I want unless I go to Europe— To whom should I write to choose my materials— I have thought of Mr Carlyle but still more of Goethe's friend Von Muller—[4] I dare say he would be pleased at the idea of a life of G. written in this hemisphere and be very willing to help me. If you have any-thing to tell me you will and not mince matters— Of course my impressions of Goethe's works cannot be influenced by information I get about his *life* but as to this latter[n] I suspect I must have been hasty in my inferences— I apply to you without scruple— These are subjects on which *gentlemen* and *ladies* usually talk a great deal but apart from one another— you, however, are well aware that I am very destitute of what is commonly called modesty. With regard to this, how fine[n] is the remark of our present subject. "Courage and modesty are virtues which every sort of society reveres because they are virtues which cannot be counterfeited, also they are[n] known by the *same hue*"—[5] When that blush does not come naturally into my face I do not drop a veil to make people think it is there All this may be very *"unlovely"* but it is *I*. As to sending the 40 vols, do not, till you know [cer]tainly that I shall not go to

Europe—[6] That will be decided the first of June and I will write and tell you— When I wrote for the Goethe I thought it *was* decided but it is not. My mind is much harassed by anxiety and suspense— add to this that my health has been most miserable for two or three months back. So I do not accomplish much— If I thought my constitution was really broken and that I must never again know my natural energy of body and mind I should be almost overcome, but the physician says it is only the extreme cold winter acting on a frame debilitated by a severe illness and all the painful emotion which came after and that the summer will[n] probably restore me.

What subjects do you wish me to write upon for your mag. and how can I send if I *do* write.[7] It seems to me I have but little to give the West. I have left myself no room for critiques on your writing but by and by I will do what you desire— Would you not like me to wait till I have read your N. American piece. Be assured you have heart and mind sympathy from me.—[8] I should like to come to the West very much perhaps if I do not go abroad, I might for a time if I could do something to pay my way. Perhaps you do not know that I am to have scarce any money.— I suppose if I have health I can earn it as others do— I have a protege that I wish you could get a place for. She is a farmer's daughter, far from elegant or pretty but with a sterling heart and mind and really good education. She knows Latin, French and Italian and could teach the common English branches and something of Mathematics I have taken some pains with her and feel a desire that her earnest wish to go and teach at the South or West should be gratified.— She is persuaded it would do her good and I know enough of the misery of being baffled and hemmed in on every side by seemingly insignificant barriers to feel an interest in giving her a chance to try her experiment too. She would make a good governess or assistant— if any thing of the sort[n] falls in your way think of *her* an thou lovest *me*.[9]

I know you must hate these crossed letters—

M. F.

I have been reading, with delight, Herschell's discourse on Nat. Philosophy— Do you know it?

ALS (MHi). Published in part in *Memoirs*, 1:128–29; Miller, p. 48; and *Letters of MF*, 1:244, 248. *Addressed:* Revd J. F. Clarke. / Louisville. / Kentucky. *Postmark:* Groton Ms / Apr 19. *Endorsed:* M. F— / Ap. 19th.
view perhaps] view ⟨possibly⟩ ↑ perhaps ↓
very ten] very ⟨three⟩ ↑ ten ↓
this latter] this la⟨st⟩tter
this, how fine] this, ⟨latter⟩ ↑ how fine ↓
they are] they ⟨have⟩ ↑ are ↓
summer will] summer ⟨b⟩ will
thing of the sort] thing ↑ of the sort ↓

1. Clarke said in his letter of 28 March, "You once said it was out of my power to live without an imaginative love— this is very true." He went on to say that he often fell in love, but always when he was away from Louisville (*Letters of JFC*, p. 119).

2. Clarke wrote: "Go on with your task, fear not, you can do it" (*Letters of JFC*, p. 117).

3. Replied Clarke, "As to what you say on the subject of Goethe's license, I have little to communicate. There is evidence enough in his Italian letters, elegies, etc., that his moral code was not of the strictest kind" (*Letters of JFC*, p. 119).

4. Friedrich von Müller was a Weimar political figure.

5. From Goethe's "Maximen und Reflexionen aus Wilhelm Meisters Wanderjahren." Clarke responded: "Your ideas upon modesty are very correct" and told her a story of a shy young man he met on a steamboat (*Letters of JFC*, pp. 120–21).

6. The set of Goethe's works that Clarke offered to lend.

7. Clarke closed his letter of 4 May by saying, "Write for the Maga—write—write— whatever you think best" (*Letters of JFC*, p. 121). Fuller ignored him and sent her work in 1836 to the *American Monthly Magazine*, which published three of her substantial articles (on Mackintosh, Heine, and modern British poetry). Since the Mackintosh essay was published in June and "Present State of German Literature" in July, Fuller must have been working on both as she wrote this letter. Her silence to Clarke in the face of his plea was deliberate, for he first learned of the essays from George Davis (*Letters of JFC*, p. 121).

8. In his letter of 28 March, Clarke specifically asked for criticism: "You have never told me your opinion of my writings in the *W. Messenger*. I wish much for a little sharp, discriminating criticism on what I am doing" (*Letters of JFC*, p. 118). He mentioned his review of Mann Butler's *History of the Commonwealth of Kentucky* and James Hall's *Sketches of History, Life, and Manners in the West*, in *The North American Review* 43 (July 1836): 1– 28. Clarke, who knew both Hall and Butler in Louisville, called the former a graceful but inaccurate writer and the latter a clumsy writer but an accomplished historian.

9. Clarke replied, "Everyone who comes to the West has to run a risk. Send out your young friend with a letter to me" (*Letters of JFC*, p. 121). On 29 July 1836 he mentions a "Miss Wilby," whom Fuller knew and who had come from the East to teach but did not stay (*Letters of JFC*, pp. 121–22).

1047. To James F. Clarke

Avon place
19th[n] Septr—[1836][n]

Dear James,

I was much disappointed that I could not speak to you after service yesterday afternoon. I hope, since[n] you are to be in town today, this note may find you. If it had not been for the liberals meeting at Mr Ripley's I think I might have asked you to take me out to Mt Auburn this afternoon when the Barkers go. As it is you must not go off to Newport without seeing me. I am sorry you think of going to Newport at all for I have said scarce any thing to you yet of what I intended, sorry I mean on my own acct—for, no doubt, you will be very happy with Dr Channing and Mrs Channing and the Glen. You must not linger ther[e] as I did, however, lest[n] you see no more of your friend

M.

ALS (MHi). *Endorsed:* (47).

19th] ⟨17⟩ 19th

Dated by the contents: Fuller writes here on a Monday, which must be either 1836 or 1842. The Barkers were in Boston in September 1836; the "liberals" were the men who formed the "Transcendental Club": Emerson, Hedge, George Putnam, and George Ripley. They met for the first time at Ripley's home on 19 September 1836 (Joel Myerson, "A Calander of Transcendental Club Meetings," American Literature *44 [May 1972]: 200).*

hope, since] hope, ⟨?⟩since

however, lest] however, ⟨or⟩ lest

1048. To James F. Clarke

Boston 21st March
1837,

Dear James,

As Dr Jarvis is going tomorrow morng I think I must e'en scribble a few lines althoug[h] too tired and busy this eveg to communicate much except that I am still your friend.[1]

I received you letter with heart as well as head. I had sympathized with you ere I received it and in the still watches of the night thought of you and your loss. I had thoughts which could we have met I might have expressed. I will not do it now; my present mood is not in unison with their solemn fragrance.[2]

You ask me to tell you what I am "doing, thinking and feeling." Just[n] now I am only doing and feeling, not thinking, if by thinking reflecting be meant.— I have done, I have learned a great deal this winter. Outwardly my efforts have not been in vain. I believe when I wrote to Sarah I was in a "wan and heartless mood." I was very sick— I was or seemed[n] in heart and aim completely isolated. And there lay not gleam of light on my onward way.

> "But fear not, God will still provide
> For every[n] being in his empire wide."

The clouds have rolled off— Several paths of fair promise open before me and my only difficulty is how to choose the best where all seem to betoken good.

New hearts have linked themselves to me and all at present goes well with me except as to my bodily health. That is even worse but the wise man of medicine flatters me that *if* I can but repose this summer even there I may be renewed. Meanwhile this bad health and my position whose fatigue is more than I can bear, without a great deal of management, must be my excuse for avoiding all exertion which is not absolutely necessary, and among others writing you a letter which is good for any thing. My engagements in Boston terminate by the first of May,[3] if indee[d] I can sustain myself till that time I shall then go home for a time and hope to write you a long letter on one of those famous folio sheets, giving an account of myself more psychological[n] than this present and of various other[n] persons and things interesting either to you or me. At present I can do no better than this— I shall write to Mr Eliot, if I possibly can, in a few days for his two lovely letters call hourly for an answer and will not be denied. But you, my friend James, you will wait, will you not?

Tell Sarah that Miss Peabody mourns and marvels over her silence, and 'tis a pity she should not do what would give so much pleasure.

Farewell, the heavens be with ye!

Margaret F.

ALS (MHi). *Addressed:* Revd James F. Clarke / ⟨?⟩Louisville. / Kentucky / Politeness of Dr Jarvis. *Endorsed:* S. M. Fuller— March / 21st 1837 Ky 29.

feeling." Just] feeling." ⟨?⟩Just
was or seemed] was ↑ or seemed ↓
For every] For e⟨?⟩very
more psychological] more p⟨?⟩sychological
various other] various o⟨e⟩ther

1. Edward Jarvis (1803–84) graduated from Harvard in 1826. He was a physician and writer who was in Louisville from 1837 to 1843. He contributed to and helped edit the *Western Messenger* (*DAB*; Habich, "Annotated List," p. 170). In later years he was prominent in the fields of public health and medical statistics. In 1834 he married Almira Hunt (d. 1884) of Concord (*DAB; Boston Evening Transcript*, 6 November 1884).

2. The whole of Clarke's letter of 10 February was given to the description of Martha Ruggles Zeigler Windship, a parishioner and contributor to the *Messenger*, who had recently died. Daughter of George Zeigler, she married Dr. Charles William Windship in 1817 (*CC*, 15 November 1817). Clarke wrote a memoir of her for the *Messenger* of March 1837.

3. Fuller at this time was teaching in Bronson Alcott's Temple School.

1049. To James F. Clarke

Boston 18th April
1837

My dear James,

As Mrs Greene (formerly Martha Dana, the Groton Lady Bountiful and our kind neighbor) is about to carry her husband's knapsack while he goes about the country making internal improvements, and expects to pass some time at Louisville[1] "This comes hoping" that you will, for my sake, pay her some attention yourself and promote other peoples' calling on her. I think nobody who does so[n] will regret it as she is lively, social, and very amiable.

No use in more words as I hope to write a good letter of fact and thoughts by post soon.

Yours very kindly

S. M. FULLER.

ALS (MHi). *Addressed:* Revd James F. Clarke. / Louisville. / Kentucky. / Mrs Greene. *Endorsed:* Margaret Fuller.

does so] does s⟨y⟩o

1. Martha Barrett Dana had been Fuller's school friend at Miss Prescott's school in the 1820s. On 21 February 1837 she married George Sears Greene (1801–99), who graduated from West Point in 1823 and served in the army until 1836, when he retired to become a civil engineer for a railroad. He later served with distinction in the Civil War (*DAB*).

1050.   To ?

Apr 23 [1837][n]

[   ] I earn little or nothing in this miserable school nor am I [*illegible*] toward any [*illegible*] good in it [   ]

MsCfr (MB: Ms. Am. 1450 [17]).

Higginson dated this fragment 1839, but that date clearly is an error, for by then Fuller was no longer at the Greene-Street School. The reference more probably is to Alcott's school, which she left in 1837.

1051.   To James F. Clarke

Groton 13th May 1837.

My dear friend James,

A letter recd this aftn from Sarah, though about as barren and careless as mine to you by Miss Goddard's friends, brings you two so forcibly to my mind that I can no longer defer my promise of writing you a long letter from this place.[1]

I have now been at home ten days and am still quite unwell, yet, I think, better and growing better. I suppose I shall never entirely recover from the shock my constitution received at the time of my Father's death. The fatigue and excitement of that period came upon me at a time when I was so ill able to bear it, and all my pursuits and propensities have a tendency to make my head worse. It is but a bad head; as bad[n] as if I were a great man. I know I am not entitled to so bad a head by any thing I have done; but I flatter myself it is very interesting of me to suffer so much and a good excuse for not writing pretty letters and saying to my friends the good things[n] I think about them. Indeed it is not exaggeration to say that what with my engagements and what with my head I could barely[n] live from day to day and that there was no time when I *could* write any letter.

I was so new to a public position and so desirous to do all I could that I took a great deal more upon myself than I was able to bear. Yet now the twenty five weeks of incessant toil are over I rejoice in it[n] all and would not have done an iota less. I have fulfilled all my engagements faithfully.[2] I have acquired more power of attention, self-command and fortitud[e] I have acted in life as I thought I would in my lonely bower. I have acquired some kn[ow]ledge of means, and, blessed be the fat[   ] of our spirits! my aims are the same as they were in the happiest flight of youthful fancy.

I have learnt too at last to rejoice in all past pain. I have now found its practical benefit. I see that my spirit has been so judiciously tempered for its work— In future I may sorrow but can I ever despair?—

The beginning of my winter was forlorn. I was always ill. I often thought I might not live. The work but just begun perhaps I must die. The usual disappointments were about me. Those from whom I had expected aid disappointed me. Others who aided did not understand me. My enthusiasm fled about the things I loved best when I seemed to be buying and selling it. I could not get the proper point of view— I could not keep a healthful state of mind. Mysteriously a gulf seemed to have opened between me and my most intimate friends. For the first time for so many years I felt entirely, absolutely alone. My own character and designs lost all romantic interest in my eyes. I felt vulgarized, profaned forsaken, and was obliged to smile so brightly and[n] talk so wisely all the while.

But all these clouds past away. I hope, I trust these[n] were the last agonies of factitious life and that I shall now repose in the arms of nature and destiny, that my heart will now vibrate in unison with the soul of the world. Leben im Ganzen [is] to be my motto— can I be disappointed?—

I will try to tell you what I have done with my classes in the way of study. To one class I taught the Gn language in the way I tried with Sarah and the Randalls. S. will remember. I thought myself very successful;[n] at the end of three months they could read 20 pages of Gn at a lesson and very well. This, class[n] of course, was nothing to me except in the way of observation and analysis of language.

With my more advanced pupils I read in 14 weeks, Schiller's Don Carlos, Schiller's[n] artists and Song of the Bell besides one lesson in wh I gave a sort of lecture on Schiller,— Goethe's Hermann and Dorothea, Goetz of Berlichingen, Iphigenia, First part of Faust (three weeks of thorough study this as valuable to me as to them) and Clavigo, thus comprehending[n] samples of all his efforts in poesy &c bringing forward some of his prominent opinions. Lessing's Nathan, Minna, Emilia Gaelotti, parts of Tieck's Phantasus, and nearly the whole firs[t] vol. of Richter's Titan.—[3] With my Italn class I read parts of Tasso, Petrarch, (whom they came to almost adore) Ariosto, Alfieri, and the whole hundred cantos of the Divina Commedia with the aid of the fine Athenaeum copy and all the best commentaries. This last piece of work was and will be truly valuable to myself.

I had besides three private pupils, Mrs G.[n] Lee, (who became very interesting to me) E. Shattuck, and little E. Bond who had not the use of his eyes I taught him Latin orally and read the Hist of England and Shakespeare's histl plays in connection.[4] I gave this lesson every day for ten weeks; it was very interesting, but very fatiguing to me. Mr Alcott's school wa[s] also very fatiguing. I, however, loved the chi [   ] had many valuable thoughts suggested there. I cannot have room to write about this now, nor about Mr Alcott whose society was much to me. By the way, dear James, I rejoice in the warm interest you have taken for Mr A. It was like you and has not been lost on his heart as I saw from a passage in his journal.[5]

—As you may imagine I have not yet written the Life of Goethe but have studied and thought about it a great deal. It grows in my mind with every thing that does grow there. It is now engaged to Mr Ripley on such terms as I could desire.[6] Three years are given me to write it in and it can be recd as much sooner into the series as I may wish. My friends in Europe have sent me the books I need on the subject[7] I am now beginning to work in good earnest. I see is possible my task may be taken from me [o]r somebody in England[n] that in doing it I may find myself in compe[tition] but I go on in hope, secure at all events [   ] will be the means of the highest culture.

I fear I am injuring you and trespassing on your generosity in keeping your Goethe, but I have not been able to send for it till now. I trust to receive it from Europe in Autumn and shall then return yours with a thousand thanks.

My readings with Dr C. amounted to but little except that this gave me oppory of seeing him a great deal.[8] When I went to bid him good bye he asked my how he could send to you and I told him

I hope correctly. I made many agreeable acquaintances and several dear friends whom I have no time or room[n] to tell about now. Mr and Mrs Ripley I enjoyed delightful hours with. I am very sorry— I did not see this ink on my writing desk till it was too late will you forgive so bad-looking a letter rather than not have any?— I know you will but do, please, burn it—

I have not answered your letter as I meant— perhaps I never shall now[n] till we meet. When will that be? I wish I had room to tell you about Mr Emerson's lectures and the week I have just passed at[n] his house and his beautiful baby—[9]

When Sarah returns she will not find me in Boston, though possibly I may be there next winter I shall be in Providence R. Island.[10] She must stop and see me as she comes— I depend upon it. I know she has a friend lives there and at Revd Mr Hall's she will hear where I am.[11] I do not yet know myself where I shall board[n] but shall go to Providence the first of June. I have been tempted there by the liberal salary offered me and other inducements. I am offered a thousand dollars a year for teaching four hours a day in my own department. But if it does not suit my health or tastes, or interferes with my main project I shall not stay I have only promised to try it. If I find a letter from you there I think I shd answer it soon.

Do not speak to any one but Sarah of my engagement with Mr R. about the Life of G.— it is indeed like the secrets of the stage so many know it, yet I wish[n] to avoid all unnecessary publicity. For often I am ashamed and think I am too, *too* unfit for so great a work.

Lebewohl mein Jungende Freund.—

M. F.

ALS (MHi). Published in part in *Memoirs*, 1:172–75, and *Letters of MF*, 1:278–79. *Addressed:* Revd James F. Clarke. / Louisville. / Kentucky. *Postmark:* Groton Ms / May ⟨?⟩ 14. *Endorsed:* S. M. F. her winter's work / May 37—

as bad] as ⟨p⟩ bad
good things] good thin⟨k⟩gs
could barely] could ⟨p⟩barely
in it] in ⟨?⟩ it
brightly and] brightly ⟨&⟩ and
trust these] trust the⟨y⟩se
very successful;] very ⟨suffi⟩ ↑ successful ↓ ;
This, class] This, ↑ class ↓
Carlos, Schiller's] Carlos, ⟨s⟩Schiller's
thus comprehending] thus ⟨re⟩ comprehending
pupils, Mrs G.] pupi⟨s⟩ls, Mrs ⟨S⟩G.
[o]r somebody in England] [o]r ↑ somebody in England ↓

time or room] time ↑ or room ↓
shall now] shall ↑ now ↓
passed at] passed ⟨th⟩ at
myself where I shall board] myself ↑ where I shall board ↓
I wish] I ⟨mu⟩ wish

1. Miss Goddard's friends are unidentified, but she is probably the sister of Francis E. Goddard (1791?–1845), one of Clarke's closest Louisville friends. Goddard graduated from Harvard in 1812 and became a teacher in Louisville (Harvard archives).

2. Fuller had just ended her teaching at Alcott's school.

3. Her reading and teaching emphasized late-eighteenth-century German literature.

4. In 1837, Hannah Farnham Sawyer Lee wrote a popular book, *Three Experiments of Living*. She later published a number of historical sketches and stories (*DAB*). In 1807 she married George Gardner Lee (1774–1816), a former naval officer and merchant, who had graduated from Harvard in 1792 (*CC*, 24 January 1807; Harvard archives). Eleanor Elizabeth Shattuck (1818?–42) was the daughter of Dr. George C. and Eliza Davis Shattuck. He was Boston's leading physician (Mt. Auburn; *DAB*).

5. Clarke, in his notice of Alcott's controversial *Conversations with Children on the Gospels*, had said that "a more interesting series of conversations we have never seen" (*Western Messenger* 3 [March 1837]: 540). In response, Alcott wrote in the journal passage Fuller mentions: "The editor of this fresh and free periodical, gave a favorable notice of my '*book*' in the No. of the 'Messenger' for this month. This is the first d[e]cided and hearty praise which the book has received. Mr. Clark[e], the editor, has heretofore taken a generous view of my enterprize, and labours. He is a free and high-minded young man, bent on finding truth where-ever it shall chance to spring up. His field of labour is ample;— and unencumbered by the conventions of older society, his spirit seems to expand in the west" (Larry A. Carlson, "Bronson Alcott's 'Journal for 1837,'" in *Studies in the American Renaissance, 1981*, ed. Joel Myerson [Boston, 1981], p. 81).

6. George Ripley had begun to edit a series of books, *Specimens of Foreign Standard Literature*. Fuller's comment here implies that he had contracted for her Goethe biography. She had, however, begun discussing a translation of Eckermann's *Gespräche mit Goethe* with Ripley early in April (*Letters of MF*, 1:268–69). It was the latter that he published in July 1839, the fourth volume of his series.

7. Sam Ward and the Farrars.

8. Fuller had read with Dr. William Ellery Channing (*Letters of MF*, 1:269).

9. Emerson had given his twelve lectures "The Philosophy of History" in Boston from 2 December to 2 March. He then gave seven individual lectures that spring at Charlestown, Salem, Concord, Cambridge, and Boston (William Charvat, "A Chronological List of Emerson's American Lecture Engagements," *Bulletin of the New York Public Library* 64 [1960]: 501).

10. She began teaching at Hiram Fuller's Greene-Street School in June.

11. Edward Brooks Hall, minister of First Church, Providence.

1052. To James F. Clarke

Providence 24th Septr
1837.

My dear James,

I left word with[n] Belinda that I hoped you would make an exchange for this place and come here on your way to your Louisville.

—But I think I will write as I[n] feel a much stronger wish to see you than I did then. I am not so languid and weary. I have had rest now and can talk. I shall be sorry to have you go back and not see you again for so long and not have interchanged any rational words with you. Besides[n] I want to hear you preach; and this place wants preaching as much as any.[1] Mr Hall is now absent; no doubt you can possess yourself of his pulpit, if you will. I might prefer you to come to Mr Farley's because it would be nearer me.[2] You will come, will you not?— and arrange matters to[n] see me as much as possible— and write a letter to tell me when you will come. I would[n] be glad to have Sarah whom also I wish to see and Belinda accompany you. They could return without you.

Affectionately your friend

S. M. FULLER.

ALS (MHi). *Addressed:* Revd James F. Clarke / Boston / Mass. *Postmark:* Providence Sep 25. *Endorsed:* S. M. Fuller— Sept 25 / 183[7]. (32).

word with] word ⟨b⟩ with
as I] as ⟨if⟩ I
you. Besides] you. ⟨A⟩ Besides
matters to] matters ⟨as⟩ to
I would] I ⟨sh⟩ would

1. Clarke delivered six sermons in Providence before he left for Kentucky (*Letters of MF*, 1:304).
2. Frederick Augustus Farley, minister of the Second Unitarian Church, Providence.

1053. To James F. Clarke

Providence 1st Octr 1[837]

Mrs Georgiana Nias is by birth an English woma[n][1] She is niece to— Davy, well-known to Unitarians who have been in England.[2] She was educated prin[ci]pally in France till the age of fourteen and is well qualified to teach the French language. After her return to England she passed four years at a boarding school of high reputation where she was instructed carefully that she might teach again as she was a dependant and an orphan. She did not, however, have more than a year or two of experience in teaching before her marriage and has had none since till she came to this country, where[n] she has been employed in the Greene St school, Providence, where she would remain if the salary given her were adequate to her support and that of her children. She can teach the common English branches, French, drawing, dancing and needle work— I think her ideas refined, and her manner of teaching judicious and thorough. Her drawings are carefully finished, her dancing graceful, her prounciation of French pure. In her own language she is a model for clear enunciation and beauty of modulation.

Her manners and address are remarkably [e]legant, and her knowledge of the little arts which are known in polished society such as to make her a most valuable guide to young ladies. So few Amern ladies have been educated with those exact and refined habits that Engh ladies are, that we shall find it very difficult to supply her place in these respects.

Reference may be made, if any further information is desired respecting her, to Revd Charles Upham, Salem, Mass or to H. Fuller, Principal of the Greene St school in this place.[3]

SARAH MARGARET FULLER

My dear Friend,

I have made out, according to agreement with you an account of Mrs Nais's qualifications. I have taken especial care not to sin on the side of exaggeration and have said no more in behalf of her as a teacher than I thought myself secure to be strictly just. I would add, if Mr Butler[4] is desirous of information about her as an individual, that her character and history are marked by traits that have excited in myself, as they did in Mr and Mrs Upham of Salem, strong affection an[d] esteem.

S. M. F.—

I was so interested about the affair I thought I must send my paper after you lest you should not return here—

21st Octr,

My dear James,

Mr Ripley brought back my letter yesterday much to my vexation, as I had supposed it on its way long since.

I have not written a word for your Messenger ye[t.] It is, literally, a fact that I have had *no* time, except one Sunday and one Saty morng I hope however to do some thing yet— I intend writing upon Mr Emerson's Oration and one delivered this autumn, here, on a similar occasion by Alexander Everett.[5]

I think you will, after seeing Miss Brackett, feel much interested in Mr Hartshorn's second number from Deleuze just out in this place. The appendix contains almost all we know here on the subject—[6]

I have finally decided to remain in Providence. [   ]y new subjects admired *you* so much that I think they cannot fail to receive *me*.

Our conversations this last time were, to me, more satisfactory broken as they were[n] than any intercourse we have had since you went to the West. There was more of real life and truth and kindliness about them—[7] May you prosper!

It is true I did not read letters or tell adventures, as I should have liked to have done; I never shall now, but let that pass. I am here a pilgrim, and born to feel it more constantly than most people. Why should I seek to grasp the hand of any one, or value ties according to their permanence— In one sense my friends must ever be mine—

Mr Ripley says he promised you a bundle of writing and you, careless Editor, never came to take it— You dont deserve to be helped.

M. F.—

ALS (MHi). *Addressed:* Revd J. F. Clarke. / ⟨Boston⟩ Louisville / ⟨Mass.⟩ Kentucky. *Postmark:* Providence R.I. / Oct 24. *Endorsed:* S. M. F. about Mrs Nias. (Ky 33).

country, where] country, ⟨a⟩ where
satisfactory broken as they were] satisfactory ↑ broken as they were ↓

1. Georgiana Nias was Fuller's colleague at the Greene-Street School.
2. Fuller refers either to William Davy (1743–1826), whose *System of Divinity* was published in 26 volumes from 1795 to 1807, or to his son, Charles Davy, who published sermons and *A Plain Discourse on the Nature, Evidences, and Means of Edification* (London, 1823) (*DNB*).
3. Charles Wentworth Upham, the Unitarian minister in Salem. He married Ann Susan Holmes.
4. Probably Mann Butler (1784–1852), lawyer and writer who wrote for the *Messenger* and whose work Clarke reviewed (Habich, "Annotated List," p. 172).
5. Emerson delivered the annual Phi Beta Kappa address at Harvard on 31 August. On 6 September Alexander Everett addressed the Philermenian Society as part of the Brown University commencement exercises. His address, "The History of the Literature of the Past and Present Century," was delivered at Edward Brooks Hall's First Church (*Providence Journal*, 8 September 1837). Everett (1790–1847) was Edward Everett's brother, a diplomat, and the former editor of the *North American Review* (*DAB*).
6. Loraina Brackett was a blind somnambulist who had performed for Clarke and Fuller in Providence, where interest in mesmerism was intense. The *Providence Journal* published excerpts of Thomas Hartshorn's translation of Joseph Philippe François Deleuze's *Instruction pratique sur le magnétisme animal*, which went on sale in Providence on 6 September.
7. In his reply of 20 November, Clarke said, "I enjoyed being with you very much, and think we might be very happy in each other's society, if it were not the law of this world for all who love each other to be separate" (*Letters of JFC*, p. 127).

1054. To John Neal

Providence R. Island
10th Jany 1838—

Dear Sir,

I hope you will not think me over bold if I avail myself of our brief acquaintance to transmit to you one of these leaves. (alas! how far from sibylline— As I was scattering them in all directions towards which I could bid the wind blow, it struck me that the "great man of a little town" would be the very man whom I should assail, he too, being at leisure unlike most Amern citizens" except some trifling divertisements, such as attending to Portland sidewalks, chastising inhuman teamsters, prosecuting the study of Phrenology, Magnetism, and the like "open secrets" &c— Then too as you went to Boston to "finish your education" I conclude it may have become a fashion in Portland. Otherwise I should not have dared to send such a paper lest Maine should hurl back indignant answer of being sufficient to herself.

I could not, indeed, promise that any young person under the Misses Tilden should have similar advantages to what you enjoyed.[1] Only in rare instances do the stars prepare education, discipline so propitious!— But according to the common scheme of life, the advantages would be great— I am anxious too for these poor ladies who are delicate, refined, not used to bear like myself. I am sure, for reasons that it would be tedious to detail, that they will not get a large day-school in Boston and am very desirous they should have boarders from elsewhere.— And you, dear Sir, are my friend, are you not? and wish to please me so if" you know any "young things" doomed to leave their "mammies" for their accidence and like to go to the Literary Emporium, will you not cast this paper on the waters and send bread therefor—

My sister Ellen is with these ladies wh sufficiently expresses my opinion of them. [   ]

We want you very much here to scintillate through the fog of our common prose world. Be sure and not forget that you promised to come and bring Mrs Neal in the spring.[2] Meanwhile believe me yours

S. MARGARET FULLER.

I am sure you must be desirous for your own sake to come and recant some of the monstrous heresies you uttered here.[3]

ALfrS (MH: bMS Am 1949 [103a]). *Endorsed:* Miss Fuller.

leisure unlike most Amern citizens] leisure ↑ unlike most Amern citizens ↓

me so if] me ↑ so if ↓

1. Catherine Brown Tilden, who had a school in Jamaica Plain, and her sister Maria Dall Tilden.

2. John Neal married his cousin Eleanor Hall (1809–77), daughter of Joel and Mary Porter Hall, in 1828 (Emma E. Brigham, *Neal Family* [Springfield, Mass., 1938], p. 255; *CC*, 18 October 1828).

3. Neal had visited Providence in 1837, at which time Fuller had been strongly affected by him, as she recorded in her journal: "We had a regular fight. Mr. Neal does not argue fairly, he uses reason while it lasts, and then, if he has got into a scrape, helps himself out as he can by wit, by sentiment or strings of assertions. . . . I told him when

we were going home that I liked him very much, knew only three or four men whom I liked better— I might have added that I knew none who was so truly a *man*" (MB).

1055. To James F. Clarke

Providence, 18th March
1838—

My dear James

I suppose if your little friends are coming hither, they have already set forth, but, in case that should not be so, I write to say that, if they come, they will be more favorably situated than I had expected at the time of Mr Fuller's letter as Mrs Aborn has taken a nice[n] new house.[1] I hope they will come. Since I must pass my time and spend my strength in a way so little fit for me, I would gladly that you might reap somewhat of such seed as I can sow; and shall take pleasure in communicating with you through the minds of your elevés. Indeed I believe you are right in wishing them sent here. The school in some important particulars is better than[n] any I know. You saw how agreeable and convenient were its arrangements. Mr F's is a living influence, (which can be said of few teachers) the two ladies who assist compare very favorably with those who have reputation in Boston. For myself, giving my soul to such business is out of the question, but what I do I do conscientiously, and, though often wearied in body and mind, by this school, yet feel in it while there sincere interest and often love the human beings whose eyes speak the possibilities of their souls; larvae though they be at present.

I thank you, my friend, for your tribute.[2] Such are my best consolations amid the petty trials of an uncongenial lot, to feel that I have served souls as you say I have served yours— While such words are so often spoken to me I suppose I ought not to feel that I live in vain. But this feeling does beset me; so inadequate is my life to the aims prescribed by my youthful aspirations.

"What interests me?— whom do I chiefly love?— how is it with Goethe?"—

Nothing deeply interests me, for imperious duty forbids me to give my soul to what is calculated to kindle my enthusiasm. The hydra conflict between the Needful and the Beautiful[n] still is waging in my bosom as in others, nor can I wish it to cease for I[n] cannot s[ee] how it should without some valued par[t] of my nature being stifled. I do not murmur; mine is the common lot of such natures, but I die. I know

301

not how long I shall be in dying, some years perhaps— Do not you care. I bide my time, and shall never be, as I never yet have been at home on earth. Whom do I chiefly love;— you know them not; their names would be words to you, except Mr Emerson's. He is to me even nobler than he was, wise, steadfast, delicate, one will neither disappoint my judgement nor wound my taste. From him, as from all I most love, I am separated, separated by my own act, because the most finite considerations make it seem a duty. Some glimpses I have of presences beauteous and beloved, and I know that high thoughts follow me. Better separation too, than that custom should stale the perfection of true intercourse. So again let me not murmur; it is my own choice, so called!

For Goethe you ought to be answered either by a book, or a billet doux from my coffin now do not misunderstand me as Miss Martineau and Mrs Farrar did because I answered their questions sincerely. There is so much to write about me" that I cannot give a fair view of myself in a few lines. If you saw me you would think me cheerful. I saw Louisa, Amelia and George in Boston, but got nothing from either except that A. also has a son Willie by name.[3] I wish you would send me the two sets of verses on Louisa's ring for I cant get them from the others. Did you ever get my Palmyra and your Faust.[4]

With blessings yours always

M. F.—

ALS (MHi). *Addressed:* Revd J. F. Clarke / Louisville. / Kentucky— *Postmark:* Providence R.I. Mar 19. *Endorsed:* Miss S. M. Fuller— / March 19th— / (Ky letter 3⟨2⟩4).

a nice] a ↑ nice ↓
better] than] better th⟨?⟩an
conflict between the Needful and the Beautiful] conflict ↑ between the Needful and the Beautiful ↓
cease for I] cease ⟨n⟩ for ⟨c⟩ I
about me] about ⟨s⟩ me

1. The two Louisville girls, Emma Keats (the poet's niece) and Ellen Clark, did not go to Providence until later. They eventually followed Fuller to Boston as private students. Susan Aborn was Fuller's landlady in Providence.

2. In his letter of 1 March, Clarke said, "Whatever we owe to those who give us confidence in ourselves, who make us believe we *are* something distinct and can do something special, who arouse our individual consciousness by an intelligent sympathy with tendencies and feelings, we ourselves only half understand—all this I owe to you. You gave me to myself" (*Letters of JFC*, p. 129).

3. Louisa is probably Maria Louisa Russell, who later married Wendell Thornton Davis; Amelia is Amelia Greenwood Bartlett; George is probably George Davis. William Pitt Greenwood Bartlett (1837–65) graduated from Harvard in 1858 (Isaac John Greenwood, *The Greenwood Family of Norwich, England, in America* [Concord, N.H., 1934], p. 143).

4. Fuller's review of William Ware's *Letters from Palmyra*, published in the April issue of the *Messenger*, was her last contribution to Clarke's journal. When he replied, he admitted that he "altered the second paragraph" because "our readers generally would not understand." He went on to criticize her writing: "I think it wants condensation and point; it is too Latinized. It is the reverse of Mr. Emerson's in these particulars" (*Letters of JFC*, p. 130).

1056. To James F. Clarke

Providence 13th May 1838—

Dear James,

I have received my own Goethe from Germany, posthumous works and all. I now wish to return yours with a thousand thanks.[1] Will you indicate to me some proper oppory— perhaps if one of your friends comes with the little girls I can send the books[n] then.—

Your sketches of them interested me and I will do what I can.— I am not, however, kind and generous now in exerting myself for others— I cannot be— the state of my health forbids at present. I looked forward when my father died to various pains but I had no idea of what I was to suffer from merely physical causes, from debility and pain which make it impossible for me to use a third part of the day to any good purpose— The effect of this on my mind is most pernicious— Always feeling doom[ed] to be less than myself, having exchanged the excitement of struggling[n] for the weariness of enduring, unable to do any beautiful thing which might cheer me, I am no longer upborne by my natural enthusiasm, and think that the last few months, on the whole, are the most miserable part of my existence as yet.—

Your little girls will not suffer from this in school as I have perfect self-command, while there, but they will see little of me out of school. I have for some weeks been obliged to pass great part of my time in bed when out of school.— I shall now, however, try riding and may perhaps be stronger for it.— I have writing to do in every well moment. But can keep my eye over them, and I can depend on the Aborn's to take care of them.

The summer term begins, I think the eleventh of June and lasts nine weeks When there will be a month's vacation. My mother will probably begin to keep house here in December— she intends to take two little girls as boarders, and if the parents of your little girls are particularly desirous they should be with me, she can take them. Sister Ellen would be an advantage to them; she has grow[n] into a fine young woman.

I was much pleased with your spirited little pieces in the last Messenger—[n2] I thank you for[n] your critiques on my style, but I want you to define more precisely what you mean by my "sentimentalism" and quote two or three passages as instances—[3] Do not forget this, as otherwise your remark will lie in my mind to hamper and perplex me. Sentimentality is what I most detest, yet I may, unconsciously exhibit it a[nd] I find it far more difficult than I had supposed to keep the sana mens without th[e] corpore sano.— I do not wish to write on Animal Magnetism as 'tis a subject in which I take no interest at present, but will write a piece on Dr Wayland's late work, if you like and I can—[4]

Please send me my trans— from the German wh you took. They are useless to you and I often want lines from them.—

Elizh Cumming is coming home in June— I hope then to see her and other of our mutual friends— I will then write to you something better than this.— Say to Mr Eliot with my best regards that I will then write to him also—

Letter-writing is at present very irksome to me and I can do nothing properly in that line.— but I hope to blossom in June like other plants.

As ever yours

M. F.

ALS (MHi). *Addressed:* Revd James F. Clarke. / Louisville / Kentucky.— *Postmark:* Providence R.I. MA 14. *Endorsed:* S. M. Fuller— (no 35 Ky.).

send the books] send ⟨them⟩ ↑ the books ↓
of struggling] of ⟨suff⟩ struggling
last Messenger—] last ⟨m⟩Messenger—
you for] you⟨r⟩ for

1. *Goethe's Werke: Vollständige Ausgabe letzter Hand* (1827–30) was expanded by the addition of *Goethe's nachgelassene Werke* from 1832 to 1842.

2. Fuller knew that Clarke wrote "An Essay on Miracles," "Unanimity of Faith," and "Lady Hewley's Charity" in the April issue, for all were signed or identified on the cover.

3. As part of his criticism, Clarke had said, "There is a kind of sentimentalism, shall I call it? which I always wonder at, in your elaborate articles. Perhaps this is lady-like, yet somehow it likes me not" (*Letters of JFC*, p. 130). In reply to Fuller, he explained that "by 'sentimental' I meant a predominance of feeling over thought. You express the feeling, the effect upon the eye or taste, but the cause, the idea, that which produces the effect is not so distinct and pointed." He went on to illustrate the point from the "Palmyra" article (*Letters of JFC*, p. 132).

4. Francis Wayland, *The Limitations of Human Responsibility* (Boston, 1838). When she lived in Providence, Fuller knew the president of Brown, who was also a Baptist minister and author.

1057. To Edward Brooks Hall

Groton 21st August 1838—

Dear Sir,

Mrs Emerson is desirous to place her niece, Sophia Brown, at the Greene St school for the autumn term.[1] She has but a limited sum for her education, and Mrs E wishes to board her for two dollars and a half per week. Can you receive her on such terms. I fear not.

I received your kind note from Louisa and thank you, but we have decided against the removal of the family to Providence and I shall leave the school at the end of the autumn term.[2] Do not regret this. I could not do good there or elsewhere in my present weak and nervous state. Perhaps a few months of repose will make me what I have been, if not what I ought to be. And I may revisit Rhode Island a calmer and a brighter being.

I hope you are better and that your sister is still with you.[3] If so, please tell her I had a very pleasant day at Medford and was enamored of its beautiful elms and still green meadows. I did not see your home. I asked to go there, but they said it lay in an opposite direction to the one we took to see Mrs Farley and I should be too tired.[4] I shall go there next time. Please remember me to Miss Procter and Miss Ames when you see them.[5]

Truly yours

S. M. FULLER.

If Mr Fuller is absent from Providence will you have the kindness to desire the Postmaster to forward any letters which may come for me.[6] I am anxiously expecting one from Europe, which should come just now.

ALS (MHi). *Addressed:* Revd E. B. Hall, / Providence / Rhode Island. *Postmark:* Groton Ms / Aug 21. *Endorsed:* Miss Fuller—Aug. 1838— / *Groton* / Ansd at once—

1. Sophia Brown (1821?–42) was the daughter of Charles and Lucy Jackson Brown (*Plymouth Church Records, 1620–1859* [New York, 1920–23], p. 684).

2. Fuller's reference is unclear. Hall's first wife, Harriet, died in June. He married Louisa Jane Park, daughter of John Park, Fuller's teacher in the 1820s, in October 1840. She may be the Louisa Fuller mentions.

3. Probably Hall's sister Mary Brooks Hall (1796–1872). The family home was the Samuel Lawrence farmhouse in Medford. Their mother, Joanna Cotton Brooks Hall, was Peter Chardon Brooks's sister (Medford VR; Middlesex probate; *Medford Historical Register* 30:18).

4. Lucy Rice Farley of Groton.

5. Miss Ames may be Anne C. Ames, who, like Fuller, attended the Coliseum club in Providence (Tess Hoffman, "Miss Fuller among the Literary Lions: Two Essays Read at 'The Coliseum' in 1838," in *Studies in the American Renaissance, 1988*, ed. Joel Myerson [Charlottesville, 1988], p. 52). Miss Procter is unidentified.

6. Hiram Fuller.

1058. To James F. Clarke

Providence 15th Septr
1838—

Dear James

You have by this time seen Mr Clark and know that I shall leave this position in Decr—[1]

You will, I suppose, be sorry on acct of your little friends. I wish they had come six months earlier. I could have done much for them in that time. Yet the few months they will pass with me may not be useless.—

If they are to remain at[n] the East, I suppose their parents would scarcely wish them to be in so exposed a position as this, unless they were under the care of some lady[n] on whom they could rely. I do not know at all who may be my successor, but in case it should not be a suitable guardian for them, I think I *can* recommend a good place. Catharine Tilden, daughter of[n] Bryant T. has opened a school at Jamaica Plains.[2] The family is, as you know, of the first respectability and the little girls would be brought under this influence of good Boston society. We have lately seen much of the family. Ellen was six months under their care, and I cannot speak too highly of the benefits she has recd, in point of character. Their habits are refined, their views liberal and Christian, their rule would be one of love. Catharine T. could not give them such a mental impulse as I could, but her character is strong, she would offer them high aims, and in details[n] would, probably, be a better teacher than I, as she loves teaching and has an accurate, careful mind. The best instruction would be provided from Boston in any branch where it is desired and yet they will not have the temptations of a city.[n] If I had the responsibility I should place them there in preference to any school I know[n] in Mass. at present.

306

They both interest me. Ellen has lively perceptions and may be made, I think, a[n] very valuable practical character. Emma seems to me susceptible of a high degree of polish and cultivation

I have not yet seen eno' of them to make up my opinion fully.

A teacher in music and a piano (which they like) have been secured, and they begin to get under weigh a little in their studies. I will write more particularly about them in three or four weeks. I was requested to take care of their affairs; no arrangement was made about remittances, as, indeed, I was too ill to talk the night I saw Mr Clark. I suppose he or Mr Keats will write to me on the subject.[3]

I am much pleased with your lines to Emma, but am sorry you should have made that public use of them.[4] T'is pity to run the risk of destroying the very charm you praise, and to no purpose that I can see.

I have[n] been staying at Dr Channing's and Wm was there. He is as noble as ever. Do exchange with him, dear James, and pass the winter here. Sarah and I have been talking over this plan, and think it would be an excellent one. You would refresh yourself and lay in a stock of new ideas and impressions of which you seem to feel the want.[5] Five years are[n] quite long eno' to be turning outwards you should retire for a while and draw fresh sap from your root. you would have peace to write many good pieces. Do come. If I am here, I will[n] tell you many things, but perhaps I may go to the South. A change of climate is recommended, but I do not, myself believe that is what I need.[n]

You know how they have been baying at Mr Emerson, 'tis pity you could not see how calmly he smiles down, on the sleuth-hounds of— public opinion That "professedly religious periodical" [The] W. M. came in for its share.[6] You see it was not well to rob Mr Norton of the benefit of your article on[n] Goethe. Time, at present, permits no more from your faithful friend

M. F.

Thanks for the ring which Emma gave me in the prettiest way.[7] I shall scarce earn[n] it by what I can do for your "lambs" however, she "will do what she can."

I find I have not attended to your requests about complimenting or encouraging you!! We will try next time.[8]

ALS (MHi). *Addressed:* Revd J. F. Clarke / ⟨Louisville⟩ Boston / ⟨Kentucky⟩ Mass. to be forwarded if / Mr C. is not to return very soon. *Postmark:* Cincinnati O Nov 3 Louisville Ky. Nov 6.

remain at] remain ⟨in⟩ at
some lady] some ⟨person⟩ ↑ lady ↓

daughter of] daughter ↑ of ↓
in details] in ⟨poin⟩ details
desired and yet they will not have the temptations of a city.] desired. ↑ and ↑ yet ↓
they will not have the temptations of a city ↓
I know] I ⟨n⟩know
think, a] think, ⟨into⟩ a
I have] I ⟨s⟩ have
years are] years ⟨is⟩ are
I will] I w⟨o⟩ill
I need.] I nee⟨e⟩d.
article on] article ⟨at⟩ ↑ on ↓
scarce earn] scarce ⟨?⟩ earn

1. L. B. Clark, Ellen's father.
2. The Fuller family and the Tildens were friends.
3. George Keats, Emma's father.
4. "To a Poet's Niece," *Western Messenger* 5 (August 1838): 298.
5. A depressed Clarke wrote: "I stiffen in routine, I am choked by custom, I lack mental stimulus—all around me are flat, heavy, worldly, like Dutch marshes, and my feeble taper expires in this moral miasma" (*Letters of JFC*, p. 133).
6. Emerson's address of 15 July to the seniors of the divinity school was published on 21 August. In a vigorous attack on him, Andrews Norton used the *Messenger* as an example of the "New School in Literature and Religion" that "owes its origins in part to ill-understood notions, obtained by blundering through the crabbed and disgusting obscurity of some of the worst German speculatists, which notions, however, have been received by most of its disciples at second hand, through an interpreter. The atheist Shelley has been quoted and commended in a professedly religious work, called the Western Messenger, but he is not, we conceive, to be reckoned among the patriarchs of the sect" (*Boston Daily Advertiser*, 27 August 1838). The offending article was Osgood's "Shelley and Pollok" in the February 1837 *Messenger*.
7. The ring was inscribed "Feed my lambs."
8. "Can you not praise my *Messenger*," wrote Clarke, "or tell me what pretty little pieces of poetry I write?" (*Letters of JFC*, p. 133).

1059. To Edward Brooks Hall

Tuesday—[October 1838][n]

Dear Sir,

I thank you very much for showing me the letters.[1] Such prodigality of thought and of love, graced by such playful sweetness, I have rarely seen. Should you find any other memorial not too sacred for my eyes, I shall rely on your promise to show it me.

I shall not go to the ordination on Wednesday eveg as I do not like to miss the close of Hamlet with Mr D.[n,2] Should you like to have me bring my sister that eveg to tea or had you rather I should defer it till Friday or some other eveg when you will have less company?

S. M. FULLER.

ALS (MHi). *Addressed:* Revd Mr Hall. *Endorsed:* Miss Fuller— Oct. 183⟨9⟩8— / Miss Fuller / Margaret.

Dated by the endorsement.

close of Hamlet with Mr D.] close. ↑ of Hamlet with Mr D ↓

1. Probably letters from Hall's wife.

2. Richard Henry Dana, Sr., lectured in Providence in October. Of this lecture on *Hamlet*, Fuller wrote in her journal, "I greatly enjoyed his readings in Hamlet, and have reviewed in connection what Goethe and Coleridge have said. . . . I regret that the whole course is not to be on Shakespeare, for I should like to read with him all the plays" (*Memoirs*, 1:185; Capper, *Margaret Fuller*, pp. 248–49).

1060. To James F. Clarke

Groton, 7th Jany 1839

Dearest James,

I think my delay in answering your letter must have put your faith in my affection and sympathy to a severe trial (c est a dire) if you have had time to think about it.— But perhaps, like me, you have been too much engrossed by the outward life to be truly conscious of any incidents or pauses in the inward.

I received your Baltimore letter, amid all the tumult which preceded my departure from Providence. I could scarce live through the fatigue of that time, for indeed, my friend, empty as the world seems at times, it is no easy matter to break the ties which an intelligent being *must* form in the course of a year and a half. Then in Boston, it was all tea and dinner parties, and long conversations and pictures, not possible to sequester my mind and be with you in any grove or grot fit for such meeting.— Now I have been at home two or three days, and my papers which I have not been at leisure to examine for some months are still lying in heaps about my room. I [do] not like to write to any one whom I value [w]hen in dishabille of any kind. I have feelings corresponding with those of Hayden who always[n] put on the ring given him by the emperor before he sat down to his piano to compose.[1] I like to have every thing arranged about me, before I touch a pen, and no more like to call the image of my friend than I should like to invite him in bodily presence into an apartment all littered with books and papers.

But you desired me to write "by the love I bear you," and as I never felt so much for you as now, I will not delay any longer to say that much at least.

It is such a relief to me that I have been able to speak to you on a subject which I thought could never lie open between us. Now there will be no place which does *not* lie open to the light. I can always say what I feel. And the way in which you took it so like yourself, so manly and noble gives me the assurance that I shall have the happiness of seeing in you that symmetry, that conformity in the details of life with the highest aims of which I have some times despaired. How much higher, dear friend, [   ] "mind the music breathing" from" the *life* than [   ] thing we can say." "Character is higher than [   ] this I have long felt to be truth; may we live as if we knew it!

I have just been looking over your letters [   ] the journal you once gave me. It seems when [I] read them as if I had never prized you at [   ] due rate. I hope and believe we may yet be y[   ] much to one another. Imperfect as I am, I feel myself not unworthy to be a true friend. Neither of us is unworthy. In few natures does such love for the good and beautiful survive the ruin of all youthful hopes, the wreck of all illusions.

I wish you would send me your other journal and any other record you may have kept of you[r] life. I shall be, I hope, quiet for a time, and would like to live with you.

In this journal— 1830 I find the words, "if I have been able to affect so forcibly such a mind as M's I am sure that I have powers which may one day be brought to bear upon men, and make them thrill while I speak. I do not believe that I am *now* of much worth.— I know the weaknesses, the inconsistences, the follies of my character but too well, but if I see the germs of the future oak, I am encouraged to labour, to say "it shall come out" I think" I may say without its being an idle boast that M. herself should see a crowd hanging on my tones and when that happens I shall come to her and say "you encouraged me to labour to you I owe it."

This has happened, you have returned, having realized all you attempted; you have equalled your own desire and surpassing *my* expectations. I [wit]nessed your success with pride and pleasure. [It s]eems I am a sybil for my friends, Cassandra only [to my]self. Let me predict once more, that my friend [   ] carry his self respect into little things as [well] as great, and return to tell me that the lower[?] [   ]ne is chained at the feet of the true Ich.

[I g]ave your message to Emma who, as is her wont, [ans]wered never a word.[2]

[I] think it right to tell you before quitting this unpleasant subject that I found after your departure that it would have been very wrong if I had said nothing for the circumstance" of which you thought so little was very much talked off. I believe I set things on their right

The Letters of Margaret Fuller

footing however.— This though the part of least consequence, you will not despise. Do "whatever is *lovely and* what is of *good report*, says a respected teacher.[3]

And now farewell to this. I will in a few days write again, and I pray you, let me get your news as soon as possible.

Your faithful friend

M. F.

ALS (MHi). Published in part in *Memoirs*, 1:81–82. *Addressed:* Revd James F. Clarke. / Louisville / Kentucky. *Postmark:* Groton Ms / Jany 8. *Endorsed:* Groton / Jan 1839. Ky no 37.

Hayden who always] Hayden ⟨when he⟩ ↑ who always ↓
music breathing] music⟨?⟩ breathing
can say.] can s⟨ee⟩ay.
I think] I ⟨m⟩ think
the circumstance] the ⟨ex⟩ circumstance

1. Fuller found the anecdote in L. A. C. Bombet, *The Life of Haydn*, trans. William Gardiner. The work was first published in London in 1817; Fuller reviewed the 1839 Boston edition for *The Dial*. Bombet describes Haydn's habits: "Frederic the Second had sent him a diamond ring; and Haydn confessed that, often, when he sat down to his piano, if he had forgotten to put on his ring, he could not summon a single idea. The paper on which he composed must be the finest and whitest possible, and he wrote with so much neatness and care, that the best copyist could not have surpassed him in the regularity and clearness of his characters" (p. 76). Bombet was one of the pseudonyms, Stendhal being the best known, of Henri Marie Beyle.

2. Emma Keats.

3. Phil. 4:8: "Finally, brethren, whatsoever things are true, whatsoever things are honest, whatsoever things are just, whatsoever things are pure, whatsoever things are lovely, whatsoever things are of good report; if there be any virtue, and if there be any praise, think on these things."

1061.   To James F. Clarke

Groton[n] 8th Jany 1839—

My dear James,

I believe I am not too tired tonight to write you my second letter.

Let me tell you first a little about Emma.— The acquaintance between us never grew after the letter I showed you, but we were on a pleasanter footing than before; I left her with little regret, for I could do little for her, and I want a softer and more genial atmosphere[n] round me. The public ways of life present rough inaccessible places in plenty without bringing them so near home.

Natheless I had a great esteem for her I hope she is as well placed now as she can be.— I fear they may be a little too fussy for her, but I think she cannot fail to get some advantage from that position.

Little Ellen grew much upon me the latter part of the time, so arch and winning were her ways. Very soon I shall write both fathers.

You asked me if you might copy any verses you liked from my journal and I gave you an over hasty assent. When it was returned I found a pencil mark (which I supposed might be yours) against one or two which I cannot be willing to know in the possession of another. If you have[n] those beginning "In this sad world &c or those beginning "The brilliant day draws to a brilliant close[,] I must ask you, as you love me and value my feelings to destroy the copies immediately.

And this reminds me to ask whether any lines by me on the promise "I will not leave you comfortless" were ever published in the W. Messenger.[1] Mother is positive they have been and with my signature. I cannot believe it, but wish to ask you and do not forget to answer me.

And I wish now as far as I can to give my reasons for what you consider absurd squeamishness in me. You may not acquiesce in my view, but I think you will respect it *as* mine, and be willing to act upon it as far as I am concerned.

Genius seems to me excusable in taking the public for a confidant. Genius is universal and can appeal to the common heart of man; But even here I would not have it too direct— I prefer to see the thought or feeling made universal. How different the confidence of Goethe, for instance from that of Byron.—

But for us lesser people who write verses merely as vents for the overflowings of a personal experience, which in every life of any value craves occasionally[n] the accompaniment of the lyre, it seems to m[e] that all the value of this utterance is destroyed by a hasty or indiscriminate publicity. The moment I lay open my heart and tell the fresh feeling to any one who chooses to hear— I feel as much profaned as if I were to go into the midst of a Providence party and talk as I did to you one night about my want[n] of Christian humility— When it has passed into experience, when the flower has has gone to seed, I dont care who knows it, whither they wander.— I am no longer it— I stand on it.— I do not know whether this is peculiar to me or no, but I am sure the moment I cease to have any reserve or delicacy about a feeling; it is on the wane.

About putting beautiful verses in your maga— I have no feeling except what I shd about furnishing a room— I should not put a dressing case into a parlor,[n] or a bookcase into a dressing room, because however good things in their place, they were[?] not in place there—[n] And this not in consideration of the public, but of my own

James F. Clarke. Courtesy of the Harvard University Archives.

sense of fitness and harmony. I do not undervalue your pet, but its whole character is popular. I would use for it such a poet as Milne rather than Tennyson and Bryant rather than R. W. E.— Yet, for this latter, as his view is entirely[n] opposed to mine, and he assumes in theory at least that there is no need of adaptation and gradation, my feeling was simply that I had scarce ever known him show his verses and I had no right to give them away without his leave—

Dear friend truly yours

S M. F.

ALS (MHi). Published in part in *Memoirs*, 1:73–74; Miller, pp. 47–48; and *Letters of MF*, 2:33–34. *Addressed:* Revd James F. Clarke. / Louisville. / Kentucky. *Postmark:* Groton Ms / Jany 9. *Endorsed:* (38 Ky).

Groton] ⟨Providence⟩ ↑ Groton ↓
genial atmosphere] genial ⟨cl⟩ atmosphere
If you have] If ↑ you have ↓
craves occasionally] craves ↑ occasionally ↓
my want] my ⟨?⟩ want
a parlor,] a par⟨?⟩lor,
place there—] place the⟨ir⟩re—
is entirely] is ⟨g⟩ entirely

1. Clarke published the unsigned poem "Jesus, the Comforter" in the September 1837 issue of the *Messenger* (pp. 20–21).

1062. To James F. Clarke

Jamaica Plains
June 26th 1839—

My dear friend James,

To answer to the first part of your letter.— The excuses you made for my silence were well founded. But the principal reason why I delayed to write till I forgot it was that you said you had a great deal more to tell me and should write again. So I waited to receive that letter!

It is true I was hurt to hear the news of circumstances so important to you from a stranger.[1] But, as even then the pleasure I felt at your happiness dispelled in a moment all other feelings, you may imagine I willingly accept your pretty apologies.— Dear friend, who at times have seemed to me a true brother your letter gave me great peace. Could it have been that you and my dear Elizabeth might have stood in such a relation to one another, I should have been happy for her as now for you. But I always knew that could not be. She is not unhappy, but neither is she so placed as to unfold to the fair proportion Nature intended. You, I trust, will have in the truest sense a home, a home where the thoughts may rest, and the affections be called out, and the noblest aspirations be quickened. Such a home, and work suited to the capacity are all that the best human beings should claim. That you are so favored quickens my faith. For I have sometimes felt as if there was an iron destiny upon you. For eight years you have almost invariably been mentioned in my prayers, whenever I have had goodness enough to venture to pray for any beside myself. Now you will be so full of cheer you will need to pray for others, and we need only *think* of you.

Surely, I shall love your Elect, if I can, and shall wish to win her regard. But in no event need either of us be disturbed. I, at least, have seen enough of human nature to know that its finest qualities rarely display themselves except to the eye of love, and that beautiful characters do not wear labels. If you are happy, if you become wiser, purer, more refined, I shall feel, of course, that all is right.

You will be glad to hear that I have been really well for several weeks past, and that feelings of cheerful energy begin to flow back upon me. If I can only be free from so much pain, if I can repose long enough to recover from the long trance of exhaustion, I will yet be worthy of the hopes and aims we shared in earlier days. Meantime let me rejoice for others.— You have found a home.— William Channing a place—[2] The advancing sun casts a golden ray even into the low valley of my experience.—

Dear friend, farewell, for I do not feel like words, and would fain I might have spoken by a look. Shall we see you here this summer—

MARGARET F—

I am sorry that I have not spoken of Emma and Ellen; yet this letter seemed sacred to ourselves. Perhaps I shall write again.— Sister Ellen cannot write to you, for she has lost the use of her eyes by a strain I believe. Mother and she think of you with affectionate regard— I have not seen your address, but shall endeavor to do so.[3]

ALS (MHi). *Addressed:* Rev J. F. Clarke. / Louisville / Kentucky. *Postmark:* Jamaica Plain Jun 27.

1. Clarke was engaged to Anna Huidekoper of Meadville, Pennsylvania, whom he married on 15 August 1839.

2. William Henry Channing was ordained in Cincinnati on 10 May. He quickly joined with Clarke to produce the *Messenger*.

3. Clarke gave the "Right Hand of Fellowship" address at Channing's ordination (and published it in the June *Messenger*), and William Greenleaf Eliot gave the charge to the new minister. The sermon was preached by Frederick A. Farley, minister at Second Church, Providence (*James Freeman Clarke: Autobiography, Diary, and Correspondence*, ed. Edward Everett Hale [Boston, 1891], pp. 129–30; Frothingham, *Memoir of William Henry Channing*, p. 146; *Heralds*, 3:197).

1063. To James F. Clarke

Jamaica Plain
28th Septr 1839—

My dear James,

George writes that he has a letter from you, and I would have been glad of one too, yet do not wish you to write— I have the satisfaction of thinking you are happy, and when people are living, I do not wish them to be writing. So though I should have been glad of the letter for mine own pleasure I am well content to be without it for yours.

I saw the new friend,[1] as she will have told you but it was only for a brief half hour, but[n] I could see that she was sweet and calm[n] and pure, and was well pleased to have the picture of my friend James's bride to hang up in my hall of imagery even though I knew not yet what verse to inscribe beneath it.

But I hope we shall all know and be known soon, for I hear that they have their eye on you to succeed Dr Walker and hope you will be induced to leave the West, where in the opinion of Me, Sybilla and Makaria to the state of Masstts and the sons thereof, you have staid long enough for others weal and your own.[2]

But on these topics more anon, with the year 1840.

I write now apropos to our friend Emma.

In the middle of the summer I told her that I hoped, if her father would like it, to take her back this winter. It was her own earnest wish that I should do so. She wrote to her father immedy and now the first day of her vacation has come and she has recd no decisive answer.

I had the vanity to suppose that Mr Keats[n] would accept the proposal with great joy. Had I supposed there was room for doubt I would not have thought of it. The uncertainty has already been a source of great annoyance to me. And now we really do not know how to proceed about Emma. If she comes, we have domestic arrangements to make about it, which *ought* to be attended too at this moment. She herself is much troubled and will be in a very uncomfortable situation if left at Miss T's.[3] If Mr Keats was here I am confident he would not hesitate, but it is not for me to say that to him. What I wish now is to know his intentions as soon as possible.— I shall regr[et it] if Emma is not to come as only my interest in her, Ellen's strong attachment, her own wishes, and a perception that the time had come when I could be of real use to her would have induced me to take her back under the circumstances. But her father will decide. I know he is too much of a gentleman to make me wait, if he were in the least aware how inco[n]venient and unpleasant it is. But the statement was not so made to him that he could realize this, and he probably thinks she can come at any hour— What I wish of you, my dear friend, is to ascertain if he has sent his answer, and, if not, to get it, if possible the very day you receive this. And then it will not come before the time when Emma should go back to Miss Tilden's if she is to go.

[I] have had a good deal of trouble on^n Emma's account especially since she has been at the Tildens^n which but that it was^n for your sake I should regret. But now I begin to take pleasure in her. Her mind is much unfolded and her character matured. If she comes to me now I think to be able to realize what you hoped for her.—

I have written in great haste dear James, because I saw no other way of helping myself than through you.

Next letter I believe I have much, much to say to you

Adieu, dear Benedict,[4] when you write to any one remember above all your faithful friend

MARGARET F.

ALS (MHi). *Addressed:* Revd James F. Clarke / Louisville / Kentucky. *Postmark:* Boston MS Sep 30. *Endorsed:* (Ky 40).

hour, but] hour, ⟨y⟩ but
and calm] and ca⟨?⟩lm
Mr Keats] Mr ⟨?⟩ Keats
trouble on] trouble ⟨for⟩ on
account especially since she has been at the Tildens] account ↑especially since she has been at the Tildens ↓
but that it was] but ↑that it was ↓

1. Anna Huidekoper Clarke.
2. Rev. James Walker resigned his Charlestown pulpit on 15 July to devote his whole time to his professorship at Harvard. He later became president of the university.
3. The Tilden school.
4. The character in *Much Ado about Nothing* who has come to symbolize a confirmed bachelor who finally marries.

1064. To James F. Clarke

Jamaica Plain,
15th Octr 1839—

My dear James,

This note will be delivered to you by your former pupil W. H. who leaves me now much happier about him than I have ever been before.[1] He is engaged to a most lovely and excellent girl, his business prospects are very flattering and I think his character is unfolded and improved, though still, as you may guess,ⁿ his *aims* are not such as to make him my true brother. I hope you will be able to have some conversation with him and, if he has time, will introduce him to Mr Keats.

Emma recd an answer from her father just after I wrote to you, and is now to be established with us. I think really to be of use to her now, for she herself has broken down the wall.

I did not offer to take back little Ellen, because I think she is very well placed now, and she is too young for my private teaching, though I could have seen to her in a school. Tell her father she seems much improved, in her studiesⁿ and she is as engaging and playful as ever.—

You known the loss our friend George has sustained.[2] I felt it much for him. But for you he is alone now. I intend writing to him today.

My friend Anna Barker has been staying with me and we have both been in celestial happiness.[3] The fragrance lingers yet upon my spirit, though I am now immersed in preparations for my winter engagements.[4] Anna saw a great deal of your brother Wm and became strongly interested in him.[5] Why have you never made him known to me? my brother.

I have very much to say to you— O if you would come to the East next year and help me in one of my plans. Will you not come?

Commend me to our new friend and write soon to yours always

MARGARET [   ]

ALS (MHi). *Addressed:* Revd J. F. Clarke / Louisville / Kentucky. / Care W. H. Fuller. *Endorsed:* S. M. Fuller. (Ky 41).

may guess,] may ⟨s⟩guess,
improved, in her studies] improved, ↑ in her studies ↓

1. Her brother William Henry Fuller, who was engaged to Frances Elizabeth Hastings.

2. George is probably George Davis, but his loss is unknown: his father died in 1830. His wife lived far past 1839.

3. This was an intense emotional time for Barker and Fuller, both of whom loved Sam Ward. In a letter to him written on this same day (but perhaps not sent), Fuller acknowledged his lack of love for her. She probably knew from Barker that the two younger people were in love (*Letters of MF*, 2:95–96; Tilton, "True Romance," pp. 64–67).

4. Fuller began the first of her "conversations" on 6 November 1839, with Greek mythology as the topic (*Letters of MF*, 2:97, 101–2).

5. William Hull Clarke had been living in Chicago since 1835. He accompanied Fuller and Sarah Clarke on their western tour in 1843.

318

1065. To James F. Clarke

Jamaica plain
1st Jany 1840.

O Benedict, thou married man, little did I think when exulting in thy happiness that it would mak[e] thee so negligent of the friend wh[o] strewed flowers so lavishly for thy "spirit when *first* it was wed."[1] Why most Pagan divine, have you not written an ode on the presence of *my* Anna, and an elegy on her departure and sen[t] me to solace my solitude withal, [   ] But thou art altogether an noi[   ] Faineant[n] and on dit both in y[   ] and other places, dost send[n] news— [   ] instead of letters to thy best friends and soil all thy intima[   ] with printer's ink. I adjure th[ee] by the Thanes of our departed [co]rrespondence make me a new years present now of a good letter "fit [to] eat" as George used to say.

And this reminds me to tell you the news. George and I are friends again [A]ll the clouds of misunderstanding [a]re rolled away. Are you not glad?

But what I am after saying now is this.— We "calculate" to have a [n]ew periodical here and hope to [i]ssue the first no. in spring.[2] I [s]uppose your "brother" of Cincinnati [h]as told you of all the talk we [h]ad about it in Autumn.[3] If you [c]ould have come on as I desired [an]d left your parish and the ["d]istrict school" you might have [he]lped me edite it and realized [an] old prophesy of yours about [   ] joint forces of our *Maga* [sc]attering all chaff before the [wi]nd"—[4] I have kept that letter of yours in my journal, and alw[ays] thought if I did any such thing it would be with you. But you would not come and I am going to work with Mr Emerson and Mr Ripley. The periodical is to be the size of Xn Examiner, literary rather than Theological, but perf[ectly] free. It is the old plan of which you have heard so much, and it is said this 1840, is the millennial time when it must succeed. But you know, James, at any rate *"Julian* was one who *must succe[ed."]* Now can you do any thing for [it?] I very much fear you have n[ot] time, yet I want some vigoro[us] work from your hand. I do [not] like the idea of setting sail [a]t all unless you are on board. Will [y]ou write directly and say whether you can do any thing at all, and if so whether for the first No.[5]

Emma desires her love. She grows now quite rapidly, and we are very good friends. I can do for her now [as] much as is ever worthwhile for one [pe]rson to do for another. She is much [m]ore reasonable about social relations [as] well as in earnest about her own [m]ind.

319

All near her love her, she is so [   ] and just, and, in substantials, kind

Little Ellen seems to improve, she is very engaging in her manners and seems more just and reverent than she was, but I have little time to see her.

With your sister Sarah I have had some fair hours. Indeed, she is happy now, ripened in knowledge, established in peace and with work and will commensurate.— I pray my regards to Mrs Clarke. I was grieved to hear of her grief.—[6] Dear James, write soon and fully of her your love, of yourself, of Anna B, of myself, of the journal, of heaven on earth, and earth the way to heaven.— And love always Your faithful friend

M. F.

ALS (MHi). *Addressed:* Rev. J. F. Clarke. / Louisville. / K.Y. *Postmark:* Jamaica Plain Ms Jany 2.

noi[   ] Faineant] noi[   ] Faine⟨?⟩ant
dost send] dost sen⟨t⟩d

1. Probably an allusion to Tennyson's "Ode to Memory":

> Large dowries doth the raptured eye
> To the young spirit present
> When first she is wed.

(Alfred Tennyson, *Poetical Works* [London, 1953], p. 11)

2. The *Dial*, which Fuller edited for two years.

3. William Henry Channing.

4. Probably Fuller's memory of Ps. 35:5, "Let them be as chaff before the wind: and let the angel of the Lord chase them."

5. Clarke contributed poems for the second, third, and fourth numbers of the first volume of the *Dial*. Now married and soon to leave Louisville, he spent less time on his writing than in the 1830s (Myerson, *New England Transcendentalists*, pp. 304–5).

6. Anna Clarke's mother, Rebecca Colhoon Huidekoper, died on 22 October 1839. Daughter of Andrew and Esther McDowell Colhoon, Rebecca was born on 15 October 1779. She married Huidekoper in 1806 (Bolster, *James Freeman Clarke*, p. 120; Nina Moore Tiffany and Francis Tiffany, *Harm Jan Huidekoper* [Cambridge, Mass., 1904], p. [361]).

1066.   To Caroline Sturgis

Jamaica Plain,
26th May 1840.

My dear Cary,

I did not receive your note till today. Your room was ready and all around so beautiful that I was quite disappointed not to see you. To-day has been one of the bits of heaven on earth. Every tree, shrub and blade of grass in its highest perfection of shape and color, the goldenest of suns, the most caressing of breezes, all the birds at the acme of bliss, and the perfection of song. I also have been in Arcadia, and I wish you had been with me.

This morning Amelia Jackson brought me a note from Marianne about reading the Italian poets with me.[1] She wants to begin immedy. I am[n] quite pleased with the prospect. I shall give her the best part of a morng each week, for I think she will enjoy all the best things, and, pour moi, I am determined to indulge my tastes this summer, and live with these men, who speak my native tongue. I have Dante's prose works now and it looks like a promise of great pleasure, but I am used to being baffled in my splendid schemes. I have not however planned large. I cannot realize now that I shall live long and it dont seem worth my while to build the card houses high.

Amelia[n] also told me of Susan's engagement; it looks well for Charles,—does it not?[2]

I wanted very much to write both to you and Mr E. from Providence, but I suffered cruelly there, and could hardly keep up, much less hold a pen. I did not go till Saty and was quite ill the eveg before. Saty afternoon I went to walk with Charles through a world of orchards in full blossom.[3] We saw the sunset near the river and then came on the heights to see the moon rise. It was not a queenly moon, but tender and tearful. We came back about nine, and I found some persons waiting, but I had to send them away while I paid for my moons and suns by a spasm in the side. After that I went to a little party where I was engaged There the circle was formed around me, and they began about Mr E.— this indeed they kept up all the time I was there as if it was I who

> "torni ambo le chiavi
> Del ambo di Federigo e chi le volri
> Serrando e disserrando, si soivi[n]
> glorioso ufizio"[4]

Now you have learned Italian you can make out these words enough to wonder why I did not write it in English

But in truth it is amusing enough through somewhat stale to see what a clattering and crackling is roused among each new set of larvae each time that this one[n] simple and noble being takes a step forward into limbo. There is no surer proof that the world lieth in wickedness[5] than all this nonsense about[n] Mr E, no surer proof that it is yet capable of redemption than his growing influence.[6]

Yet I must say that the Philistency of my P. interlocutors is not so deeply ingrained, though more coarse and obtrusive, as that of the citizens of Boston.

Mr Greene would say to those that asked him what they could make of it, "Make—*you*—nothing,—sit still and let *him* make it and be thankful for what you can get." To another, "I'll tell you the case. He's got matches and knows how to light them— you only sit still and let him throw them in, if you've any combustibles stored up you'll catch fire, but if you sit long enough and dont find yourself burning, go home and dont trouble yourself to come back; you've lost your money"[7]

I amused myself with destroying two or three gnats which were trying to make themselves of consequence by buzzing about the lion, but I can't say I performed the office Sybilline thus put upon me in a very pious spirit.[8]

I suppose I was indebted[n] to all this idle talk for a divine dream. I never dreamt of Mr E. before though[n] I have so often of the other beautiful persons whom I love that at times

> My days[n] are dim in the shadow cast
> By the memory of the same[9]

I thought I was with him on the rocks near a castellated place on the sea shore. I was dying and had that transparent spiritual feeling that I do after I have been in great pain, as if separated from the body and yet with memory enough of its pressure to make me enjoy the freedom. Mr E. was in his most angelic mood. We talked on every subject, and instead of that perpetual wall which is always grieving me now, the talk led on and on like [   ]

ALfr (MB). *Endorsed:* 26 May 1840.

I am] I ⟨want⟩ am
Amelia] ⟨?⟩ Amelia
si soivi] si soi⟨?⟩vi
larvae each time that this one] larvae ↑ each time that ↓ ⟨as⟩ th⟨?⟩is ⟨?⟩one
nonsense about] nonsense ⟨of⟩ about
was indebted] was inde⟨p⟩bted
before though] before ⟨for⟩ ↑ though ↓
My days] ⟨Those visions are r⟩ My days

1. Amelia Lee Jackson (1818–88), daughter of Judge Charles and Fanny Cabot Jackson (1780–1868), married Oliver Wendell Holmes on 15 June 1840 (Briggs, *Cabot Family*, pp. 266–67). Marianne, her sister, was Fuller's pupil.
2. Charles Jackson, Jr. (1815–71), Marianne and Amelia's brother, married his cousin Susan C. Jackson (1817–90), daughter of Dr. James Jackson, on 16 February 1842 (Mt. Auburn; Davis, *Suffolk County*, 1:134).

3. Charles Newcomb.

4. From Dante's *Inferno*, Canto XIII, where Pier della Vigna speaks these words to Dante and Vergil from Circle VII, the place of suicides. Pier describes his service as the private secretary of Frederick II before his arrest and imprisonment:

> Io son colui che tenni ambo le chiavi
> del cor di Federigo, e che le volsi,
> serrando e diserrando, sì soavi,
>   che dal secreto suo quasi ogn' uom tolsi;
> fede portai al glorioso offizio,
> tanto ch'i' ne perde' li sonni e' polsi.

> I am he who held both keys to Frederick's heart,
>   locking, unlocking with so deft a touch
>   that scarce another soul had any part
> in his most secret thoughts. Through every strife
>   I was so faithful to my glorious office
>   that for it I gave up both sleep and life

(Dante Alighieri, *La Commedia*, ed. Arnoldo Mondadori [n.p., 1966], pp. 213–14; *The Divine Comedy*, trans. John Ciardi [New York, 1970], pp. 66–67)

5. 1 John 5:19, "And we know that we are of God, and the whole world lieth in wickedness."

6. Emerson had lectured in Providence from 20 March to 1 April, drawing from his "Human Life" and "Present Age" series. In a letter to him, Fuller described the enthusiasm he let loose: "You have really got up a revival there, though they do not know it" (*Letters of MF*, 2:135).

7. Albert Gorton Greene was a Providence writer.

8. One of her victims was William Jewett Pabodie, "who offered himself as a prey to the spoiler" (*Letters of MF*, 1:135).

9. Shelley's "Rosalind and Helen," written in 1818:

> His name in my ear was ever ringing,
> His form to my brain was ever clinging:
> Yet if some stranger breathed that name,
> My lips turned white, and my heart beat fast:
> My nights were once haunted by dreams of flame,
> My days were dim in the shadow cast
> By the memory of the same!

(*Complete Poetical Works of Shelley*, p. 181)

1067. To James F. Clarke

Jamaica Plain.
7th June, 1840.

Dear James,— Your letter had been long wished for and was most welcome. There is something in your tone nowadays which suits me well— May we meet to our mutual satisfaction!

I suppose I shall not see Anna, for two or three weeks.[1] The Farrars will not be settled in their Cambridge house for a fortnight or so, but then she will come to stay with them and I shall be there too.

Elizabeth is sitting by my side and send[s] her love to you. She has come, probably,ⁿ for the summer. She seems wiser, happier and as pure and lovely as ever.

Emma improves rapidly. I wish very much it had been consistent with her father's convenience that she should stay another year, her mind is so open now to improvement. But say nothing to him about it, for I see that he is in earnest very desirous to have her at home, and she will improve now wherever she is. If she could return, afterⁿ having visited her home that were still better, but I fear that may not be either. I hope her father will not fail to come for her. I want to know him, myself, very much and her journey home with him and the sight of Niagara would be of more value to her than many a learned tome!

The little Ellen has been staying with us. She is an amusing, pretty child, but I see no improvement in her character.

I write principally to send you our prospectus, and do not tell you any thing, because I am not well enough to write more than a few lines today, and hope to see you soon and have worlds of talk. We will then agree what you shall do. I am rejoiced you are so well disposed to us ward,— Your poem I have not received; by whom did you send it?[2]

Farewell, dear James, I shall wait impatiently for your coming. Will *your* Anna accompany you?

Your friend

M. F.

ALS (MHi). *Addressed:* Rev J. F. Clarke. / Louisville / K.Y. *Postmark:* Jamaica Plain Ms Jun 8. *Endorsed:* ⟨Ky 43⟩.

come, probably,] come, pro⟨ss⟩bably,
return, after] return, ⟨I⟩ after

1. Anna Barker had stopped in Louisville on her way to New York (*Letters of JFC*, p. 138).

2. In his letter of 24 May, Clarke said: "You wished for the Dream Poem, and so I sent it, imperfect as it is, for I should be glad to help you in any way" (*Letters of JFC*, p. 138). Fuller published "Dream" in the April 1841 issue of the *Dial* (Myerson, *New England Transcendentalists*, p. 305).

1068. To James F. Clarke

Jamaica plain
26th July 1840,

My dear friend, James,

I hoped I should not write to you again for I was looking to some long drives with you through the lanes of Brookline or some long walks in the woods of Newton these golden summer days and— when lo! yesterday I had the vexation of hearing that you had gone to Chicago instead of coming here.— Now when *will* you come. Dont wait till next summer; we shall all be dead then. You ought to see me now. I am comparatively at leisure. I am tolerably well. I am calm[n] with thought; we could talk to some purpose, better than ever before since you went to the west, I think.

—I recd the Meadville letter, thank you. I like very much such leaves out of your life. Much of the life of each is now[n] unknown to the other, but though strangers, we can never be strange one to another. If all my strength were not used up from day to day by inevitable affairs, I suppose I should like sometimes to write to you also[n] in this, the only genuine way.

I have taken great pleasure in the book of poems for myself, and am most glad you give me the administration of it for others. I only fear you will not be satisfied with my alterations; it is a delicate office, and I should not have consented to assume it,[n] only that I see you have almost always injured them where you tried to mend, as indeed, it seems to me you do every thing best by a few vigorous strokes,[n] and are not by nature intended to retouch, and fill up. Ein skizzist.—[1]

Some of those I like best have already been published. Those I wish to use are, First crossing the Alleghanies— The Dream— Ohio River,— Three landscapes— Genuine Portrait— Hymn and Prayer (very noble) To Elschen— the two poems on the Ring (which as one of my friends justly said are more in the *troubadour* style than any of the others) and one of the sonnets.—[2]

Will you not also get, or give me leave to get the Jacob's Well which, Sarah says, is good. We want these Art-poems very much— I should like to take the Dedication but suppose it should not be forced out of its natural relations.— If any of these have been published and in such a way that they cannot be used again, let me know. The poem to Elschen is one of your best, as indeed the *crisis poems* are always your best, your character being of the volcanic sort, and I suppose with *your* creed on such matters you can have no objection to my using it, and heading it with its own sweet nom d'amour, still sweet in my ear at least.[3]

I want you to write more hex- and pentameters. This sort of poem would be truly homogenous[n] with Amern thought. I have put the First Crossing &c into the Dial with great pleasure. I wish you would finish your trans of Hermann[n] and Dorothea and let me publish that.

The Dial is quite favorably recd, some of its friends fear *too* favorably. All other nos will be better than this, of course.[4]

I am most glad that you have become better acquaint with *my* Anna.

Was the Belphoebe yours or Spensers—[5] a naive question n' est ce pas?

I intend writing to W. Channing, but in case I should not find time, will you ask him to send the 2d chapter of Ernest by the 20th August, or earlier, if may be.[6]

I want to bespeak of you some friendship in behalf of Ellen.[7] She is to return with Emma and make a short visit to Louisville She then wishes to remain at the West and be thrown on her own resources for a while as a teacher, and has fixed her eye and heart on Cincini. I have not room now to tell you the reasons why I have acquiesced in this plan, nor why I write to you about it rather than to W. C. suffice till we meet to say I am sure you would think them good. I wish to ask whether you may not be here in time (in case as I hear you return to Louisville) to take charge of her and Emma and introduce her to some friends in Cincini, and if you have a lady friend to whom you could write as to a prospect of employment for her. Her wish is to take charge of children any where under fourteen and have a school by herself. Her talent for teaching young children is remarkable, she has had a good education; if she could have eight or ten engaged to begin with and should be well, I doubt not she would succeed. The reasons are such as to make it desirable for her to try this experiment whether she fails or succeeds. I think it cannot fail to do her good, but I wish her to try it under favorable circumstances. I wish her brought into connexion with good and kind persons, and I wish, especially, that some kind and wise lady of mature age might take an interest in her success and happiness. Can you aid me, this time, my dear James, if so please answer soon, as otherwise I must try other friends.

In the hope of soon meeting truly your friend

M. F.

am calm] am cal⟨?⟩m
is now] is ⟨?⟩ now
you also] you ⟨?⟩ also
have consented to assume it,] have ↑ consented to ↓ assume⟨d⟩ it,
a few vigorous strokes,] a ⟨v⟩few vigorous ⟨to⟩ strokes,
truly homogenous] truly homog⟨o⟩enous
of Hermann] of Herm⟨m⟩ann

1. A sketcher.
2. Of these poems, Fuller published "First Crossing," "Dream," "Three Landscapes," and "Hymn and Prayer."
3. Only "Poems on Art" appeared in the *Dial*.
4. The first number appeared at the end of June. Emerson seemed cool toward the

issue; Ripley was unenthusiastic, and Fuller herself was disappointed with the printing (Myerson, *New England Transcendentalists*, p. 49).

5. In his letter of 24 May, Clarke had substituted "Anna" for "Alma" in quoting the *Faerie Queene* to describe Anna Barker: "*Alma* she called was, a virgin bright" (bk. 2, canto IX, chap. xviii, l. 1; *Letters of JFC*, p. 138).

6. Fuller had published the first part of Channing's "Ernest the Seeker" in the first number of the *Dial*; the final installment appeared in the second number.

7. Ellen Fuller arrived in Louisville in October 1840 and lived with the George Keats family. Ill and unhappy, she left for New Orleans in February 1841, returned to Louisville (where she quarreled bitterly with Emma Keats) in April, and moved on to Cincinnati. There she taught school for James Perkins, and met and married Ellery Channing (Frederick T. McGill, Jr., *Channing of Concord* [New Brunswick, 1967], pp. 47–63).

1069. To William H. Channing

Saturday morng
October 10th [1840]

Dear William, Ellen has just shown me your letter.[1] I see the text is the same as of one I have given her, only the comment is more sweet-toned.— I felt singular pleasure in seeing you quote those lines from Hood. I though nobody knew and loved his serious poems except myself and two or three others to whom I have imparted them. Do you love also the ode to Autumn and

"Sigh on, sad heart, for love's eclipse"[2]

It was a beautiful time when I first read these poems. I was staying in Hallowell, Maine, and could find no books that I liked except Hood's poems and a novel, "De Lisle," which I also remember with deep interest.[3] You know how the town is built, like a terraced garden on the rivers bank; I used to go every afternoon to[n] the granite quarry which crowns these terraces and read till the sunset came casting its last glory on the opposite bank. They were such afternoons as these in Septr and Octr clear, soft and radiant; Nature held nothing back. 'Tis many years since and I have never again seen the Kennebec, but remember it as a stream of noble character. It was the first I ever sailed up, realizing all that emblem discloses of life. Greater still would it have been to sail along an unknown stream in the opposite direction, seeking, not a home, but a[n] ship upon the ocean. Both are beautiful both are ours. The sun shines bright, tomorrow I shall be on the little river. The only aunt worthy to be mother's sister will pass Sunday with her.[4] The next, and last I shall. On both I shall think of you saying holy words to men.—[5] And now a last, a sigh, a holy, a serene Farewell.

AL (collection of Joel Myerson). Published in part in *Memoirs*, 2:44, and *Letters of MF*, 2:162–63; published entire in *Manuscripts* 39 (Summer 1987): 242–47. *Addressed:* W. H. Channing / New York / by Ellen.

afternoon to] afternoon ⟨and read in⟩ ↑ to ↓
but a] but ⟨your⟩ ↑ a ↓

1. Ellen Fuller.
2. "Ode: Autumn" appeared in 1823. Fuller quotes the opening line of Hood's "Ballad."
3. Elizabeth Caroline Grey's *De Lisle; or, The Distrustful Man*.
4. Given favorable comments in other letters, Fuller probably refers here to Elizabeth Crane.
5. Channing soon returned to Cincinnati.

1070. To Bettina Brentano von Arnim

Boston, U S.—
2d Novr 1840.

Dear Bettine,

For how can I address you by any title less near than that by which you have become so familiar to our thoughts. I write to you in the name of many men and many women of my country for whom you have wrought wonders. How many have read the records of your beautiful youth and ceased to distrust the promptings of their own young hearts![1] How many have looked back from maturer years and wondered that they also did not dare to *live*! How many have counted each pulse of your heart of love, how many more been kindled into flame at the touch of your genius!

We want to know more of you, Bettine. In your youthful ideal we see such promise! Your childhood was so prodigal a May-time, we want to know that you have bloomed into an eternal youth. Since you have trusted us with the secret of your love, will you not trust us farther? We have read again and again the manifold records of those early years of inspiration. We drink deep of the nectar cup, and yet long for more. We ask all men who come from your land, Have you seen Bettine?— What know you of the Child?— Is she weeping beside the monument of Goethe, or has she ascended a pedestal of her own?— But they do not speak intelligently of thee! They do not tell us what we want to hear. Thou art dear to us, thou art the friend of our inmost mood. We do not wish to hear street gossip about thee. We will not hear it. Speak to us thyself.

Give thyself to us still farther. There lives none perhaps now who could speak fitly of thee but many who would listen intelligently.

I do not believe you will refuse to gratify our desire. Though expressed by an obscure individual it is the desire of many hearts. I would say of a new world,— but all worlds are new to ardent natures like yours. Writ[e] to me or print it in a book. Tell us how the years have flown, what brought on their wings. There is one question above all we would fain ask. You will divine and, I trust, answer it. I give my name, though it will be a word without significance, in hope that you will address yourself to me and thus enable me to give the great pleasure to others of hearing more from their friend. We have written here no book worthy to send you; should any printed leaves accompany this, it will be merely as a token of respect.[2] But you are wise, you have the spiritual sight, the breath of our love will be wafted to you and you will see whether we are yours. The bearer[3] of this will tell you how to direct if you are disposed to fulfil the hope of yours in faith

S. MARGARET FULLER.

My messenger may miss you. Address to care of Hilliard, Gray and company and I shall receive the letter.[4] Or to that of Rev George Ripley Boston.

ALS (Goethe- und Schiller-Archiv der Stiftung Weimarer Klassik). Published in *Internationales Jahrbuch der Bettina-von-Arnim-Gesellschaft* 4 (1990): 61–62. *Addressed:* For / "Bettine".

Bettina Brentano knew Goethe well from 1807 to 1811, when he broke the friendship. In 1835 she published *Goethes Briefwechsel mit einem Kinde*, "a free and imaginative rehandling" of the letters between the two. She later wrote other books, one of which, *Die Günderode*, Fuller partially translated. She was involved in social reform, especially the emancipation of women. In 1811 she married Achim von Arnim (*OCGL*).

1. On the popularity of *Goethes Briefwechsel mit einem Kinde*, see Konstanze Bäumer, "Margaret Fuller (1810–1850) and Bettina von Arnim," *Internationales Jahrbuch der Bettina-von-Arnim-Gesellschaft* 4 (1990): 47–69.

2. On 7 November, Fuller told Emerson that she sent copies of John Dwight's *Select Minor Poems* and the *Dial* with this letter to von Arnim (*Letters of MF*, 2:181–82).

3. Joseph Coolidge Shaw, who was going to Rome, was probably her messenger (ibid.).

4. The publishing firm that Emerson called "the best publishers in Boston" (*Emerson-Carlyle Correspondence*, p. 121).

1071. To James F. Clarke

Feby 2d 1841

James, my friend, I wish you would finish this poesy and give it for the next no. of the Dial.

I hoped you would be here so as to give your sanction to some slight alterations in "The Dream" but now I have sent it to press, and you will be obliged to bear with them whedder or no, so remember you gave me carte blanche Can I publish the Genuine Portrait, lines on the broken Ring and dedication to my Friends, if I like, I believe these are all I want[1]

Your friend

MARGARET.

ALS (MHi). *Addressed:* Rev James F. Clarke / Central Court. *Endorsed:* Ky 45.

1. "Poems on Art. The Genuine Portrait. The Real and the Ideal" appeared in the April number. The other two were not published. Clarke had moved from Kentucky to Boston, where he founded the Church of the Disciples.

1072. To William H. Channing

[21 February 1841][n]

Like a desperate gamester I feel, at moments, as I cling to the belief that he cannot have lost this great throw of Man, when the lesser hazards have ended so successfully. Men disappoint me so, I disappoint myself so, yet courage, patience, shuffle the cards, Durindarte.[1] There was an Epaminondas, a Sidney,—[2] we need the old counters still.

I wish I were a man, and then there would be *one*. I weary in this play-ground of boys, proud and happy in their balls and marbles. Give me heroes, poets, lawgivers, Men.

There are women much less unworthy to live than you, Men; the best are so unripe, the wisest so ignoble, the truest so cold!

Divine Spirit, I pray thee, grow out into our age before I leave it. I pray, I prophesy, I trust, yet I pine.

ELfr, from Higginson, *MFO*, pp. 111–12.

Higginson dates the fragment, which is part of letter 299 (Letters of MF, 2:204).

1. Fuller refers to *Don Quixote*, chap. 23, pt. 2, in which the legendary Durindarte speaks the gambler's proverbial lines.

2. Epaminondas (c. 410–362 B.C.) was a hero and lawgiver; Sir Philip Sidney (1554–86) was a hero and poet.

1073.   To William H. Channing

[ca. March 1841][n]

Gunderode is the ideal; Bettina, nature; Gunderode throws herself into the river because the world is all too narrow. Bettine lives, and follows out every freakish fancy, till the enchanting child degenerates into an eccentric and undignified old woman. There is a medium somewhere. Philip Sidney found it; others had it found for them by fate.

ELfr, from Higginson, *MFO*, p. 192.
Dated by the reference to Günderode and Bettina, about whom Fuller had written Channing in February 1841 (Letters of MF, 2:202–3).

1074.   To Richard F. Fuller

16th April. [1841][n]

Dear Richard,

I shall be very glad to see you on Sunday. Come directly here in the morning, if I am not at home, call again between twelve and one.

I miss you very much and should like to see you every day.

No more letters from N. O. as yet, but perhaps one will come before Sunday.—

I will tell you then what I think about signing the Pledge.—

Very afftly your sister

MARGARET.

I think you would like Mr. Clarke's church far better than Uncle H's, I will tell you about it on Sunday.—[1]

MsC (MH: fMS Am 1086 [Works, 2:623]).
Dated by the reference to letters from New Orleans, where their mother was visiting Eugene, and by the reference to the Church of the Disciples, which had been organized in February 1841.

1. Henry Holton Fuller was a member of the Hollis Street Church, whose minister was John Pierpont.

1075.   To ?

March 22nd 1842.

[   ] Rejoice with me; for that which was lost is found! Waldo has done that, which I never expected him to do. He has given himself back to me in perfect trust, in the only way I could ever have received him. I had quite abandoned the hope of this and had steeled myself to bear our separation; but I cannot tell how painful it has been to meet continually on so intimate a footing,— to feel so great a mutual regard, and yet with no understanding, at least on my part. I had no hope that he himself would bridge over the gulf between us, and yet felt that I would never do anything more myself, than be firm to my own thought of him.

Now he has been so generous, and so given up, so his sceptical waiting, that I feel we might meet at anytime, though there are such differences to reconcile. [   ]

MsCfr (MH: bMS Am 1280.235 [136, pp. 19–20]).
It is not certain that this fragment is a letter, though the language suggests it may be one.

1076.   To Mary G. Ward

Saty morng.
[9 April 1842][n]

Dear Mary

I am sorry not to find you in your pretty room, though I could hardly expect it so fine a morning. If you want to see me I shall be at the house in[n] Avon place, packing up from 1/2 past one to 1/2 past three.

I like your friend's letter, and I do not like it.[1] In some respects her view of these matters pleases me much.—What does she mean by Coterie &c? I know of none such here at least;— surely there never was a place where there was less of approximation to a harmony in views and tastes than here in Boston. It is a time of dissonance, of transition, of aspiration. No three persons think alike. The preference, to be given to this over another place I should think would be that there is here a restless *almost* earnest spirit of inquiry as to[n] What shall a man do to worthily[n] fill the place assigned him in the universe?

I think the poem had best be published in N. York. If done in the way that has generally seemed best to Miss Ward, she will be more likely to be satisfied with the results.

I inclose the bill for copying. It seems to me too much, and if you think so you must say so. The copy[n] seems well done.

I have never employed a copyist, as my brother while here, and, since he went away, private friends have elected to be my scribes. But it is, as you know, hard labor. Still the person whom I employed has charged only from the information of others, and will not be happy in receiving the money if you or Miss W. think it an undue charge,[n] nor should I be happy to have her. So be sincere as you would to your shoemaker.

Adios

MARGARET F.

ALS (PSt). *Addressed:* Miss Mary G. Ward.

Mary Gray Ward was Samuel Gray Ward's sister. They were not related to Julia Ward's New York family.

Dated by the contents: she was staying with Henry Holton Fuller at 2 Avon Place during the spring of 1842. She left there on Monday, 11 April. Thus this letter was probably written on the previous Saturday (Letters of MF, 3:58).

at the house in] at ↑ the house in ↓
inquiry as to] inquiry ↑ as to ↓
to worthily] to ⟨a⟩worthily
The copy] ⟨It⟩ ↑ The copy ↓
undue charge,] undue charg⟨?⟩e,

1. The friend is almost certainly Julia Ward, who had been sending poems to Mary Ward for comment.

1077. To Caroline Sturgis

3d June [1842][n]

Dear Caroline, I have Hoffmann's works belonging to W. Story; it is a great heavy book with only a paper cover, and I have broken the back all to pieces.[1] I thought you might like to read it, as though[n] many of the stories are ill-wrought and fantastic, others are beautiful, and contain interesting passages on the[n] arts, especially music. And it is a good book to read now and then when you are tired, for the wild humorousness stirs the blood and would while away an hour else wasted. Now after you have done with it, (if you please take it with you for the summer.) and if not *now*, will you have a new back pasted on and return it to W. S.— Tis of no use, for no doubt he will have it bound and not try to read it in this clumsy form, but I cant return it in this condition. I enclose a demi-dollar having had such jobs done for less, they will see to it from any booksellery. I shall send the book to Miss Peabody for you.[2]

Of late I have been able to bear the heat of noon out doors and I think of you every day in the fields spangled with their myriad golden flowers, and where wild geranium and even the aster are already seen, or lying beneath the pines and junipers so ambrosial in the heat of noon. You often told me how beautiful noon was, but I had not felt it; the sun then seemed to me merciless and cruel, and the aching temples longed for the cool shadows and breezes. But now I have enjoyed it, it seems the best, cruel things seem beautiful when we can suddenly bear them.

Yesterday, I took with me all your poems and read them often in the day, it is the first time for long. I felt you near and dear. The harmony of the world sounded again within, and the destinies of those I love seemed clustered round, not too near, but gracefully, and decorously grouped full of life and silent love like the trees. My friends are certainly real existences to me, and immortal for when I look on them again after a separation I know them better as I do the trees. Yesterday I knew you better than ever before. Reconcile dear Waldo to me, if he is vexed with me, interpret to him since you know his language, and my thought has not been veiled from you. I do not mean, tell him what he does not know, but let him understand Some demon urged me to a sally of haughty impatience towards him; it was that. The wave plunging deeply rises to assault the pure serene, to challenge its distance, its vague, and ask if it be really blue. Returning from the thicket, thorny and tangled but where grows the *healing plant* let them receive me into their houses, for I am weary. I could not knock a great while, I would have all love and promise now[n] like the June day. How many flowers there are, how fearless they look. I am not fearless enough yet to put out a flower, else I would give it you. Even the oaks this spring put forth too soon, and one day I found them black with frost. Adieu, dear Cary, how do you bear the absence of the angel child?[3] It has seemed to me I could not bear to see his vacant seat. These flowers grow on his grave. I think of it very often, yet still his life seems with me like the others.—

M.

ALS (MB). *Addressed:* Miss Caroli[ne] Sturgis.
Dated by the reference to Waldo Emerson's death. She clearly writes from Boston to Concord, so the year must be 1842, for Fuller was on her western trip on 3 June 1843, and Sturgis was in Boston, not Concord, on 3 June 1844.
as though] as ↑though↓
on the] on ↑the↓
promise now] promise ⟨?⟩ now

1. Fuller had for some time known the work of E. T. A. Hoffmann. Story probably owned a copy of *Sämtliche Werke in Einem Bande* (Paris, 1841), which had 1,157 pages.

2. Elizabeth Peabody opened her bookstore on West Street in Boston on 31 July 1840 (Louise Hall Tharp, *The Peabody Sisters of Boston* [Boston, 1950], p. 135).
3. Emerson's first child, Waldo, died on 27 January.

1078. To James F. Clarke

Cambridge, 31st July
1842.

My dear James,

When I told Sarah how far I had gone in my communications to you, she expressed pleasure at your knowing these things, but some anxiety as to your discretion. This has troubled me since, and the more on account of some words said by me to you that might put you off your guard, therefore permit a few lines addenda

I said "I was happy in having no secret". It is my nature, and has been the tendency of my life to wish that all my thoughts and deeds might lie, as the "open secrets" of nature free to all who are able to understand them. I have no reserves, except intellectual reserves, for to speak of things to those who cannot receive them is stupidity rather than frankness. But, in this case, I alone am not concerned, but one whose nature is unfolded in the solitudes of reserve, whose delicate feelings, so different from mine, I ought to fear to violate. There is, also, another whose peace might be disturbed by the disclosure of facts which few, I fear, have hearts to understand. My own peace for the remainder of my days might be deeply wounded by any carelessness here. Therefore, dear James, give heed to the subject. You have received a key to what was before unknown of your friend, you have made use of it, now let it be buried with the past, over whose passages, profound and sad, yet touched with heaven-born beauty, "let Silence stand sentinel."

I reflect with satisfaction on the intercourse we have had on this journey.[1] You will better know how to pardon the probable wreck of my life's health and purposes, and the non-fulfilment of its earthy promise. You will not refuse[n] for inscription to my funeral stone, She hath done what she could.

I have been happy in the sight of your pure design, of the sweetness and serenity of your mind. In the inner sanctuary we met.— But shall I[n] say a few blunt words such as were frequent in the days of intimacy and, if they are needless you will let them fall to the ground. youth is passed, with its passionate joys and griefs, its restlessness, its

335

vague desires. You have chosen your path, you have sounded out your lot, your duties are before you. *now* beware the mediocrity that threatens middle age, its limitation of thought and interest, its dulness of fancy, its too[n] external life, and mental thinness. Remember the limitations that threaten every professional man, only to be guarded against by great earnestness and watchfulness.— Your parish is not composed of minds that will call on you for your best mentally, though for a sincere, and reverent temper worthy your desire.— You have lost Mr Keats, and I see not that you have any other friend who will call on you for your best, and feed the mind languid with continual exertion.[2] So take care of yourself, and let not the the intellect more than the spirit be[n] quenched.— I am obliged unwillingly to hurry to a close. Your faithful friend

MARGARET.

ALS (MHi). Published in part in *Memoirs*, 1:74, 81, and *Letters of MF*, 3:79, 111. *Addressed:* Rev J. F. Clarke. *Endorsed:* S. M. Fuller— / (after our journey to the / White Hills) *July 1842*. (Ky 48).

not refuse] not refu(?)se

shall I] shall ⟨s⟩I

its too] its ⟨ex⟩ too

the the intellect more than the spirit be] the ↑ the intellect more than the ↓ spirit ⟨more or⟩ be

1. She described her journey to the White Mountains in a letter to Charles Newcomb (*Letters of MF*, 3:77–78).

2. Clarke had returned to Boston, where in February 1841 he organized the Church of the Disciples. He retained its pulpit until his death. George Keats died on 29 December 1841.

1079. To William H. Channing

[25 August 1842][n]

[   ] I began to tell you about my life with Waldo. The conclusion of that was very noble. You will see the change, if I am successful in producing anything. What did you mean by saying I had imbibed much of his way of thought? I do indeed feel his life stealing gradually into mine. And it sometimes seems, as if the work of my own life would have been more simple, and my unfolding to a temporal activity, more rapid and easy, if we had never met. But when eternal growth is thought of I am conscious[?] of having become far larger and deeper for his influence. He has been to me a lofty assurance and sweet serenity.

He says: "I come to him as the European to the Hindoo, or as the gay Trouvere to the Puritan in his steeple hat." Of course this implies that our meeting has been partial. I present to him the many forms of Nature and solicit with music, he melts them all into Spirit, and reproves performance with prayer. He stops me from doing and makes me *think*. When I am with those who trust me, I feel capable of all things. With Nature I am filled and grow. With most persons I bring words of past life, and do actions suggested by the wants of their natures. I need all, as all need me. When with God alone I adore in silence. Let us ever lend to one another a gentle and assured hand. Let us still travel together towards the heavenly city. [   ]

MsCfr (MH: bMS Am 1280.235 [136, pp. 17–19]). Published in part in *Memoirs*, 2: 67–69, and *Letters of MF*, 3:90–92.
This is a more complete copy of the letter, probably to W. H. Channing, written on 25 August 1842. Though this copy is dated Dec 1840, the contents place it in 1842.

1080.   To Caroline Sturgis

Concord, August 30th 1842.
Cary dear your letter did not come till it had often been wished for. Though you seem now always near and dear, joined by invincible bonds to my life, long silences are somewhat sad, and I am always glad when they are broken.

We are having, I think, a^n pleasant time. W. and E. and I all scribble^{nl} or pretend to scribble in our several apartments all the morning. I generally see one or the other of them some part of the day. Waldo is very lovely, though in a subdued tone of spirits, and rather passive in thought, he softly shines upon the day. He thinks of you with his unbroken affection. I think he does not feel towards any one so strongly as he has sometimes. Perhaps the loss of his boy makes all ties seem less real to him, perhaps it is only a long still time.—Ellery is very fond of him, is with him in the most easy, familiar way, and occupies his thoughts agreeably. I see much of Ellery; often he charms me. I love his face, the feeling in^n his cheek, and the wild light of his eyes. But there is a touch of the goblin in his beauty. I like the demon better, black chasms and crater fires, rather than wild ignes fatui of the swamp. He is fresh every day. While the moon lasted, we used to sit on the east door step till quite late evenings. E. talked all

337

the time and sometimes said the finest things. Since then, it has not been so good;— I must always take the tone of his mind, not bring him to mine, sometimes I like this much, entirely to be taken from myself, but at deeper times I should like to bring him to me rather. Yesterday was a day sacred to me. E. asked me to walk in the afternoon and I went with him, but great part of the time it seemed to hurt my day, but the last hour was good. It was a calm golden afternoon and one of the solemn refulgent sunsets. E. was inspired by it,— when I came home I was glad I went with him. I often wish the things he says to me were written into poems instead. The more they charm me, the less I can keep them in mind, the flowers fade in an instant. But his presence has led me to many thoughts.— You are much in his mind, he wrote to you a week ago Sunday. I dont know why he did not send the letter, it must have been good, for every thing else he wrote that day was. As to his doing any thing, his plan is to write a few months for the magazines and see if he can get engagements to write for money; I dont know whether he will do any thing of it; he is so changeable.[2] It is terrifying to a more snail-like nature, (I mean as to some house always at hand) to see any one so sensitive, moody, and plastic to every change. I suppose there are defences I do not see, else such an one could not live from day to day. I think he really loves Ellen, and that this connection is one that ought to come in the course of his experience. He says she is never out of his thoughts a moment. He does not over rate her, I believe, but he likes her action upon him. She accommodates herself to all his fancies[?], yet, having so much will, she stimulates him. He says he always feels when she comes in or goes out of the house.— His thoughts of S. W. are beautiful, far better he expresses the truth than it has ever been expressed.[3] He loves to dwell on the thought of him, but slighted him now in Boston, just as heretofore.— Of William, too, he says fine[n] things, discussing the genius of his life, though not seeing him wholly.[4]

Of Charles I hear that he is getting well.[5] W Story's lecture on music at Commencement was much admired.[6] I mean to borrow and see if I like it.

Farewell, I hope you will write again. Your first summer's letters from your island are dear to memory as angel visits in dark days. I love to think of you there. Now you write from the beech tree and not the grape vine, though you say you prefer grapes to beech nuts.— I have a verse of yours here, which is sublime, it paints the situation with a firm grasp, on the reality no preaching, no O be loyal, or be lofty &c— it begins "Bound in the prison of my own sad soul."[7]

I should be peacefully happy, here, but I cannot forget little Waldo, yet I am peaceful, and in[n] far better health than before, this summer. May the days be sweet to you!

MARGARET.

ALS (MB). *Addressed:* Miss Caroline Sturgis / Care Wm Swain Esq / New Bedford, / Mass. *Postmark:* Concord Mas. Aug 31. *Endorsed:* (*in Emerson's hand*) August 1842.
think, a] think, ⟨?⟩ a
all scribble] all scri⟨?⟩bble
feeling in] feeling ⟨?⟩ ↑ in ↓
says fine] says ⟨the⟩ fine
and in] and ↑ in ↓

1. Emerson and Ellery Channing. Fuller described her stay in Concord in her journal (Myerson, "Margaret Fuller's 1842 Journal," 320–40).
2. Though a prolific writer, Channing never made a living from his poems.
3. Samuel Gray Ward, who was Channing's close friend.
4. William Henry Channing.
5. Charles King Newcomb.
6. Story lectured before the Harvard Musical Society on 24 August (*Boston Daily Advertiser*, 25 August 1842).
7. Apparently the poem never appeared in the *Dial*.

1081. To James F. Clarke

Concord
9th Septr, 1842.

My dear James,

I should like to have a class this winter, if a class would like to have me. The subject which grew most naturally out of last winter's meetings, and which some present expressed a wish to hear discussed may be thus stated.

How can constancy, or fixedness of purpose and perseverance in action be made to consist with a free development of character?[1]

If we began with this, those subjects which are connected with it would be suggested from week to week.

I accept your kind offer of your house with many thanks in case a class should be collected.— But I earnestly hope that none will continue to go, merely from personal regard for me. I want a class who find the meetings of use to them beyond a doubt, or I want none. Therefore I left them as free as I[n] could at the end of the winter, and

339

I want any friend interested in my behalf to bear this in mind. To be in possession of my powers I *must* feel that these meetings are important to those present.

I meant to have written to you at some length, but will not now because desirous to close this letter in season for this morning's stage which will be here in a few minutes. I have a favor to ask of you.— Will you go to Dr Walter Channing's and ascertain whether Ellery is there, or if they know where he is.[2] Ask this from yourself not from me, and be careful to raise no breeze. If you find he is gone to Concord to day or will come tomorrow do nothing more. But if you find he is ill, or any thing the matter, will you let me know tomorrow p.m by the Concord accommodation stage which leaves, I think, *East tavern Hanover St*ⁿ at three or half past three.

Ellery left here last Saty, for N. Bedford, fully intending to return Tuesday morng *at least*. He has not returned, nor have I heard from him. He then expected my sisterⁿ to arrive here any day after Wednesday. She has not yet come, but letters recd since he went, lead me to expect her today orⁿ tomorrow. If she arrives and does not find him, you may imagine, how painful for her and for me. Beside, he was as anxious she should not, as I am; he was all impatience to see her, and our last conversation was such that I am filled with anxiety lest some accident has happened to him. Still I dont want to cause a sensation in B. by sending to ask after him, so I commend it to your discretion dear friend, to ascertain what I wish, quietly, and that I may be out of suspense tomorrow, if he should not come today as I earnestly hope he will.— With affece regards to your wife

Yours always

M. F.

ALS (MHi). *Addressed:* Rev J. F. Clarke / Boston / Mass. *Postmark:* Boston Sep 9. *Endorsed:* S. M. Fuller— / about her winter's class / &c. &c.— Sept. 9th / Ansd Sept 10th.

as I] as ⟨they⟩ I

think, *East tavern Hanover St*] think, ⟨Elm St⟩ ↑ *East tavern Hanover St* ↓

my sister] my ⟨?⟩ sister

her today or] her ↑ to⟨m⟩day or ↓

1. In the *Memoirs,* Emerson lists several specific topics, among them "Mistakes," "Faith," "Woman," and "Daemonology," but no uniting theme (*Memoirs,* 1:350).

2. Fuller sent a similar letter to Sturgis, Channing's old flame (*Letters of MF,* 3:94). Dr. Walter Channing, Ellery's father, was Dr. William Ellery Channing's brother and an accomplished physician and teacher. Fuller was able to smooth over the delicate situation until Channing appeared the next morning. "Ellery told Ellen at once how it was," wrote Fuller in her journal, "and she took it just as she ought" (Myerson, "Margaret Fuller's 1842 Journal," p. 336).

1082.   To William H. Channing?

Tuesday September 20th [1842][n]

[   ] I have arranged Mr Emerson's letters anew and put together almost all of the last two years. I am sorry you [*illegible*] I have mislaid his last letter about the Dial, for in that you would have seen how noble and free he is; how he remains the same through every change; [*illegible*] how in every detail he is serenely true to his own high object, and regardless of the lower aims of the inner man. In these letters you will be charmed also, by his grace and sweetness, "he," indeed "compares with no man's ways," as E[llery] expressed it.

I have reserved two beautiful letters which I should like to read aloud. They are sacred to me! The first is addressed to his brother Charles, several years before his death. The second is to his Aunt, Miss Mary Emerson. These show the innermost heart, as well as his fair life and seeking mind. I prize these letters more than I can tell. [   ]

MsCfr (MH: bMS Am 1280.235 [136, pp. 6–7]).
As often happens, the copyist confuses the date. The manuscript has "Tuesday September 20th 1840," but 20 September fell on Sunday in 1840 and on Tuesday in 1842. The contents suggest the later date, for in 1840 Fuller was not quoting Ellery Channing (whom she had seen often in the late summer of 1842).

1083.   To ?

[ca. 30 January 1843][n]

I congratulate myself that I persisted, against every persuasion, in doing all I could last winter; for now I am and shall be free from debt, and I look on the position of debtor with a dread worthy of some respectable Dutch burgomaster. My little plans for others, too, have succeeded; our small household is well arranged, and all goes smoothly as a wheel turns round. Mother, moreover, has learned not to be over-anxious when I suffer, so that I am not obliged to suppress my feelings when it is best to yield to them. Thus, having more calmness, I feel often that a sweet serenity is breathed through every trifling duty. I am truly grateful for being enabled to fulfil obligations which to some might seem humble, but which to me are sacred.

ELfr, from *Memoirs*, 2:119–20.
Several phrases duplicate those in letter 405 to Elizabeth Hoar. The overall language is differ-ent enough to permit the conjecture that this is a separate letter written on the same day (Letters of MF, 3:118–19).

1084.   To James F. Clarke

Tuesday eveg 14th Feby 1843

My dear James, To have mislaid my best pen seems to warn that I shall postpone writing you a few lines that I had in my mind, but I perversely decline listening to the Daemon, friendly though he might be so perhaps I shall be let from expressing myself.

As to what we were saying *of forms*, I am reminded of the descrip-tion of the constantly changing abodes of the peasant at the mouth of the Indian river. As its great sweep casts up fresh islands, the peasant goes higher in his boat, plants his grain, builds his light hut, and gar-lands it speedily with the large-leaved vines of that climate. A season or two[n] he rejoices in the verdure and fruit of his garden when lo; he discerns the river which gave is[n] taking it away again. He obeys the hest of the bounteous stream, enters his boat and seeks out another island. Thus, says the observer, if the benefits of his care be often taken from him, he is, on the other hand, constantly presented with a virgin soil. And if he does not sigh for the forests and cities of the mainland, but uses the[n] peculiar advantages of his own position, he is a happy man.

Just so with us at present, we are in the stress of a great stream of change which gives on one side but takes away on the other. Let us keep ready then our light boats, and our bag of seed-grain well pro-tected from the water, that is furniture enough for life at present We will not sigh[n] for the sacred depths of the slow growing forests,[n] for its secret springs and glades, and wild-flowers. Those are beauteous, but *not ours* and have[n] not this quick springing verdure and these strange wild fowl and fish, and the loud rushing music of the stream enough to tell for one day?[1]

But let us be wholly in the spirit of the stream since we are in it. Let us not stiffen in our innovations! It was not, as you said "to pick to pieces your form." that we thought the other day. Neither to demand from it "*perfection, as a form*" But that a pliant medium should be pre-sented for the ever present spirit, not *brittle* but *plastic*

Tiresome is our life at times, perhaps forlorn, when we would lean

342

on a pillar of strong marble seeking the heavens, and find nothing but a reed. But the wiser mind rejoices that it can noway be excused from constant thought, from an ever springing life, and must in this day stand beneath a naked heaven whose light no dome built by the energy of man is able to intercept.

I never wrote you the letter I meant on the little door and its inscription which is indeed the one yourself[n] does realize. The substance would have been this. Having once read it (the inscription)[n] through, we must again begin to read, understanding the better to *be bold*, that we have now learnt not to be *too bold*. Is it not so? that when we begin to be bold under God we will not again be over-bold as man.

Farewell, dear James. I will hope a letter from the great Babel, a letter of good tidings from your hand.

MARGARET.

ALS (MHi). *Addressed:* Rev J. F. Clarke / Chestnut St. / Boston. *Endorsed:* S. M. Fuller / Feb 15th 1843. No 50.

or two] or t⟨o⟩wo
gave is] gave ⟨it⟩ is
uses the] uses ⟨its⟩ ⟨?⟩ the
not sigh] not s⟨ay⟩igh
growing forest,] growing forest⟨s⟩,
and have] and ha⟨s⟩ve
one yourself] one yoursel⟨e⟩f
it (the inscription)] it ↑ (the inscription) ↓

1. Clarke answered her from New York on 24 February: "A strong and healthy man can make a home for himself anywhere. In a skeptical or a believing age—in a society of fixed or tumbling forms. A man at rest in himself, with clear aims, who has a thought and word of his own can always collect his audience and become the centre of somewhat" (*Letters of JFC*, p. 142).

1085. To James F. Clarke

Chicago, 9th July, 1843.

My dear James,

We returned last night from our visit to the enchanting regions, watered by the Fox and Rock rivers where we have passed a fortnight happy as[n] mortals are seldom permitted to be.[1] On my way back I went to Belvidere saw the academy and talked with some of the leading men.[2] Your mother whom we left at Geneva, has also talked with many persons competent to advise in this case and I feel now able to form a judgment with tolerable confidence.

343

Returning, I find your paragraph, in appeal to the Unitarians for aid.[3]

Now as to that, it seems to me that it would be well for Arthur to hold this property himself, if he can do so on the payment of the $400.[n] It is not sure that he can do so for this sum precisely. The accounts are not all proven, though they cannot, it is supposed, vary much from this estimate Some evil-intentioned person may bid against him. But it is probable that he can get it for this and with a clear title to a property worth about $1000

The people are much in earnest about it, so much so, that six of these Christians are willing, if Arthur will advance the money now and make a fair experiment to repay it him with interest at the end of two years, if he is not satisfied.[4]

I am so far pleased with the location and the circumstances that I think it would be every way advisable for A[n] to take this risk. It seems to me an opening which may enable him to do just what he wants. Also, as he must have a female assistant, to associate his sister Ellen with him to open a path for others of his family and to relieve me of many uncertainties.

Persons there, even Mr Conant, are of opinion that he had better hold it himself, that it should *not* belong to the Unitarian Association both as likely to be valuable property to him, that it is better he should be quite untrammelled in his plans and efforts, and that the school should not appear as the agent of a sect[5] It is enough, they all think, that Unitarianism should have fair play in it, but not best that it should stand foremost in the matter. Let what is done be done for the sake of education and the spread of liberal views. Let Arthur, if he is to head it, lay[n] claim to success as a good teacher, one anxious to know truth and aid his fellow men.— The majority of those from whom he will have aid are the Christians, if the Unitarians could reciprocate their spirit, and go hand in hand with them in this matter, it will go well.

But beside the money to be advanced for the building as it stands, a considerable sum is needed for apparatus, books, and refitting[n] of the building, for it has been a good deal abused. I estimated this in my own mind[n] at about $200 and found the people here did the same. Now[n] if this sum could be got for Arthur in any way that would not fetter him; it would be of great use.

It is not thought that it will be any disadvantage for Arthur to preach also, as he will have oppory of doing for Mr Conant, and in the same places that Mr Conant does, but only that his school shall not stand as a Unitarian school, but merely as a good school with no exclusive theological bias.

I shall write to Arthur by this same post, to raise the money for the building, to come out immedy, if possible, so that I may go out to Belvidere with him to be there at the time of sale (this is fixed for the 31st July, but they expect to be able to postpone it so that it may take place in the course of August) and to aid in planning out the school.[6] Will you see him directly if you can, and (no easy matter I fear) get $200 or $250 out of philo liberality and philo education pockets to give the school a good set out if you can. Adieu, dear brother my rare and kind friend. This prospect flatters me almost too much with an end to many perplexities. I hardly dare be in spirits about it lest the Belvidere should prove a mirage. But I know it will not be for want of your help and intelligence if it does. Your Mother will say what I may have omitted. Ever yours

MARGARET.

I write to Arthur at Cambridge by todays mail.

ALS (MHi). *Addressed:* Rev James F. Clarke / Boston / Mass. *Postmark:* Chicago Ill. Jul 11. *Endorsed:* S. M. Fuller— / July 9. 1843. (51).
happy as] happ⟨ier⟩y ⟨than⟩ ↑ as ↓
the $400.] the ↑ $ ↓ 400.
advisable for A] advisable ↑ for A ↓
it, lay] it, ⟨cl⟩ lay
and refitting] and re⟨pa⟩fitting
abused. I estimated this in my own mind] abused. ⟨Now, if you could get⟩ ↑ I estimated this in my own mind ↓
same. Now] same. ⟨?⟩ Now

1. Fuller was traveling with Sarah Clarke through the Midwest, a journey chronicled in *Summer on the Lakes, in 1843.*

2. Fuller was eager for her brother Arthur to become headmaster at the Belvidere Academy in Belvidere, Illinois.

3. Clarke published his appeal in the *Christian Register* of 1 July 1843, in which he described the opportunity "to make . . . a theological Institution, of a liberal character, where Unitarians, Christians, Baptists, or others could acquire that education which would make them far more useful as ministers than they can be with their present limited opportunities."

4. "Christians" was the common term for the Christian Connexion, an antisectarian movement also called "Disciples" or "Reformers." The Christians and the Unitarians were deeply suspicious of each other (Habich, *Transcendentalism and the "Western Messenger,"* p. 35).

5. Augustus Hammond Conant was a Unitarian missionary in the West. He warmly supported Arthur Fuller's acquisition of the school (*Letters of MF,* 3:190–92).

6. No letter from Fuller to her brother survives from this period. Later in the year Arthur Fuller paid $455 for the school, a two-story building, and two acres of land (*Letters of MF,* 3:192).

1086. To James F. Clarke

Milwaukie, 16th July 1843.

My dear James,

Your Mother, ever full of resource, wishes me to suggest your applying to the Society for propagating the Gospel among the Indians AND *others* in North America in behalf of the Belvidere plan. Unto this she is moved by seeing in the Monthly Miscellany[n] that a legacy of seven thousand dollars has been bequeathed to the society this past year, and that Judge Shaw, with whom your opinion would have weight, is its president.[1]

We have had a letter from Belvidere; the sale is appointed for the 19th August; a postponement of ten days will be given, if we ask it. They think now the debts will amount to four hundred and fifty dollars, instead of four[n] hundred, and as[n] they have not all been examined they may to more. Still as the property is to be sold[n] at public sale; he may get it for less, unless some one bids against him, and it is thought they certainly will not, if it is understood he cannot be drawn beyond a certain sum.

Since I wrote, I have listened to many opinions as to the chances of the school's success,[n] varying as the various men, but mostly favorable, and I still think them sufficient to make it desirable to take the risk.

I am very impatient to hear from Arthur; whether he will come on and how soon. Will you say to him that if he comes soon, I shall probably be at Milwaukie, that the boats stop here some time, that at any rate[n] he had better come on shore, inquire for Abraham's[2] store, find whether I am here, and if I am, have his baggage brought on[n] shore, and stay till the next boat with me, when, if I can, I shall go with him to Chicago and Belvidere And ask him to bring letters from all my friends, for I am homesick with hearing so little

Farewell, I would gladly write more, but am really sick tonight with the heat and fatigue I have endured this past week. Your Mother and I came yesterday, Sarah some days before; we had literally had no sleep the night before and next to none for several. Thermometer a hundred and two, dogs barking all night. Here it is quiet; we shall have rest. Sarah has written you word how we are situated, rather a droll location for your Mother; she can scarce keep her Unities in the back ground. We have grace before and after meat, six graces per diem, two long prayers, but the clerical man is a merry soul. Sarah and I have taken a delightful drive this aftn Abraham has shown us the beauties of this place, with which his heart seems bound up; he is as bright and clear as a sunbeam. After all, I forgot to say that I was scrawling now because if I dont the letter wont go for two days, and I hope you will have a chance soon to enlighten Arthur with its contents Affecy your friend

M. F.

ALS (MHi). *Addressed:* Rev J. F. Clarke / Boston / Mass. *Postmark:* Milwaukie WnT Jul 21. *Endorsed:* S. M. Fuller / July 16. 1843. 53.

seeing in the Monthly Miscellany] seeing ↑ in the Monthly Miscellany ↓
of four] of f⟨e⟩our
and as] and ↑ as ↓
as the property is to be sold] as ↑ the property ↓ ⟨it⟩ is to be ⟨?⟩sold
school's success,] school's, ↑ success ↓
that at any rate] that ↑ at any rate ↓
brought on] brought ⟨to⟩ on

1. Lemuel Shaw (1781–1861), later Melville's father-in-law, was chief justice of the Commonwealth of Massachusetts. On 1 June he was reelected president of the Society for Propagating the Gospel among the Indians, a position he held from 1837 to 1861. Though he held Unitarian beliefs and attended New South Church, Shaw was not a member of a Unitarian church (Frederic Hathaway Chase, *Lemuel Shaw* [Boston, 1918], pp. 253, 314). The announcement in the *Monthly Miscellany of Religion and Letters* spoke of a legacy of $7,000 left the society by "the late Mrs. Haskell of Ipswich" and said that the society had appropriated $500 to be distributed "in aid of schools or missions among the Western Indians" (*Monthly Miscellany* 8 [June 1843]: 411–12). Eunice Caldwell (1785–1843) married Mark Haskell in 1823 (Ipswich VR).
2. Abraham Clarke.

1087. To James F. Clarke

Milwaukie, 28th July 1843.

Dear James,

Your letter came to me one morning with most sweet influence. I warmly thank your affectionate thoughtfulness of me, and will avail myself of it, should it be necessary to enable me to see all I wish to see, and I suppose it will so far as I can judge.[1] I am desirous to remain till the payment of the tribes at Mackinaw this takes place early in Septr; there are then four or five thousand[n] Indians assembled and I should have an opportunity to see this remnant of a great past, such as may never occur again.[2] We wish to go previously to the Sault, Green Bay &c on the Indiana which makes a trip there the 14th August, for, as to the canoe voyage to the pictured rocks, that appears to be quite given up, and your brother S. speaks coldly of going even to the Sault, and William, I suppose, cannot go away again, as he was absent so long at Rock River. But to Mackinaw if not to the Sault[n] Sarah and I can go by ourselves, be there at the time of the Indians are and pass some days in enjoying the natural beauties of the place. Thence I shall set my face homeward.

Tomorrow, I *hope*, for there is much changing of plans from day to day, as must be when ladies depend on men of business we go into the country as far as Madison and shall see something of Wisconsin.

This place is beautifully situated, there are many fine walks, and one close at hand upon the bluff, on the edge of the lake. The light house too is at our will to ascend and lock the door on the rest of the world. There Sarah and I watched the progress of a thunder-shower over this magnificent lake, the Buffalo was coming in and the scene much alive with other craft; it was a glorious scene— I much enjoy the lake now, and shall leave it with grief. I love to go each day and watch the changes of color upon it, for each day it wears a new face.

Dear James, you cannot think how much I enjoyed receiving your beautiful verses, seeing you inspired once[n] more.[3] The daily track of theological life, I love not to tread, but on the green and flowery field beneath this mellow July moon, how sweet to find my friend of many years. Yes! it was such a moon, so mellow in its glorious brightness as this last, which has kept me awake many successive nights, that shines in your verse, none of a colder narrower beam. You have never written better, so finely, yet simply is the image kept up, the versification full and free, the feeling soft and manly. They came just at the right moment. Sarah and William and I enjoyed them in full, and then came a letter from your Anna, saying how she had just received them.

I have become a friend to your brother William, too. I always thought I should and now I am. I do not know whether he is most engaging as a companion, or most to be loved as a man; he[n] is so open and free and sprightly, yet large and noble in all his feelings.

With Sarah I enjoy being the same as ever. Your mother too is the kindest, most affective, and amusing companion. She puzzled a great deal about your verses. Whom can they be about, who has *the whitest forehead*?[4] &c &c like Goethe's friends finding out the innumerable[n] Lottchens.

She bids me to tell you to write the moment you have any thing to tell about selling her place, as this will affect all her plans, if it is sold, she wishes to go to Meadville and thence home in September, if not to return to Chicago and stay there till late (I do hope the Wards will buy it, I should like to see them there) Also to charge you to go to the sea shore and scold you violently for not having gone already."— Sarah has been greatly moved by Mr Allston's departure.[5] Nothing could have been so sad for her. Send any particulars you can about him. Adieu, my friend.— I have no letter from Arthur but hear he is surely coming. Affectionately yours

S. M. FULLER.

ALS (MHi). *Addressed:* Rev J. F. Clarke / Boston / Mass. *Postmark:* Milwaukie [*illegible*] WnT. *Endorsed:* S M. Fuller / July 28th / 1843. (Ky 52).

five thousand] five tho⟨n⟩usand
Mackinaw if not to the Sault] Mackinaw ↑ if not to the Sault ↓
inspired once] inspired ⟨much⟩ ↑ once ↓
man; he] man; h⟨is⟩e
the innumerable] the in⟨u⟩numerable
gone already.—] gone.— ↑ already ↓

1. Clarke had sent Fuller $50, "so that you may not be hurried by want of means" (*Letters of JFC*, p. 143).
2. Fuller visited Mackinac Island in August 1843, at a time when almost 2,000 Indians had arrived for the annual event. She later wrote in *Summer on the Lakes, in 1843:* "I have not wished to write sentimentally about the Indians, however moved by the thought of their wrongs and speedy extinction. I know that the Europeans who took possession of this country, felt themselves justified by their superior civilization and religious ideas. Had they been truly civilized or Christianized, the conflicts which sprang from the collision of the two races might have been avoided; but this cannot be expected in movements made by masses of men. The mass has never yet been humanized, though the age may develop a human thought" (p. 234).
3. Clarke sent his poem "Triformis," which Fuller published in *Summer on the Lakes.* The poem compares a young woman to the moon.
4. "Triformis" begins "So pure her forehead's dazzling white."
5. Washington Allston, with whom Sarah Clarke had studied, died on 9 July.

1088. To James F. and Sarah A. Clarke

New York 13th Septr 1843.

Dear James,

This letter though intended chiefly to acquaint your Mother and Sarah, according to promise with the news of my safe arrival is addressed to you, partly lest it should reach Meadville after they are gone, and partly because I did not write to you, a note, as I intended by them. I wanted to tell you, myself, how much that part of my Western life which I owe to you was to me. More, in point of *pleasure*, was the time at Mackinaw than all the rest except the two or three weeks of Rock River. As to *use*, in giving materials for thought, *all* was of use. The time spent in town hotels, and in casual intercourse, though not at the time agreeable, will, I already feel, bear fruit in memory.

Already I feel the difference between hearing and seeing; much that I seemed to know before has never been truly mine, till I had such limited means of observation as this summer has afforded. Now I have some inkling what is meant by the West, and what its prospects and tendencies are.

And I am enriched not only[n] in mere knowledge as to what regards men, but in a succession of pictures, wide shifting shadows of natural beauty, which shall refresh me to my latest day.

And now postponing further communication till we meet I turn to My dear Sarah,

I found an excellent care taker in Mr D'Wolf, also a fine steward, for wishing[n] to save his money, as a clergyman with small money salary, albeit a *farmer* of some 1700 acres Illinois land, must, he brought me back for half the money I spent going on, and quite as pleasantly.[1]

Some queer characters I met on the route, of whom sketches when we meet.

In one way I was indeed unfortunate. That absurd launch, which detained us at Detroit, prevented my reaching Albany in time for the Saty morning boat or cars. I was detained in Albany from twelve o clock till seven, eveg and then went down the North River in the night. I did not see a thing; this was a little too bad. I came down on the Knickerbocker, the most splendid boat I ever saw. The lake boats are shabby, in comparison. Arriving Sunday morng, I breakfasted and went to W. Channing's church. The Revd Episcopal not only attended me to the door but chose to go in. I happened to be there the first Sunday the church was opened after a six weeks'[n] recess. W. C. spoke with great power and beauty. Looking round, at the end of service, who should I see but Messrs Alcott Lane, and Thoreau.[2] The effect of this was queer enough.

I was at the City Hotel, a very good house where I could see my friends pleasantly and did so all the time till next afternoon when, by invitation from Wm Emerson, I went out to Staten Island. There I passed yesterday, walking and riding to see Mr Emerson's (Waldo's)[n] view from the Telegraph office, ah Sarah, I wish you had been there to see this view of the sea and shipping and the grand old fort. They were such splendors as we have not seen elsewhere.

W. C. came for me, in the aftn and we went to the meeting of his society in N.Y. for conversation Mr Lane was present and talked a great deal but not so well as usual.

This morning I am at the Graham-house Barclay St. I had a curiosity to try it. It is clean, still, and the breakfast excellent for one who can dispense with tea and coffee. The dinner I am yet to see[3]

This morning I am to receive some visits, from Mr Vathek (the author of the essays on *Femality*) who has been to see me once, and with whom I am much pleased and others.[4] This aftn I am going to Staten Island again and going home from there.

I am, you see two or three days longer on the road than I expected, but have written home to say just when I shall be there. There were so many inducements offered for me to remain here awhile, that I thought I ought to stay as I have not been here before for six or seven years, and may not for as long again.

I wish I could hear from you how you got on from that *Grand* place, and how Mother likes the promised stillness of Meadville Tell her Mr Lloyd mourned much for her absence but consoled himself as well as he could, part of the time with Butler's analogy, part with the Detroit singing girls.[5] In less than a fortnight I shall see you; with love to Anna, Hermann and Lilly,[6] dear Sarah, adieu

MARGARET.

Tell your Mother I saw the yellow pamphlet constantly sticking out of Mr. D. W's pocket, but I fear little passed from the pocket to the head! much less the heart!

I am to see all the beauties of Staten Island tomorrow and they are many, such lovely winding wooded roads and grand sea views with processions of gliding sails caught at the openings. Mr Emerson's is a sweet place.[7] A high hill behind the house and on his farm commands one of the finest views.

James, may not your verses about the Moon be printed either in the Dial, or the Present, write to me about this. William C. admires and wants them, if you are willing[8]

ALS (MHi). *Addressed:* Rev James F. Clarke / Meadville / Pa. *Postmark:* New York Sep 15.

not only] not ⟨m⟩ only
for wishing] for ⟨?⟩ ↑ wishing ↓
six weeks'] six ⟨months⟩ ↑ weeks' ↓
Emerson's (Waldo's)] Emerson's ↑ (Waldo's) ↓

1. The identity of her clerical companion is not clear, but she later calls him "Episcopal," which suggests Erastus DeWolfe (1808?–64), son of Wylys and Waity Brown De Wolfe. He was an Episcopal minister who later became a chaplain in the Union army and died at the battle of the Wilderness (Calbraith B. Perry, *Charles D'Wolf of Guadaloupe* [New York, 1902], pp. 70, 128, 139).

2. Bronson Alcott, Charles Lane (who had lived with the Alcotts at Fruitlands), and Henry Thoreau. Fuller met them at a meeting of the Christian Union, a society William Henry Channing formed in April 1843.

3. The first Graham boardinghouse opened in New York City in 1833. It offered two vegetarian meals a day, with no spices, condiments, tea, coffee, or stimulants. Horace Greeley lived there for a time (Stephen Nissenbaum, *Sex, Diet, and Debility in Jacksonian America* [Westport, Conn., 1980], pp. 142–43).

4. Parke Godwin's *New York Pathfinder* published a two-part essay on women on 11 and 18 March 1843, signed only "Vathek." Fuller commented on the essay in *Woman in*

the Nineteenth Century: "He views Woman truly from the soul, and not from society, and the depth and leading of his thoughts are proportionably remarkable" (*Woman in the Nineteenth Century,* ed. Joel Myerson [Columbia, S.C., 1980], p. 102).

5. Joseph Butler, *Analogy of Religion, Natural and Revealed, to the Constitution and Course of Nature* (London, 1736).

6. Clarke's wife, son, and daughter.

7. She visited the home of William Emerson, Waldo's brother.

8. Despite Channing's admiration, he did not publish Clarke's poem in the *Present.* Fuller, however, did (though without attribution), in *Summer on the Lakes.*

1089. To Georgiana Bruce

[27? February? 1844?][n]

[   ] loose; much is thus gained, there is some temporary loss. Here is friction, here circulation, but in silence alone can the liberty of law be duly felt. Nature prepares her marble and gold out of sight, and yields them only to the patient and strong. You will let me preach a little, I am by nature not less ardent than you. I am older and have lived very forcibly for my years. Time has not subdued, but it has tempered and assured me. I will not say *re*assured, for I was always faithful as I see you are. With best wishes yours

M. F.

I shall see you at Brook Farm by and by. Be very careful of your health. You will need some apprenticeship to teach you how, for it is very unnatural to guard against harm, and you should ask at once the best advice. Tis pity to let the body become a clog instead of a pliant vestment and organ to the Spirit.

ALfrS (ViU). *Addressed:* Miss Bruce / at Mr Gannett's / Cambridge Port. *Endorsed:* Margaret Fuller / Feby 27—45.

The endorsement is incorrect, for neither Fuller nor Bruce was in Boston in 1845. The date is uncertain, but since Bruce was at Gannett's home, it was before she went to work at Sing Sing.

1090. To James F. Clarke

Cambridge 3d April
1844.

This morning, my dear James, I received a letter from Arthur, in which he says Mr Conant, he finds, has written a letter to you about his position &c. That he had no thought of troubling you again, and is very desirous nothing should be done till I have told you all the facts as he has stated them to me, lest he should either be deprived[n] of his liberty or seem to those who become interested very fickle on account of what he must do.

I am going to N. York this afternoon for a short time, and cannot see you first. I write therefore merely to ask that if you have recd or shall receive Mr Conant's letter you will do nothing till I return and can talk with you. I should like too that this may be as soon after my return as may be. If that should be by Monday's boat, I may come in and see if you are at leisure[n] Tuesday morng But if you do not see me[n] then, will you leave a note at Miss Peabody's saying whether you can give me an hour from your busy life on Thursday aftn of next week.[1]

With affection yours

S. M. FULLER.

ALS (MHi). *Endorsed:* S. M. Fuller.

be deprived] be d⟨r⟩eprived
at leisure] at le⟨e⟩isure
see me] see ↑ me ↓

1. On the 22nd, Fuller wrote Arthur to say that she had seen Clarke, that he had read Conant's letter to her, and that the Unitarian Association might donate $100 to the Belvidere school (*Letters of MF*, 3:189–92).

1091. To Rebecca Buffum Spring

Cambridge
April 17th 1844.

Dear Mrs Spring,

It was a source of true regret to me that I could not comply with your cordial invitation. Should I be in N. York again, and time permit, I shall certainly come to see you.

Jane and her friend I have not seen, but hear they are well and singing merrily.[1]

Yours

S. MARGARET FULLER.

ALS (CSt). *Addressed:* Mrs Spring / Care Wells & Spring / Pine St / New York. *Postmark:* April 24.

1. Probably Jane Tuckerman King and her daughter Alice, who was born on 20 February 1844 and died on 10 May 1846 (Chelsea VR).

1092. To Caroline Sturgis

Concord July 25th 1844.

Where art thou, Caroline?— on what black sea art floating now away from me? Black *or* Red?

I am constantly reminded of that game (Rouge *et* Noir I mean) which fascinates the player so, to madness sometimes.[1] Which ever colour they get upon they dont like to leave and try the other, but double their stakes on that.

Yet with me the board has been tri-colored. I began with Rouge, then played a foolish while, and prodigal stakes of thought and feeling and night-watches upon Noir, and now I have got upon Blanche, O Saint, not St Theresa, but Catharine, wedded to the child, please keep[n] me there till I have won back my gold and silver and pearls of price.[2]

What ails this ink? It is Ellery's ink and wont flow from my pen.

Ellery is at Lenox. Ellen is at Cambridge, I am living in their house alone; it is very pleasant. I write and muse and sleep much and study a little and go sit among the trees in Sleepy Hollow and the breeze flows around and the birds sing a few contented notes and the light streams in more and more gently and I feel cradled,— with me the rarest, happiest of feelings. I am borne along on the stream of life I have no weaving to do for myself.

At home here I go sit in the room where Ellery is accustomed to write and enjoy his presence more than ever before. There are old broken pictures against the wall, a dark ladye whose sidelong gaze is somewhat marred by the suppression of part of her nose, a foot alone gleaming from one dingy canvass. Here is Ellery's pipe, breathing through which he orientalizes himself and finds the Sun! Here are the Ledgers betwixt whose dull thick leaves he hides a Poet's Hope.[3]

Ellen has the baby with her, but it is not much loss yet as she has hardly variety enough now.[4] In about a month she will be interesting. She looks like Ellery; her eyes are full of quick sad soul already.

Waldo has been a good playmate singing me long chants of laws and causes and the Metamorphosis. They are the same keys, mostly G. majors, I think, but rich and full strains of Pindaric loftiness if not of Orphic searching stress. Now he is getting up an oration which stammers in its first days and teazes the Father's listening eager ear—[5]

Before I came here I staid with the Hawthornes and enjoyed it much. The river side and the old whispering trees and their wise life of mutual thought and H's all-seeing mellow eyes and stilly growing mind and human heart. And the child worthy the name of Una.[6] She is beautiful and of a calm, harmonious beauty, which will stand. Over her face the smiles beam as light upon the equal heavens. She is tender too, shows as yet no passion, but a full determined nature.—

I would like to hear from you; would you not like to write? Has the cloud opened yet and showed a face of angel or of demon. Have you not written some poems you will send me. Give my love to those ex[c]ellent friends there Ss whose word we will take for a million to whom we may lend the heart in an uncovered dish.[7] And thou, O maid of deepest Fate hast thou again let the curtain fall between us? If so paint it over with symbolic figures, that looking, I may muse and musing the fire may burn.—

I shall be here till 2d August.

AL (MB). *Addressed:* Miss Caroline Sturgis / Care Geo. Russell Esq. / West Roxbury / Mass. *Postmark:* Concord Mas. Jul 24. *Endorsed:* 1844 S M F.

please keep] please ⟨?⟩ keep

1. Rouge et Noir is a solitaire in which the ranks are built in alternate colors (John Scarne, *Scarne's Encyclopedia of Games* [New York, 1973], p. 416).

2. St. Teresa of Avila (1515–82), who rejuvenated the Carmelite order, was a renowned mystical writer. St. Catharine of Bologna (1413–63) was said to have been visited by the Virgin, "who placed the newborn Christ in her arms" (*New Catholic Encyclopedia* [Washington, D.C., 1967], p. 254). Fuller echoes Matt. 13:45–46: "Again, the kingdom of heaven is like unto a merchant man, seeking goodly pearls: Who, when he had found one pearl of great price, went and sold all that he had, and bought it."

3. The title of one of Channing's poems.

4. Margaret Fuller Channing, called Greta by the family.

5. In a letter written to Emerson this same month, Fuller clearly refers to his lecture, "Address Delivered in Concord on the Anniversary of the Emancipation of the Negroes in the British West Indies," which he read on 1 August (*Letters of MF,* 3:213).

6. Una Hawthorne, the original for Pearl.

7. Sturgis was staying with the family of George and Sarah Russell in Roxbury. She would have visited Russell's brother-in-law, Francis George Shaw, and his wife, Sarah (Caroline's distant cousin), both Fuller's close friends.

1093. To [Marcus Spring]

[1845?][n]

[   ] [I] am truly obliged by y[   ] wife's affectionate interest [   ] With regard to coming on Wedn[   ] Mr Channing[1] intended to see for me the relatives of the lady who was so much benefitted in a case of curvature and, if I judged by an exact report of the case that the cure was such as to afford *me* a hope of[n] chance of real *cure*, I intended to try the Dr.[2]

But I am not desirous to try magnetism, merely as a means of soothing or strengthening m[e] for my case is exactly this

I no longer suffer severely and when I can take excellent care of myself suffer scarce at all.

But this weakness disables me from doing or enjoying what would be natural to me and when I have to make *great* exertions, or at the wrong time [   ]

[   ] pay for is a [   ] me.

[   ] I do not wish to spend two hours daily in going to the Dr nor to spend money merely for a benefit which might be of value to another, because that time and that money I should have to redeem by exertions which would hurt me more than the aid of the magnetism would help me.

But if there is a prospect of *cure*, i e of straightening and strengthening the spine, I would do almost any thing to ensure it, for nothing that could now happen could make me so happy.

[   ] time it dem[   ] Shall I ask the favor [   ] to call after receiving this [   ] talk with Mr Greeley who has some suggestions to make on the subject?

If I decide to go and I shall be much influenced by what I hear from you in reply, I will transport myself and inkstan[d] to your house on Wednesday for the remainder of the week, and however I decide, please accept the thanks of your friend

S. M. FULLER.

ALfrS (CSt). *Addressed:* To / Marcus Spring / 52 Pine St / N.Y.—

Dated by the contents: Fuller was in New York, but the formality of the signature suggests a date earlier than 1846.

The top half of the letter has been burned away.

a hope of] a ↑ hope of ↓

1. William Henry Channing.

2. Her reference probably is to Théodore Léger, a New York hypnotist who treated her in 1845 (*Letters of MF,* 4:47).

1094. To James F. Clarke

9th Jany
45.

My dear James,

The sagacious seem to think it is not desirable to send the "Xn World" to Sing-Sing, at present.[1] The nomination of William C. to the office of secretary in the new society has roused a good deal of ignorant affright among the so called orthodox.[2] In order to carry into effect what is so desirable for the prisons, care must be taken not further to distress these good people," 'or they will either refuse to cooperate with the liberal, or throw daily obstacles in their way. Now, they would not believe that your paper will not exercise a sectarian influence, and would much rather continue beating the prisoners &c than admit such perilous stuff to their *souls*.

It will, therefore, be best to leave your offer in abeyance for awhile and make use of it by and by, when the proposed improvements shall be confirmed in practice, and the society be convinced that these "good *moral* men" are too useful to be dispensed with. *Now*, sending the paper might do more harm, in one way, than good in another.

I must say, all this kind of nonsense seems to me worse than vice, but I am not impatient, now, with it. Life is so short and so much to be done, we cant spare time to be impatient.

I am very glad you sent books; that will do good. Miss Robbins is, indeed, exceedingly disagreeable," but is, I understand, efficient.[3] She has really done a good deal for Sing Sing. She is, certainly, no charming specimen of the Magdalen. A *conceited* Magdalen is a sad sight. And her history would make her the very person to instruct the women in these places; if she had only a beautiful character. Her friends, here, esteem her, and say she is better than she seems.

I am now to visit all the public *benevolent!* institutions of N.Y, and write" about them, when I see fit.[4] This will interest me. I was just beginning, but stopped short by Influenza, of which I am not yet quite well.

What you say of my writing seems to be very true. I dont know whether I can make it of use or not, but shall bear it in mind. I have a [mu]ch better chance, as to writ[in]g now than ever before. You know I have, constantly, written in bodily pain, and pressed for time. Little pieces, that have been written in a single day when I was well and every way at ease, such as "The Two Herberts" the story of Mariana in "Summer on the Lakes," the "Magnolia" in the "Dial" seem to me to have flow and an obvious unity. One of my long" pieces in the Dial "The Great Composers" is satisfactory to myself.[5] I do not expect to write better than that. But now, that I can choose my own times, and have a public of sufficient range or disposition and powers to interest me, also am in much better health. I hope my average writing will be better than it has been. Still, I suspect, from the nature of my mind, *coherence* is the best you will get from me. I should always like to know how things strike you; it will aid my judgment, if it does" not improve my effect.

I thank heartily for the New Years wishes and reciprocate them in full. Your sympathy is dear to me, your honor and happiness no less so. The common life we enjoyed while growing up so near to one another was rich in seeds whose harvest will not fail[n] us and whose bounties it must eternally be a happiness to impart to one another And so, dear James, farewell from

MARGARET.

ALS (MHi). *Addressed:* To / Rev James F. Clarke / Mt Vernon St. / Boston / Mass. *Endorsed:* (56).

these good people,] the⟨m⟩se, ↑ good people ↓
exceedingly disagreeable,] exceedingly disa⟨?⟩greeable,
and write] and ⟨?⟩ write
my long] my ↑ long ↓
it does] it do⟨n⟩es
not fail] not f⟨e⟩ail

1. In 1843 Clarke and some of his parishioners founded the *Christian World*. He was its chief author, editor, and publisher.

2. In 1844 Channing was one of the founders of the New York Prison Association (W. David Lewis, *From Newgate to Dannemora* [Ithaca, N.Y., 1965], p. 232).

3. Probably Eliza Robbins (1786–1853), daughter of Edward H. and Elizabeth Murray Robbins of Milton, Massachusetts. She was the author of a number of children's schoolbooks and had been a matron at Sing-Sing for some years (*History of Milton, Mass., 1640 to 1887* [n.p., n.d.], pp. 513–14).

4. Fuller first wrote about the public institutions on 19 March, when she discussed the Bellevue Alms House, the Farm School, the Asylum for the Insane, and the penitentiary on Blackwell's Island (*New-York Daily Tribune*, 19 March 1845).

5. "The Two Herberts," *Present* 1 (March 1844): 301–12; "The Magnolia of Lake Pontchartrain," *Dial* 1 (January 1841): 299–305; "Lives of the Great Composers, Haydn, Mozart, Handel, Bach, Beethoven," *Dial* 2 (October 1841): 148–203.

1095.   To Charles K. Newcomb

Saty p.m.
[10 May 1845]

Dear Charles,

I have had a very pleasant visit from your mother.[1] All right. Your ever affece

MARGARET.

ALS (MH: fMS Am 1086 [10:125]). *Addressed:* C. K. Newcomb. *Endorsed:* May 10 1845.

1. The Newcombs were visiting in New York. Fuller wrote Emerson that she had seen Charles "and we have had a good meeting" (*Letters of MF*, 4:103).

1096. To Rebecca Buffum Spring

Thursday June 12th [1845]

Dear Rebecca

Anna Ward will be at her grandmother's in Beekman St till Saty; would like much to see you.[1]

I shall not be at Dr's after tomorrow, so when you want me to come and meet E. Hoar, please leave a note at the Tribune office the day previous.

in haste yr friend

MARGARET F.

ALS (CSt). *Addressed:* Mrs Spring / Care Wells & Spring / 52 Pine St. / please send this immedy.

1. Anna Barker Ward's maternal grandmother, Anna Rodman Hazard, lived at 80 Beekman Street.

1097. To James F. Clarke

[14 August 1845]

My dear friend James,

With a start came to me the thought this evening; if you wish to write to James at Chicago; you must do it at once, for this is the 14th August. Indeed, it *is* "in my heart" to write. Your letter was of cordial sweetness to me, as is ever the thought of our friendship, that sober suited friendship, where the web was so deliberately and well woven, and which wears so well.

I was pleased with your sympathy about The[n] Tribune; I do not find much among my old friends.[1] They think I ought to produce something excellent, while I am well content for the present to aid in the great work of mutual education in this way. I never regarded literature merely as a collection of exquisite products, but as a means of mutual interpretation. Feeling that many are reached and in some degree aided the thoughts of every day seem worth writing down, though in a form that does not inspire me. Then I like to feel so fairly afloat in mid-stream, as I do here.[n] All the signs of life appear to me at least superficially, and, as I have had a good deal of *the depths*, an abode of some length in *the shallows* may do me no harm. The sun comes full upon me.

Mr Greeley is all you say.[2] He is in other ways interesting for me to know, "A born and thorough Plebeian" as he declares himself to be, he teaches me many things, which my own influence on those who have hitherto[n] approached me, as also that we attract in mutual relations those congenial with ourselves, has prevented my learning. He and I are in business and friendly relations there is a solid good will and natural respect without intimacy. I think him the most disinterestedly generous person, except my own Mother, that I have ever known.

You speak justly of Rousseau too.[3] With earliest instincts he was so prized by me, all development has confirmed the feeling. But natures so earnest and with the central fire so deeply enkindled will never be believed in by the world in general till men have far more manhood than now. Some of us, James, were not unlike the personages of Rousseau, the children of his Soul. We never tampered with our feelings we never falsified their expression, nor borrowed an unworthy help from false pride.

I wish you joy of your little one.[4] Your marriage is a good one, and I feel as if your children would be of value. I can congratulate you, which I could few persons. Since Anna Parsons[5] discovered the name, it must be the right one, else[n] I should say W. Eliot is not good enough to be associated with W. Channing. I am not pleased with much that I have heard and the little I have seen of him these later years. He seems to have grown narrow and conceited in the absence of equal and superior minds that might have checked him.

I was very sorry for[n] those poor conscientious people that left you last winter except that foolish vain George Channing.[6] He ought to go through the water cure,[n] no less would eradicate the taint from his system. I could not help feeling Poor Jesus! it seemed so much more sacrilegious to utter such meannesses in his name than all the crimes of the Jesuits. I declare that nothing in the world is to me so revolting as religious vanity.

Dear James, I do not want to write much more. I go to Rockaway tomorrow for sea air, as I am not strong and have preparations to make[n] Have been today over the Great Britain; it is a majestic sight; as fine as I expected. But I would rather cross in a smaller boat; she cannot be very manageable.

Tell Sarah Mr Emerson has just been here a delightful visit.[7] He enjoyed my rocks with free heart. Tell me what is Sarah painting; she never tells Adieu ever affecy

Your friend

MARGARET.

ALS (MHi). Published in part in *Memoirs*, 1:98, 164, 151, and *Letters of MF*, 4:39, 40.
about The] about ⟨t⟩The

do here.] do. ↑ here ↓
have hitherto] have hither ↑ to ↓
one, else] one, e⟨e⟩lse
sorry for] sorry ↑ for ↓
water cure;] water cur⟨r⟩e;
strong and have preparations to make] strong ↑ and have preparations to make ↓

1. Of her writings in the *Tribune*, Clarke said on 26 July: "They seem to me to be better written than anything of yours I have read. There is more ease, grace, freedom and point to them. The thoughts and sentiments are such as must do good" (*Letters of JFC*, p. 145).

2. Horace Greeley began the *New-York Daily Tribune* in 1841 with the goal of making it intellectually substantial. Clarke said: "Mr. Greeley I admire and esteem very much. It is so rare that we find one who combines with noble purposes and disinterested striving so much practical energy, tact, and adroitness" (ibid., p. 145).

3. Clarke was reading *La Nouvelle Héloïse* for the first time. In his letter, he said: "Rousseau is the commanding mind of our century. He seems to me to have great wisdom and balance of mind; to me he does not seem disposed to overstate or exaggerate" (ibid., p. 145). Fuller and Clarke had read Rousseau together at the beginning of their friendship in Cambridge.

4. Eliot Channing Clarke (1845–1921) was born on 6 May. Named for William Henry Channing and William Greenleaf Eliot, Clarke graduated from Harvard in 1867 and became a civil engineer. In 1878 he married Alice de Vermandois Sohier (MVR 1921 1:294; *Harvard College Class of 1867. Secretary's Report. No. 14. 1918* [Boston, 1918], p. 36).

5. Anna Parsons was a friend who experimented with Mesmerism.

6. On 12 January 1845 Clarke informed his congregation that he intended to exchange pulpits with Theodore Parker (with whom almost no Unitarian minister would exchange because of his radical theology) on the last Sunday in the month. He was then obliged to meet on 22 January with several of his parishioners who were angry over the Parker exchange, but Clarke held to his principles and exchanged on the 26th. As a result, sixteen of his people, including George Channing (who called Clarke a "monomaniac"), withdrew and later formed the Church of the Savior in Boston (Bolster, *James Freeman Clarke*, pp. 153–56). George Gibbs Channing (1789–1881), son of William and Lucy Channing, was the youngest brother of Dr. William Ellery, Edward Tyrell, and Walter Channing. A successful businessman, Channing was also a Unitarian missionary and an ordained evangelist who served churches in Massachusetts, Connecticut, and New Hampshire. Once one of Clarke's close friends and an original parishioner at the Church of the Disciples, Channing was the editor of the *Christian World*. In 1814 he married Elizabeth Parsons Sigourney (1794?–1870) (MVR 329:260; *Christian Register*, 22 January 1881; MVR 230:268; Henry H. W. Sigourney, *Genealogy of the Sigourney Family* [Boston, 1857], p. 14).

7. Emerson, who had lectured in Middletown, Connecticut, on 6 August, arrived at his brother's home on Staten Island on the 7th to find that William and Susan Emerson were departing that evening for New England. Waldo returned to Concord on the 13th (Rusk, *Letters of RWE*, 3:294–96).

1098. To James F. Clarke

New York.
16th Novr 1845.

Dear James,

Did you ask me to get a Daguerreotype made for you from the Ivory Christ.[1] I am going to have one made for another friend and I had the impression I was asked to see about *two*— I thought the other might be for you. What should you be willing to give to have one made, if you do want it?— I do not know certainly whether they are five or ten dollars, as I have not been to the man myself yet, and informants vary to that extent. Please answer this, at once, if you want me to see to it for you.

I called at your house, saw Anna and the children. Herman looked lovely as ever. Lilla looked darkly upon me, as I came in the wrong hour.[2] I hope to see her in a happier time, when she has the use of that little foot again.

I enclose a billet which please give to Ellen Hooper, saying it is what I spoke of to her and please dont forget sometime to send me your poem and hers.

Ever, dear James, your friend

MARGARET

ALS (MHi). *Addressed:* Rev. J. F. Clarke. / Boston / Mass. *Postmark:* New York 16 Nov. *Endorsed:* (55).

1. In a *Tribune* column Fuller briefly noted a carved ivory crucifix, 3 feet long and 14 inches wide, that had been on display in New York City and was then taken to Boston (*New-York Daily Tribune,* 27 November 1845; *Christian Register,* 29 November 1845).

2. Lillian Clarke (1842–1921), his daughter (MVR 1921 2:315).

1099. To James F. Clarke

New York.
5th Decr 1845.

My dear James,

I had, before receiving your letter already sent you a note about the Daguerreotype. My good[n] genius suggested that you might not care so much for one after seeing the statue.

Thanks for the dried flowers. I wish you would send such often.

I did not know that William C. was ill. I infer from your letter that he is not dangerously so, yet feel some anxiety, for he is not subject to serious illness of this kind. Will you, dear James, write a line on Monday or Tuesday to let me know whether he is getting better, and take upon yourself to let me know of any important change, for there is no one else there who understands enough about the closeness of spiritual kindred to let me know whatever might happen.

Ever affecy

MARGARET

ALS (MHi).
My good] My ⟨d⟩ good

1100.   To William C. Russel

4 Amity place
Wednesday eveg
4th Feby [1846]

Dear Mr Russel,

I went yesterday to see the poor English woman. I found her intoxicated and the scene that followed was very sad. I should say she was so much enslaved and her character so weakened by the bad habit, that there is no hope of her doing any better, from her own resolves[n] and that she ought to be separated from her children. I saw what her temper is, when excited, and it must be ruinous to them.

in haste, your friend

S. M. F.

ALS (PSt.) *Addressed:* To / William C. Russel Esq / Wall St. *Endorsed:* S. M. Fuller / 4 Feb. 1846.

William Channing Russel (1814–96), son of William Washington and Lucy Channing Russel (Dr. William Ellery Channing's sister), graduated from Columbia in 1832 and became a lawyer in New York. From 1867 to 1881 he was first, professor of History, then Vice President and acting President of Cornell. He married Matilda Howland (1824–76) of Charleston, South Carolina (*NEHGR* 8:319; *The Ten-Year Book of Cornell University 1868–1908* [Ithaca, 1908], p. 56; Cornell archives; *Columbia Catalog*, p. 103).

better, from her own resolves] better, ↑ from her own resolves ↓

1101.   To William C. Russel

Wednesday
June 3d. [1846]

Dear Mr Russell,

Harro finds himself in great distress, because of the absence of Mr Jordan just as he hoped his trial was coming on at last.[1] Will you listen to him a little and give him a word of counsel in case he changes his lawyer who to choose. It is all important to him, and he says Stallknecht takes no interest.[2] I do not understand why because S. was

William C. Russel. Courtesy of the Division of Rare and Manuscript Collections, Cornell University Library.

exceedingly so, but do you listen to him a little with your own good heart, and for my sake too, for I do want him to get out of this part of the miseries of his life.

Will you, if disengaged, come tomorrow eveg and go with me to Mr Templeton's concert.[3] If not convenient or agreeable[n] to you to do so, please send a line *today* through Mr Manning[4]

in haste your friend

S. M. F.

ALS(PSt). *Endorsed:* Miss Fuller / 3 June / 46.

or agreeable] or a⟨?⟩greeable

1. Harro Harring was a Dane who published a novel, *Dolores*, but then sued his New York publisher (*Letters of MF*, 4:211). The New York City directory lists Ambrose L. and Philip Jordan as lawyers. Ambrose (1789–1865) practiced in Hudson before moving to New York City in 1838. He was a member of the state constitutional convention in 1846 (*National Cyclopedia*); Philip Jordan is otherwise unidentified.

2. Frederick Stoud Stallknecht (1819?–75), a New York lawyer, immigrated from Denmark when he was sixteen, attended Brown but did not graduate, and was admitted to the New York bar in 1843 (*Historical Catalogue of Brown University, 1764–1904* [Providence, 1905]; *New York Times,* 21 December 1875).

3. John Templeton (1802–86) gave a concert on the theme "Reminiscences of Grand Opera" on 4 June 1846. A Scottish tenor, Templeton was on a North American tour (*Baker's Biographical Dictionary of Musicians,* 5th ed. [New York, 1971]; *New-York Daily Tribune,* 3 June 1846).

4. Richard Henry Manning was a New York businessman and Fuller's good friend.

1102. To Rebecca Buffum Spring

Brooklyn, N Y
7th June 1846.

Dear Rebecca,

I was right glad to get thy little note all about Jeanie and the pleasant times you were having with the birds and flowers and meant to have answered it before Marcus went, but some interruption prevented. Since I hope you have been having just so good a time and with Eddie, too.[1]

All goes on pretty smoothly with me. I hear the business world still is much harassed though prospects as to peace with England look favorable.[2] I hope Marcus will be here or that I shall hear from you soon. I suppose all looks, still, as if we should go and by the time and in the way proposed. I have written to Miss Martineau and expect an answer by middle of July.

I shall seriously begin my preparations by the middle of next month. I did not go to Lenox, or get your veil, because just as I was going Anna Ward's children were seized with scarlet fever. The little boy was dangerously ill, but they are safe now.[3]

Dr Vanderveer told me that yr sister is almost well, and[n] that she had just had a letter from you.[4] The Dr did entirely forsake me, but I go now to Mrs Fairchild's twice a week.[5] I detest going there, but it was my only way. I generally have to wait several hours, but take my books to look over and the Dr sends me home in his carriage.

I was just thinking of writing to you when Harro sent these things to be forwarded Poor Harro! he is fifty times more worn and harassed and fevered than ever. Mr Jordan being absent, he has [   ] change to a new [a]dvocate,[n] or wait several months for his trial and that, I suppose, would kill him. Now it only remains for him to lose it. "Dolores" sells very well. I long for the 4th No to be out and for him to make a visit to you and the gentle Maggie. You will comfort him, I know.

Tell Maggie my brother Eugene is just going to be married in La so I shall not be able to offer him to her as I should have liked to.[6] I can offer her only my love.

Napoleon &c send back to me, when done with[7]

Interrupted, have only time for a word more. Mr Walker the pianist thinks he shall join us in Paris; that may on many accts be very pleasant. Love to pet Jeanie, is she still as cunning!— Write a note please

ever affecy

M. F.

No news of a place for that Louisa?

ALS (CSt).
well, and] well, ↑ and ↓
to a new [a]dvocate,] to ↑ a ↓ new [a]dvo⟨t⟩cate,

1. The Springs' children.
2. On 23 April the Congress approved a resolution to end the Anglo-American joint jurisdiction of the Oregon Territory. On 6 June the British draft treaty to end the crisis arrived in Washington. Congress and Polk accepted it on 15 June. The treaty set the 49th parallel as the boundary, and defined navigation rights for both countries (*Encyclopedia of American History*, ed. Richard B. Morris [New York, 1953], pp. 195–96).
3. The Wards' children were Anna Barker, Lydia Gray, and Thomas Wren.
4. Which of Rebecca Spring's six sisters Fuller means is not clear. Adrian Vanderveer (1796?–1857) graduated from Columbia in 1816 and became a doctor in 1818. On 25 March of that year he married Eliza Lott, daughter of Henry I. Lott (*Columbia Catalog; New-York Evening Post*, March 1818, July 1857).
5. The New York City directory lists three widow Fairchilds in 1846. It is not clear to whom Fuller refers.
6. Eugene Fuller married Anna Eliza Rotta later in June.

7. Fuller had probably lent her copy of Joel T. Headley's *Napoleon and His Marshals*, which she reviewed in the *Tribune* on 2 May and 18 June.

1103.　To Parke Godwin

43 Middaugh St
Brooklyn
14th July 1846.

Dear Mr Godwin,

Returning this morng I find the bearer of this, Mr Taylor an Englishman, formerly an English clergyman, now with the better profession of *man only*. He came with a letter of introduction from a valued friend, who hopes I shall offer him some inducement to remain in this country.

I should like to do so, for we need such men, but see not my way clear. He regretted much that he was likely to leave this country (he expects to sail on Thursday)[n] without seeing William Channing, Mr Ripley &c &c. and thought I would send him to you, as (meseems!!)[n] you will tell him many things they would and hear in turn many things you will like to hear. I hope you will have leisure for a good talk with him.

　truly yours

S. M. Fuller

The memory of the woods and waters and smiles of Hempstead[1] seem already, fresh indeed as if in a work of art, but distant as the song of other days! O blessed seclusion inaccessible to errand boys; how, how, was it possible to quit thee? Where the errand boy enter not, the Muse may dare to set her foot, but here!

ALS (NN-M)

Parke Godwin (1816–1904), a writer, editor, and translator, shared many interests with Fuller. He warmly supported Brook Farm, edited the *Harbinger,* the Fourierist journal, and translated the first part of Goethe's autobiography. An 1834 Princeton graduate, Godwin became a lawyer and practiced in Louisville but moved to New York City because of his detestation of slavery. An author of several volumes, he was for 45 years associated with the *New-York Evening Post* with William Cullen Bryant, whose daughter Fanny he married in 1842 (*DAB*).

country (he expects to sail on Thursday)] country ↑ (he expects to sail on Thursday) ↓
as (meseems!!)] as ↑ (meseems!!) ↓

1. Godwin's home.

Parke Godwin. Published with the permission of the Manuscripts Division, Department of Rare Books and Special Collections, Princeton University Libraries.

1104. To William C. Russel

London
30th Octr 46.

My dear friend
William Russel

I never acknowledged your farewell letter but the truth is I was almost killed with hurry before leaving the U.S. I thought then I would write immedy on arriving here, but could not till *now* and *now* time presses and I must only say the needful as to the interest you promised to take in my affairs.

Harrow Harring has just been here and returns tomorrow to the U.S.[n] As well as I can judge from his statement, neither he nor I will ever receive a penny from his book.[1] I should like, however, that you should talk the matter over with Mr Stallknecht and let me clearly understand how the matter is. Mr S. knows that I expected he would take some care of me, but I fancy he got wearied out with Harro's impracticability. My wishes are simply these. I would rather lose the money entirely than that anything should be added to the pressure on Harro. Let nothing whatever be done that can trouble him or weaken his confidence in me as an ever affece friend, for such I really am to him. But I ought to have been secured so that if there is to be any profit from the work it should come to me and not to Marenner and Lockwood, beyond the just commission on their sales.[2] I do not, at this moment, need the money, but shall very much within a year from this time and if I cannot have it, must work hard to make up the loss. Do, then, whatever you can for me that is consistent with perfect kindness and delicacy towards Harro, and do not blame him for making your interposition necessary, for he is a wrong-headed child as to the affairs of this world, and I never had confidence except in the supposition that Stallknecht as a man of business wd manage the affair, and as a man of honor and good feeling wd wish to protect my interests But, if you find I must lose the money, I shall make no complaint, for I lent it, supposing this must, probably, be the result only[n] I then took a different view of Harro and his position from what I do now and supposed that by the sacrifice I shd be able to do an essential[n] service to a fellow man, such as I would sometimes have wished might be done to me.

As to the other little affairs I mentioned, they require no attention at present. I shall write to you again by and by. Will you, can you write to me and tell me something of yourself and our friends as well as of business? My address is Care Brown Shipley & Co Liverpool. I am very happy, almost perfectly well, learning a great deal, hoping to do good with it some time.

May all be the same with you and believe me always with affece regard yours

S. M. FULLER.

ALS (PSt). *Endorsed:* Margaret Fuller / London 30 Oct / 46.

here and returns tomorrow to the U.S.] here. ↑ and returns tomorrow to the U.S. ↓
result only] result ⟨though⟩ ↑ only ↓
an essential] an essenti⟨?⟩al

1. As she acknowledged in a letter to Marcus Spring in 1849, Fuller lent money to Harring for the publication of *Dolores (Letters of MF,* 5:296).
2. David J. Marrener and James L. Lockwood had a bookshop at 459 Broadway.

1105. To George Palmer Putnam

Paris.

28th Nov. 1836 [1846].ⁿ

To Mr Putnam,

Dear Sir,

Proposals have been made to me for translatingⁿ some fragments of my writings into the French journals, and I think that, at least, the sketch of Amern lite and some part of "Woman in the 19th Century" might be interesting here.[1] Will you have the kindness to send me five copies of the "Papers on lite & Art" and to purchase for me as many of "Woman" &c to send with them. I can give them away, much to my advantage and pleasure toⁿ the persons with whom I am making acquaintance. As I have already givenⁿ away the copies I brought with me, would you have the kindness to send the parcel as early as possible and in some safe way to my address here

Hotel Rougemont

No 2 rue de Rougemont

Boulevard Poissoniére

Please charge to my account whatever the expense may be of the books you buy and of sending theⁿ parcel. Perhaps you will have also the kindness to write a line, if there is any interesting news from America. We are enjoying a great deal here; it is truly the city of pleasures. Mademoiselle Rachel I have seen with the greatest delight.[2] I go whenever she acts and when I have seen the entire range of her parts intend to write a detailed critique which shall also comprehend comments on the high French tragedy. With compliments to Mrs Put-nam[3] very truly yours

S. M. FULLER.

ALS (NjP). Published in part in *Putnam's*, n.s. 4 (October 1869): 473; in George Haven Putnam, *A Memoir of George Palmer Putnam* (New York, 1912), pp. 398–99; and in *Letters of MF*, 4:252.

1846] *Fuller misdated the letter.*
translating] translati⟨o⟩ng
pleasure to] pleasure ⟨?⟩ ↑ to ↓
already given] already ⟨hea⟩ given
sending the] sending ↑ the ↓

1. "De la littérature américaine" appeared in *La Revue Indépendante* for 10 December 1846.

2. Rachel (Élisa Félix) was the most celebrated actress of her day. For Fuller's extended comments, see her letter to Caroline Sturgis (*Letters of MF*, 4:250–52).

3. In March 1841 Putnam married Victorine Haven (1824–91), daughter of Joseph Haven of Boston (*National Cyclopedia; New York Times*, 17 June 1891).

1106. To William Cullen Bryant

Rome
22d May 47

Dear Sir,

One of the editors of the *Contemporaneo*, which may be esteemed the organ of the present liberal movement in the Papal States, has consulted me as to an exchange with some American journals.[1] I told him I thought yours, with the Natl Intelligencer[2] and Tribune, would give a fair" representation such as they wish to see of the state of things in the U.S. and I thought that you" from your knowledge of foreign languages and foreign affairs would take pleasure in receiving their paper. Some numbers have, accordingly, been forwarded to you through Wiley and Putnam. If you are, as I hope, disposed to an exchange, will [you] forward the N[ew York] Evening Post to their agent in London, whose name" you will find on their paper.

Mr and Mrs Spring are well and desire their best regards With mine, also, to Mrs Bryant and your daughters[3] I am, dear Sir, yours with great respect

S. M. FULLER.

ALS (NN-M). *Addressed:* To / William C. Bryant, Esq / New York/ U. S. A. *Postmark:* New-York / Jul 7. *Endorsed:* S. M. Fuller / Miss ↑ S M ↓ Fullers Letter / May 1847.

William Cullen Bryant (1794–1878) was a preeminent poet and influential editor of the *New-York Evening Post*, for which he began work in 1826. Politically he was a Jacksonian Democrat who bitterly opposed both slavery and the annexation of Texas. In 1848 he broke with the Democrats to support the Free-Soil ticket. During the Civil War he was one of the New York radicals who pressed Lincoln to fight the war with more vigor (*DAB*).

a fair] ⟨an⟩a fair
thought that you] thought ↑ that you ↓
whose name] whose ⟨?⟩name

1. Luigi Masi was a founder and editor of *Il Contemporaneo*, a reformist Roman newspaper. Fuller made these same comments to a Mr. Page (*Letters of MF*, 5:62–63, where it is misdated as 1848).
2. The *National Intelligencer* was a Washington paper published by Joseph Gales, Jr., and William W. Seaton.
3. Bryant married Frances Fairchild (1797–1866), daughter of Zachariah and Hannah Pope Fairchild, in 1821 (*The Letters of William Cullen Bryant*, ed. William Cullen Bryant II and Thomas G. Voss [New York, 1975], 1:12). Their daughters were Frances (1822–93), who married Parke Godwin, and Julia Sands (1831–1907) (ibid.; *New York Times*, 24 June 1893 and 25 July 1907).

1107. To Marcus Spring

Rome. 1st Feby 1848

My dear Marcus,

Your letter by the steamer of 1st Jany gave me a great deal of satisfaction; it is pleasant indeed to think of you all settled again beneath the hospitable roof at Brooklyn and enjoying so much "dear comfort." You do not mention how you and Rebecca are, but I conclude from your cheerful tone, uncommonly well. Long and full as your letter was it was not half long enough and I hope very soon to receive another containing all the things you say you had to leave out and that Rebecca, too, will do her part. As to Eddie, let him bide his natural time. I would not have such a good friend urged to write to me, what he does not write I dare say he will tell me, if we ever meet again.

I do not take a big sheet of paper to begin an answer, because I am so unwell that writing is a great effort.[1] The first two months here when it was sunny and dry I had very good health and spirits. I thought myself quite recovered from the gastric troubles I had in Lombardy and Florence. But now in the rainy season these are worse than ever, with constant nervous headach, often of my worst kind. Nature has driven me round to the Greeley diet, at once I gave up meat wine, strong tea or coffee.[2] I live on a little rice cooked with milk and such vegetables as Rome supplies, but even this light food hurts me.

Under these influences I feel very depressed and so I will not say any thing about myself now, but only I am rejoiced we did not come to Italy last winter. I should have been too grieved to see Rome first in its present state, so gloomy and reeking with malignant vapors. And bad as the climate of Paris is, it is not so bad as this sultry damp, which no breeze ever drives away. Miss Shaw says it took[n] her 3 winters to learn to bear it; you were fortunate to come in the glorious spring. (apropos to Miss S. I shall send Rebecca's book so soon as I have oppory.)

Your account of your vision of Marquette quite cheered me. I hope I too may sometime be able to look back on this past Jany of Rome only as an ugly painful dream.

My public news you will read in my Tribune letters[n] (the suggestions you make about them are good, but I dont know when I shall feel equal to writing any thing full or[n] sustained. I wish the letters were better for the sake of my reputation, but I think them quite good enough for the rec[om]pense I receive, and, if not entertaining, they contain information which not every one could give. But drop any other hints that occur to you; perhaps should heaven grant me better days, I may make use of them.

I know Mr Stralt *did* send your box long since, but will go there and inquire by what ship and give him your message. They have a great regard for you; good old people; Mrs S. comes to see me every other Sunday eveg, with the English son an intelligent man, but all stiff and bristling with Anglicism. As there are a great many people here I dont mind it and beside[n] Mrs Story and Mrs Cropsey have rather taken a fancy to the old lady and help entertain her.[3] She always comes in her frightful hat, and at first all strangers think her Mrs *Trollope* and laugh when they find her only *Stralt*[?]![4]

Our friends often inquire about you. Mrs Cranch expects another little one in April or May; she seems quite courageous, forgetful of bye-gone woes. Her child is very handsome now.[5] Hicks has never got well after his fever; he looks very pale and says he cannot work.[6] Terry flourishes serenely as usual.[7] I have made a number of acquaintances, of famous ones, Gibson, and the Princess Belgiojoso[8]

[B]ut I pay very dear for a whistle when I go to parties. [I] am obliged to have both a carriage and servant which makes it a dollar each time. This is in [*illegible*] to American The friends are thoughtful and attend me. I have reason to be glad of all the "toggery" I got at Paris and Florence[n] I have needed it all here. Well good bye. Think sometimes in the peaceful hours of your friend

MARGARET

373

Thanks for the acct. I was indeed glad it turned out so well, especially as it encourages me a little about another fear. I had no servant after Domenico, when I need one I hire from Milani

ALS (CSt). *Addressed:* Marcus Spring Esq / New York / U. S. A. *Postmarked:* Boyd's City Express Post / Mar 2.

Miss Shaw says it took] Miss Shaw ↑ says it ↓ took⟨s⟩
Tribune letters] ↑ Tribune ↓ letters
full or] full ↑ or ↓
and beside] and ↑ beside ↓
Paris and Florence] Paris ↑ and Florence ↓

1. She was almost certainly pregnant at this time.
2. The Greeleys followed the Sylvester Graham diet, which excluded stimulants.
3. Emelyn Story and Maria Cooley Cropsey, who married the painter Jaspar Cropsey in 1847.
4. Frances Trollope outraged American sensibilities in her *Domestic Manners of the Americans* (London, 1832).
5. Fuller often saw Christopher Pearse and Elizabeth De Windt Cranch. Their daughter Leonora was born on 4 June of that year. The child Fuller mentions here is George William Cranch (1847–67), who was named after George William Curtis (Leonora Cranch Scott, *The Life and Letters of Christopher Pearse Cranch* [Boston, 1917], pp. 117, 258).
6. Thomas Hicks was an American painter living in Rome.
7. Luther Terry had settled in Italy in 1837 to pursue a career in painting.
8. John Gibson (1790–1866) was an English sculptor. Cristina Belgioioso was a scholar, nationalist, and the feminist center of a brilliant intellectual circle in France and Italy.

1108. To ?

[ca. 29 March 1848][n]

In all the descriptions of the Roman Carnival, the fact has been omitted of daily rain. I felt, indeed, ashamed to perceive it, when no one else seemed to, whilst the open windows caused me convulsive cough and headache. The carriages, with their cargoes of happy women dressed in their ball dresses and costumes, drove up and down, even in the pouring rain. The two handsome *contadine*, who serve me, took off their woollen gowns, and sat five hours at a time, in the street, in white cambric dresses, and straw hats turned up with roses. I never saw anything like the merry good-humor of these people. I should always be ashamed to complain of anything here. But I had always looked forward to the Roman Carnival as a time when I could play too; and it even surpassed my expectations, with its exuberant gayety and innocent frolic, but I was unable to take much part. The others threw flowers all day, and went to masked balls all night; but I went out only once, in a carriage, and was more exhausted with the storm of flowers and sweet looks than I could be by a storm of hail. I went to the German Artists' ball, where were some pretty costumes, and beautiful music; and to the Italian masked ball, where interest lies in intrigue.

I have scarcely gone to the galleries, damp and cold as tombs; or to the mouldy old splendor of churches, where, by the way, they are just wailing over the theft of St. Andrew's head, for the sake of the jewels. It is quite a new era for this population to plunder the churches; but they are suffering terribly, and Pio's municipality does, as yet, nothing.[1]

ELfr, from *Memoirs*, 2:234–35.

Although the language echoes Fuller's Tribune *dispatch of 29 March, this fragment may be part of the letter to Emerson of 14 March.*

1. Pius IX.

1109. To Horace Greeley

[May 1848][n]

[   ] well. And dont trouble to send any more, for there are too many obstacles. Even these sent from England some how miss me. If ever I get back to Paris, I shall be more in contact with the rest of the civilized world But dont fail to write me now and then.

[   ] and postage. Perhaps I shall write him and his mother a letter, if I feel like it when in the mountains.

Goodbye, get a good President, and collect from the eternal sea a little salt day by day to keep our big U.S. from putrefying[1] Ever in earnest friendliness and good hope

yours [   ]

[   ] reced you.—

—Baring and Brothers was just right. I have as yet no advices from them, but shall, no doub[t] before leavin[g] for the country I stay here days[n] yet

ALfr (CtT-W). Published in *American Renaissance Literary Report* (Hartford, 1991), pp. 171–72.

here days] here ⟨11⟩ days

1. General Zachary Taylor defeated Martin Van Buren and Lewis Cass, Sr., in the 1848 presidential campaign. He died ten days before Fuller, in July 1850.

1110. To Marcus Spring

Rome
9th March, 1849.

Dear Marcus,

I wish you had written by this last steamer. I confidently expected to hear. Am anxious to know how Rebecca fared and, beside, it would have put me in the humor for writing, which, unluckily, I seldom am, when, as now, I have a private popportunity.

I send you by some poppo a pair of screens, selected principally because Eddie liked so much this pin-pricked St Peters and now he can keep it constantly between him and the light, if he likes.

I am anxious you should send this letter direct to my friend Caroline.[1] I believe she is at Newburgh.[n] You can detect her address through Dr Hull, who is her physician.[2] She always forgets to send it to me. I send you also 1 no[n] of Roman Advertiser, that you may see how we go on at Rome. You will see our good friends, the Stralts, edit. They deserve credit for being quite alone among the English in showing fairness towards Italy and have lost many a subscriber in consequence. I say they; it is the young man that guides the team, but Ma and Pa help push a little. The paper presents a refreshing contrast to the nauseous adulations and catholic out catholicized sentimentalities with which Hemans[?] used to stuff it.

But what I write for now is to tell that last night Mazzini came to see me.[3] You will have heard how he was called to Italy, and received at Leghorn like a Prince as he is. Unhappily, in fact, the only one, the only great Italian. It is expected that if the Republic lasts he will be President. He has been made a Roman Citizen, and elected to the Assembly, the labels bearing[n] in giant letters *Giuseppe Mazzini Cittadino Romano*, are yet up all over Rome. He entered by night on foot to avoid demonstrations, no doubt, and enjoy the quiet of his own thoughts at so great a moment. The people went under his windows next night and called him out to speak, but I did not know about it. Last night, I heard a ring, a German artist who lives here opened, the people of the house being out, I heard somebody say my name, the voice struck upon me at once I rushed. He looks more divine than ever, after all his new strange sufferings. He asked after all of you, lamented that he had never written. I told him you knew how impossible it was for him in these times, that you held him dear and would[n] value his message of remembrance.

If he comes here again before I send this letter I shall get him to write his name for Rebecca, as she used to wish, but I felt last night, perhaps this is all he will be permitted to give me. He staid two hours and we talked through rapidly of every thing. He hopes to come often, but the crisis is tremendous and all will come on him, as, if any one can save Italy from her foes, inward and outward, it will be he. But it is very doubtful whether this be possible, the foes are too many, too strong, too subtle. Yet heaven helps sometimes. I only grieve I cannot aid him, freely would I give my life to aid him, only bargaining for a quick death! I dont like slow torture. I fear that is in reserve for him to survive defiant. True he can never be utterly defeated, but to see Italy bleeding prostrate once more will be very dreadful for him.

What would I not give that my other two brothers, Mr Emerson and William Channing could see him. All have in different ways the celestial fires, all have pure natures. They may have faults, but no base alloy. To me they form a triad. I know none other such.

Mickiewicz is a great poet, an inspired man, but he belongs to a different order of spirits from them.[4]

All this I write to you, Marcus, because you said when I was suffering to leave Mazzini, "you will meet him in heaven".

This I believe will be, despite all my faults. My other brothers will meet him, too.

17th Another steamer and no letter from you, do write Marcus, I feel disappointed. O if I could possibly have some good news some word to cheer me from any body on earth. You cant think how much I have had to suffer since we parted.

I have only seen Mazzini again in the Assembly; he has sent me tickets twice to hear him speak: it was a pure commanding voice, but when finished he looked very exhausted and melancholy. He looks as if the great battle he had fought the past year had been too much for his strength, and that he was only sustained now by the fire of his soul.

This little picture is for Jeanie; her mother can tell her the story. Ever affecy yrs

M<small>ARGARET</small>

I have not got the autograph. he is overpowered with affairs at this moment; if I ever get, I shall keep it for Rebecca.

ALS (CSt). Published in part in *Memoirs*, 2:262–63; Frothingham, *Memoir of William Henry Channing*, p. 181; Van Doren, 294–96; and *Letters of MF*, 5:201. *Endorsed:* This letter was not received for a year—and—when received & for a long while before Mrs Spring was very ill—

Newburgh] *Fuller later wrote across this comment*: have recd her address since writing this.

1 no] ⟨2 nos⟩ ↑ 1 no ↓
labels bearing] labels ⟨?⟩bearing
and would] and ↑ would ↓

1. Caroline Sturgis Tappan.
2. The New York City directory lists a Dr. R. M. Hull at 284 Spring Street.
3. Fuller first met Giuseppe Mazzini in London at Carlyle's home. She consistently praised him in her *Tribune* dispatches.
4. Adam Mickiewicz was a Polish poet and patriot whom Fuller had met in Paris. They corresponded afterward, and he became her son's godfather.

1111. To Christopher P. Cranch

[April? 1849][n]

Dear friends,

I have only a moment to acknowledge receipt of the order for the money.[1] Excuse my having troubled you. I felt a little anxious when I found Cropsey had remitted it to Florence, lest it should arrive there after you had gone and I have no way to get at it except the long one of writing to U. S.[2] All right now. I have only a moment to write; these for me are troubled days one hour I thought of going home with you, but the objections and losses seem too great. Please write as soon as you can of your safe arrival and how you find yourselves to your ever affece friend

MARGARET.

James Clarke has lost his dear little boy, Hermann.[3] Did you know the child Pearse?[n] Why must children die?

ALS (Buckminster Fuller Archives; courtesy, Buckminster Fuller Institute, 2040 Alameda Padre Serra, Suite 224, Santa Barbara, CA 93103). *Addressed:* C. P. Cranch Esq / ⟨11⟩ 18 Via Val Fondia / Firenze. *Postmark:* [   ] Apr 1849.

Christopher Pearse Cranch, an artist and writer, had been living in Italy but soon left for Paris and then New York. After his work was published in the *Dial*, he and Fuller became good friends.

Dated by the postmark.
Pearse?] Pear⟨?⟩se?

1. Though the postmark clearly says "Apr," the contents suggest that the letter was written shortly after the one Fuller sent the Cranches on 9 March. There Fuller says

that Cropsey was to leave Rome on 18 March and that he had sent money for her to Florence. She then asked Cranch to send it to her in Rome by James C. Hooker, her banker at Maquay, Packenham (*Letters of MF,* 5:204).

2. Jaspar Cropsey was an American landscape painter.

3. The Clarkes' eight-year old son died on 15 February.

Unrecovered Letters

Letters that Fuller is known to have written but that are not known to survive are listed here chronologically and then, if necessary, alphabetically by recipient. The place where the letter is mentioned follows the recipient in parentheses.

1819

16 January, to Ellen Kilshaw (Margarett C. Fuller to Timothy Fuller, 17 January 1819. MH: fMS Am 1086).

6 February, to Margarett C. Fuller (Margarett C. Fuller to Timothy Fuller, 8 February 1819. MH: fMS Am 1086).

18? February, to Timothy Fuller (Margarett C. Fuller to Timothy Fuller, 19 February 1819. MH: fMS Am 1086).

28 December, to Timothy Fuller (*Letters of MF*, 1:93). Fuller may refer to hers of 25 December (*Letters of MF*, 1:90–91).

1820

2 February, to Timothy Fuller (*Letters of MF*, 1:95). In Latin.

11 October, to Ellen Kilshaw (Ellen Kilshaw to Margaret Fuller, 15 November 1820. MH: fMS Am 1086).

9 November, to Ellen Kilshaw (Margarett C. Fuller to Timothy Fuller, 9 November 1820. MH: fMS Am 1086).

December, to Sarah W. Fuller (Margarett C. Fuller to Timothy Fuller, 19 December 1820. MH: fMS Am 1086).

1821

3 February, to Ellen Kilshaw (Margarett C. Fuller to Timothy Fuller, 4 February 1821. MH: fMS Am 1086).

31 December, to Timothy Fuller (Timothy Fuller to Margaret Fuller, 22 January 1822. MH: fMS Am 1086).

1822

16 January, to Timothy Fuller (Timothy Fuller to Margaret Fuller, 22 January 1822. MH: fMS Am 1086).

8 December, to Timothy Fuller (Timothy Fuller to Margaret Fuller, 15 December 1822. MH: fMS Am 1086).

1823

2 February, to Ellen Kilshaw (*Letters of MF*, 1:129).

October, to Ellen Kilshaw (Timothy Fuller to Margaret Fuller, 7 July 1824. MH: fMS Am 1086).

1824

1 February, to Timothy Fuller (Timothy Fuller to Margaret Fuller, 12 February 1824. MH: fMS Am 1086).

14 February, to Timothy Fuller (Margarett C. Fuller to Timothy Fuller, 2 March 1824. MH: fMS Am 1086).

17 February, to Amelia Greenwood (Paul Richards Sale Catalogue, 1970).

28 March, to Timothy Fuller (Timothy Fuller to Margaret Fuller, 3 April 1824. MH: fMS Am 1086).

ca. 12 May, to Timothy Fuller (Timothy Fuller to Margaret Fuller, 15 May 1824. MH: fMS Am 1086).

31 May, to Timothy Fuller (Timothy Fuller to Margaret Fuller, 1 June 1824. MH: fMS Am 1086).

4 June 1824, to Timothy Fuller (Timothy Fuller to Margaret Fuller, 7 June 1824. MH: fMS Am 1086).

6 June, to Margarett C. and Timothy Fuller (Timothy Fuller to Margaret Fuller, 9 June 1824. MH: fMS Am 1086).

6 June, to Susan Williams (Timothy Fuller to Margarett C. Fuller, 9 June 1824. MH: fMS Am 1086).

11 June, to Timothy Fuller (Timothy Fuller to Margaret Fuller, 12 June 1824. MH: fMS Am 1086).

25 June, to Timothy Fuller (Timothy Fuller to Margaret Fuller, 26 June 1824. MH: fMS Am 1086).

2 July, to Timothy Fuller (Timothy Fuller to Margaret Fuller, 7 July 1824. MH: fMS Am 1086).

8 July, to Timothy Fuller (Timothy Fuller to Margaret Fuller, 17 July 1824. MH: fMS Am 1086).

21 July, to Timothy Fuller (Timothy Fuller to Margaret Fuller, 23 July 1824. MH: fMS Am 1086).

2 August, to Timothy Fuller (Timothy Fuller to Margaret Fuller, 4 August 1824. MH: fMS Am 1086).

13? August, to Margarett C. Fuller (Margarett C. Fuller to Margaret Fuller, 20? August? 1824? MH: fMS Am 1086).

11? September, to Margarett C. Fuller (Margarett C. Fuller to Margaret Fuller, 13 September 1824. MH: fMS Am 1086).

ca. 13 September, to Timothy Fuller (Timothy Fuller to Margaret Fuller, 15 September 1824. MH: fMS Am 1086).

19 September, to Timothy Fuller (Timothy Fuller to Margaret Fuller, 26 September 1824. MH: fMS Am 1086).

ca. 30 September, to Timothy Fuller (Timothy Fuller to Margaret Fuller, 2 October 1824. MH: fMS Am 1086).

13 October, to Timothy Fuller (Timothy Fuller to Margaret Fuller, 16 October 1824. MH: fMS Am 1086).

ca. 28 October, to Timothy Fuller (Timothy Fuller to Margaret Fuller, 30 October 1824. MH: fMS Am 1086).

ca. 28 October, to Miss Prescott (Timothy Fuller to Margaret Fuller, 30 October 1824. MH: fMS Am 1086).

ca. 28 October, to Mr. Trowbridge (Timothy Fuller to Margaret Fuller, 30 October 1824. MH: fMS Am 1086).

1 November, to Timothy Fuller (Timothy Fuller to Margaret Fuller, 4 November 1824. MH: fMS Am 1086).

6 November, to Timothy and Margarett C. Fuller (Margarett C. Fuller to Margaret Fuller, 7 November, 1824. MH: fMS Am 1086).

December?, to Margarett C. Fuller (Margarett C. Fuller to Timothy Fuller, 30 December 1824. MH: fMS Am 1086).

December?, to Margarett C. Fuller (Margarett C. Fuller to Timothy Fuller, 30 December 1824. MH: fMS Am 1086).

1? December, to Margarett C. Fuller (Margarett C. Fuller to Margaret Fuller, 21 December 1824. MH: fMS Am 1086).

ca. 20 December, to Ellen Kilshaw (Timothy Fuller to Ellen Kilshaw, 27 December 1824. MH: fMS Am 1086).

27? December, to Margarett C. Fuller (Margarett C. Fuller to Timothy Fuller, 30 December 1824). MH: fMS Am 1086).

1825

ca. 5? January, to Margarett C. Fuller (Margarett C. Fuller to Timothy Fuller, 9 January 1825. MH: fMS Am 1086).

ca. 6? January, to Margarett C. Fuller (Margarett C. Fuller to Timothy Fuller, 9 January 1825. MH: fMS Am 1086).

ca. 10 January, to Elisha Fuller (Margarett C. Fuller to Margaret Fuller, 21 January 1825. MH: fMS Am 1086).

16 January, to Timothy Fuller (Timothy Fuller to Margaret Fuller, 27 January 1825. MH: fMS Am 1086).

ca. 19 January, to Margarett C. Fuller (Margarett C. Fuller to Margaret Fuller, 21 January 1825. MH: fMS Am 1086).

ca. 23 January, to Harriet H. Peck (Margarett C. Fuller to Margaret Fuller, 21 January, 1825. MH: fMS Am 1086).

5? February, to Margarett C. Fuller (Margarett C. Fuller to Timothy Fuller, 8 February 1825. MH: fMS Am 1086).

8 February, to Margarett C. Fuller (Margarett C. Fuller to Timothy Fuller, 15 February 1825. MH: fMS Am 1086).

23 February, to Margarett C. Fuller (Margarett C. Fuller to Timothy Fuller, 26 February 1825. MH: fMS Am 1086).

ca. 1 March, to Harriet H. Peck (Margarett C. Fuller to Margaret Fuller, 6 March 1825. MH: fMS Am 1086).

1827

Fall, to Lydia Maria Francis Child (Child to Margaret Fuller [1827]. CtY).

1829

13 November, to George T. Davis? (Higginson list of mss. MB: Ms. Am. 1450 [18]).

1830

ca. March, to Louisa [Hickman] (*Letters of JFC*, p. 12).

25? October, to Rebecca Hull Clarke (*Letters of JFC*, p. 22).

1831

ca. October, to James F. Clarke (*Letters of JFC*, p. 31).

1832

ca. August, to James F. Clarke (*Letters of MF*, 6:188).

1834

Winter?, to Sarah A. Clarke (Clarke, "Letters of a Sister").
7 February, to Anna Barker (*Letters of MF*, 6:239).
7 February, to Elizabeth Randall (*Letters of MF*, 6:239).
Early? April, to Sarah A. Clarke (Clarke, "Letters of a Sister").
ca. October, to Harriet Russell (*Letters of MF*, 6:245).
6? December, to Sarah A. Clarke (Clarke, "Letters of a Sister").

1835

January, to Sarah A. Clarke (Clarke, "Letters of a Sister").
ca. August, to Ellen K. Fuller (*Letters of MF*, 1:232).
ca. August, to Timothy and Margarett C. Fuller (*Letters of MF*, 1:232).
27? September, to James F. Clarke (*Letters of JFC*, p. 104).
6? November, to ? (*Letters of MF*, 1:238).
ca. December, to Helen Davis (*Letters of MF*, 6:273).
19? December, to Helen Davis (Davis to James F. Clarke, 20 December 1835. MH: fMS Am 1569 [923]).

1836

ca. April?, to Margarett C. Fuller (*Letters of MF*, 1:250).
May, to James F. Clarke (Clarke ms. journal. March 1836–February 10. MHi). May be letter 129.
ca. 18 September, to Ralph Waldo Emerson (Rusk, *Letters of RWE*, 2:36).

1837

ca. 21 March, to Sarah A. Clarke (*Letters of MF*, 6:290).
25 March, to James F. Clarke (Clarke journal, 1837–39. MHi).
24? April, to Ralph Waldo Emerson (Rusk, *Letters of RWE*, 2:71).
ca. 17? May, to Ralph Waldo Emerson (Rusk, *Letters of RWE*, 2:76).
July?, to Elizabeth Peabody (*Letters of MF*, 1:292).
Autumn?, to Anna Jameson (*Letters of MF*, 1:317).
ca. 15 October, to James F. Clarke (Clarke ms. journal, March 1836–February 10 1839. MHi).

ca. 15 October, to Ralph Waldo Emerson (Rusk, *Letters of RWE*, 2:98).

ca. November?, to Thesta Dana (*Letters of MF*, 1:316).

ca. 30 November, to Ralph Waldo Emerson (Rusk, *Letters of RWE*, 2:104).

1838

ca. February to James F. Clarke (*Letters of JFC*, p. 128).

ca. 20 May, to Ralph Waldo Emerson (Rusk, *Letters of RWE*, 2:134).

ca. 15 July?, to James F. Clarke (*Letters of JFC*, p. 133).

ca. 13 September, to Rhoda M. Newcomb (Rhoda M. Newcomb to Charles K. Newcomb, 14 September, RPB).

17 September, to Ralph Waldo Emerson (Rusk, *Letters of RWE*, 2:163).

ca. 1 October, to Ralph Waldo Emerson (Rusk, *Letters of RWE*, 2:167).

ca. 1 November, to James F. Clarke (Clarke journal, May 10 1836. MHi).

1839

ca. January?, to Ralph Waldo Emerson (Rusk, *Letters of RWE*, 2:180).

8 March, to Christopher P. Cranch (Cranch Papers, list of mss. MHi). May be 1840.

ca. 15 April, to Ralph Waldo Emerson (Rusk, *Letters of RWE*, 2:197).

ca. 20? July?, to Ralph Waldo Emerson (Rusk, *Letters of RWE*, 2:211).

4 August, to Margarett C. Fuller (Hudspeth, "Margaret Fuller's 1839 Journal," p. 460).

6 August, to ? (Hudspeth, "Margaret Fuller's 1839 Journal," p. 462).

6 August, to ? (Hudspeth, "Margaret Fuller's 1839 Journal," p. 462).

10? August, to Ralph Waldo Emerson (Rusk, *Letters of RWE*, 2:216).

September?, to Sarah A. Clarke (Clarke, "Letters of a Sister").

ca. 1 September, to Ralph Waldo Emerson (Rusk, *Letters of RWE*, 2:221).

ca. 29 September, to Ralph Waldo Emerson (Rusk, *Letters of RWE*, 2:226).

ca. 14 October, to Ralph Waldo Emerson (Rusk, *Letters of RWE*, 2:228). May be letter 234.

14? October, to A. Bronson Alcott (Margaret Fuller MsC journal. MH: 58m-308 [13]).

ca. 21 December, to Ralph Waldo Emerson (Rusk, *Letters of RWE*, 2:245).

1840

ca. 16 January, to James F. Clarke (Clarke journal, 1839. MHi).

1? February, to William H. Channing (William H. Channing to Julia A. Channing, 5 February. MH: bMS Am 1755 [158]).

ca. 13 March, to Ralph Waldo Emerson (Rusk, *Letters of RWE*, 2:261).

ca. 27 March, to Ralph Waldo Emerson (Rusk, *Letters of RWE*, 2:270).

ca. 5 April, to Ralph Waldo Emerson (Rusk, *Letters of RWE*, 2:275).

ca. 20 April, to Ralph Waldo Emerson (Rusk, *Letters of RWE*, 2:291).

ca. Summer, to Sarah A. Clarke (Clarke to Fuller, [15 August 1840]. MH: fMS Am 1086).

ca. Summer, to Sarah A. Clarke (Clarke to Fuller, [15 August 1840]. MH: fMS Am 1086).

ca. 25 July, to Ralph Waldo Emerson (Rusk, *Letters of RWE*, 2:318).

ca. 1 August, to Rhoda M. Newcomb (RPB).

8 August, to Rhoda M. Newcomb (Rhoda M. Newcomb to Charles K. Newcomb, 9 August 1840. RPB).

ca. 14 August, to Ralph Waldo Emerson (Rusk, *Letters of RWE*, 2:324).

26 August, to Ralph Waldo Emerson (Rusk, *Letters of RWE*, 2:327).

ca. 4 September, to Ralph Waldo Emerson (Rusk, *Letters of RWE*, 2:329).

ca. 12? September, to Ralph Waldo Emerson (Rusk, *Letters of RWE*, 2:332).

ca. 23 September, to Ralph Waldo Emerson (Rusk, *Letters of RWE*, 2:336).

22? October, to Ralph Waldo Emerson (Rusk, *Letters of RWE*, 2:352; *Letters of MF*, 2:167).

ca. 26 October, to Samuel G. and Anna B. Ward (*Letters of MF*, 2:175).

2 November, to Margarett C. Fuller (Margarett C. Fuller to Margaret Fuller, 22 November 1840. MH: fMS Am 1086).

22 November, to Margarett C. Fuller (Margarett C. Fuller to Margaret Fuller, 6 December 1840. MH: fMS Am 1086).

ca. 30 November, to Margarett C. Fuller (Margarett C. Fuller to Margaret Fuller, 29 and 30 December. MH: fMS Am 1086).

December?, to George Keats (Madeleine B. Stern, "Four Letters from George Keats," *PMLA* 56 [1941]: 213).

1841

January?, to Margarett C. Fuller (Margarett C. Fuller to Margaret Fuller, 20 January 1841. MH: fMS Am 1086).

1? January, to Margarett C. Fuller (Margarett C. Fuller to Margaret Fuller, 20 January 1841. MH: fMS Am 1086).

ca. 17 January, to Ralph Waldo Emerson (Rusk, *Letters of RWE*, 2:377).

ca. 10 February, to Margarett C. Fuller (Margarett C. Fuller to Margaret Fuller, 26 February 1841. MH: fMS Am 1086).

24 February, to Ralph Waldo Emerson (Rusk, *Letters of RWE*, 2:383).

5 April, to Margarett C. Fuller? (Margarett C. Fuller to Margaret Fuller, 20 April 1841. MH: fMS Am 1086).

8 April, to Eugene Fuller? (Margarett C. Fuller to Margaret Fuller, 20 April 1841. MH: fMS Am 1086).

ca. 20 April, to Ralph Waldo Emerson (Rusk, *Letters of RWE*, 2:394).

May?, to Margarett C. Fuller (Margarett C. Fuller to Margaret Fuller, 6 June 1841. MH: fMS Am 1086).

ca. June, to Sarah Whitman (Rhoda M. Newcomb to Charles K. Newcomb, 13 June. RPB)

July?, to Harriet Martineau (Martineau to Fuller, 9 August 1841. MH: fMS Am 1086).

ca. 11 July, to Ralph Waldo Emerson (Rusk, *Letters of RWE*, 2:422).

ca. 29 July, to Ralph Waldo Emerson (Rusk, *Letters of RWE*, 2:437).

ca. 7 August, to Richard F. Fuller (Richard F. Fuller to Margaret Fuller, 13 August 1841. MH: fMS Am 1086).

ca. 14 August, to Ralph Waldo Emerson (Rusk, *Letters of RWE*, 2:441).

late August?, to Ellen K. Fuller (Ellery Channing to Fuller, 17 September [1841]. MH: fMS Am 1086).

13 September, to ? (Higginson list of mss. MB: Ms. Am. 1450 [18]).

ca. 20 October, to Arthur B. Fuller (Arthur Fuller to Richard F. Fuller, 26 October 1841. MH: fMS Am 1086 [13:7]).

ca. 1? November?, to Ralph Waldo Emerson (*Letters of MF*, 2:251).

ca. 13 December, to Arthur B. Fuller (Margarett C. Fuller to Margaret Fuller, 16 December, 1841. MH: fMS Am 1086).

1842

January?, to Ellery Channing (Channing to Fuller, 26 February 1842. MH: fMS Am 1086).

ca. 28 January, to Ralph Waldo Emerson (Rusk, *Letters of RWE*, 3:9).

ca. late February?, to Ellery Channing (Channing to Fuller, 20 March 1842. MH: fMS Am 1086).

April?, to Ellery Channing (Channing to Fuller, 7 May 1842. MH: fMS Am 1086 [9:128]).

April?, to Eugene Fuller (Eugene Fuller to Margaret Fuller, 8 May 1842. MH: fMS Am 1086).

ca. 1 May, to Margarett C. Fuller (Margarett C. Fuller to Margaret Fuller, 15 May 1842. MH: fMS Am 1086).

12? May, to Eliza Farrar (*Letters of MF*, 3:64).

23? May, to Sarah A. Clarke (Clarke to Fuller, 25 May 1842. MH: fMS Am 1086).

ca. 1? June, to Ralph Waldo Emerson (Rusk, *Letters of RWE*, 3:62).

ca. 7? June, to Ralph Waldo Emerson (Rusk, *Letters of RWE*, 3:62).

ca. 7 July, to Frances H. Fuller (Margarett C. Fuller to Margaret Fuller, 13 July 1842. MH: fMS Am 1086).

ca. 7 July to Margarett C. Fuller (Margarett C. Fuller to Margaret Fuller, 13 July 1842. MH: fMS Am 1086).

ca. 29 December, to Ralph Waldo Emerson (Rusk, *Letters of RWE*, 3:107).

1843

ca. January?, to Ralph Waldo Emerson (Rusk, *Letters of RWE*, 3:137).

ca. 17 January, to Ralph Waldo Emerson (Rusk, *Letters of RWE*, 3:128). *May be the preceding unlocated letter.*

ca. 19 February, to Ralph Waldo Emerson (Rusk, *Letters of RWE*, 3:148).

13 April, to ? (C. F. Libbie catalogue, 10 January 1912).

ca. July, to Eliza Farrar (Farrar to Fuller, 25 July 1843. MH: fMS Am 1086).

ca. July, to Margarett C. Fuller (Eliza Farrar to Fuller, 25 July 1843. MH: fMS Am 1086).

July, to Ellery Channing (Channing to Richard F. Fuller, 2 August 1843. MH: fMS Am 1086 [9:130]).

July, to Ralph Waldo Emerson (Rusk, *Letters of RWE*, 3:193).

July, to Mr. Wilson (William Clarke to Fuller, 2 August 1843. MH: fMS Am 1086).

9 July, to Arthur B. Fuller (*Letters of MF*, 6:345).

28 July to William Clarke (Clarke to Fuller, 2 August 1843. MH: fMS Am 1086).

August?, to William Clarke (Clarke to Fuller, 20 September. MH: fMS Am 1086).

September?, to Sarah A. Clarke (Clarke to Fuller, 14 September 1843. MH: fMS Am 1086).

ca. October, to Arthur B. Fuller (Arthur Fuller to Richard F. Fuller, 1 November 1843. MH: fMS Am 1086 [13:17]).

ca. November, to William Clarke (Arthur B. Fuller to Richard F. Fuller. MH: fMS Am 1086 [13:18]).

ca. 1 November?, to Ralph Waldo Emerson (Rusk, *Letters of RWE*, 3:220).

ca. 1 November, to Eugene Fuller (Eugene Fuller to Margarett C. Fuller, 11 December 1843. MH: fMS Am 1086).

8 November, to Ralph Waldo Emerson (Higginson list of mss. MB: Ms. Am. 1450 [18]).

27 and 28 November, to Eugene Fuller (Eugene Fuller to Margarett C. Fuller, 11 December 1843. MH: fMS Am 1086).

ca. December?, to Peter Crane, Jr. (*Letters of MF*, 3:166).

1844

13 April to Horace Greely (Greeley to Fuller, 13 April 1844. MH: fMS Am 1086).

ca. late April, to Eugene Fuller (Eugene Fuller to Margarett C. Fuller, 5 May. MH: fMS Am 1086).

15 May, to Eugene Fuller (Margaret Fuller MsC diary, 15 May 1844. MB: Ms. Am. 1450 [99]).

June?, to Lloyd Fuller (Lloyd Fuller to Margaret Fuller, 16 June [1844]. MH: fMS Am 1086).

ca. 14 June, to Margarett C. Fuller (Margarett C. Fuller to Margaret Fuller, 15 June 1844. MH: fMS Am 1086).

ca. 26 June?, to Margarett C. Fuller (Margarett C. Fuller to Margaret Fuller, [28 June 1844?]. MH: fMS Am 1086).

ca. 4 July, to Jane Tuckerman King (King to Fuller, 6 July [1844]. MH: fMS Am 1086).

4 July, to Caroline Sturgis (Berg-Perry, " 'Impulses of Human Nature,' " p. 70).

ca. 12 July, to Lloyd Fuller (Lloyd Fuller to Margaret Fuller, 14 July 1844. MH: fMS Am 1086).

16 July, to Samuel G. Ward (Berg-Perry, " 'Impulses of Human Nature,' " p. 85).

31 July, to Sophia Hawthorne (Berg-Perry, " 'Impulses of Human Nature,' " p. 107).

ca. August, to Lydia Maria Francis Child (Child to Fuller, 23 August 1844. MH: fMS Am 1086).

8 August, to ? (Berg-Perry, " 'Impulses of Human Nature,' " p. 114).

9 August, to Horace Greeley (Berg-Perry, " 'Impulses of Human Nature,' " p. 116).

1845

ca. 21 February, to Lloyd Fuller (Lloyd Fuller to Margaret Fuller, 25 February 1845. MH: fMS Am 1086).

22 July, to George Bancroft (*Letters of MF*, 4:133).

1 August, to James Nathan (*Letters of MF*, 4:156).

ca. October, to Samuel Gridley Howe (*Letters of MF*, 4:168).

ca. November?, to Caroline Sturgis (Sturgis to Fuller, 10 December 1845. MH: fMS Am 1086).

ca. 16 November, to Ellen Sturgis Hooper (*Letters of MF*, 6:362).

1846

ca. 1 January, to Lydia Maria Francis Child (Child to Fuller, [1846]. MH: fMS Am 1086).

ca. 1 January to Caroline Sturgis (Sturgis to Fuller, [February? 1846]. MH: fMS Am 1086).

ca. mid-January, to Arthur B. Fuller (Arthur B. Fuller to Richard F. Fuller, 4 February 1846. MH: fMS Am 1086 [13:24]).

4 May, to Richard F. Fuller (Richard F. Fuller to Margaret Fuller, 7 May 1846. MH: fMS Am 1086).

ca. 1 June, to Harriet Martineau (*Letters of MF*, 6:365).

14? July, to Edward Everett (*Letters of MF*, 4:217).

ca. Autumn?, to Margaret and Mary Gillies (*Emerson-Carlyle Correspondence*, p. 479).

October, to Jane Carlyle (Detti, p. 347).

25 October, to James Nathan (Nathan to Fuller, 6 November 1846. MH: fMS Am 1086).

November, to Giuseppe Mazzini (Detti, p. 264).

ca. 3 November, to Eliza Farra (*Letters of MF*, 4:237).

ca. 3 November, to Arthur B. Fuller (*Letters of MF*, 4:237).

ca. 3 November, to Margarett C. Fuller (*Letters of MF*, 4:237).

11 November, to James Nathan (Nathan to Fuller, 27 November 1846. MH: fMS Am 1086).

December?, to Giuseppe Mazzini (Detti, p. 266).

1847

ca. 1847, to Margarett C. Fuller (*Emerson-Carlyle Correspondence*, p. 475).

ca. January?, to Giuseppe Mazzini (Detti, p. 269).

26 January, to Horace Greeley (Greeley to Fuller, 8 February 1847. MH: fMS Am 1086).

ca. March?, to Adam Mickiewicz (Wellisz, p. 16; Detti, p. 312).

ca. March, to Caroline Sturgis (*Letters of MF*, 4:290).

ca. 15 March, to Elizabeth Hoar (*Letters of MF*, 4:293).

ca. April, to Adam Mickiewicz (Wellisz, p. 19; Detti, p. 309).

ca. 1 April?, to Giuseppe Mazzini (*Mazzini's Letters to an English Family*, ed. E. F. Richards [London, 1920], p. 53).

ca. May, to Horace Greeley (Greeley to Fuller, 27 July 1847. MH: fMS Am 1086).

Summer, to Horace Greeley (Greeley to Fuller, 27 September 1847. MH: fMS Am 1086).

ca. 20? June?, to Elizabeth Hoar (Rusk, *Letters of RWE,* 3:412).

22 June, to Benedetta Mazzini (Detti, p. 348).

ca. late June, to Arthur B. Fuller (*Letters of MF,* 4:277).

ca. late June?, to Benedetta Mazzini (Detti, p. 348).

July?, to Adam Mickiewicz (Wellisz, p. 22; Detti, p. 310).

3 July, to Benedetta Mazzini (Mazzini to Fuller, 5? July 1847. MH: fMS Am 1086 [11:94]).

August?, to Adam Mickiewicz (Wellisz, p. 24; Detti, p. 313).

September?, to Costanza Arconati Visconti (Detti, p. 286).

September?, to Margarett C. Fuller (Margarett C. Fuller to Margaret Fuller, 8 October 1847. MH: fMS Am 1086).

ca. 6? September, to Richard F. Fuller (*Letters of MF,* 4:295).

ca. 13? September, to Richard F. Fuller? (*Letters of MF,* 4:295).

ca. October, to Harriet Martineau (Martineau to Fuller, 25 October [1847]. MH: fMS Am 1086).

October?, to Adam Mickiewicz (Wellisz, p. 27; Detti, p. 314).

21 October, to ? (Higginson list of mss. MB: Ms. Am. 1450 [18]).

ca. November?, to Thomas Carlyle (*Emerson-Carlyle Correspondence,* p. 434).

ca. November?, to Ralph Waldo Emerson (*Emerson-Carlyle Correspondence,* p. 434).

ca. November, to Giuseppe Mazzini (*Emerson-Carlyle Correspondence,* p. 434).

November?, to Jane Wilhelmina Stirling (Stirling to Fuller, 6 December 1847. MH: fMS Am 1086).

November?, to Costanza Arconati Visconti (Detti, p. 288).

November?, to Costanza Arconati Visconti (Detti, p. 291).

December?, to Giuseppe Mazzini (Detti, p. 270).

ca. December, to Benedetta Mazzini (Mazzini to Fuller, December 1847. MH: fMS Am 1086 [11:101]).

17 December, to Horace Greeley (Greeley to Fuller, 27 January 1848. MH: fMS Am 1086).

17? December?, to Jonathan Phillips (*"These Sad but Glorious Days,"* ed. Larry J. Reynolds and Susan Belasco Smith [New Haven, 1991], p. 177).

1848

1848?, to Rhoda M. Newcomb (Charles K. Newcomb to Fuller, 15 May 1848. MH: fMS Am 1086).

ca. January?, to the American Consul at Civita Vecchia (*Letters of MF,* 5:70).

8 January, to Costanza Arconati Visconti (Detti, p. 292).

9 February, to Horace Greeley (Greeley to Fuller, 4 April 1848. MH: fMS Am 1086).

ca. 25 February, to Elizabeth B. Browning (Detti, p. 350).

25 February, to Horace Greeley (Greeley to Fuller, 4 April 1848. MH: fMS Am 1086).

ca. March, to Giuseppe Mazzini (Rusk, *Letters of RWE,* 4:63).

8? March, to Cristina di Belgioioso (*Letters of MF,* 5:54).

27 March, to Richard F. Fuller (Richard F. Fuller to Margaret Fuller, 2 May 1848. MH: fMS Am 1086).

Spring?, to Sarah A. Clarke (Clarke to Fuller, 13 June [1848]. MH: fMS Am 1086).

April, to Margarett C. Fuller (Margarett C. Fuller to Margaret Fuller, 3 October 1848. MH: fMS Am 1086).

April?, to Adam Mickiewicz (Wellisz, p. 33; Detti, p. 315).

ca. late April?, to Adam Mickiewicz (Wellisz, p. 33; Detti, p. 315).

ca. 25? May, to Baring & Brothers (*Letters of MF,* 5:82).

ca. June, to Caroline M. Kirkland (William S. Osborne, *Caroline M. Kirkland* [New York, 1972], p. 92).

Summer, to Arthur B. Fuller (*Letters of MF,* 5:186).

Summer, to Eugene Fuller (*Letters of MF,* 5:186).

Summer, to Lloyd Fuller (*Letters of MF,* 5:186).

13 July, to ? (*Letters of MF,* 5:88).

September?, to Horace Greeley (Greeley to Fuller, 29 November 1848. MH: fMS Am 1086).

December?, to Richard F. Fuller (Richard F. Fuller to Margaret Fuller, 9 February 1849. MH: fMS Am 1086).

7 December, to Caroline Sturgis (*Letters of MF,* 5:160, 209).

1849

January?, to Costanza Arconati Visconti (Detti, p. 300).

16 January, to Eliza Farrar (Farrar to Fuller, 20 March 1849. MH: fMS Am 1086).

25? January, to Sarah Fisher Clampitt Ames (*Letters of MF,* 5:181).

27? January, to Costanza Arconati Visconti (*Letters of MF,* 5:189).

May, to Costanza Arconati Visconti (Detti, p. 301).

ca. May, to Sarah A. Clarke (Clarke to Fuller, 29 July 1849. MH: fMS Am 1086).

22? May, to Eliza Farrar (*Letters of MF*, 5:231).

June?, to Giuseppe Mazzini (Detti, pp. 277–78).

Summer?, to Anna B. Ward (*Letters of MF*, 5:273).

July, to Thomas Carlyle (*Emerson-Carlyle Correspondence*, p. 456).

August, to Adam Mickiewicz (Wellisz, p. 37; Detti, p. 316).

ca. 1 October, to Costanza Arconati Visconti (Detti, p. 302).

Fall, to Richard F. Fuller (Richard F. Fuller to Margaret Fuller, 4 December 1849. MH: fMS Am 1086).

ca. November?, to Margarett C. Fuller (*Letters of MF*, 6:58)

ca. December?, to Sarah A. Clarke (Clarke to Fuller, 5 March 1850. MH: fMS Am 1086).

ca. December, to Arthur B. Fuller (Arthur B. Fuller to Eugene Fuller, 8 March 1850. MH: fMS Am 1086 [13:143]).

1850

ca. March, to Ralph Waldo Emerson (Rusk, *Letters of RWE*, 4:198).

16? April, to Mary Clarke Mohl (*Letters of MF*, 6:78).

ca. 3 June, to Elizabeth Barrett Browning (Moncure Daniel Conway, *Autobiography, Memories and Experiences* [Boston, 1904], 2:25).

UNDATED

To Mary Channing (Channing to Fuller, 18 July, n.y. MH: fMS Am 1086).

To Sarah A. Clarke (Clarke to Fuller, n.d. MH: fMS Am 1086).

To Sarah A. Clarke (Clarke to Fuller, n.d. MH: fMS Am 1086).

To Abby Adeline Manning (*Letters of Ellen Tucker Emerson*, ed. Edith E. W. Gregg [Kent, Ohio, 1982], 1:37).

ERRATA

The following corrections and additions to the previously published volumes are noted. Volume and page numbers, separated by a colon, are followed by a period and line number. The key to the printed version follows the line number. The correction or addition follows the square bracket.

1:51.8 trip] ship

1:96.36] Published in part in Nicholas, "Thomas Fuller," p. 26.

1:104.23] Ibid.

1:119.32] Ibid., pp. 26–27

1:124.28] Her reference may be to Paley's *Views of the Evidences of Christianity* (London, 1794).

1:130.38 Mr Emerson's school] Probably not William Emerson's school but that of George Barrell Emerson, who had established his school that year (*DAB*).

1:134.1] Published in part in Nichols, "Thomas Fuller," p. 27.

1:154.17 George Gordon, Lord Byron] George Gordon Byron, sixth Baron Byron

1:164.36 T. Hook] Theodore Edward Hook (1788–1841), a writer of satiric novels and editor of *John Bull,* a caustic comic journal (*DNB*).

1:170.27 Almia] Almira

1:178.7 *letzer*] *letzter*

1:182.39 German] Prussian

1:186.18 1? July] 2? July

1:230.18 Thornton Davis] George Davis's brother, John Thornton Kirkland Davis, who later changed his name to Wendell Thornton Davis.

1:235.45 Miss Jeffrey's note] Louisa Jeffry, niece of Francis Jeffry, a founder of the *Edinburgh Review* and England's lord advocate. She was Martineau's traveling companion (Vera Wheatley, *The Life and Work of Harriet Martineau* [London, 1957], p. 148).

1:236.33 $18,098.50] $27,198.50 [Value of land added to other assets.]

1:241.11] Probably [ca. May 1833] (Capper, *Margaret Fuller*, p. 378n11).

1:242.6] Published in part in Higginson, *MFO,* pp. 41–42, where it is described as a diary.

1:244.14] Published in part in Higginson, *MFO,* p. 54.

1:256.32] Published in part in Sanborn and Harris, *Alcott,* 1:244–45.

1:269.38 pp. 86–87,] pp. 68–69, 86–87,

1:274.14 Robert Hooper] Robert William Hooper, who was not the duelist.

1:275.15] MsCfr (MH: 59m-308 [10], p. 383. Published in part in Sanborn and Harris, *Alcott,* 1:245–46, and Larry A. Carlson, "Bronson Alcott's 'Journal for 1837' (Part Two)," in *Studies in the American Renaissance, 1982,* ed. Joel Myerson (Boston, 1982), p. 80.

1:277.24] Published in part in Higginson, *MFO,* p. 69.

1:280.12 Summer 1837] Probably May 1837, for her letter of 13 May to James Clarke has similar language.

1:283.27] Published in part in Higginson, *MFO,* p. 80.

1:284.1 Bartlett] Probably Rebecca Bartlett.

1:289.3] Published in part in Higginson, *MFO,* p. 284.

1:320.34] Published in part in Nichols, "Thomas Fuller," p. 28.

1:328.39] Fuller refers to Emerson's lecture "Being and Seeming," given in Cambridge on 15 March.

1:335.22] Published in part in Higginson, *MFO,* p. 88.

1:339.35] The lecture is undoubtedly the one delivered at the divinity school on 15 July.

1:351.14 Lord Houghton] Richard Monckton Milnes, later first Baron Houghton.

1:353.4] Published in Ida Gertrude Everson, *George Henry Calvert* (New York, 1944), p. 274.

2:32.13 "Lying broad awake] Fuller slightly misquotes part of Tennyson's "The Mystic," a poem he published in 1830 but suppressed in all subsequent editions of his works.

2:40.30–31 Chaos and old night] Milton, *Paradise Lost,* bk. 1, l. 543.

2:46.14] Published in part in *Memoirs,* 1:281.

2:76.18 two paintings] copies of two paintings

2:81.23] MsCfr (MHi).

2:91.23] MsC (MHi).

2:95.1] Published in part in Sanborn and Harris, *Alcott,* 1:293.

2:96.35] MsC (MHi).

2:98.13 Anne Bates] Nancy Bates

2:100.24 1821–84] 1821–84)

2:133.37 but —— had not] [Fuller refers to Sam Ward, then in New Orleans.]

2:145.17] Published in part in Higginson, *MFO,* p. 154.

2:148.10 pp. 154–56;] pp. 72, 154–56;

2:155.2 Bluebell] Sturgis was staying at the Samuel Curzon mill at Newburyport, a favorite vacation spot for both women.

2:162.17] The ill sister-in-law must have been Frances Hastings Fuller, William Henry's wife, for Eugene did not marry until 1846.

2:164.27 James Russell Lowell] Most probably Robert Traill Spence Lowell (1816–91), James's brother, who became an Episcopal priest (*DAB*).

2:169.33 To Caroline Sturgis] Perhaps not a letter, but a set of notes Fuller wrote to herself.

2:176.19 pp. 183–84.] pp. 180, 183–84; and Charles R. Crowe, "Transcendentalist Support of Brook Farm: A Paradox?" *Historian* 21 (May 1959): 284.

2:176.38] Probably von Arnim's *Goethes Briefwechsel mit einem Kinde*, which had been very popular among Fuller's friends.

2:182.1 "Nature,"] Fuller called von Arnim "Nature" and Günderode "Ideal."

2:184.28 339–40,] 339–40; and in Higginson, *MFO*, p. 96.

2:188.20] Published in part in Higginson, *MFO*, p. 301.

2:214.10 in the past] in the part

2:215.27 to Lidian Emerson] to Emerson's aunt Mary Moody Emerson, a letter that Fuller copied.

2:249.31] Published in part in Higginson, *MFO*, p. 167.

3:52.8–9] Not published in Higginson, *MFO*.

3:65.7 p. 105.] pp. 17, 105–6.

3:66.35] Published in Lathrop, *Memories of Hawthorne*, pp. 187–88.

3:87.10 the book] Fuller had returned to Sturgis William Story's copy of Browning's *Pippa Passes* (Francis B. Dedmond, "The Letters of Caroline Sturgis to Margaret Fuller," in *Studies in the American Renaissance, 1988*, ed. Joel Myerson [Charlottesville, 1988], p. 224).

3:106.11] MsC (MCR-S).

3:117.27] Published in Lathrop, *Memories of Hawthorne*, pp. 188–89.

3:119.22] A fragment with quite similar wording appears in *Memoirs*, 2:119–20. It is probably an altered version of part of this letter.

3:138.22–23. *MFO*, pp. 166, 193–94,] *MFO*, pp. 193–94,

3:212.35] Published entire in Berg-Perry, " 'Impulses of Human Nature,' " pp. 87–88.

3:212.42 Ellis Gray Loring] Fuller probably refers to the Boston bookseller James or Benjamin Loring (Berg-Perry, " 'Impulses of Human Nature,' " p. 88).

3:217.1 Tuckerman] Tuckerman King

3:218.16] Published entire in Berg-Perry, " 'Impulses of Human Nature,' " p. 100.

3:227.20] Published in part in *Century Magazine*, n.s. 23 (April 1893): 926.

3:242.38] Published in part in *Memoirs*, 2:139.

4:81.41 1 May] 2 May

4:266.22 In July] In late June [Richard wrote Margaret on 9 July that he had had a "honeymoon" letter from Eugene, which must have been written in June.]

5:47.22] Published in part in *Memoirs*, 2:231.

5:62.35 ca. May 1848] ca. May 1847 [The letter Fuller wrote to William Cullen Bryant in 1847 discusses this same exchange of papers.]

5:68.14–15 "City of the Soul"] Fuller quotes canto IV, stanza 78, of Byron's *Childe Harold's Pilgrimage*, as she does on p. 147 in a letter to her mother.

5:69.32] The entire text derives from *Memoirs,* 2:240–41. The MH version is a fragment.

5:182.35 married in 1845.] married in 1846.

5:186.39] Published in part in Higginson, *MFO,* p. 156.

5:195.32 Jasper] Jaspar

5:240.16 "Cursed with every granted prayer,"] From the second of Pope's Moral Epistles, "To a Lady: Of the Characters of Women," l. 147.

5:301.33 *Memoirs,* 2:334–35, 337.] *Memoirs,* 2:311–12, 334–35, 337.

5:305.7–8 Harry Sorrequer (Sever)] Fuller refers to Charles James Lever, who wrote *The Confessions of Harry Lorrequer* (Dublin, 1839). In the winter of 1842 Fuller apparently had read his second novel, *Charles O'Malley, the Irish Dragoon* (*Letters of MF,* 3:32).

INDEX

Brook Farm, **I**: 52, 134n; **II**: 57n, 174,
206, 210, 240; **III**: 37n, 41, 42n, 76, 77,
82, 83, 87, 94, 97, 111–13, 125, 144,
145n, 161, 201, 208n; **IV**: 15, 143, 158,
174n, 188n, 202n, 203n, 294n, 307; **V**:
275, 277n; **VI**: 59, 60n, 94n, 112, 114,
352, 367n; Emerson on, **II**: 164n, 195n;
fire destroys, **IV**: 198–99; Fuller on, **II**:
163, 180, 194, 205; visits to, **II**: 209, 211,
212, 217, 237, 238. *See also* Ripley,
George: and Brook Farm.
Brooks, Peter Chardon, **I**: 115n, 116n; **VI**:
306n
Brough, Mr., **II**: 190
Brougham, Henry Peter, Baron Brougham
and Vaux, **III**: 103, 104n; **VI**: 226,
227n–28n
Brown, Mrs., **II**: 227
Brown, Adeline, **I**: 126, 127n
Brown, Ann Frances, **I**: 326, 327n
Brown, Caroline Clements, **V**: 233, 234n;
VI: 94n
—letter to, **VI**: 94
Brown, Charles, **I**: 341n; **VI**: 305n
Brown, Charles Brockden, **I**: 153; **VI**: 162,
164n
Brown, Hugh H., **I**: 327n
Brown, John, **IV**: 49n
Brown, Dr. John, **IV**: 245, 249n
Brown, Lucy Jackson, **VI**: 305n
Brown, Nicholas, 3d, **V**: 230n, 233, 269n;
VI: 94n
Brown, Shipley & Co., **V**: 177, 179–80,
193
Brown, Sophia, **I**: 341; **VI**: 305
Brown, Thomas, **I**: 151, 152n, 245; **VI**:
281, 283n
Brown, Uriah, **I**: 127n
Browning, Elizabeth Barrett, **I**: 50; **IV**: 9,
16, 207n, 220, 235, 236n, 244, 268, 272;
V: 14, 75, 159, 170, 189, 204, 275, 279,
280, 282, 288n; **VI**: 6, 7, 51n, 54, 62; on
Fuller, **IV**: 220n; Fuller on, **VI**: 77
—letters to, **V**: 289–90; unrecovered, **VI**:
393, 394
Browning, Robert, **I**: 50, 60; **III**: 104; **IV**:
9, 16, 145, 200, 212, 220, 235, 236n,
244, 268, 272; **V**: 14, 149, 159, 170, 181,
185n, 189, 204, 275, 279, 280, 282, 287,
289, 307; **VI**: 6, 7, 51, 54, 63, 71, 73n,
86; Fuller on, **VI**: 62, 72, 77
—works of: *Bells and Pomegranates*, **IV**:
145n, 212n; **V**: 181, 185n, 189, 204; **VI**:
73n; *Dramatic Romances and Lyrics*, **IV**:
145n; *Luria*, **IV**: 212; *Paracelsus*, **III**:
104; **IV**: 145n; **VI**: 73n; *Pauline*, **IV**:

145n; *Pippa Passes*, **IV**: 145n; **V**: 307;
VI: 397; *Poems*, **VI**: 72, 73n; *Sordello*, **IV**:
145n; *A Soul's Tragedy*, **IV**: 212n
Browning, Robert Wiedeman Barrett
(Pen), **V**: 275, 277n, 280, 282
Brownson, Orestes Augustus, **I**: 328, 329n;
II: 95n, 118, 120n, 150; **III**: 124n, 175n;
V: 174, 175n; **VI**: 243, 244n
—letter to, **III**: 174
Bruce, Georgiana, **III**: 207, 208n; **IV**: 59,
60n–61n, 80–81, 89, 140–41; **VI**: 94n,
119, 120n
—letters to, **III**: 210–11, 221–23, 235–37,
250–51; **IV**: 143–44, 166–67, 180; **VI**:
94, 352
Brunelleschi, Filippo, **V**: 305, 307n
Brunetti, Angelo (Ciceruacchio), **V**: 10,
150n
Brunetti, Luigi, **V**: 150n
Bryant, Frances, **VI**: 367n, 372n
Bryant, Frances Fairchild, **VI**: 372n
Bryant, Julia Sands, **VI**: 372n
Bryant, William Cullen, **IV**: 6, 16n, 217n;
V: 63n; **VI**: 314, 367n, 372n, 397
—letter to, **VI**: 371
Buchanan, James, **IV**: 140n, 142
Buchanan, Joseph Rodes, **II**: 63, 64n; **III**:
177–78, 180n
Buch der Lieder (Heine), **I**: 242n
Buckingham, Joseph T., **VI**: 218n
Buckminster, Joseph (father), **I**: 236n
Buckminster, Joseph Stevens, **III**: 177,
180n; **VI**: 224n
Buffum, Arnold, **IV**: 49n
Buhle, Johann Gottlieb, **I**: 245; **VI**: 276,
277n, 281
Buke of the Howlat (Holland), **II**: 171, 176n
Bull, Ole Bornemann, **III**: 201, 249, 251,
256; **IV**: 129, 130n, 164, 167, 168, 170–
71, 172n, 173n
—works of: "Adagio Religioso," **III**: 201;
"Ciciliano e Tarentelle," **III**: 251;
"Niagara," **III**: 256; "Solitude of the
Prairie," **III**: 256; "Tribute to Washington," **IV**: 170, 171
Bullard, Mary Ann Barrett, **I**: 282n
Bullard, Silas, **I**: 282n
Bulwer-Lytton. *See* Lytton, Edward George
Bulwer-.
Bunyan, John, **VI**: 124
Buono, Luigi Del, **VI**: 63n
Burbidge, Thomas, **V**: 287, 288n
Burditt, Cordelia, **III**: 153
Burditt, James W., **II**: 118, 120n; **III**: 153
Burditt, Mary, **III**: 153
Bürger, Gottfried August, **V**: 75, 76n

Harvard Rebellion of 1834, **I**: 204, 206n
Hastings, Daniel, **I**: 82n, 316, 317n, 350
Hastings, Deborah Hammond, **I**: 82n
Hasty, Catherine Thompson, **VI**: 89–92
Hasty, John, **VI**: 76n
Hasty, Libby, **VI**: 76n
Hasty, Seth Libby, **I**: 50–51; **VI**: 7, 75, 76n, 87, 88; death of, **VI**: 89–92
Hasty, William, **VI**: 76n
Haven, Ann Woodward, **II**: 63n
Haven, Experience Parker, **I**: 320n
Haven, John, **II**: 63n
Haven, Luther (father), **I**: 320n
Haven, Luther (son), **I**: 320, 350
Haven, Susan Woodward, **II**: 63n
Hawthorne, Nathaniel, **I**: 51–53, 56, 198n, 228n; **II**: 155n, 238; **III**: 5, 40n, 58, 70, 71n, 211, 217; **IV**: 7, 14, 167, 278n; **V**: 5, 92n; **VI**: 49n, 354; Fuller on, **III**: 65–66, 70; on Fuller's marriage, **VI**: 9–10
—letters to, **III**: 115–17; **IV**: 103
—works of: "The Gentle Boy," **I**: 198; *Twice-Told Tales*, **III**: 58
Hawthorne, Sophia Peabody, **I**: 203n; **II**: 92n, 129n, 153, 155n; **III**: 40n, 70, 71n, 117n, 188, 217; **VI**: 354
—letters to, **III**: 65–66; **IV**: 103; unrecovered, **VI**: 390
Hawthorne, Una, **III**: 188, 189n, 210, 211, 217, 218, 220; **IV**: 103, 169n; Fuller on, **VI**: 354–55
Hayden, John C., **I**: 85n
Haydn, Franz Joseph, **VI**: 309, 311n
Hayes, Thomas, **I**: 131n
Hays, Matilda, **IV**: 267, 268n
Hayward, Catharine S. Frisbie, **I**: 118n
Hayward, Charles L., **I**: 203n
Hayward, James, **I**: 117, 118n, 126
Hazard, Anna Rodman, **IV**: 115n–16n; **VI**: 359
Hazard, Eliza, **VI**: 120
Hazard, Margaret Avery, **VI**: 120n
Hazard, Thomas Rodman, **VI**: 120n
Hazlitt, William, **II**: 152, 153n; quoted, **VI**: 227n
—works of: *Lectures on the English Comic Writers*, **II**: 152, 153n; *The Spirit of the Age*, **VI**: 226, 227n
Headley, Joel Tyler, **IV**: 5, 6, 81, 178; Fuller on, **IV**: 178
—works of: *The Alps and the Rhine*, **IV**: 81n; *Napoleon and His Marshals*, **IV**: 81n; **VI**: 366, 367n
Heard, Miss, **I**: 117
"Heart, The" (Emerson), **I**: 328
Heart and the World, The (Marston), **IV**: 293

Heath, John Francis, **II**: 191; **V**: 199–200, 233–34; **VI**: 79, 81n
Hedge, Caroline, **I**: 267n
Hedge, Charlotte, **I**: 267n
Hedge, Edward, **I**: 135, 136n
Hedge, Ellen, **I**: 267n
Hedge, Frederic Henry (father), **I**: 29, 32, 35, 64–65, 128n, 136n, 190, 208, 210, 283, 297; **II**: 5, 114n, 227–28; **III**: 7, 162n; **V**: 54; **VI**: 119, 164n, 221, 242, 247n, 250n, 252n, 254, 255n, 273n, 290n; on Clarke, **I**: 187; **VI**: 248; Fuller on, **VI**: 163; quoted, **VI**: 258n, 259; and *Western Messenger*, **VI**: 253
—letters to, **I**: 188, 211, 212, 215, 222, 225, 228, 235, 259, 265, 292; **II**: 113–14, 124–25; **III**: 106–9; **V**: 41, 54–55
—works of: "Coleridge's Literary Character," **I**: 190n; "An Introductory Lecture Delivered at the Opening of the Bangor Lyceum," **I**: 266, 267n; "Pretensions of Phrenology Examined," **I**: 213, 215n; *Prose Writers of Germany*, **V**: 55; review of Carlyle's *Life of Friedrich Schiller*, **I**: 216, 217n; "A Sermon Preached before the Ancient and Honourable Artillery Company," **I**: 213, 215n
Hedge, Frederic Henry (son), **I**: 267n
Hedge, Levi, **I**: 127, 128n, 139, 140n, 189, 190n; **VI**: 110n, 163, 164n
Hedge, Lucy Pierce, **I**: 189, 259, 292; **II**: 115n
Hedge, Mary, **I**: 189, 190n, 198, 211, 216, 226
Hedge, Mary Kneeland, **VI**: 109, 110n, 163
Heine, Heinrich, **I**: 242, 243n
—works of: *Buch der Lieder*, **I**: 242n; *Letters Auxiliary to the History of Modern Polite Literature in Germany*, **I**: 242, 243n; **VI**: 274, 275n, 289n; *Die Romantische Schule*, **I**: 243n; *Zur Geschichte der neueren schönen Literatur in Deutschland*, **I**: 242, 243n; **VI**: 261, 262n, 274, 275n
Heinrich von Ofterdingen (Novalis), **I**: 178, 255n; **II**: 107, 157, 158n; **VI**: 190
"Helena" (Goethe), **II**: 69, 70n, 75
Helvétius, Claude Adrien, **I**: 151, 152n
Hemans, Mr., **VI**: 376
Hemans, Felicia Dorothea, **I**: 195, 197n; **VI**: 131, 197, 198n, 205
Henry, Mr., **II**: 207, 208; **III**: 64
Henry, Caleb Sprague, **I**: 227n; **VI**: 188
Henry the Fourth, pt. 1 (Shakespeare), **II**: 124, 125n
Heraud, John, **II**: 136, 138n

Index

Sewel, William, **III**: 122
"Sexton's Daughter, The" (Sterling), **II**: 70n
"Shadows" (Milnes), **II**: 54, 55n
Shah Nameh (Firdawsi), **II**: 122
Shakers, **VI**: 214
Shakespeare, William, **I**: 108n, 186, 279, 325n; **II**: 42, 53, 55n, 116, 119, 243; **III**: 108, 126, 224; **IV**: 98, 248; **VI**: 294, 309n
—works of: *As You Like It*, **I**: 108n; **VI**: 268n; *Coriolanus*, **II**: 110; *Hamlet*, **I**: 325n; **II**: 110; **III**: 156; **VI**: 230n, 243n, 308, 309n; *Henry the Fourth*, pt. 1, **II**: 124, 125n; *Julius Caesar*, **II**: 110; *The Merchant of Venice*, **III**: 126; *A Midsummer Night's Dream*, **VI**: 145; *Much Ado about Nothing*, **II**: 116; **VI**: 317n; *Othello*, **II**: 42, 44n; *The Tempest*, **I**: 186; *The Two Gentlemen of Verona*, **III**: 108, 110n
Sharpe, Charles Kirkpatrick, **I**: 327n
Shattuck, Amelia, **III**: 39n
Shattuck, Daniel, **I**: 303n
Shattuck, Eleanor Elizabeth, **III**: 38, 39n; **VI**: 294, 296n
Shattuck, Eliza Davis, **VI**: 296n
Shattuck, Frances, **I**: 302, 303n
Shattuck, George C., **III**: 39n; **VI**: 296n
Shattuck, Sarah Edwards, **I**: 303n
Shaw, Miss, **VI**: 373
Shaw, Anna, **III**: 211n, 226, 227n; **VI**: 117n
Shaw, Anna Blake. *See* Greene, Anna Blake Shaw.
Shaw, Elizabeth Palmer, **I**: 140n
Shaw, Elizabeth Parkman, **II**: 74n, 178n; **III**: 42n
Shaw, Elizabeth Willard, **III**: 188
Shaw, Ellen, **III**: 227n; **IV**: 127, 128n
Shaw, Francis George, **II**: 175, 178n, 190, 211n; **III**: 39, 40n, 209, 226, 246; **IV**: 15, 51, 52n, 127, 168, 169n, 203; **V**: 215; **VI**: 117, 355n
—letter to, **IV**: 307–8
Shaw, John, **I**: 140n
Shaw, Joseph Coolidge, **II**: 181, 182n; **V**: 72; **VI**: 329n
Shaw, Josephine, **III**: 168, 227n; **IV**: 127
Shaw, Lemuel, **VI**: 346, 347n
Shaw, Mary Breed, **I**: 138, 140n
Shaw, Pauline Agassiz, **V**: 277n
Shaw, Quincy Adams, **V**: 275, 277n
Shaw, Robert Gould (father of Francis George), **II**: 74n, 178n; **III**: 33n, 42n
Shaw, Robert Gould (son of Francis George), **II**: 178n; **III**: 227n; **IV**: 127; **VI**: 117n

Shaw, Sarah Sturgis, **II**: 175, 178n, 190, 211n; **III**: 7, 39, 209; **IV**: 207; **VI**: 117n, 119, 120n, 355n
—letters to, **III**: 127, 168, 221, 225–27, 245–46; **IV**: 51, 126–27, 163–65, 203–4, 305–6; **V**: 214–15; **VI**: 116–17
Shaw, Susanna, **III**: 227n; **VI**: 117
Shaw, Virginia, **I**: 138, 140n, 146; **VI**: 63n
Sheafe, Jacob, **III**: 159n
Sheafe, Margaret, **III**: 158, 159n
Sheafe, Mary Haven, **III**: 159n
Shelley, Mary Wollstonecraft, **I**: 164, 165n, 197n; **II**: 134n; **VI**: 110n
Shelley, Percy Bysshe, **I**: 55, 164, 165n, 242n; **II**: 133, 134, 136, 138n, 144, 145n; **III**: 165, 167, 224, 225n; **IV**: 111, 123, 146, 190, 213; **V**: 297n; **VI**: 70, 194, 217, 226, 308n; Fuller on, **VI**: 205
—works of: *Alastor*, **I**: 242n; "Defence of Poetry," **II**: 133, 134n, 136, 138n; *Essays, Letters from Abroad, Translations and Fragments*, **II**: 133, 134n; "Lift not the painted veil," **VI**: 70, 71n; "On Death," **I**: 241, 242n; **III**: 165, 167; "Prince Athanase," **VI**: 110, 111n; "Reality," **V**: 297n; "Rosalind and Helen," **VI**: 322, 323n; "The Sunset," **VI**: 136, 137n; "To —," **IV**: 123, 125n
Shelley, William, **III**: 224, 225n
"Shelley and Pollok" (Osgood), **VI**: 308n
Shepherd, Honora, **IV**: 80–81, 84, 85, 86n, 89, 127
"She Walks in Beauty" (Byron), **II**: 49–50, 51n
"She was not fair, nor full of grace" (Cornwall), **VI**: 225
Shirley (Brontë), **VI**: 63, 72
Shirley, James, **I**: 159, 160n
"Short Essay on Critics, A" (Fuller), **II**: 145
Sidney, Philip, **VI**: 330, 331
Sigourney, Charles, **I**: 312n
Sigourney, Mary Greenleaf, **I**: 312n
Silenus, **III**: 202
Silsbee, Mary, **I**: 233, 235n
Silsbee, Mary Crowninshield, **I**: 233, 235n
Silsbee, Nathaniel, **I**: 233, 235n
Simmons, George Frederick, **II**: 37, 148
Simmons, William, **II**: 37n
Simmons, William Hammatt, **I**: 304, 305n
Simms, William Gilmore, **I**: 43; **IV**: 6, 7, 222
Simrock, Karl, **VI**: 146n
Sing Sing Prison, **III**: 221–23, 236, 237, 247–48; **VI**: 356–57
Sismondi, Leonard Simonde de, **I**: 151, 152n
Six Etchings from Salvator-Rosa, **II**: 33n

Index

454

AACO524

PS
2506
A4
1983
v.6